MODELS OF SHORT-TERM MEMORY

Models of Short-term Memory

Edited by

Susan E. Gathercole
University of Bristol, UK

Psychology Press
An imprint of Erlbaum (UK) Taylor & Francis

Copyright © 1996 by Psychology Press, an imprint of
Erlbaum (UK) Taylor & Francis Ltd

Psychology Press
27 Church Road
Hove
East Sussex BN3 2FA
UK

British Library Cataloguing in Publication Data

A catalogue record for this book is available from the British Library

ISBN 0–86377–416–4 (Hbk)

Typeset by DP Photosetting, Aylesbury, Bucks.
Printed and bound in the UK by Biddles Ltd., Guildford and King's Lynn

Contents

List of Contributors

Alan D. Baddeley, Department of Psychology, University of Bristol, 8 Woodland Road, Bristol BS8 1TN, UK

Philip Beaman, School of Psychology, University of Wales College of Cardiff, PO Box 901, Cardiff CF1 3YG, UK

Gordon D.A. Brown, Department of Psychology, University of Warwick, Coventry CV4 7AL, UK

Neil Burgess, Department of Anatomy, University College London, Gower Street, London WC1E 6BT, UK

Nelson Cowan, Department of Psychology, 210 McAlester Hall, University of Missouri, Columbia, MO 65211, USA

Clive Frankish, Department of Psychology, University of Bristol, 8 Woodland Road, Bristol, BS8 1TN, UK

Susan E. Gathercole, Department of Psychology, University of Bristol, 8 Woodland Road, Bristol, BS8 1TN, UK

Lawrence Geuntert, Department of Biological Sciences, Purdue University, West Lafayette, IN 47907-1364, USA

David W. Glasspool, Department of Psychology, University College London, Gower Street, London WC1E 6BT, UK

Tom Hartley, Department of Psychology, University College London, Gower Street, London WC1E 6BT, UK

Cathrin Hayt, Mission Insurance Companies' Trust, 3333 Wilshire Boulevard, Los Angeles, CA 90010, USA

Lora Hersberger, Department of Psychological Sciences, Purdue University, West Lafayette, IN 47907-1364, USA

Graham J. Hitch, Department of Psychology, Lancaster University, Lancaster LA1 4YF, UK

George Houghton, Department of Psychology, University College London, Gower Street, London WC1E 6BT, UK

Charles Hulme, Department of Psychology, University of York, Heslington, York YO1 5DD, UK

Dylan M. Jones, School of Psychology, University of Wales College of Cardiff, PO Box 901, Cardiff CF1 3YG, UK

Robert Kail, Department of Psychological Sciences, Purdue University, West Lafayette, IN 47907-1364, USA

Mary F. Lesch, Department of Psychology, Rice University, PO Box 1892, Houston, TX 77251, USA

William J. Macken, School of Psychology, University of Wales College of Cardiff, PO Box 901, Cardiff CF1 3YG, UK

Amanda J. Martin, Department of Psychology, University of Bristol, 8 Woodland Road, Bristol, BS8 1TN, UK

Randi C. Martin, Department of Psychology, Rice University, PO Box 1892, Houston, TX 77251, USA

Bennet Murdock, Department of Psychology, University of Toronto, Toronto, Ontario M5S 1A1, Canada

Richard Schweickert, Department of Psychological Sciences, Purdue University, West Lafayette, IN 47907-1364, USA

Preface

Susan E. Gathercole
University of Bristol, UK

The chapters in this volume represent some of the newest theoretical developments in the area of short-term memory. Short-term memory research has occupied an important place in the profile of cognitive psychology for almost 40 years. Throughout this period, research activity in the area has been vigorous and strongly theoretically motivated. What is particularly exciting at present is that the new theoretical perspectives being developed are the products of much broader perspectives on theory-building than those that dominated previous decades.

The touchstone for models of short-term memory has always been empirical studies based in the experimental laboratory. Unless the models can account for key data in this domain, they are of little use. However, other sources of information are now also being used to motivate the provision of much more complete theoretical accounts, resulting in the present profusion of models of short-term memory that are detailed and highly distinctive from one another.

Probably the single most important influence on the current theories is the development of computational models of short-term memory. There are a number of reasons why this approach has had such an important impact in the area. First, the building of such models forces the modeller to provide an explicit account of the mechanisms and processes present in verbal theoretical accounts. This process and its benefits for theory are clearly demonstrated in the chapter by Burgess and Hitch, in which they present their revised connectionist model of the articulatory loop. This model is capable of simulating many core phenomena of serial verbal recall such as the serial position function and order and item errors, in addition to showing more detailed sensitivity to the characteristics of memory lists. No previous verbal model could match this model for its twin features of detailed specification and breadth of scope in accommodating key empirical phenomena. Similarly, Murdock's TODAM model, a distributed memory account of storage and retrieval of many basic kinds of information, provides an impressively broad and tractable account of human memory performance.

A second contribution of the computational approach is to identify what mechanisms and processes are necessary to provide an adequate theoretical account of empirical findings. Brown and Hulme's chapter, for example, provides an excellent demonstration that the well established sensitivity of immediate memory performance to word length can be adequately simulated in a trace decay model with no rehearsal component. Similarly, Schweickert, Hayt, Hersberger, and Geuntert present a simple mathematical model which makes few assumptions but which is nonetheless capable of effectively predicting differences in short-term memory span in different experimental conditions.

Computation approaches to modelling can bring with them a degree of theoretical parsimony rarely matched by purely verbal accounts. Houghton, Hartley, and Glasspool simulate the serial output characteristics of immediate recall of nonwords by using a seriating mechanism developed originally for the domain of speech production. In showing that the same basic mechanism embedded in a common architecture captures well immediate memory behaviour, these authors make a compelling argument for considering verbal memory as a part of the language system rather than a separate mechanism. In my own chapter with Martin, I make a similar argument concerning the parallel characteristics of speech perception of verbal short-term memory, pointing to simplicity of computational simulations of phenomena in the perception of speech that are also ubiquitous in immediate memory. Frankish, in a chapter reporting new findings which suggest that echoic memory is a genuine acoustic record, also speculates on how a neural network model could capture these findings and also readily accommodate developmental changes in speech perception ability.

The strength of current models of memory does not only lie in the impact of computational approaches. A further critical feature is the use of a much broader empirical base to inform theory. Data to be addressed by models of short-term memory no longer originate solely in the laboratory. Since the early 1980s, findings from neuropsychological studies of patients with acquired brain damage resulting in impairments either of short-term memory or of other cognitive skills have been playing an increasingly important role in theory. The capacity to accommodate patterns of performance in such patients is now viewed as providing a critical test for any model of short-term memory, as demonstrated clearly in the chapters in the present volume by Baddeley and by Martin and Lesch.

The broadening of the empirical base informing theory in the area of short-term memory also extends to developmental evidence. Cowan and Kail work towards a theory of how short-term memory develops during childhood, which is embedded in a basic framework of adult short-term memory, and in doing so elucidate both the fundamental nature of short-term memory as well as its development. Evidence from studies of short-term memory in children also plays significant roles in many other chapters in this book, where it is considered alongside both laboratory data from skilled adult subjects and from neuropsychological patients. Previous distinctions concerning the domains of models of short-term memory, to adults, children, and so on, are diminishing. The value of providing more complete accounts of how memory develops, how its skilled operation functions, and how it degrades with accidental damage, is now being recognised, resulting in a much richer and broader perspective of short-term memory function.

Of the models presented in this volume, the majority provide accounts of short-term memory for verbal materials such as words, nonwords, and digits. The reason for this bias towards verbal short-term memory is that it reflects the predominance of verbal memory research within cognitive psychology more generally. Quite simply, there is much more known, and theoretical accounts in the short-term memory domain are considerably more advanced, for verbal rather than nonverbal materials. The chapter by Jones, Beaman, and Macken is, however, an honourable exception. These authors present a model designed to account for serial recall behaviour with verbal and nonverbal memory sequences, following an object-oriented approach. The approach advanced in this chapter is intriguingly at odds with many of the other purely verbal perspectives in the book, and provides a powerful critique of the empirical basis of many dearly held assumptions concerning modularity in short-term memory.

The contribution of this volume will, I hope, be to provide the reader with an advanced understanding of both the theoretical issues of the critical findings that are currently at the forefront of research in short-term memory.

Susan E. Gathercole
3rd August 1995

1

The concept of working memory

Alan D. Baddeley

Medical Research Council Applied Psychology Unit, Cambridge, UK*

INTRODUCTION

In the 1880s Joseph Jacobs, a London schoolmaster with an interest in the new science of psychology wanted to have a measure of the individual differences among the mental capacities of his pupils. He devised a test in which the subject was presented with a string of numbers, and attempted to repeat them back verbatim. If correct, the string was increased to a point at which errors began to occur; the subject's digit span. The digit span paradigm has continued to be important, both practically, as it forms a subtest of the WAIS, probably the most widely used measure of adult intelligence (Wechsler, 1955), and theoretically, where the technique continues to play an important role in contemporary theorising about short-term or working memory (Baddeley, 1986). The term *working memory* refers to the system or systems involved in the temporary storage of information in the performance of such cognitive skills as reasoning, learning, and comprehension. It has evolved from the earlier concept of short-term memory, and can probably best be understood in the context of its development over the last 30–40 years. Before going on to examine this however, it is important to point out that the term "working memory" is also used in other ways. These will be described briefly before we consider the early development of the concepts of short-term and working memory.

---

* Now at the Department of Psychology, University of Bristol.

1

In research on learning in animals, the term working memory is most closely associated with the work of Olton, Walker, and Gage (1978), and in particular with work involving the radial maze. This piece of apparatus involves a series of runways each of which radiates out from a central choice point. In a typical experiment, all the arms are baited with food, and the animal placed in the centre. The optimal strategy is to take the food from each limb of the maze, and then not return to that limb again. In order to perform this task, the animal, typically a rat, must remember which arms have already been visited. Because the animal is likely to be tested repeatedly on the same maze, it is important to base a given day's judgements on performance on that particular day. The term working memory is used by Olton to refer to the system responsible for holding this information for that particular day, hence allowing the animal to perform effectively. Although this has proved to be a very valuable paradigm for studying animal learning and memory, it is not at all clear how the paradigm maps onto the working memory research that forms the bulk of the present chapter; indeed attempts to develop an analogue for use with human subjects suggest that there may be a substantial long-term rather than working memory contribution to the way in which humans perform the task (R.Morris personal communication).

A second use of the term working memory is concerned with the computer-based modelling of cognition, based on the production system approach initially developed by Newell and Simon (1972). For example Anderson's (1983) model of cognition ACT*, as with all production system models, assumes a working memory system within which the production systems operate. Such an assumption appears to be essential to this approach to modelling. However, such models do not necessarily make any attempt to identify and study an equivalent working memory system in humans. In the case of Anderson's model for example, the capacity of working memory does not appear to be limited in any important way, whereas the concept of limited capacity lies at the heart of empirical research on short-term and working memory.

It is important to note however, that other cognitive models based on a production system architecture do make assumptions about working memory and its limitations. A good example of this is the model of comprehension developed by Kintsch and van Dijk (1978) which assumes that comprehension capacity is constrained by the assumption that working memory can hold only a limited number of propositions, and that this varies from one individual to the next. Kintsch and Vipond (1979) present an intriguing demonstration of this aspect of their model in a study contrasting the speeches of Eisenhower and Stevenson in their respective Presidential campaigns. Given a large working memory, the two sets of speeches are found to be equally "comprehensible" by the model, whereas when the working memory capacity of the model was reduced, then it began to have difficulty in coping with Stevenson's speeches. Even here, however, the model assumes a limited-capacity working memory as part of a model of language comprehension, rather than being directly concerned with investigating the nature of the working memory system that is assumed.

Long- and Short-term Memory

Despite the continued psychometric use of digit span, short-term memory was comparatively neglected until the late 1950s when interest in the temporary storage of information developed as a result of the practical need to study such real-world tasks as air traffic control or telephony as part of the application of experimental psychology to military performance during World War II. This coincided with the development of the information processing approach to human cognition as reflected in Broadbent's seminal book *Perception and communication* (Broadbent, 1958), and subsequently by Neisser's equally influential text, *Cognitive psychology* (Neisser, 1967). Broadbent suggested that it was necessary to assume two kinds of memory: a short-term system in which items were held in a temporary buffer from which the memory trace would fade spontaneously unless revived by rehearsal; and long-term memory, where forgetting was assumed to occur as a result of mutual interference between long-term memory traces. This distinction appeared to be supported by the demonstration by Brown (1958) in Britain and Peterson and Peterson (1959) in the US that small amounts of material, well within the memory span, would be forgotten within seconds unless actively rehearsed.

During the 1960s, controversy raged as to whether it was or was not necessary to assume more than one kind of memory. Melton (1963) showed that traditional short-term memory tasks such as digit span were capable of reflecting long-term learning. If, for example, a given sequence were surreptitiously repeated from time to time, then the probability of its being correctly repeated would increase (Hebb, 1961). He concluded on the basis of this and similar evidence that it was unnecessary to assume two memory systems. Short-term memory (STM) was simply a weaker version of long-term memory (LTM). In both cases, he proposed that forgetting was the result of interference, citing cogent evidence from Keppel and Underwood (1962) in support of the view that the rapid forgetting observed by Brown and the Petersons was the result of proactive interference—disruption of memory by early items rather than resulting from trace decay.

By the mid 1960s however, the evidence seemed to be favouring a dichotomous view. Waugh and Norman (1965) pointed out the need to distinguish between a hypothetical short-term memory store, which they labeled *primary memory*, and the experimental STM paradigm that was assumed to reflect it. As they point out, there is no reason to assume that any given experimental paradigm is a pure measure of anything, hence the demonstration that digit span may have components of both long- and short-term memory is unproblematic. They agree with Melton in suggesting that short-term forgetting is not due to trace decay, but rather than the traditional associationist interference theory interpretation offered by Melton, they prefer a model that assumes that short-term forgetting occurs because of the limited capacity of STM; as new items enter, old ones are displaced.

During the next few years, a number of new sources of evidence in favour of a dichotomous view appeared, among the most cogent were:

Two-component Tasks.   Certain experimental tasks appear to have two quite separable components, one brief and the other durable. One example is the task of free recall; subjects are presented with a list of words and attempt to recall them in any order, typically resulting in a relatively low level of recall for earlier and middle-order words, together with excellent recall of the last few items presented. If recall is delayed by a distracting task however, the good recall of the last items, the so-called *recency effect*, is disrupted, whereas recall of earlier items remains at approximately the same level (Glanzer & Cunitz, 1966). In general, recall of the earlier items is dependent on a wide range of variables that are known to influence long-term learning, such as rate of presentation, word frequency, and imageability, whereas the recency effect is sensitive to delay but is unaffected by these variables. A simple interpretation is that earlier items are recalled from LTM, whereas the more recent items reside in a temporary short-term store (Glanzer, 1972).

Acoustic and Semantic Coding.   Immediate memory span for verbal materials suggested that memory was based on the sound of the material rather than its meaning; errors tended to be phonologically similar to the item they were replacing (e.g. *V* substituting for *B*), even though presentation was visual (Conrad, 1964). Furthermore, sequences that are similar in sound, whether comprising letters (e.g. *P D C V G*), or words (*man, cat, cap, mat, can*), lead to poorer immediate serial recall than dissimilar sequences (*K Q W L Y*, or *pit, day, cow, pen, tub*) (Baddeley, 1966a; Conrad & Hull, 1964). In contrast, the long-term serial learning of word lists tends to rely on meaning, to be disrupted by semantic similarity, and to be unaffected by similarity of sound (Baddeley, 1966b). Sachs (1967) showed that a similar phenomenon occurs in remembering prose passages, when subjects are required to decide whether a sentence is an exact repetition of an earlier section of the passage. Changes to the surface structure of the passage which maintain meaning are readily detected only when tested virtually immediately, whereas semantic changes are detected after substantial delays. Finally, Kintsch and Buschke (1969), using a two-component probed memory task, demonstrated that the earlier LTM component of the task was sensitive to semantic coding, whereas the recency component was susceptible to similarity of sound.

Neuropsychological Evidence. Perhaps the most powerful evidence for a distinction between long- and short-term memory however, came from brain-damaged patients. It had been known for many years that patients suffering from the classic amnesic syndrome typically have preserved digit span, despite their substantial impairment in long-term learning and memory capacity. This point was demonstrated particularly cogently by the classic amnesic patient, HM, who became amnesic following bilateral hippocampal and temporal lobe excision carried out to relieve an intractable epilepsy (Milner, 1966). Subsequent research showed the pattern of deficits predicted by a dichotomous view of memory systems. Two-component tasks such as free recall showed the recency component to be preserved, while the long-term component was grossly impaired (Baddeley & Warrington, 1970). Performance on the Peterson task is also preserved in amnesic patients, provided their deficit is relatively pure, with no impairment in the executive functions that are typically mediated by the frontal lobes (Baddeley & Warrington, 1970; Warrington, 1982). In short, patients suffering from a pure and classic amnesic syndrome appeared to have a deficit in LTM, but preserved STM.

At the same time, patients with the opposite pattern of deficits were reported by Shallice and Warrington (1970). One such patient, KF, had normal long-term learning ability, coupled with a digit span of only two items, and markedly impaired recency in free recall, together with very poor performance on the Peterson short-term forgetting task. Such patients were assumed to have a specific deficit in STM.

The Modal Model

By the late 1960s, evidence seemed to be accumulating for a division of memory into three subsystems: (1) sensory memory, a series of brief sensory buffers lasting for less than a second, and feeding into (2) short-term or primary memory, which in turn fed (3) long-term memory. There were many such models, all approximating more or less closely to that of Atkinson and Shiffrin (1968), which for that reason has been termed the "modal model".

However, despite its apparent success in accounting for a wide range of data, by the early 1970s the modal model was itself running into problems. These centred on the learning assumption made by the model, namely that long-term learning involved transfer from the short-term store, and that the longer an item resided in the short-term store, the greater its probability of being learned. A series of experiments that required subjects to maintain items in short-term storage by rote rehearsal failed to find the predicted relationship between time in store and long-term learning (e.g. Craik & Watkins, 1973).

Such studies led Craik and Lockhart (1972) to re-interpret the data in terms of *levels of processing*. This view argues that the probability of an item being learned increases as it is processed at progressively deeper and more elaborate levels. Hence, given a printed word such as *dog*, the requirement to make a superficial judgement of the typeface will lead to rather poor long-term learning; a slightly "deeper" judgement as to whether it rhymes with the word *log* or not, will lead to somewhat better recall, whereas even better learning results from a deeper judgement based, for instance, on its semantic characteristics (e.g. *Would the word "log" make sense as a completion of the sentence "The lumberjack chopped the ...?"*) (Craik & Lockhart, 1972; Craik & Tulving, 1975).

The levels of processing framework was extremely influential during the 1970s, and absorbed much of the research effort that had previously been directed to understanding short-term memory. Indeed, in some cases it was argued that it obviated the need for a concept such as short-term memory, although Craik and Lockhart themselves continued to assume a short-term or primary memory system that plays an important part in the process of encoding and recoding. Although the theoretical power of the framework has been questioned (e.g. Baddeley, 1978), it remains a useful broad framework that ties together a good deal of evidence on the relationship between coding and long-term memory.

A second source of problems for the modal model came from a closer examination of the data from patients with STM deficits. If, as the model proposes, good short-term storage is necessary for long-term learning, then STM patients should also have LTM deficits. This did not appear to be the case, whether performance was measured in terms of the long-term component of free recall, standard clinical memory tasks, or everyday cognitive performance, on which STM patients often appear to be remarkably normal. Such patients clearly presented a challenge to the dominant view that STM acts as a working memory that is necessary for the performance of a wide range of other cognitive tasks. For that reason, a colleague Graham Hitch and I decided to study the working memory hypothesis in more detail, not through the examination of STM patients, as such patients are rare and were not available to us, but rather by an attempt to simulate STM deficit in normal subjects.

WORKING MEMORY

The section that follows will be concerned with the general concept of working memory, and attempts that have been made to investigate its usefulness. The account will start with the work of Baddeley and Hitch

(1974), which led to the assumption of a specific model of working memory. In this section however, we will not be concerned with the details of this or any alternative model, but rather with the general usefulness of the concept of working memory. Hence, some of the work described stems from investigators who assume a single relatively monolithic system; others assume they are investigating a system that is specific to language; whereas I myself favour a view of working memory as a general purpose system that can be fractionated into subsystems.

Baddeley and Hitch (1974) began by attempting to simulate in normal subjects the deficit found in STM patients. They did so by using a secondary task technique, whereby subjects attempted to perform a digit span task at the same time as they were reasoning, comprehending, or learning. Virtually all existing models agreed that STM was limited in capacity, and that this limitation in capacity was responsible for the limit in digit span. It followed from these assumptions that the more digits the subject was required to remember, the less working memory capacity should be left for any other task such as reasoning or comprehension. Subjects therefore were required to remember and rehearse continuously one, three, or six random digits, at the same time as they were performing a number of other tasks, each selected because it was assumed to be dependent on working memory. In one study for example, subjects attempted to learn lists of unrelated words, which they subsequently tried to recall in any order. In another study, subjects performed a verbal reasoning test that had previously been shown to be highly correlated with intelligence, attempting to verify statements about letter pairs AB or BA. The sentences could be simple (*A follows B— BA*), or relatively complex (*B is not preceded by A—AB*). In a third study, subjects attempted to understand prose passages, and in a fourth they attempted to make semantic judgements on the veracity of sentences, some of which were obviously true (e.g. *Hammers can be bought in shops*) and some false (e.g. *Nuns are sold in pairs*).

The pattern across all these tasks was broadly similar; performance progressively deteriorated as concurrent memory load was increased, but even when the load approached and exceeded span, performance was far from totally decimated. We concluded that digit span, and the various cognitive tasks with which it was combined, all loaded on a common working memory system. However, the fact that subjects could still perform demanding cognitive tasks with concurrent digit sequences of span length, suggested that we should abandon the previous assumption that the STM system that was responsible for digit span was synonymous with a general working memory. As will become clear, we ourselves opted to tackle this problem by assuming a multi-component working memory system. Others have accepted that digit span is not a good measure of the capacity of working memory, but have been less concerned about why this should be the case. Much of the work in this area has used an approach based on individual differences in working memory capacity, and probably the most influential group using this approach has been that of Carpenter and Just (Carpenter, Just, & Shell, 1990; Daneman & Carpenter, 1980, 1983; Just & Carpenter, 1992).

Individual Differences in Working Memory

The essence of this approach to the study of working memory is the identification of subjects who are high or low in capacity. This contrast can then be used to understand the role of working memory in a range of important tasks such as comprehension and reasoning. This approach clearly depends on a good measure of working memory capacity, and the most frequently used has been the working memory span measure developed by Daneman and Carpenter (1980). The subject is presented with a series of sentences which must be either read, or else heard and verified. After several sentences have been presented, the subject is then asked to recall the final word of each; working memory span is defined as the largest number of sentences that can be processed, and their final words correctly recalled. In an initial study, Daneman and Carpenter (1980) showed a correlation of +0.72 between working memory span and prose comprehension as measured by a standardised test. This finding has been replicated using a range of different subject populations, although in my own experience the correlation does not always emerge. This may be because the sentential material used varies from study to study, which may allow a range of different strategies to be employed. However, there is no doubt that given appropriate material the correlation does appear, and as we shall see, groups selected on this basis show interesting differences in performance on a range of tasks.

One study (Daneman & Carpenter, 1983) examined the capacity of high and low WM span subjects to cope with ambiguity. A polysemous word such as *bat* was incorporated in a prose passage, which provided either a helpful or misleading context. Subjects with low WM spans were much more readily misled, an effect that was particularly marked when the misleading information and the critical word came in separate sentences, suggesting that low WM span subjects are less able to keep their semantic options open while reading a passage.

A similar line of investigation has been pursued by Oakhill and her colleagues, investigating children who are good readers in that they can pronounce printed words very well, but who are poor comprehenders (Oakhill, Yuill, & Parkin, 1988). These children were shown to be characterised by low working memory span, and to be very poor at drawing inferences from the passages they read. High- and low-span children were equivalent at recognising verbatim repetition of components of a passage that they had read, but differed in the nature of their errors. High-span children were likely to falsely identify passages that were valid inferences, whereas low-span children were equally likely to accept as repetitions sections that were semantically unrelated to the original text.

A third source of evidence for the importance of working memory in comprehension comes from the work on ageing and comprehension of Kemper and her colleagues. There is substantial evidence to suggest that working memory capacity falls with age (Craik, 1977), and Kemper has been interested in the implications of this for language processing in the elderly, for whom there is evidence to suggest that certain complex syntactic forms create problems by overloading working memory capacity (Kemper & Rash, 1988; Morris, Craik, & Gick, 1990). In one ingenious study, Kemper (1990) examined the prose of a number of 19th-century diarists who had kept a record of their lives from youth to old age. One of the syntactic features that she had studied was that of anaphora, whereby a subject is subsequently referred to by a pronoun such as *he* or *it* rather than re-specifying the subject directly, for example: *John bought an old jeep when he inherited a house in the country, but it proved very inconvenient when he changed jobs.* "He" and "it" involve anaphoric reference; "he" is clear, there is only one animate noun, but reference to "it" is ambiguous. Kemper found that as diarists got older they tended to avoid anaphora, and when they used it, were more likely to introduce ambiguity, a phenomenon she attributes to the decline in working memory capacity with age.

So far, all the work on individual differences in WM span have concentrated on language processing. Is the system involved one that is specialised for language, or does it reflect just one area of operation of a general working memory system? Daneman and Tardif (1987) opt firmly for a language-specific working memory, Carpenter and Just (1977) also lean in this direction, although emphasising that analogous systems are likely to be responsible for other tasks of a less linguistic nature (Carpenter et al., 1990). On the other hand, Turner and Engle (1989) and Oakhill et al. (1988) argue against the view that working memory is a language-specific system. They both find that replacing the sentences in Daneman and Carpenter's span task with arithmetic operations leads to a measure that approximates closely to sentence span. This suggests that the important factor is to have demanding cognitive operations combined with memory, and that it is of secondary importance whether these operations are made difficult because of the linguistic operations involved, or for other reasons. Our own findings broadly agree with this, suggesting that the crucial factor is the need to coordinate information from a number of different sources, regardless of whether these are language and memory span, or solving chess problems while attempting to press keys at random (Baddeley, in press; Robbins et al., in press).

Working Memory and Intelligence.   The obvious question raised by the differences in working memory span between individuals is the extent to which individual differences in the classical concept of intelligence might possibly be reducible to differences in working memory capacity. This issue is discussed by Duncan (1993) who describes one of a number of current attempts to use measures of working memory capacity as a means of extending and supplementing more traditional psychometric measures. Kyllonen and Christal (1990) have explored this issue extensively, collecting data from a large sample of US Air Force recruits on a range of tests that have been proposed to load heavily on working memory capacity, and then relating the results to performance on conventional measures of intelligence, typically based on reasoning ability. They found a very high correlation between the two sets of measures, concluding that the traditional intelligence tests and the newer working memory measures were very similar in what they measured, with the exception that the traditional tests probably relied slightly more on experience, whereas the working memory measures were slightly more loaded in speed of processing. In a subsequent study, Christal (1991) attempted to use measures of working memory to predict the success of students taking a course in logic gates, and found that the measures provided a better prediction of subsequent success than the standard Air Force battery that is currently used. It appears therefore that the concept of working memory is already in a position where it is likely to play a useful role in the practical field of psychometric selection.

Fractionating Working Memory

It may be recalled that the studies carried out by Baddeley and Hitch (1974) suggested two conclusions; first that there was evidence for a general working memory system underlying a range of cognitive tasks, but second that this was synonymous with the process underlying digit span. The studies described in the previous section lend further support to the usefulness of a concept of working memory, but have said little about its relationship to the earlier concept of STM. There is of course, no necessary reason why they should, given that most of the investigators were primarily interested in aspects of cognition other than memory. For that purpose, it is sufficient to note that digit span is not a particularly helpful measure, and to opt for an alternative measure that is more satisfactory. For anyone whose primary interest is in memory however, this approach is rather limited, and for that reason, a good deal of my own work has been concerned with attempting to understand the relationship between traditional short-term memory measures and the evolving concept of working memory.

As a first step, Baddeley and Hitch (1974) proposed that the concept of a unitary working memory system be abandoned, and replaced by a tripartite system. As shown in Fig. 1.1, this assumes an attentional controller, the *central executive*, aided by two slave systems, each of which is capable of actively maintaining information of a particular kind. The *visuo-spatial sketchpad* is assumed to hold and manipulate information about objects and locations, while the *articulatory* or *phonological loop* is a system that is assumed to be capable of storing and manipulating speech-based information. Digit span is assumed to depend principally on this latter system, although executive processes will be required to maintain the operation of the loop, with evidence suggesting that executive demand is particularly large when errors begin to occur and need to be "repaired" if performance is not to disintegrate (Hitch & Baddeley, 1976). Hence, as the digit load increases, the demands made on the executive will increase, resulting in a general impact of concurrent span on any task that demands working memory capacity. However, even when a subject is performing at the limit of span, this does not necessarily imply that executive processes are fully stretched. It seems likely that level of performance on a task such as digit span which involves relatively little complex processing will be determined by storage rather than executive limitations, with the result that subjects performing at the limits of digit span will still have some executive capacity left over for performing other tasks such as reasoning or comprehension.

Patients with impaired STM performance are assumed to have a deficit in the phonological loop system; this will not of course prevent the executive or the sketchpad being used, thus explaining why an STM deficit does not lead to general cognitive impairment. The three proposed subsystems will be described in turn, starting with the central executive which has most in common with the general working memory systems assumed in the previous section.

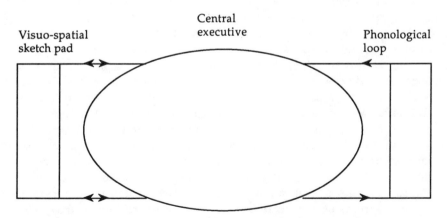

FIG. 1.1.   The tripartite working memory system proposed by Baddeley and Hitch.

The Central Executive. This is the most complex and least understood component of the working memory model. It is assumed to be an attentional processor that serves as an interface between the slave systems and long-term memory. I have argued elsewhere (Baddeley, 1992, 1993a;) the value to an organism of a system that is capable of reflecting on information available from both the environment and from episodic memory in order to create an adequate mental model or representation of the situation and to use this in order to select the most appropriate action. I have speculated that conscious awareness has evolved as part of this process, and that the central executive component of working memory is intimately associated with this process (Baddeley, 1993b).

There is clearly a danger in postulating anything as powerful as that implied by the previous paragraph. Am I not simply postulating a homunculus that sits within the system and is capable of performing any task that happens to be required, a concept that can "explain" everything and predict nothing? This is clearly an important problem, but one that I think can be handled.

Let us begin by assuming that the central executive is nothing but a convenient homunculus; then I would suggest that it is still useful as it allows one to accept the complexity of working memory without being overwhelmed by it. During our first few years of investigating working memory, we used the central executive very much in this way, concentrating on the simpler slave systems, while accepting that they were not entirely self-sufficient in either their operation or their strategic application to specific problems. I would argue that this approach has proved justified on the basis of the progress made in understanding the slave systems.

More recently, we have begun to move away from the use of the central executive as a convenient label for a pool of residual ignorance, and towards a concerted effort to understand its operation. It seems likely that the system will prove complex and multi-faceted, and we have opted to deal with the issue of complexity by attempting to chip away specific aspects or roles of the executive. We have not sacked the homunculus, but are in process of gradually attempting to understand the tasks he undertakes, thereby reducing the residual pool of ignorance. We are thus working towards a point at which the homunculus will become redundant and retire. Whether that will leave a system that has some form of central controller, a cognitive dictatorship, or an oligarchic system, or possibly something more democratic in which subcomponents interact in some form of constructive symbiosis, remains to be seen. For present purposes, the use of the term central executive acts as a reminder that executive control presents a real problem to be solved, but one that can be separated from the understanding of the less central visual and verbal slave systems.

In attempting to model the central executive, I looked to the attentional literature, as attentional control clearly forms one of its principal functions. However, despite the elegance and subtlety of much of the recent work on selective attention, most of it is tied to a detailed analysis of a relatively narrow range of phenomena, typically concerned with the processes of perception. The aspect of attention that seems closest to working memory, however, concerns planning and the control of action; areas that have been much less extensively investigated. One exception however, was the model proposed by Norman and Shallice (1980) which was developed to account for slips of action, and for the disruption of attentional control in patients suffering from damage to the frontal lobes (Shallice, 1982). Norman and Shallice assume that routine activity is controlled by means of a series of over-learned schemata whereby past experience interacts with environmental cues and prompts; when two schemata require action that is inconsistent, then conflict-resolution procedures come into operation so as to allow the schema with the highest priority to gain precedence. However, when novel situations arise, either in emergency or through encountering situations that are non-routine, a second system comes into operation, the supervisory attentional system or SAS. This system operates by changing the probabilities of actions so as to allow the existing schema to be overridden, as for example when you are driving to work and your companion happens to ask if you have remembered to bring a crucial document that you have in fact left behind.

Slips of action are explained on the basis of the triggering of inappropriate schemata, for example, setting off to drive to the supermarket and finding yourself driving to work instead; the routes have a common start and given that your SAS system is occupying itself with other matters, a more frequent work-driving plan takes over.

Patients with frontal lobe damage tend to show a curious combination of distractibility and perseveration. The distractibility is illustrated by the phenomenon of *utilisation behaviour*, in which the patients will respond, often inappropriately, by manipulating any object that comes to hand. Thus, if there is a glass on the table then they will pick it up and drink from it, if there is paper and a pen they will begin to write, and so forth (Shallice, Burgess, Schon, & Baxter, 1989). Perseveration occurs when the subject appears to have great difficulty in breaking away from a given pattern of responding. For example, one frontal patient describing an accident referred to a conversation between himself and the driver of a lorry that he had hit, along the lines "So I said to the driver 'Don't worry, it was my fault', and he replied 'That's alright mate I was just as much to blame', so I said 'Right then but don't worry I was to blame' whereupon he said, 'Don't worry' etc. etc." generating what threatened to be an endless loop of mutual apologies (Baddeley & Wilson, 1986).

Shallice suggests that patients with frontal lobe damage have a deficit in the operation of the SAS, which results in difficulty in the attentional control of action. Utilisation behaviour occurs because the system is captured by any triggering stimulus that occurs, in the absence of long-term SAS control. In a situation where there are many stimuli, then a succession of different schemata are triggered. Perseveration occurs when one schema dominates, and captures the attentional system. In its original formulation two separate subprocesses are proposed for routine and novel actions. Later formulations, however, are probably at least as consistent with a view that replaces a dichotomy between either control by schema or control by the SAS with one in which *both* processes play a simultaneous role; over-learned and routine tasks will rely more on schema-based control processes, whereas novel tasks will place heavier demands on the SAS (Shallice & Burgess, 1993). The more a task is practised, the less demand it is likely to place on the SAS, a process sometimes known as automatisation (Shiffrin & Schneider, 1977).

It was therefore proposed that the central executive operated in broadly the same way as Norman and Shallice's SAS system (Baddeley, 1986). Adoption of the model provided an explanation of an otherwise puzzling phenomenon, namely the limited capacity for random generation. If subjects are asked to produce a stream of random letters at a rate of one per second, they rapidly find that they are deviating from randomness and producing sequences that follow the alphabetic stereotype (e.g. *PQR*), or generating common acronyms such as *USA* and *BBC*, etc. The effect is not due to a false concept of randomness, as it disappears if subjects are allowed to respond more slowly. It appears to be linked to available attentional resources, as randomness declines systematically with speed of generation, and is lawfully related to the demands of a concurrent task such as choice reaction time. Finally, the capacity to generate appears to decline with age and is correlated with intelligence (Baddeley, 1966c, 1986).

This pattern of results can be explained on the assumption that the task picked requires the rapid selection of responses, while avoiding the stereotypy that would be produced by existing habits; the greater the capacity of the SAS, or the more the available time, the better the chance of selecting a novel response and avoiding a stereotyped letter, or the repetition of items that are readily available because recently used.

If random generation is dependent in this way on the SAS, then it should prove a powerful way of disrupting the operation of the central executive; this proves to be the case. For example, in a range of studies of the role of working memory in chess, random generation has proved to be a particularly potent way of disrupting performance, whereas articulating a predictable stream of spoken items at the same rate has no effect (Robbins et al., in press). The effectiveness of random generation does not depend on using letters, or indeed on verbal output. We have recently been exploring a task in which subjects are required to attempt to generate random keypresses in contrast to a condition in which the keys were pressed in a systematic order (Baddeley, in press). Degree of randomness is substantially disrupted by a range of tasks that would be expected to depend on the functioning of the central executive, ranging from problem solving to generating items from semantic categories. The pattern is broadly similar for generating random numbers or random keypresses, although the two tasks differ in one interesting way. Subjects who are generating digits or letters tend to be painfully aware of their deviation from randomness, whereas when pressing keys they seem to be unaware of the extent to which their output is deteriorating.

A prime feature of the function of the central executive is to coordinate information from a number of different sources. We have attempted to utilise this assumption in designing tests that aim to elucidate the role of the central executive in Alzheimer's disease (Baddeley et al., 1986; Baddeley et al., 1991). Earlier studies had suggested the possibility of an executive deficit in this disease, and we planned to explore it by choosing two tasks that loaded respectively on the visuo-spatial sketchpad and phonological loop, adjusting the level of performance on each so that the patients were functioning at a similar error rate to the controls, and then requiring the two tasks to be combined. Normal elderly subjects are no more disrupted by the requirement to combine the two sources of information than are young subjects, provided the level of difficulty is matched. On the other hand, Alzheimer patients are markedly impaired, with the degree of dual-task disruption increasing systematically as the disease progresses, in contrast to their relatively static performance on the individual component measures.

It seems unlikely that the two tasks described capture anything like the full range of capacity of the executive, but as the first stages in a strategy of divide-and-rule they appear to be proving reasonably satisfactory.

The Visuo-spatial Sketchpad.   While the traditional digit span tends to rely on verbal coding and the phonological loop, there are a number of paradigms that appear to rely on visuo-spatial coding. One of these is Corsi's Block Tapping Test in which the subject is presented with an array of nine blocks scattered in a quasi-random manner (Milner, 1971). The experimenter taps a sequence of blocks, and the subject attempts to imitate the sequence. As with digit span, performance is measured by the longest sequence that can successfully be replicated. This task seems to rely principally on right-hemisphere coding, and Corsi span is typically about two items less than digit span.

A good deal of work in this area has been carried out in connection with the attempt to explore visual imagery, frequently employing a technique devised by Brooks (1967). The subjects are shown a four by four matrix of cells, with one cell designated the starting square. They are then asked to remember a sequence of sentences such as *"In the starting square put a 1; in the square to the right put a 2; in the square beneath put a 3"* etc. Most subjects remember this by recoding the sentences in terms of a path through the matrix, and can typically remember about eight items. Visual recoding can be prevented by substituting non-spatial adjectives for "up", "down", "left", and "right", giving sequences such as *"In the starting square put a 1; in the next square to the good put a 2; in the next square to the weak put a 3; in the next square to the bad put a 4"*, etc. Subjects typically manage to recall a sequence of about six sentences, and appear to depend on rote verbal recall. Evidence for this comes from a number of sources. Brooks himself showed that the spatial task was best recalled with auditory presentation rather than visual, whereas the reverse pattern operated for the rote memory task. He argued that this was because visual processes and the imagery system use overlapping resources, as do rote memory and the auditory system.

Baddeley, Grant, Wight, and Thomson (1973) required subjects to perform the Brooks task with auditory presentation under either control conditions, or while simultaneously performing a visuo-spatial tracking task in which they had to keep a stylus in contact with a moving spot of light. Tracking had no effect on memory for the "nonsense" sequences which was assumed to depend on rote memory, but led to a marked decrease in performance on the visuo-spatial task. A subsequent study showed that disruption did not need to be visual, as a spatial tracking task in which the subject pointed to a moving sound source disrupted the imagery condition substantially more than the rote task, whereas a visual but non-spatial task in which the subject made judgements about the brightness of a field of light had the opposite effect (Baddeley & Lieberman, 1980). Baddeley and Lieberman concluded that the system was spatial rather than visual, but this has since been questioned by Logie (1986) who, using an imagery mnemonic task, showed that imagery could be disrupted by material with relatively little spatial information, such as patches of colour. The pattern of results therefore suggests that the sketchpad either comprises two separate subsystems, or possibly a single system with separable dimensions for visual and spatial information.

Probably the strongest evidence for a multi-component visuo-spatial sketchpad comes from the neuropsychological evidence. Holmes (1919) reports cases of soldiers suffering from gunshot wounds in World War I who appeared to show evidence of separable disruption of visual and spatial coding. Hence one patient was able to locate objects accurately, but not identify them, whereas a second showed exactly the opposite pattern, suggesting the separate coding of *what* and *where*. More recent evidence has lent further support to this, and is summarised by Farah (1988), who reports results from psychophysiological measures involving blood flow within the brain, or cortical evoked responses, to indicate at least two subsystems underlying visual imagery. One system appears to be dependent on the occipital lobes of the brain and is involved in representing the physical appearance of objects such as their colour and shape. The other subsystem which is responsible for spatial information appears to be more dependent on the parietal lobes. Evidence that the frontal lobes are also involved in visuo-spatial working memory comes from studies by Goldman-Rakic (1988), who has recorded from single units in the cortex of awake monkeys. She observes the involvement of certain frontal areas in tasks that require the monkey to continue to maintain visuo-spatial information over a brief period of time.

More recently, positron emission tomography (PET) scanning studies have further extended knowledge of the anatomical basis of the sketchpad, indicating the involvement of occipital parietal, pre-frontal, and frontal lobes, primarily in the right hemisphere (Jonides et al., 1993).

It seems probable then that the sketchpad is a relatively complex system that involves the active utilisation of parts of the two visual systems that have been identified as responsible for coding information about what and where respectively. Performance can be disrupted by requiring concurrent visual or spatial activity that is inconsistent with the image being maintained (Brooks, 1967; Byrne, 1974).

The Phonological Loop.   Much of the early work on short-term memory utilised verbal information, for which performance is assumed to be mainly dependent on the operation of the phonological loop. The loop is assumed in the Baddeley and Hitch model to have two components, a verbal store and an articulatory rehearsal process. The store is assumed to hold speech-based information represented in traces that fade away over a period of about two seconds. The traces can be maintained by subvocal articulatory rehearsal, a process that can also be used to enter information into the store, for example by articulating the names of the objects to be remembered either overtly or subvocally. Evidence on the nature of the store comes principally from two phenomena. The first is the phonological similarity effect described earlier, whereby similar sounding items such as the letters *P G V C T* are harder to remember accurately than a dissimilar sequence such as *K Y B R W*. This is assumed to occur because the items are stored in terms of a phonological or speech-based code; as the items fade, the similar items have fewer distinguishing features and hence are more subject to error.

A second phenomenon supporting the concept of a store is the *irrelevant speech effect*. If a subject is trying to remember a sequence of visually presented numbers, then performance will be disrupted by the presence of simultaneous irrelevant spoken material. The disrupting effect is just as great if the irrelevant material comprises nonsense as if it contains real words, and even other digits cause little additional problem over and above that of any other spoken items. The effect was assumed to occur because spoken material gains obligatory access to the phonological store, where it is able to corrupt the memory trace, although an extensive recent research programme by Jones and his colleagues has led to his development of an alternative view (see Jones 1993 for a review). The irrelevant speech effect does not appear to reflect simple distraction, as bursts of white noise have no effect on performance, nor does the intensity of the irrelevant stimulus, provided that it is clearly audible (Colle & Welsh, 1976; Salamé & Baddeley, 1982).

Characteristics of the articulatory control process are indicated by two other phenomena, the *word length effect* and the effects of *articulatory suppression*. If a subject's memory span for words is measured, then it becomes clear that span for long words such as *opportunity, individual, university*, etc. is substantially greater than that for short words such as *sum, harm, wit* (Baddeley, Thomson, & Buchanan, 1975). Indeed, memory span is linearly related to the spoken duration of the constituent items. This leads to consistent differences in digit span across different languages, dependent on how long digits take to articulate in that language (Ellis & Hennelly, 1980; Naveh-Benjamin & Ayres, 1986). Furthermore, the development of digit span over childhood parallels an increase in articulation rate, suggesting that much of the increase may be due to the capacity of the child to rehearse more rapidly (Hitch, Halliday, & Littler, 1984; Nicolson, 1981). Baddeley et al. proposed that the word length effect occurs because subjects maintain the memory trace by recycling the items, with span being set by the joint function of the rate of decay of the trace and the speed with which it can be refreshed by rehearsal. As rehearsal occurs in real time, long words are rehearsed more slowly, allowing more forgetting and hence leading to a reduced span. However, as Cowan et al. (1992) have pointed out, a major part of the word length effect may result from the delay in recall due to longer time taken to produce the long word sequences at recall, an effect that is also clear from earlier studies in which the length of an irrelevant verbal suffix was manipulated (Baddeley & Hull, 1979).

If subjects are prevented from rehearsing the material to be remembered, by the requirement to utter some irrelevant sound such as the word *the*, then performance is impaired (Murray, 1968). Overt articulatory suppression does, of course, also lead to irrelevant speech. However, Gupta and Macwhinnie (1995) have shown that suppression has a powerful effect that is over and above any influence of irrelevant speech. Suppression also obliterates the word length effect, provided it occurs during both input and written recall (Baddeley, Lewis, & Vallar, 1984). If the subject is not subvocally rehearsing, then it does not matter how long the words are.

Articulatory suppression also interferes with the phonological recoding of visually presented materials. Hence, the phonological similarity effect occurs with visual or auditory presentation, but when a subject is required to suppress articulation, then phonological similarity has no influence on visual presentation, although it continues to have an effect when presentation is auditory (Baddeley, et al., 1984). If the subject cannot name the visually presented material, then it must be stored in some non-phonological code. With auditory presentation, direct phonological representation however is guaranteed, without the need to recode through articulation.

Finally, the simple phonological loop model offers a clear interpretation of the previously reported patients with defective STM performance. Such patients typically show reduced memory span, particularly with auditory presentation. With visual presentation they typically show no evidence of phonological similarity and no word length effect (Vallar & Shallice, 1990). It is suggested that such patients have an impairment in the phonological loop system, which may reflect either a defective store, as suggested in case PV by Vallar and Baddeley (1984), or in other cases a defective operation of the articulatory control process, typically in association with dyspraxia reflecting problems in the setting up of speech motor programs (Caplan, Waters, & Rochon, 1992; Waters, Rochon, & Caplan, 1992). However, although the capacity to initiate articulatory programs does appear to be necessary, the evidence suggests that it is not necessary that the subject is able to realise such articulatory programs by overt verbal output; patients who are dysarthric, having lost the power to vocalise without disruption of higher-level language processes, typically show normal phonological loop performance (Baddeley & Wilson, 1985; Nebes, 1975).

The Function of the Phonological Loop.   Although the phonological loop is probably the best understood component of working memory, until relatively recently its function remained unclear. It has been suggested that STM plays a crucial role in language comprehension (Clark & Clark, 1977), although the evidence for this remains equivocal. In general patients with a deficit to this system appear to have problems with certain types of long and complex syntactic structures, but not to have a major deficit with straightforward sentential material (Vallar & Shallice, 1990).

An alternative hypothesis as to the functional significance of the phonological loop was proposed by Baddeley, Papagno, and Vallar (1988) in a study using patient PV who had a very pure deficit to the phonological loop system. The hypothesis was that the loop is important for new phonological learning; it was tested by attempting to teach PV Russian vocabulary, contrasting this with her capacity to learn to associate pairs of words in her native language of Italian. She proved to have normal capacity for Italian paired-associate learning, but to be dramatically impaired in her capacity to acquire words of a foreign language, suggesting that the phonological loop may indeed be important for vocabulary acquisition.

Further evidence for the role of the phonological loop comes from the case of a girl suffering from Down's syndrome, whose impaired level of general intelligence was atypically accompanied by an apparently normal phonological loop, as measured by verbal memory span. She had lived abroad and spoke three languages. When tested on paired-associate tasks devised for PV, she showed exactly the opposite pattern, namely normal performance on novel vocabulary coupled with impaired learning of pairs of words in her native language, a task that typically relies on semantic coding (Vallar & Papagno, 1993).

Other studies have been concerned with the role of the phonological loop in the acquisition by children of the vocabulary of their native language. One study (Gathercole & Baddeley 1990) involved children with a specific language disability, that is, they had normal or above average non-verbal intelligence, coupled with a level of verbal development that was at least two years behind that which was normal for their age. When the memory performance of these children was studied in more detail, they were found to have a particularly marked impairment in the capacity to hear and repeat back unfamiliar pseudo-words. On this task, the 8-year-old subjects tested who had the language development of 6-year-olds, performed like 4-year-olds, suggesting that this may be a crucial weakness. The deficit in this group did not seem to result from perceptual or speech production problems, but was associated with impaired verbal memory span. This study was therefore consistent with the hypothesis that the children's poor language development was a direct result of the impaired functioning of the phonological loop. More recent studies of two single cases of subjects with developmental STM deficit also broadly support this hypothesis (Baddeley, 1993c; Baddeley & Wilson, 1993).

A subsequent investigation was concerned with the development of vocabulary in a sample of normal children. They were tested at age 4 on non-verbal intelligence, sound mimicry, the nonword repetition task mentioned previously, and on vocabulary (Gathercole & Baddeley, 1989). Nonword repetition correlated more highly with vocabulary than did intelligence. However, an association between vocabulary and nonword repetition could imply either direction of causality; the capacity to remember nonwords could help a child learn new vocabulary items, or conversely a rich vocabulary might help the child to retain unfamiliar new material. We therefore re-tested the children a year later, comparing the capacity for nonword repetition at age 4 to predict vocabulary a year later with the opposite pattern. There was a significantly higher correlation between nonword repetition and later vocabulary acquisition than there was for the reverse, suggesting that at this age, nonword repetition is more likely to be the basic factor leading to good vocabulary. It is important to note however, that as children get older, the relationship changes, with the result that in 6- and 8-year-olds, good vocabulary is at least as likely to be helping nonword repetition as the reverse (Gathercole, Willis, Emslie, & Baddeley, 1992).

There is evidence that nonword repetition is also a good predictor of second language learning. In a study concerned with the learning of English by young Finnish children, a number of measures taken at the beginning of the course were correlated with a range of indicators of English language skill two years later. The best predictor proved to be the child's capacity to repeat unfamiliar pseudo-words, in short a nonword repetition task (Service, 1992).

We have implied that the capacity for the acquisition of vocabulary is related to the operation of the phonological loop, and in particular to short-term phonological storage. The capacity for nonword repetition could however, be dependent on many other factors, and Snowling, Chiat, and Hulme (1991) have argued that it is at least as plausible to assume that it reflects general phonological maturity rather than the phonological loop. Although we do not accept this interpretation (Gathercole, Willis, & Baddeley, 1991), we do accept that the existing developmental data remain open to a range of interpretations.

Fortunately, however, the presence of a reasonably well-developed model of the phonological loop allows us to test the influence of the system on vocabulary acquisition in other ways, using normal adults, who cannot be assumed to have defective phonological development. In one study, Papagno, Valentine, and Baddeley (1991) replicated the vocabulary learning experiment carried out initially on PV, but this time using normal subjects with and without articulatory suppression. Suppression should disrupt the operation of the loop, leading to clear impairment of the learning of novel vocabulary items, while having little effect on the acquisition of pairs of familiar words, as this is assumed to depend principally on semantic coding. The predicted pattern of results was observed. In a subsequent study, Papagno and Vallar (1992) studied the effects of phonological similarity and word length on both the acquisition of the vocabulary of a foreign language, and native language paired associated learning. As predicted by the phonological loop hypothesis, both similarity and word length impaired the rate of acquisition of foreign language vocabulary, but had no influence on native language learning. Articulatory suppression, word length and phonological similar-ity are all known to influence the phonological loop, and all have the predicted effect on the acquisition of foreign language vocabulary. It is hard to see how an explanation in terms of general phonological development could account for these results. On the other hand, the phonological loop hypothesis can account for these as well as the data on first and second language vocabulary acquisition in both normal and language-disordered children. There therefore appears to be a good prima facie argument for the view that the phonological loop has evolved as one of a range of language acquisition devices.

CONCLUSION

The concept of a working memory capable of holding and manipulating information in performing a range of more complex tasks thus continues to be a fruitful one. It sits at the intersection of research on memory with that of perception and action, and its future would seem to depend at least in part on its continuing capacity to integrate with the surrounding fields. Hence an adequate understanding of the phonological loop is likely to depend on a better understanding of the processes of speech perception and production. Our understanding of the visuo-spatial sketchpad is likely to evolve together with our improved analysis of the processes of object recognition and imagery, while the executive is clearly intimately tied into the role of attention in the control of action. All of these in turn are likely to depend to a greater or lesser extent on the relationship between working memory and long-term memory. Viewed from this perspective, working memory is likely to offer a fruitful area of interaction between cognitive psychology and other neurosciences for many years to come.

REFERENCES

Anderson, J.R. (1983). *The architecture of cognition*. Harvard: Harvard University Press.

Atkinson, R.C., & Shiffrin, R.M. (1968). Human memory: A proposed system and its control processes. In K.W. Spence (Ed.), *The psychology of learning and motivation: Advances in research and theory Vol. 2*, (pp. 89–195). New York: Academic Press.

Baddeley, A.D. (1966a). Short-term memory for word sequences as a function of acoustic, semantic and formal similarity. *Quarterly Journal of Experimental Psychology, 18*, 362–365.

Baddeley, A.D. (1966b). The influence of acoustic and semantic similarity on long-term memory for word sequences. *Quarterly Journal of Experimental Psychology, 18*, 302–309.

Baddeley, A.D. (1966c). The capacity for generating information by randomization. *Quarterly Journal of Experimental Psychology, 18*, 119–129.

Baddeley, A.D. (1978). The trouble with levels: A re-examination of Craik and Lockhart's framework for memory research. *Psychological Review, 85*, 139–152.

Baddeley, A.D. (1986). *Working memory*. Oxford: Oxford University Press.

Baddeley, A.D. (1992). Working memory. *Science, 255*, 556–559.

Baddeley, A.D. (1993a). Working memory or working attention? In A. Baddeley & L. Weiskrantz (Eds.), *Attention: Selection, awareness and control. A tribute to Donald Broadbent* (pp. 152–170). Oxford: Oxford University Press.

Baddeley, A.D. (1993b). Working memory and conscious awareness. In A. Collins, S. Gathercole, M. Conway, & P. Morris (Eds.), *Theories of memory*, (pp. 11–28). Hove, UK: Lawrence Erlbaum Associates Ltd.

Baddeley, A.D. (1993c). Short-term phonological memory and long-term learning: A single case study. *European Journal of Cognitive Psychology, 5*, 129–148.

Baddeley, A.D. (in press). Exploring the central executive *Quarterly Journal of Experimental Psychology*.

Baddeley, A.D., Bressi, S., Della Sala, S., Logie, R., & Spinnler, H. (1991). The decline of working memory in Alzheimer's Disease: A longitudinal study. *Brain, 114*, 2521–2542.

Baddeley, A.D., Grant, S., Wight, E., & Thomson, N. (1973). Imagery and visual working memory. In P.M.A. Rabbitt & S. Dornic (Eds.), *Attention and performance V*, (pp. 205–217). London: Academic Press.

Baddeley, A.D., & Hitch, G. (1974). Working memory. In G.A Bower (Ed.), *The psychology of learning and motivation, Vol. 8*, (pp. 47–89). New York: Academic Press.

Baddeley, A.D., & Hull, A.J. (1979). Prefix and suffix effects: Do they have a common basis? *Journal of Verbal Learning and Verbal Behavior, 18*, 129–140.

Baddeley, A.D., Lewis, V.J., & Vallar, G. (1984). Exploring the articulatory loop. *Quarterly Journal of Experimental Psychology, 36*, 233–252.

Baddeley, A.D., & Lieberman, K. (1980). Spatial working memory. In R.S. Nickerson (Ed.), *Attention and performance VIII*, (pp. 521–539). Hillsdale, NJ: Lawrence Erlbaum Associates Inc.

Baddeley, A.D., Logie, R., Bressi, S., Della Sala, S., & Spinnler, H. (1986). Dementia and working memory. *Quarterly Journal of Experimental Psychology, 38A*, 603–618.

Baddeley, A.D., Papagno, C., & Vallar, G. (1988). When long term learning depends on short-term storage. *Journal of Memory and Language, 27*, 586–595.

Baddeley, A.D., Thomson, N., & Buchanan, M. (1975). Word length and the structure of short-term memory. *Journal of Verbal Learning and Verbal Behavior, 14*, 575–589.

Baddeley, A.D., & Warrington, E.K. (1970). Amnesia and the distinction between long- and short-term memory. *Journal of Verbal Learning and Verbal Behavior, 9*, 176–189.

Baddeley, A.D., & Wilson, B. (1985). Phonological coding and short-term memory in patients without speech. *Journal of Memory and Language, 24*, 490–502.

Baddeley, A.D., & Wilson, B. (1986). Amnesia, autobiographical memory and confabulation. In D.C. Rubin (Ed.), *Autobiographical memory*, (pp. 225–252). New York: Cambridge University Press.

Baddeley, A.D., & Wilson, B.A. (1993). A developmental deficit in short-term phonological memory: Implications for language and reading. *Memory, 1*, 65–78.

Broadbent, D.E. (1958). *Perception and communication*. London: Pergamon Press.

Brooks, L.R. (1967). The suppression of visualization by reading. *Quarterly Journal of Experimental Psychology, 19*, 289–299.

Brown, J. (1958). Some tests of the decay theory of immediate memory. *Quarterly Journal of Experimental Psychology, 10*, 12–21.

Byrne, B. (1974). Item concreteness vs. spatial organization as predictors of visual imagery. *Memory and Cognition, 2*, 53–59.

Caplan, D., Rochon, E., & Waters, G.S. (1992). Articulatory and phonological determinants of word length effects in span tasks *The Quarterly Journal of Experimental Psychology, 45A*, 177–192.

Carpenter, P.A , & Just, M.A. (1977). Reading comprehension as the eye sees it. In M.A. Just & P. Carpenter (Eds.), *Cognitive processes in comprehension* (pp. 109–139). Hillsdale, NJ: Lawrence Erlbaum Associates Inc.

Carpenter, P.A., Just, M.A., & Shell, P. (1990). What one intelligence test measures: A theoretical account of the processing in the Raven's Progressive Matrices Test. *Psychological Review, 97*, 404–431.

Christal, R.E. (1991). Comparative validities of ASVAB and lamp tests for logic gates learning. *Armstrong Laboratory Human Resources Directorate Technical Report AL-TP-1991-0031*. (Brooks Airforce Base, Texas 78235-5000).

Clark, H.H., & Clark, E.V. (1977). *Psychology and language.* New York: Harcourt Brace Jovanovic.

Colle, H.A., & Welsh. A. (1976). Acoustic masking in primary memory. *Journal of Verbal Learning and Verbal Behavior, 15,* 17–32.

Conrad, R. (1964). Acoustic confusion in immediate memory. *British Journal of Psychology, 55,* 75–84.

Conrad, R., & Hull, A.J. (1964). Information, acoustic confusion and memory span. *British Journal of Psychology, 55,* 429–432.

Cowan, N., Day, L., Saults, J.S., Keller, T.A., Johnson, T., & Flores, L. (1992). The role of verbal output time in the effects of word length on immediate memory. *Journal of Memory and Language, 31,* 1–17.

Craik, F.I.M. (1977). Age differences in human memory. In J.E. Birren & K.W. Schaie (Eds.), *Handbook of the psychology of aging,* (pp. 384–420). New York: van Nostrand Reinhold.

Craik, F.I.M., & Lockhart, R.S. (1972). Levels of processing: A framework for memory research. *Journal of Verbal Learning and Verbal Behavior, 11,* 671–684.

Craik, F.I.M., & Tulving, E. (1975). Depth of processing and the retention of words in episodic memory. *Journal of Experimental Psychology: General, 104,* 268–294.

Craik, F.I.M., & Watkins, M.J. (1973). The role of rehearsal in short-term memory. *Journal of Verbal Learning and Verbal Behavior, 12,* 599–607.

Daneman, M., & Carpenter, P.A. (1980). Individual differences in working memory and reading. *Journal of Verbal Learning and Verbal Behavior, 19,* 450–466.

Daneman, M., & Carpenter, P.A. (1983). Individual differences in integrating information between and within sentences. *Journal of Experimental Psychology: Learning, Memory and Cognition, 9,* 561–584.

Daneman, M. & Tardif, T. (1987). Working memory and reading skill re-examined. In M. Coltheart (Ed.), *Attention and performance XII* (pp. 491–508). Hove, UK: Lawrence Erlbaum Associates.

Duncan, J. (1993). Selection of input and goal in the control of behaviour. In A. Baddeley & L. Weiskrantz (Eds.), *Attention: Selection, awareness and control* (pp. 53–71). Oxford: Clarendon Press.

Ellis, N.C., & Hennelley, R.A. (1980). A bilingual word-length effect: Implications for intelligence testing and the relative ease of mental calculation in Welsh and English. *British Journal of Psychology, 71,* 43–52.

Farah, M.J. (1988). Is visual memory really visual? Overlooked evidence from neuro-psychology. *Psychological Review, 95,* 307–317.

Gathercole, S., & Baddeley, A.D. (1989). Evaluation of the role of phonological STM in the development of vocabulary in children: A longitudinal study. *Journal of Memory and Language, 28,* 200–213.

Gathercole, S., & Baddeley, A. (1990). Phonological memory deficits in language-disordered children: Is there a causal connection? *Journal of Memory and Language, 29,* 336–360.

Gathercole, S.E., Willis, C.S., & Baddeley, A.D. (1991). Nonword repetition, phonological memory, and vocabulary: A reply to Snowling, Chiat, and Hulme. *Applied Psycholinguistics, 12,* 375–379.

Gathercole, S.E., Willis, C.S., Emslie, H., & Baddeley, A.D. (1992). Phonological memory and vocabulary development during the early school years: A longitudinal study. *Developmental Psychology, 28,* 887–898.

Glanzer, M. (1972). Storage mechanisms in recall. In G.H. Bower (Ed.), *The psychology of learning and motivation: Advances in research and theory, Vol. V.* New York: Academic Press.

Glanzer, M., & Cunitz, A.R. (1966). Two storage mechanisms in free recall. *Journal of Verbal Learning and Verbal Behavior, 5,* 351–360.

Goldman-Rakic, P.W. (1988). Topography of cognition: Parallel distributed networks in primate association cortex. *Annual Review of Neuroscience, 11*, 137–156.

Gupta, P., & MacWhinney, B. (1995). Is the articulatory loop articulatory or auditory—re-examining the effects of concurrent articulation on immediate serial-recall. *Journal of Memory and Language, 34*, 63–88.

Hebb, D.O. (1961). Distinctive features of learning in the higher animal. In J.F. Delafresnaye (Ed.), *Brain mechanisms and learning*, (pp. 37–46). London and New York: Oxford University Press.

Hitch, G.J., & Baddeley, A.D. (1976). Verbal reasoning and working memory. *Quarterly Journal of Experimental Psychology, 28*, 603–621.

Hitch, G.J., Halliday, M.S., & Littler, J.E. (1984). *Memory span and the speed of mental operations*. Paper presented at the joint Experimental Psychology Society/Netherlands Psychonomic Foundation Meeting, Amsterdam.

Holmes, G. (1919). Disturbances of visual space recognition. *British Medical Journal, 2*, 230–233.

Jonides, J., Smith, E.E., Koeppe, R.A., Awh, E., Minoshima, S., & Mintun, M.A. (1993). Spatial working memory in humans as revealed by PET. *Nature, 363*, 623–625.

Jones, D.M. (1993). Objects, streams, and threads of auditory attention. In A. Baddeley & L. Weiskrantz (Eds.), *Attention: Selection awareness and control* (pp. 87–104). Oxford: Clarendon Press.

Just, M.A., & Carpenter, P.A. (1992). A capacity theory of comprehension: Individual differences in working memory. *Psychological Review, 99*, 122–149.

Kemper, S. (1990). Adults' diaries: Changes made to written narratives across the life-span. *Discourse Processes, 13*, 207–223.

Kemper, S., & Rash, S.J. (1988). Speech and writing across the lifespan. In M.M. Gruneberg, P.E. Morris, & R.N. Sykes (Eds.), *Practical aspects of memory: Current research and issues, Vol. 2* (pp. 107–122). Chichester: John Wiley.

Keppel, G., & Underwood, B.J. (1962). Proactive inhibition in short-term retention of single items. *Journal of Verbal Learning and Verbal Behavior, 1*, 153–161.

Kintsch, W., & Buschke, H. (1969). Homophones and synonyms in short-term memory. *Journal of Experimental Psychology, 80*, 403–407.

Kintsch, W., & van Dijk, T.A. (1978). Toward a model of text comprehension and production. *Psychological Review, 85*, 363–394.

Kintsch, W., & Vipond, D. (1979). Reading comprehension and readability in educational practice. In L-G Nilsson (Ed.), *Perspectives on memory research* (pp. 329–365). Hillsdale, NJ: Lawrence Erlbaum Associates Inc.

Kyllonen, P.C., & Christal, R.E. (1990). Reasoning ability is (little more than) working-memory capacity. *Intelligence, 14*, 389–433.

Logie, R.H. (1986). Visuo-spatial processing in working memory. *Quarterly Journal of Experimental Psychology, 38A*, 229–247.

Melton, A.W. (1963). Implications of short-term memory for a general theory of memory. *Journal of Verbal Learning and Verbal Behavior, 2*, 1–21.

Milner, B. (1966). Amnesia following operation on the temporal lobes. In C.W.M. Whitty & O.L. Zangwill (Eds.), *Amnesia*, (pp.109–133). London: Butterworths.

Milner, B. (1971). Interhemispheric differences in the localization of psychological processes in man. *British Medical Bulletin, 27*, 272–277.

Morris, R.G., Craik, F.I.M., & Gick, M.L. (1990). Age-differences in working memory tasks: The role of secondary memory and the central executive system. *Quarterly Journal of Experimental Psychology, 42A*, 67–84.

Murray, D.J. (1968). Articulation and acoustic confusability in short-term memory. *Journal of Experimental Psychology, 78*, 679–684.

Naveh-Benjamin, M., & Ayres, T.J. (1986). Digit span, reading rate, and linguistic relativity. *Quarterly Journal of Experimental Psychology, 38*, 739–751.

Nebes, R.N. (1975). The nature of internal speech in a patient with aphemia. *Brain and Language, 2*, 489–497.

Neisser, U. (1967). *Cognitive psychology.* New York: Appleton-Century-Crofts.

Newell, A., & Simon, H.A. (1972). *Human problem solving.* Englewood Cliffs, NJ: Prentice Hall.

Nicolson, R. (1981). The relationship between memory span and processing speed. In M.P. Friedman, J.P. Das, & N. O'Connor (Eds.), *Intelligence and learning,* (pp. 179–184). New York: Plenum Press.

Norman, D.A., & Shallice, T. (1980). *Attention to action: Willed and automatic control of behavior.* University of California San Diego CHIP Report 99.

Oakhill, J.V., Yuill, N., & Parkin, A.J. (1988). Memory and inference in skilled and less-skilled comprehenders. In M.M. Gruneberg, P.E. Morris, & R.N. Sykes (Eds.), *Practical aspects of memory: Current research and issues, Vol. 2. Clinical and educational implications,* (pp. 315–320). Chichester, UK: John Wiley.

Olton, D.S., Walker, J.A., & Gage, F.H. (1978). Hippocampal connections and spatial discrimination. *Brain Research, 139*, 295–308.

Papagno, C., Valentine, T., & Baddeley, A.D. (1991). Phonological short-term memory and foreign-language vocabulary learning. *Journal of Memory and Language, 30*, 331–347.

Papagno, C., & Vallar, G. (1992). Phonological short-term memory and the learning of novel words: The effect of phonological similarity and item length. *Quarterly Journal of Experimental Psychology, 44A*, 47–67.

Peterson, L.R., & Peterson, M.J. (1959). Short-term retention of individual verbal items. *Journal of Experimental Psychology, 58*, 193–198.

Robbins, T.W., Anderson, E.J., Barker, D.R., Bradley, A.C., Fearnyhough, C., Henson, R., Hudson, S.R., & Baddeley, A.D. (in press). Working memory in chess. *Memory & Cognition.*

Sachs, J.S. (1967). Recognition memory for syntactic and semantic aspects of connected discourse. *Perception and Psychophysics, 2*, 437–442.

Salamé, P., & Baddeley, A.D. (1982). Disruption of short-term memory by unattended speech: Implications for the structure of working memory. *Journal of Verbal Learning and Verbal Behavior, 21*, 150–164.

Service, E. (1992). Phonology, working memory, and foreign-language learning. *Quarterly Journal of Experimental Psychology, 45A*, 21–50.

Shallice, T. (1982). Specific impairments of planning. *Philosophical Transactions of the Royal Society London B, 298*, 199–209.

Shallice, T., & Burgess, P. (1993). Supervisory control of action and thought selection. In A. Baddeley & L. Weiskrantz (Eds.), *Attention: Selection, awareness and control* (pp. 171–187). Oxford: Clarendon Press.

Shallice, T., Burgess, P., Schon, F., & Baxter, D. (1989). The origins of utilisation behaviour. *Brain, 112*, 1587–1598.

Shallice, T., & Warrington, E.K. (1970). Independent functioning of verbal memory stores: A neuropsychological study. *Quarterly Journal of Experimental Psychology, 22*, 261–273.

Shiffrin, R.M., & Schneider, W. (1977). Controlled and automatic human information processing: II. Perceptual learning, automatic attending and a general theory. *Psychological Review, 84*, 127–190.

Snowling, M., Chiat, S., & Hulme, C. (1991). Words, nonwords, and phonological processes: Some comments on Gathercole, Willis, Emslie, and Baddeley. *Applied Psycholinguistics, 12*, 369–373.

Turner, M.L., & Engle, R.W. (1989). Is working memory capacity task dependent? *Journal of Memory and Language, 28*, 127–154.

Vallar, G., & Baddeley, A.D. (1984). Phonological short-term store, phonological processing and sentence comprehension: A neuropsychological case study. *Cognitive Neuropsychology*, *1*, 121–141.

Vallar, G., & Papagno, C. (1993). Preserved vocabulary acquisition in Downs' syndrome: The role of phonological short-term memory. *Cortex*, *29*, 467–483.

Vallar, G., & Shallice, T. (Eds). (1990). *Neuropsychological impairments of short-term memory*. Cambridge: Cambridge University Press.

Warrington, E.K. (1982). The double dissociation of short- and long-term memory deficits. In L.S. Cermak (Ed.), *Human memory and amnesia* (pp. 61–76). Hillsdale, NJ: Lawrence Erlbaum Associates Inc.

Waters, G.S., Rochon, E., & Caplan, D. (1992). The role of high-level speech planning in rehearsal: Evidence from patients with apraxia of speech. *Journal of Memory and Language* *331*, 54–73.

Waugh, N.C., & Norman, D.A. (1965). Primary memory. *Psychological Review*, *72*, 89–104.

Wechsler, D. (1955). *Wechsler Adult Intelligence Scale*. New York: The Psychological Corporation.

2 Covert processes and their development in short-term memory

Nelson Cowan
University of Missouri, USA

Robert Kail
Purdue University, USA

INTRODUCTION

Immediate, serial verbal recall could be viewed as one of the simplest tasks used by investigators of cognition and intelligence. On every trial, a list of items is presented to the subject, who is supposed to reproduce that list verbatim. The correct response is the same as the stimulus. What could be simpler? It would be tempting to try to account for performance in the task in an equally simple manner. How would that account go? Perhaps we have an internal recording of the sensory impression of the list items, along with a verbal output process that can convert the sensory impression back into spoken or written words; or perhaps each sensory impression is immediately converted into a motor plan and the motor plans are retained in a memory store, in order, until the list ends and the response can begin.

Notice that even these maximally simple accounts of performance rely on mental processes that cannot be observed directly (e.g. in these accounts, a sensory-to-motor conversion process and either sensory or motor memory storage). Such "covert" mental processes can be studied indirectly, however, through attempts to draw inferences about what must occur in the brain and mind to account for performance across a variety of test conditions. Our thesis is that progress has been made recently in understanding the covert mental processes that take place in short-term memory tasks, though we still have far to go for a complete understanding. Unfortunately for inquiring

29

minds, human performance does not appear to be as simple as the possibilities sketched here; but it does appear reasonably orderly.

In the present chapter, we will focus on recent progress in understanding immediate, serial recall tasks involving both verbal and visual stimuli. The organisation of the chapter is by the specific covert processes, which will be discussed one at a time although, in reality, multiple covert processes appear to operate together to produce an adequate response. We believe that the mnemonic processes underlying this seemingly simple sort of task may actually be important in a much broader variety of problem-solving activities.

The list of processes that we will examine is not exhaustive, but we have attempted to include the processes that have attracted researchers' attention the most. These include (1) stimulus recoding, (2) speech articulatory processes, (3) short-term memory search, and (4) the retrieval of information from long-term memory as support for immediate memory performance. We will rely on previous literature reviews where we can, allowing us to focus on what we consider to be some key findings and controversial points within the research literature.

Throughout the chapter, we also will consider how these covert processes may account for developmental and individual differences in immediate recall. The emphasis is on normal childhood development, but with some evidence from learning disabilities and adult ageing considered as well. If differences in recall can be related to other abilities, that can help us eventually to determine what the causal variables underlying immediate recall may be. The developmental and individual-difference research reflects back on our basic process knowledge and informs it considerably.

Near the chapter's end we will ask how well a simple, general factor—the overall speed of processing—accounts for an individual's level of ability in immediate recall tasks. We will conclude with a consideration of future directions for research on covert processes in short-term memory.

STIMULUS RECODING

Within the confines of the immediate, serial verbal recall task, one can present stimuli in the form of spoken words, printed words, or pictures. One can require a spoken response, a written response, or some form of manual response. At some point, the subject must decode the incoming stimulus and re-encode it in terms of the planned response modality, at least when the stimulus and response modalities differ. We refer to the decoding and re-encoding processes together as stimulus "recoding".

There are several reasons why the nature and timing of the recoding process logically could influence recall. Subjects could differ in how difficult it is for them to recode the materials, which could affect (a) the fidelity of the recoding process, or (b) the amount of various processing resources that must be taken away from strategic mnemonic activities in order to accomplish that recoding. Subjects also could differ in (c) the degree to which they have the foresight to do the recoding at convenient points in the trial, with less able subjects therefore forced to do the recoding at later, less opportune points. (We do not know, at present, what points would be inopportune.) A final possibility is that (d) there is some choice in how to recode and that the ideal route involves going through some intermediate coding modality, not directly from the stimulus modality to the response modality.

Spoken Responses to Spoken Lists

One cannot readily convert a spoken stimulus into a spoken response without going through an intermediate, abstract code. Consider how difficult it is, for example, to repeat a single word spoken in a foreign language, especially one with a phonology that is very different from one's own language. Familiarity with the phonemes helps one repeat them accurately, and familiarity with the lexical item greatly helps one recall the sequence of phonemes. These effects occur presumably because a spoken word activates phonological and lexical codes in long-term memory.

It seems quite likely that some sort of internal recoding is needed, therefore, even in the case of spoken responses to spoken lists. However, the recoding differences might be expected to be smaller than in the case of written or pictorial stimuli, for which the initial stimulus encoding is more complex. A written word needs to be read and a picture needs to be interpreted in light of one's world and lexical knowledge; and individuals differ greatly in amount of knowledge. The recoding differences might also be expected to be larger in the case of a written response, for which a knowledge of spelling is needed. The difficulty of a manual response would depend on what coding cues are being responded to manually (e.g. written versus pictorial response choices). In any case, it seems likely on an a priori basis that there would be individual and age-related differences in the speed and accuracy with which internal recoding could proceed even for spoken responses to spoken lists.

A study by Case, Kurland, and Goldberg (1982) was seminal in bringing a concern about recoding into the immediate recall literature. Their subjects (children aged 3 and 6 years, and adults) received a test of memory span for spoken lists composed of subsets of the words *star*, *ball*, *fish*, *shoe*, *tree*, *chair*, and *cup* (which, presumably, all the children knew). They also received a test in which isolated spoken words were presented and the subject was to repeat each word as quickly as possible. The correlation between span and the mean identification time (defined as the time between an isolated word and the onset of the response) was –0.74. When age was partialled out, the correlation remained significant at –0.35.

It should be pointed out that, though the repetition task demonstrates age and individual-difference effects in recoding, it is not clear what the critical covert processes are. The critical difference could be either in attaching a lexical identity to the spoken input, or in creating and initiating a motor plan based on that lexical identity. As an excellent review of the relevant literature (Henry & Millar, 1993) indicates, the results typically have been interpreted as evidence of the former. The measure is termed "identification time" even though the time of response planning is also included in the estimate.

It also is important to note that one must continually take seriously the caveat that correlations cannot be interpreted as clear evidence of causation. Henry and Millar (1991) attempted to examine the causal role of identification times by controlling for them. The subjects were children of 5 and 7 years of age. An identification-time measure similar to that of Case et al. (1982) was used to produce a set of stimuli for each subject, such that the identification times were matched across subjects and across ages. Despite a completely successful match for familiar, monosyllabic words, older children's mean span (4.13) was significantly higher than that of younger children (3.29). At the very least, this suggests that identification time is not the sole causal factor in developmental changes in memory span.

What alternative account of the correlation between identification time and span can be found? It seems quite unlikely that short-term memory skills play a critical role in carrying out the identification-time task. Therefore, the remaining hypothesis is that a third factor (or set of factors) underlies the variance common to span and identification-time tasks. For example, the time it takes to identify an item might be correlated, though imperfectly, with the time it takes to carry out other processes that are more directly relevant to memory span performance. This type of hypothesis has been prevalent in recent research and will be discussed later in the chapter.

Tasks Involving Stimuli or Responses in Other Modalities

The recoding considered so far is the minimal recoding necessary when the stimuli and responses are both in the same, spoken modality. Additional recoding processes may be necessary when they differ in modality. Aside from the obvious developmental increase in reading and writing ability in childhood, facility with verbal labelling is known to increase with age (Henry & Millar, 1993). Consequently, whenever the stimuli are pictorial in nature and verbal responses are required, young children's performance may be limited by their verbal labelling abilities.

The recent work of Hitch and his colleagues is quite consistent with this proposed factor. The results obtained in several studies (Halliday, Hitch,

Lennon, & Pettipher, 1990; Hitch, Halliday, Dodd, & Littler, 1989; Hitch, Halliday, Schaafstal, & Heffernan, 1991; Hitch, Halliday, Schaafstal, & Schraagen, 1988) suggest that children below the age of 7 years do not consistently use labels for pictorial stimuli. In all of these studies, stimuli were presented in either pictorial or spoken form, and spoken responses were required. There were specific disadvantages for younger children that occurred only with the pictorial stimuli, suggesting that the difficulty was in converting these stimuli to a verbal form.

Role of Phonological Similarity and Word Length Effects. Rather than relying solely on developmental differences in memory span, which could be attributed to many different factors, the studies by Hitch and his colleagues, cited earlier, focused on the well-established "phonological similarity" and "word length" effects. The phonological similarity effect is the finding that short-term memory performance is less accurate for lists of words that are phonetically similar to one another than for dissimilar lists (Conrad, 1964), which has been interpreted to mean that items are confused with one another in phonological storage or during retrieval from storage for recall (e.g. Baddeley, 1986). The effect is much smaller in very young children (Conrad, 1971; Hulme, 1984). The applicability to picture recall in children is that the phonological similarity effect should not occur if the subject has not recoded the stimuli into a phonological form.

The word length effect is the finding that short-term memory performance is less accurate for lists composed of phonetically longer words (Baddeley, 1986; Baddeley, Thomson, & Buchanan, 1975). Given that this effect is abolished when articulation is suppressed during both the reception of the list and written recall (Baddeley, Lewis, & Vallar, 1984), it has been assumed that the word length effect reflects the contribution of articulatory activity to recall, and that longer words permit more forgetting while words are being articulated covertly during the presentation of the list (Baddeley, 1986) or overtly in the spoken response (Cowan et al., 1992; Henry, 1991). Similar to the phonological similarity effect, the applicability to picture recall in children is that the word length effect should not occur unless a phonological recoding of the stimuli is undertaken at some point.

All of the experiments by Hitch and his colleagues cited earlier included conditions in which the stimuli consisted of line drawings, and they all required a spoken response. Hitch et al. (1988) found that visual similarity between the drawings impaired recall in 5-year-old children but not 10-year-old children, as would be expected if only the older children recoded the stimuli into a verbal form. Hitch et al. (1989) investigated word length effects at various ages in childhood and found them in children as young as 4 years when the stimuli were spoken, but not until 8 years when the stimuli were line drawings. This finding again suggests that only the older children recoded the line drawings into a verbal form, permitting the word length effect to occur. Halliday et al. (1990) used an articulatory suppression task (repeating a word over and over during the recall task) to prevent any covert articulation. This eliminated the phonological similarity and word length effects in the recall of line drawings in 11-year-olds, and reduced their performance to the level of 5-year-olds without articulatory suppression. Finally, Hitch et al. (1991) found that 5-year-old children produced word length effects and phonological similarity effects when they were required to label line drawing stimuli during their presentation, but not when the children remained silent during the presentation. All of these findings are consistent with an interpretation in which young children convert the pictures to a phonological form (and therefore yield phonological similarity and word length effects) only if they are instructed or encouraged to do so.

In all these studies, visual materials might be recoded primarily because of the requirement of verbal recall. However, Schiano and Watkins (1981) found phonological similarity and word length effects for pictures in adults, even though the response was nonverbal: Subjects were to select the pictures presented from a larger deck, and were to place the selected pictures in the correct serial order.

A developmental study by Hulme, Silvester, Smith, and Muir (1986), basically modelled after the one by Schiano and Watkins (1981), contradicts the findings of Hitch and his colleagues regarding the abilities of young children. In the Hulme et al. study, each stimulus picture was overturned after its presentation and, after the list was presented, a complete set of pictures was revealed. The subject was to match each overturned picture to the corresponding picture in the response set. The pictures had names that were monosyllabic on some trials and multisyllabic on other trials. A length effect was obtained in the youngest children tested (4-year-olds), even when the pictures were not labelled at the time of their presentation (Experiments 2 and 3). The third experiment also showed that the length effect was abolished with articulatory suppression during presentation of the list.

It is not yet clear why the studies with young children are discrepant. The response modes differ, but one would think that the use of a nonverbal response by Hulme et al. (1986) would, if anything, discourage labelling of the picture stimuli. One potentially relevant factor is that Hulme et al. (1986) did not use a span procedure, but instead presented three items per trial to the 4- and 5-year-old subjects. However, Hitch et al. (1991) also used three-item sets with 5-year-olds, with a spoken response, and they did not find a length effect in these subjects (even though the overall level of recall was higher than Hulme et al. obtained).

Hulme et al. (1986, Experiment 2) attempted to detect children's articulatory movements during the presentation of unnamed pictures, and found that naming occurred in 4-year-olds on about 73% of those trials.

Perhaps the amount of naming was greater than in other studies. However, it remains unclear what factor accounts for the difference in the likelihood of 4-year-olds to name pictures. In any case, it seems likely that word length effects and phonological similarity effects for pictorial stimuli occur only if the subject recodes the pictures into a verbal form, and that this verbal recoding is at least somewhat less readily accomplished across a variety of stimuli by young children.

These conclusions in turn lead to a more fundamental statement. It is not the stimuli or the responses *per se* that primarily govern the nature of immediate recall performance. Instead, it is the nature of the internal memory codes that is critical. To the extent that very different kinds of stimuli and responses are converted to comparable mental codes (e.g. to a phonologically based code), then they are processed in a comparable manner during the recall task. Cowan and Saults (1995) pursued this notion further, discussing the variety of sensory, phonological, orthographic, and semantic codes that can be formed for verbal stimuli and used in combination.

The act of verbal recoding cannot apply to all pictorial stimuli, as there are sure to be visual stimuli too complex for that type of recoding to be accomplished adequately. The strategies and covert processes used in retaining more complex visual stimuli have been examined in other studies (e.g. for a review see Baddeley, 1986), but we will treat them as beyond the scope of the present chapter.

SPEECH ARTICULATORY PROCESSES

The foregoing discussion indicates that at least older children and adults verbally label picture stimuli and tend to rely on that recoding of the stimuli in recall, even when the response mode is nonverbal. As yet, we have not suggested why this might be the case. One good reason, however, is that verbal recoding may allow more efficient covert articulatory rehearsal of the material to be recalled than would be the case if the material were not verbally recoded. Subjects may use rehearsal, for example, to retain the serial order of stimuli.

This notion of covert articulatory rehearsal is the cornerstone of a predominant account of short-term memory performance (e.g. Baddeley, 1986; Gathercole & Baddeley, 1993). For example, in this account it was suggested that the word length effect stems largely from rehearsal, because the effect is abolished if articulatory suppression is required during both the presentation and the written recall of word lists (Baddeley et al., 1984). The basic idea is that timely rehearsal is needed to refresh a decaying representation of the list items before it is too late (within about two seconds of the previous presentation or rehearsal of the item), and that longer words are recalled more poorly because they take longer to rehearse. In contrast, the account of the phonological similarity effect does not depend on the notion of rehearsal. Instead, it assumes that similar items are confused in the act of retrieval from phonological storage.

We will present a critical appraisal of the role of covert rehearsal within this theoretical framework. Then we will examine consequences of developmental and individual differences in the speed of rehearsal and overt articulation.

Critical Appraisal of the Role of Covert Rehearsal

Within the general constraints of the model of short-term memory developed by Baddeley (1986, and this volume), it need not be the case that word length effects occur totally because of memory decay during covert rehearsal. Another possibility is that memory could decay while words are pronounced during verbal responding. Longer words take longer to pronounce in recall, thereby allowing more time for the memory of other words to decay.

Cowan et al. (1992) obtained strong evidence that at least some of the effect of word length can result from the duration of overt verbal recall. They presented lists of words visually, following each word by a cue to recall the words either in the forward or the backward order. Adults were to repeat each list aloud following the cue. There were four types of list: those composed of short words, those composed of long words, those beginning with short words but ending with long words, and those beginning with long words but ending with short words. The finding was as predicted according to a recall delay factor. Only the length of words to be recalled first made a difference, and the length of those words affected performance throughout the list. Presumably, this occurred because the length of words to be recalled first determined the length of the delay before recalling the remaining words. However, the results did not rule out the possibility that rehearsal is also important.

Henry (1991) showed that both rehearsal and recall delay are important factors to consider in understanding developmental changes in memory span. She tested phonological similarity and word length effects for spoken lists in children, using a verbal response on some trials and a nonverbal response, pointing to pictorial representations of the words, on other trials. With a verbal response, both 5- and 7-year-olds yielded phonological similarity and word length effects. However, with a pointing response, only 7-year-olds yielded these effects. This suggests that events taking place during the recall period are the main (or only) factor underlying the effects in 5-year-olds, whereas covert rehearsal is an additional factor in 7-year-olds. It appears from this research that rehearsal is important in recall, although it may not play the central role that Baddeley (1986) suggested for it.

Of course, Henry (1991) is not alone in demonstrating that young children generally do not engage in covert rehearsal. Two recent reviews (Gathercole & Hitch, 1993; Henry & Millar, 1993) together do an excellent job of summarising evidence for this. However, the impact of Henry's study is to resolve a contradiction between the fact that word length effects are obtained with spoken stimuli in children too young to rehearse (e.g. Hitch et al., 1989) and the supposition that word length effects result from rehearsal processes.

Another account of the word length effect also has been offered. Caplan, Rochon, and Waters (1992) suggested that it might originate in the phonological complexity of words and their effect on the speech planning process. In two previous studies (Baddeley et al., 1975; Cowan et al., 1992) the word length effect was obtained even with short and long word lists matched for the number of phonemes and syllables, but differing in the necessary time for pronunciation. Caplan et al. questioned the adequacy of the match between words in the study of Baddeley et al. In experiments in which Caplan et al. used new sets of words matched for phonemes and syllables, no word length effect was obtained. However, it is important to realise that Caplan et al. had subjects respond by pointing to pictures representing the words. Perhaps a portion of the word length effect can be obtained when the lists are matched for phonemes and syllables, but only because of delays in pronouncing the longer words during recall, given a verbal response. It may well be the response modality, rather than inadequacies in previous stimulus sets, that accounts for the difference in the findings. In support of this account, Avons, Wright, and Pammer (1994) found that word length effects were much smaller in probed recall (in which the output processes cannot operate) than in serial recall. In a serial, spoken recall task, the stimuli of Caplan et al. might well yield a word length effect after all.

It can be concluded that rehearsal is one factor in immediate verbal recall, although clearly not the only covert process that matters.

The Speed of Covert Rehearsal

Baddeley et al. (1975) found a correlation between subjects' rate of speech, when asked to speak as quickly as possible, and their short-term memory ability. They also found that subjects took longer to pronounce long words, to an extent that was commensurate with the reduction in short-term memory performance for the longer words. Across individuals and words, a particular individual could recall about the same number of words of a particular type that he or she could pronounce in about 1.5–2.0 seconds. The theoretical account (further described in Baddeley, 1986) was that subjects use an "articulatory loop" mechanism in which the list of words is rehearsed in a repeating loop. Each item rehearsal can take place only if the phonological representation of the item still remains in short-term memory, which is said to be the case if less than the critical duration (1.5–2.0 seconds) has elapsed since the last rehearsal of that item. Therefore, the individual will be able to recall about as many words as can be rehearsed in 1.5–2.0 seconds, an amount that is estimated by the speeded speech task. A study by Landauer (1962) supports the basic contention that speeded overt speech is a reasonable estimate of the rate of covert speech.

Other researchers have found that age differences in recall can be accounted for by the rate of rehearsal. For example, Hulme and Tordoff (1989) found this in a study examining memory span for short, medium, and long words in children of three ages (4, 7, and 10 years). A plot of speech rate task performance against memory span resulted in approximately a straight line across the nine condition means.

There is much less of this type of research on development throughout adulthood, but the articulatory loop hypothesis is strengthened to the extent that adult development also is consistent with it. Kynette, Kemper, Norman, and Cheung (1990) obtained speech rate differences commensurate with span differences in young versus elderly adults. A simple account of these data would state that the rate of rehearsal increases with age in childhood and decreases with adult ageing, and that this rate of rehearsal accounts for age differences in short-term memory performance.

This account appears to conflict, however, with the general finding that children under the age of about 7 years do not use covert rehearsal. How can the rate of rehearsal account for recall, given that the regression line extends down to subjects who do not use rehearsal?

Two recent studies have found that if one looks at performance within a group of 4-year-olds, the expected correlation between individuals' speech rate and memory span does not emerge. Gathercole, Adams, and Hitch (1994) found no significant correlation within 4-year-olds, but a significant correlation within a group of adults. Cowan, Keller, et al. (1994) found a correlation that was opposite of the expected within 4-year-olds (i.e. slower speech rates in subjects with better memory span), although the correlation was as expected in 8-year-olds. Thus, rate of rehearsal cannot entirely explain the correlations between speech rate and memory span across ages and materials, and cannot be the sole causal factor underlying effects of various factors on memory span.

The Role of Overt Pronunciation

In line with the findings of Henry (1991) and Cowan et al. (1992) mentioned earlier, perhaps the important factor is not rehearsal, but rather the amount of time it takes subjects to pronounce items in spoken recall. This hypothesis states that subjects should only be able to recall words within about a two-second period because the phonological representation of any unrecalled items would have decayed from short-term memory by that time. (A weaker form of the hypothesis states that there is some fixed duration of memory decay, but not necessarily close to two seconds.) According to this type of hypothesis, speeded pronunciation correlates with span, not because it estimates rehearsal speed, but because it provides an estimate of the relative durations of words as they are spoken during the recall period. This hypothesis remains generally compatible with the articulatory loop mechanism proposed by Baddeley (1986), and was proposed by Schweickert and Boruff (1986). It appears to be supported by a study of digit span in Chinese and American adults (Stigler, Lee, & Stevenson, 1986) showing that the recall period for span-length lists lasted roughly two seconds on the average. It takes less time to say the Chinese digits, so more digits were included in the two-second recall period when subjects were tested in Chinese.

If the recall duration limit hypothesis were universally true, and if we assume that the rate of memory decay is comparable across subjects, then we would expect subjects of any level of ability to limit their recall to a comparable period. However, Cowan (1992) measured the duration of recall in 4-year-olds and found results that are discrepant with those expectations. More capable subjects took longer to produce their responses. In fact, the duration of recall varied from an average of less than two seconds for the children with the shortest spans to over five seconds for the children with the longest spans. Rather than a monotonically decaying memory representation, one would have to assume that some items are reactivated during the recall period, allowing more capable subjects to speak for longer without letting the memory representations lapse. Thus, it does not appear that either covert or overt articulatory speed factors, or both together, are sufficient to account for memory span. Another potential factor, the speed of short-term memory search, is discussed next.

SHORT-TERM MEMORY SEARCH

We have an apparent contradiction between the findings of Stigler et al. (1986), suggesting that word length differences across languages affect span and the duration of each item in recall, but not the total duration of the recall period, and the findings of Cowan (1992), suggesting that individual differences in ability affect span and the total duration of the recall period, but not the duration of each item in recall. Could it be that word length effects and individual differences in ability work through different mechanisms? There are reasons to believe so, and to suspect that a second mechanism playing an important role may be some sort of short-term memory search.

Providing evidence for the different mechanisms, Cowan, Keller, et al. (1994) examined memory span for short (monosyllabic), medium (bisyllabic), and long (trisyllabic) words in 4- and 8-year-olds, using a spoken response, and measured the duration of each word and each interword silent period in the correct responses, using a speech waveform editor on a microcomputer. An interesting outcome of that study was a dissociation between the speech-timing correlates of word length effects and age effects. Word length affected the duration of words in the response, as one would expect (with means of 0.52 seconds for short words, 0.60 seconds for medium words, and 0.75 seconds for long words), but it had no effect on the duration of interword silent periods. However, age affected the duration of silent periods in the response. For correct responses to lists of a particular length, older subjects had significantly shorter interword silent periods, and much shorter preparatory periods, than younger subjects did. For example, the preparatory intervals in span-length lists were an average of 1.75 seconds long in 4-year-olds, versus 1.16 seconds in 8-year-olds. Age had no effect, however, on the duration of words in the response. Older subjects were shown to be capable of saying words more quickly than younger subjects, but they did not do so in the response periods of the span task.

The data seem compatible with the hypothesis that the processes that are common during silent intervals in the response may not include covert rehearsal. If covert rehearsal were prevalent during those periods, then the length of words should have had an effect on the duration of silent periods, which was not the case.

A process that may be more prevalent during the silent intervals is memory search. Subjects might have to search through the short-term memory representation in order to determine which word to say next. Similar to the absence of word length effects on the duration of silent periods in the memory response (Cowan, Keller, et al., 1994), effects of word length on memory search were not observed in the probe task devised by Sternberg (1966), in which subjects must quickly indicate whether a probe item is present or absent from a list presented previously (Chase, 1977; Clifton & Tash, 1973).

The idea that memory must be searched before the overt repetition of elements in a list can take place is not brand new. A similar idea was proposed by Sternberg, Monsell, Knoll, and Wright (1978). They required subjects to repeat lists of various lengths as rapidly as possible on receiving a start signal. As the list length increased, the preparatory interval increased and the rate of pronunciation (in items per second) decreased. An essential aspect of the account offered for these effects was that subjects search through a representation of the entire list every time another item is to be pronounced. As list length increased, there would be more items to process during each interval between items, explaining the response slowdown that occurs with longer lists.

Analogous to the findings of Sternberg et al. (1978), Cowan, Keller, et al. (1994) found that the preparatory interval and rate of pronunciation in correctly repeated lists within the span task both depended on the list length, with longer preparatory intervals and slower pronunciation rates occurring for lists one below span than for span-length lists. The preparatory interval was, on the average, 1.24 seconds for lists at the subject's span length, versus only 1.04 seconds for lists of a length one below span. The rate of speech can be calculated (on the basis of mean word duration plus mean interword pause) as 1.02 seconds/word at span, versus only 0.84 seconds/word at one below span. Extending the effect of list length downward, in Cowan's (1992) larger sample of 4-year-olds who were to repeat lists of monosyllabic words, the rate of speech was significantly faster for lists two below span than for lists only one below span.

The type of memory search for lists to be recalled may not be the same as the type that occurs in a rapid pronunciation task. However, in both cases, one reason for proposing that a covert process such as memory search is carried out on each list item repeatedly, between items, is to account for the finding that the recall rate is dependent on the number of list items.

Sternberg, Wright, Knoll, and Monsell (1980) conducted a more detailed analysis of speech responses. They divided each response sequence into inter-word and intra-word periods. For example, if the response sequence included the two-word series "copper, token," then the period including the "-er" of copper and the "t" of token was taken to be the inter-word period, with the other segments representing intra-word periods. That analysis showed that the stimulus list length affected the duration of inter-word periods but not intra-word periods. Somewhat analogously, in spoken responses within the memory span task, Cowan, Keller, et al. (1994) found that list length affected inter-word pause durations in the response (0.38 seconds for span-length lists, versus 0.22 seconds for lists one below span) much more than word durations (0.64 versus 0.62 seconds, respectively). In both cases, apparently, a list-length-dependent covert process takes place primarily during the periods between words. In both cases, that covert process could be some type of short-term memory search.

Now the discrepancy between the effects of word length (Stigler et al., 1986) and individual and age differences (Cowan, 1992; Cowan, Keller, et al., 1994) on the timing of spoken responses in the span task can be explained. According to the articulatory loop theory (Baddeley, 1986), both word length and age effects are assumed to occur because these variables affect the rate of covert rehearsal. However, we have seen that word length and age have dissociable effects on response timing. One possible revised interpretation is that word length directly affects the duration of spoken words in the response, and therefore the amount of memory decay during the response period; whereas age affects the speed of a covert process such as memory search, and therefore affects the efficiency with which items can be retrieved (and perhaps reactivated) during silent periods in the response.

The mechanisms may be similar in the realm of adult ageing. Salthouse and Coon (1993) presented younger and older adults with lists of printed digits and letters for immediate recall through keystroke responses, and the timing of responses was analysed. Consistent with the results of Cowan, Keller, et al. (1994), they observed the biggest age difference in response timing in the preparatory intervals. Response timing was correlated with recall across individuals, and more general speed-of-processing measures accounted for most of this common variance (anticipating a theme to be discussed at the end of the present chapter).

The results of several investigators thus suggest that age across the lifespan may affect short-term memory ability through a change in the rate of covert, mnemonically related processes. Indirect evidence points to memory search as one such important process.

RETRIEVAL OF INFORMATION FROM LONG-TERM MEMORY

One well-motivated modification of the articulatory loop theory is that long-term memory representations of the items might assist in the performance of a short-term memory task (see Brown & Hulme, this volume). For example, lexical knowledge might be used to reconstruct a complete memory representation when only partial knowledge of the item remains in short-term phonological storage (e.g. see Schweickert, 1993).

Hulme, Maughan, and Brown (1991) showed how the contribution of long-term memory storage in short-term memory tasks might be observed. In one experiment, memory span and maximal articulatory rate were measured for short, medium, and long English words and nonsense words conforming to English phonology. When the two measures were plotted against one another using the group means for each of the word lengths, the functions across item lengths were linear, with the same slope for words and nonwords but with a higher Y-intercept for words.

To understand the implication of this result, consider first what the articulatory loop theory (Baddeley, 1986, and this volume) would predict. Assume that the duration of short-term memory is T seconds (T $\approx$ 2 seconds, according to previous findings). If subjects can articulate the items in a stimulus set at an average rate of R items/second, then the subjects should be able to recall on the average (T $\times$ R) of those items. Thus the plot of memory span across materials with different speech rates should follow the equation: Memory$_i$ = T $\times$ R$_i$, where i is the particular item set.

Identical slopes for words and nonwords would be expected assuming that T is the same for both' sets. (A similar argument could be made even if the measured articulation rate is indicative of the rate of a larger set of mnemonically relevant processes, as proposed for example by Cowan, Keller, et al., 1994.)

The theory also would predict that for materials yielding a pronunciation rate of zero there should be no memory; the Y-intercept should be zero. If the Y-intercept of the linear function is above zero, this indicates that some factor other than the articulatory loop contributes. Hulme found a Y-intercept of about 1 item for nonwords versus about 2.5 items for words. The difference was attributed to lexical knowledge that exists for words only.

There have been several applications of the Hulme et al. (1991) method, with varying outcomes. Roodenrys, Hulme, and Brown (1993) found a marginally significant difference in the intercept in 6-year-olds versus 10-year-olds, although far more of the age difference was accounted for by the lower position of the younger children along the regression lines as predicted by the articulatory loop theory. Although they interpreted the intercept difference as indicating the contribution of long-term memory, the graph shows that a nonsignificant difference in slope could have contributed to that pattern. When the slopes differ, there may be no simple, clear-cut interpretation within an articulatory loop framework. However, the results suggest to us that long-term memory may have given an advantage to the older subjects, beyond what the articulatory loop theory would predict, only for the long words. Another example of a data set that includes differences in slope is seen in the difference between children with and without severe learning difficulties (Hulme & Mackenzie, 1992).

An example of a data set that is more ideally suited to the Hulme et al. (1991) type of analysis (because there are no slope differences) is a study by Hulme, Lee, and Brown (1993) comparing normal adults to those with Alzheimer-type dementia. The patients had a function with a slope similar to the normal subjects, but with a slightly lower intercept (suggesting poorer use of long-term memory) and lower placement along the regression lines (suggesting slower articulatory processes).

Another approach to observing the effect of long-term memory is to manipulate factors that theoretically should influence the use of long-term memory but not articulatory processes. For example, Bourassa and Besner (1994) found that the imageability of the items to be recalled affected short-term memory performance (see also Cowan, Wood, & Borne, 1994).

To summarise, it is clear at this point that information in long-term memory plays a role in short-term memory tasks. Researchers have just begun to develop the tools necessary to determine the nature of this long-term memory contribution.

WHAT FACTORS MAY DETERMINE THE EFFECTIVENESS OF COVERT PROCESSING?

We have shown that a number of covert processes are influential in short-term verbal recall, and that the use of those processes changes markedly with age. We conclude with a discussion of what factors may determine the effectiveness of a subject's covert processing.

The question of the ultimate causes of individual differences is obviously beyond the current state of knowledge and can be addressed only speculatively. There may be myriad individual differences in the component skills that can be used in short-term memory performance, as well as myriad differences in preferred strategies. Some progress has been made, however, in discerning one factor that operates across individuals as a function of age. Specifically, there is considerable evidence that the speeds of multiple processes change together as a function of age and that this global speed of processing factor is critical in many cognitive tasks. If short-term memory ability can be viewed as one instance of the larger question of why operations change in speed with development, the conception of short-term memory becomes a more parsimonious one.

On most speeded tasks, age differences are substantial: Speed increases throughout childhood and adolescence, reaches a peak in young adulthood, and declines slowly thereafter. Considerable evidence now supports the position that a global mechanism, or perhaps a few mechanisms, limit(s) the speed with which children and older adults process information, relative to young adults (Hale & Jansen, 1994; Kail & Salthouse, 1994). The mechanism is not specific to particular tasks or domains but is, instead, a fundamental characteristic of the information-processing system.

Two lines of evidence involving children and older adults are consistent with this conclusion. One line is based on the method of statistical control. If two measures reflect a common age-related mechanism, then statistical control of the variance in one of the measures should greatly reduce the age-related variance in the other. According to this logic, if a global mechanism is responsible for age-related change in processing speed, then statistical control of one measure of processing speed should substantially reduce age effects in other measures. If, instead, each speeded process changes with age at a unique rate, then statistical control of one speeded measure should have a relatively small impact on the magnitude of age-related variance on other measures. In general, for children and older adults, age-related differences in speeds of various mental processes typically are attenuated by approximately 70–90% when the variance associated with performance on a paper-and-pencil measure of perceptual speed is eliminated (Kail & Salthouse, 1994). This result is readily reconciled with the notion of a substantial general component to the development of processing speed, but not with the view that processing speed can be explained entirely in terms of task-specific mechanisms.

Another line of evidence is based on a relation that is often found between young adults' reaction times (RTs) on the one hand and children's and older adults' RTs on the other. If children execute all cognitive processes more slowly than young adults by some constant factor, then children's RTs should be equal to adults' RTs multiplied by that constant. That is, children's RTs should increase linearly as a function of RTs from corresponding experimental conditions for younger adults. The same prediction would hold for older adults.

The general prediction of a linear increase is upheld, both for children and for older adults (Hale & Jansen, 1994; Kail & Salthouse, 1994). Furthermore, the rate of increase, which indicates the constant by which RTs for children and older adults differ from young adults' RTs, changes systematically with age. It drops rapidly during childhood and more slowly during adolescence, and then increases gradually throughout adulthood (Hale & Jansen, 1994; Kail & Salthouse, 1994).

Findings like these, along with results derived from the method of statistical control, point to the conclusion that some sort of mechanism that is not specific to particular tasks limits the speed with which children and older adults process information. Of course, the impact of such a global mechanism is particularly salient on speeded tasks but it need not be restricted to those tasks. To the contrary, much cognitive processing is temporally limited; processing must occur in a finite window of time or it fails. Consequently, the speed of processing may be critical whenever the rate of stimulation or pacing of responses is controlled externally, or, more generally, whenever a number of activities must be completed in a fixed period. In these instances, slow processing speed in children or older adults may result in reduced performance because these individuals are less likely than young adults to complete the necessary components of task performance in the time allotted.

Memory represents one domain in which performance may be particularly sensitive to age-related changes in processing speed. Recall the evidence discussed earlier concerning the articulatory loop hypothesis in which, across a variety of experimental conditions and ages, recall increases linearly as a function of articulation rate. Perhaps age-related change in articulation rate is, itself, a reflection of global developmental change in processing speed. Increased processing speed with age would yield more rapid articulation, which, in turn, would yield more accurate retention. (A similar case could be made for the dependence of other mnemonically relevant covert processes, such as memory search, on global processing speed.)

Figure 2.1 shows this general framework for the factors of global speed and articulation. The effects of age on memory might be mediated entirely

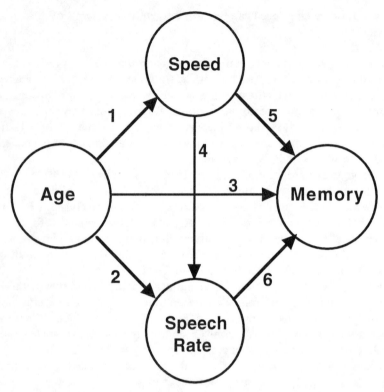

FIG. 2.1.   Possible links between age, global speed of processing, speech rate, and memory span.

by the path that runs from age to processing speed to speech articulation rate and then to memory (Path 1–4–6). However, other paths are also possible. Age might have direct effects on rate of articulation (Path 2), perhaps reflecting an age-related increase in the familiarity of information to be remembered. Moreover, processing speed might have direct effects on memory (Path 5) in addition to those mediated by speech articulation rate. For example, age-related change in processing speed might also lead to more rapid initial encoding of stimuli, independent of the rate with which they are subsequently rehearsed. Finally, if global and specific processing speeds cannot account for all of the age-related variation in memory span, then age would be linked directly to span (Path 3).

This framework was evaluated by Kail and Park (1994), who tested 7- to 14-year-olds and adults. To assess processing speed, subjects completed the Identical Pictures and Number Comparisons tasks, two measures of perceptual speed derived from the French Kit; to measure rate of articulation, subjects were timed as they repeated sets of three letters or three digits aloud; and finally, digit and letter spans were assessed in the standard way.

The key results concern analyses of the paths that link the constructs in Fig. 2.1. Consider, first, direct links to memory. As expected from work on the articulatory loop hypothesis, the path linking memory and speech rate was significant. Processing was linked significantly to speech rate but not to memory. This indicates that the impact of processing speed on memory was mediated entirely by increases in rate of articulation. However, the link between age and memory remained significant. This link means that other age-related variables not included in the general framework play a mediating role in the age–memory span relation.

In sum, the findings support the view that processing speed contributes to developmental change in memory. Processing speed may well have some interesting links with other forces that are important in the development of memory, at least during childhood. First, consider memory strategies. Much of the impact of processing speed may well be mediated by memory strategies. More rapid processing means that overt rehearsal, mental imagery, or other deliberate mnemonics are more effective because subjects accomplish more in a fixed period of time. Turning to task-relevant knowledge, here, processing speed may well work differently. Increased processing speed may be a consequence of greater task-relevant knowledge. Subjects can access highly familiar stimuli in long-term memory more rapidly than less familiar stimuli and this is independent of age-related change in global processing speed. It still must also be kept in mind that the exact mechanisms accounting for childhood development, adult development, and various types of deviance may well be different from one another.

FUTURE DIRECTIONS

The articulatory loop model by Baddeley (1986) has served as a convenient framework to tie findings together and motivate research. Some of the new processing factors that, as a result of that research, are now thought to make a difference (e.g. memory search; the involvement of long-term memory) must be explored further. However, it is our conviction that if these new factors are to contribute to our understanding of working memory, sooner or later they must be tied together into a new simple framework, similar to the articulatory loop model in intent, although probably not in exact substance.

There certainly are ways to continue to learn about each factor. For example, consider the potential role of memory search. Whereas Cowan and his colleagues have shown that there are systematic effects of age and list length on the duration of silent pauses between words within the immediate verbal recall of lists, the exact nature of processing within those pauses remains uncertain. Do these pauses relate strongly to subjects' ability to conduct memory searches, as the account of Cowan et al. (1994) implies, or not? To what extent is it true that subjects who search more quickly can recall more? Answers to these questions appear to be on the horizon.

We now know that information in long-term memory influences short-term memory performance, but the way in which it operates is far from certain. Long-term lexical memory may contribute by helping the subject to interpret the identity of a partly-faded phonological trace. Another possibility is that subjects use long-term memory to form an episodic record of the list that is completely separate from the phonological short-term memory of the articulatory loop model. Whenever the phonological store proved inadequate to retrieve an item, there would be the option to check for the item's identity in the abstract episodic record. There is interesting work to be done here.

Finally, the newer covert variables have yet to be explored within the statistical control approach. Perhaps the application of that approach would be premature until more is known about the new variables. Age differences in these variables have been examined usefully, but individual differences are still unexplored. There appear to be tremendously large differences between children within an age on memory span and on various processes that may contribute to it, despite the systematic nature of age differences.

One major question that needs to be addressed within the statistical control approach is the extent to which the various specific covert processes are merely manifestations of a common, global processing speed, and the extent to which different personal profiles of abilities exist. For example, is it possible to be very slow on memory search and very quick on covert articulation? Is there any one measure of global speed that is unbiased, or is any measure at best one of a number of imperfectly correlated abilities? Ultimately, it is not any one task that will prove central to our understanding of covert processes in short-term memory. It is the task analysis that is central.

REFERENCES

Avons, S.E., Wright, K.L., & Pammer, K. (1994). The word-length effect in probed and serial recall. *Quarterly Journal of Experimental Psychology*, *47A*, 207–231.

Baddeley, A.D. (1986). *Working memory*. Oxford: Clarendon Press.

Baddeley, A.D., Lewis, V.J., & Vallar, G. (1984). Exploring the articulatory loop. *Quarterly Journal of Experimental Psychology*, *36A*, 233–252.

Baddeley, A.D., Thomson, N., & Buchanan, M. (1975). Word length and the structure of short-term memory. *Journal of Verbal Learning & Verbal Behavior*, *14*, 575–589.

Bourassa, D.C., & Besner, D. (1994). Beyond the articulatory loop: A semantic contribution to serial order recall of subspan lists. *Psychonomic Bulletin & Review*, *1*, 122–125.

Caplan, D., Rochon, E., & Waters, G.S. (1992). Articulatory and phonological determinants of word length effects in span tasks. *Quarterly Journal of Experimental Psychology, 45A*, 177–192.

Case, R., Kurland, D.M., & Goldberg, J. (1982). Operational efficiency and the growth of short-term memory span. *Journal of Experimental Child Psychology, 33*, 386–404.

Chase, W.G. (1977). Does memory scanning involve implicit speech? In S. Dornic (Ed.), *Attention and performance VI*, (pp. 607–628). Hillsdale, NJ: Lawrence Erlbaum Associates Inc.

Clifton, C., & Tash, J. (1973). Effect of syllabic word length on memory-search rate. *Journal of Experimental Psychology, 99*, 231–235.

Conrad, R. (1964). Acoustic confusion in immediate memory. *British Journal of Psychology, 55*, 75–84.

Conrad, R. (1971). The chronology of the development of covert speech in children. *Developmental Psychology, 5*, 398–405.

Cowan, N. (1992). Verbal memory span and the timing of spoken recall. *Journal of Memory & Language, 31*, 668–684.

Cowan, N., Day, L., Saults, J.S., Keller, T.A., Johnson, T., & Flores, L. (1992). The role of verbal output time in the effects of word length on immediate memory. *Journal of Memory & Language, 31*, 1–17.

Cowan, N., Keller, T., Hulme, C., Roodenrys, S., McDougall, S., & Rack, J. (1994). Verbal memory span in children: Speech timing clues to the mechanisms underlying age and word length effects. *Journal of Memory & Language, 33*, 234–250.

Cowan, N., & Saults, J.S. (1995). Memory for speech. In H. Winitz (Ed.), *Human communication and its disorders*, Vol. 4. Timonium, MD: York Press.

Cowan, N., Wood, N.L., & Borne, D.N. (1994). Reconfirmation of the short-term storage concept. *Psychological Science, 5*, 103–106.

Gathercole, S.E., Adams, A.-M., & Hitch, G.J. (1994). Do young children rehearse? An individual-differences analysis. *Memory & Cognition, 22*, 201–207.

Gathercole, S.E., & Baddeley, A.D. (1993). *Working memory and language*. Hove, UK: Lawrence Erlbaum Associates Ltd.

Gathercole, S.E., & Hitch, G.J. (1993). Developmental changes in short-term memory: A revised working memory perspective. In A.F. Collins, S.E. Gathercole, M.A. Conway, & P.E. Morris (Eds.), *Theories of memory*. Hove, UK: Lawrence Erlbaum Associates Ltd.

Hale, S., & Jansen, J. (1994). Global processing-time coefficients characterize individual and group differences in cognitive speed. *Psychological Science, 5*, 384–389.

Halliday, M.S., & Hitch, G.J., Lennon, B., & Pettipher, C. (1990). Verbal short-term memory in children: The role of the articulatory loop. *European Journal of Cognitive Psychology, 2*, 23–38.

Henry, L.A. (1991). The effects of word length and phonemic similarity in young children's short-term memory. *Quarterly Journal of Experimental Psychology, 43A*, 35–52.

Henry, L.A., & Millar, S. (1991). Memory span increase with age: A test of two hypotheses. *Journal of Experimental Child Psychology, 51*, 459–484.

Henry, L.A., & Millar, S. (1993). Why does memory span improve with age? A review of the evidence for two current hypotheses. *European Journal of Cognitive Psychology, 5*, 241–287.

Hitch, G.J., Halliday, M.S., Dodd, A., & Littler, J.E. (1989). Development of rehearsal in short-term memory: Differences between pictorial and spoken stimuli. *British Journal of Developmental Psychology, 7*, 347–362.

Hitch, G.J., Halliday, M.S., Schaafstal, A.M., & Heffernan, T.M. (1991). Speech, "inner speech," and the development of short-term memory: Effects of picture-labelling on recall. *Journal of Experimental Child Psychology, 51*, 220–234.

Hitch, G.J., Halliday, S., Schaafstal, A.M., & Schraagen, J.M.C. (1988). Visual working memory in young children. *Memory & Cognition, 16*, 120–132.

Hulme, C. (1984). Developmental differences in the effects of acoustic similarity on memory span. *Developmental Psychology, 20*, 650–652.

Hulme, C., Lee, G., & Brown, G.D.A. (1993). Short-term memory impairments in Alzheimer-type dementia: Evidence for separable impairments of articulatory rehearsal and long-term memory. *Neuropsychologia, 31*, 161–172.

Hulme, C., & Mackenzie, S. (1992). *Working memory and severe learning difficulties*. Hove, UK: Lawrence Erlbaum Associates Ltd.

Hulme, C., Maughan, S., & Brown, G.D.A. (1991). Memory for familiar and unfamiliar words: Evidence for a long-term memory contribution to short-term memory span. *Journal of Memory and Language, 30*, 685–701.

Hulme, C., Silvester, J., Smith, S., & Muir, C. (1986). The effects of word length on memory for pictures: Evidence for speech coding in young children. *Journal of Experimental Child Psychology, 41*, 61–75.

Hulme, C., & Tordoff, V. (1989). Working memory development: The effects of speech rate, word length, and acoustic similarity on serial recall. *Journal of Experimental Child Psychology, 47*, 72–87.

Kail, R., & Salthouse, T.A. (1994). Processing speed as a mental capacity. *Acta Psychologica, 86*, 199–255.

Kail, R., & Park, Y. (1994). Processing time, articulation time, and memory span. *Journal of Experimental Child Psychology, 57*, 281–291.

Keller, T.A., & Cowan, N. (1994). Developmental increase in the duration of memory for tone pitch. *Developmental Psychology, 30*, 855–863.

Kynette, D., Kemper, S., Norman, S., & Cheung, H. (1990). Adults' word recall and word repetition. *Experimental Aging Research, 16*, 117–121.

Landauer, T.K. (1962). Rate of implicit speech. *Perceptual & Motor Skills, 15*, 646.

Roodenrys, S., Hulme, C., & Brown, G.D.A. (1993). The development of short-term memory span: Separable effects of speech rate and long-term memory. *Journal of Experimental Child Psychology, 56*, 431–442.

Salthouse, T.A., & Coon, V.E. (1993). Influence of task-specific processing speed on age differences in memory. *Journal of Gerontology: Psychological Sciences, 48*, 245–255.

Schiano, D.J., & Watkins, M.J. (1981). Speech-like coding of pictures in short-term memory. *Memory & Cognition, 9*, 110–114.

Schweickert, R., & Boruff, B. (1986). Short-term memory capacity: Magic number or magic spell? *Journal of Experimental Psychology: Learning, Memory, and Cognition, 12*, 419–425.

Sternberg, S. (1966). High-speed scanning in human memory. *Science, 153*, 652–654.

Sternberg, S., Monsell, S., Knoll, R.L., & Wright, C.E. (1978). The latency and duration of rapid movement sequences: Comparisons of speech and typewriting. In G.E. Stelmach (Ed.), *Information processing in motor control and learning*. New York: Academic Press.

Sternberg, S., Wright, C.E., Knoll, R.L., & Monsell, S. (1980). Motor programs in rapid speech: Additional evidence. In R.A. Cole (Ed.), *Perception and production of fluent speech*. Hillsdale, NJ: Lawrence Erlbaum Associates Inc.

Stigler, J.W., Lee, S.-Y., & Stevenson, H.W. (1986). Digit memory in Chinese and English: Evidence for a temporally limited store. *Cognition, 23*, 1–20.

3

A connectionist model of STM for serial order

Neil Burgess
University College London, UK

Graham J. Hitch
University of Lancaster, UK

INTRODUCTION

In recent years, support has grown for the idea that the human memory system consists of separate, functionally specialised subsystems. Fractionation of this sort is indicated by selective impairments of memory function in neuropsychological patients and complementary dissociations in normal individuals (see e.g. Shallice, 1988). Theoretical accounts of these findings typically use an information processing framework and are expressed in the form of verbal descriptions or relatively crude flow diagrams. We refer to these accounts as "conceptual models". This type of theorising usually applies at a general level, and is particularly useful where it would be premature to attempt a more detailed account. However, it is much less useful where an understanding of underlying mechanisms is required. The lack of commitment to unnecessary detail in typical conceptual models allows them to integrate large bodies of different types of data, but can make them difficult to apply in specific circumstances. For example, it can be difficult to generate precise predictions with confidence. One way round this problem, when circumstances permit, is to devise and explore explicit computational models.

We illustrate this theme in the present chapter with respect to part of the human working memory system which mediates the serial recall of verbal sequences (Baddeley & Hitch, 1974). A widely used conceptual model sees this subsystem as a "phonological loop" (Baddeley, 1986; see also Baddeley, this volume). Our starting point is the observation that despite the success of this model it does not explain important aspects of the recall process, such as its serial nature and typical patterns of order errors. Computational modelling of the system is clearly viable given the availability of extensive data concerning immediate serial recall and progress in simulating serial ordering (e.g. Houghton, 1990). We describe progress in developing a neural network model of the phonological loop, starting with an initial view of the underlying mechanisms (Burgess & Hitch, 1992) and going on to a simple extension of this basic model (Burgess, 1995). At the same time we show that the neural network model retains a clear mapping to the conceptual model of the phonological loop. The outcome is an explanatory account of a much wider range of phenomena than is captured by the conceptual model, but one that nevertheless retains a reasonable degree of simplicity and parsimony. We go on to show that the new model can be used to make novel predictions, which can readily be tested. Most striking among these is the suggestion that the serial operation of the phonological loop is driven by some form of timing signal.

The Phonological Loop

As the conceptual model of the phonological loop will be familiar to most readers of this volume, and is reviewed fully in another chapter (Baddeley, Chapter 1), we provide only a very brief background. The loop is capable of storing sequences of verbal information over short time intervals, and has two components, a phonological store and an articulatory control process, used for subvocal rehearsal. Memory traces in the phonological store decay to the level of background noise in approximately two seconds but can be refreshed by the rehearsal process. The loop is specialised for dealing with information about serial order, and subvocal rehearsal is itself a sequential process.

The conceptual model of the phonological loop successfully accounts for the following phenomena in short-term memory for verbal sequences:

1. The span of immediate recall is limited (Miller, 1956), where span is assessed by presenting lists of increasing length and noting the longest list that can be accurately recalled. This is explained by decay of traces in the phonological store (Baddeley, Thomson, & Buchanan, 1975).

2. Immediate recall is poorer for phonemically similar items than phonemically distinct ones (Baddeley, 1966). The model assumes that traces of phonemically similar items are harder to discriminate after a given amount of decay.

3. There is a linear relationship between span s (or alternatively, the number of items recalled from lists of fixed length) and the rate at which the

items can be articulated r, such that $s \approx 2r + c$ where c is a constant and articulation rate can vary across word length, development and language (Baddeley et al., 1975; Ellis & Hennelly, 1980; Hitch & Halliday, 1983; Hulme, Thomson, Muir, & Lawrence, 1984). This is explained in terms of the importance of articulation rate in determining the time between successive subvocal rehearsals. Longer intervals allow more time for traces to decay.

4. Articulatory suppression (repeating a redundant word such as "blah") and exposure to irrelevant speech both impair immediate recall, and can abolish the influence of word length and phonemic similarity on performance under appropriate conditions (Baddeley, Lewis, & Vallar, 1984; Salamé & Baddeley, 1982). This is explained by assuming that suppression blocks the use of subvocal rehearsal, and that irrelevant speech gains automatic access to the phonological store. Note, however, that recent work questions this interpretation of the irrelevant speech effect (Jones & Macken, 1993).

Positron Emission Tomography studies indicate that the phonological store is localised in the left supramarginal gyrus, whereas subvocal rehearsal involves Broca's area and some of the motor areas involved in speech planning and production (Paulesu, Frith, & Frackowiak, 1993). These findings support the conceptual model in so far as they indicate that its functional organisation is reflected in neural structures. It is notable also that the localisation is broadly consistent with the localisation of damage in neuropsychological patients who have been interpreted as showing selective impairments of the phonological store. Other evidence suggests that the phonological loop plays an important role in children's learning of new vocabulary (see e.g. Gathercole & Baddeley, 1993; Gathercole & Martin, this volume) and is involved in a range of other aspects of cognition (see Baddeley, 1986). These examples are valuable in suggesting that the system serves a useful general purpose beyond that of remembering random word lists, and they add considerably to its intrinsic scientific interest.

However, despite its strengths and successes, the conceptual model of the phonological loop has some significant limitations. Most notably, it fails to address the problem of how the system stores and processes serial order information. Thus, while the effects of internal noise and trace decay can account for the fact that errors tend to be phonemically confusable with correct items (Conrad, 1964), they cannot explain aspects of errors that relate to serial order, such as the fact that transpositions of the order of a pair of items tend to involve temporally adjacent items, the characteristic shape of the serial position curve, or the occurrence of "serial order intrusions" (see later). Notice also that the model fails to address the crucial relationship between long- and short-term memory, the importance of which is underlined by evidence that the phonological loop is involved in vocabulary acquisition (Gathercole & Baddeley, 1993) and by effects of item familiarity on immediate recall (Hulme, Maughan, & Brown, 1991).

Regarding these limitations, we considered the principal phenomena that the conceptual model of the phonological loop leaves unexplained to be the following:

5. The majority of errors are "order errors" rather than "item errors" (Aaronson, 1968; Bjork & Healy, 1974), and tend to involve transpositions of neighbouring items (Conrad, 1965; Healy, 1974).

6. The probability of correctly recalling an item varies as a function of its serial position in the list according to a bow-shaped serial position curve (e.g. Crowder, 1972)

7. The probability of correctly recalling a list declines sigmoidally with increasing list length (Guildford & Dallenbach, 1925)

8. "Serial order intrusions" occur, in which an item recalled (either correctly or in error) in a previous list occurs as an error in the current list, at the same serial position (Conrad, 1960)

9. Span increases with the familiarity of the items used, such that familiarity alters the parameter c in the equation $s \approx 2r + c$. (Hulme et al., 1991). Recall also increases if a list has previously been presented (the "Hebb Effect"; Hebb, 1961).

Taken together, these data impose strong constraints on candidate mechanisms for implementing the phonological loop.

Goals of Modelling

We chose to use mathematical/connectionist modelling because it has a number of general advantages. First, the conceptual model must become well-specified in the process of being implemented, and, once implemented, its performance can be checked in detail. This provides a much tighter constraint on theorising than is the case with purely conceptual models. A further advantage of connectionist modelling lies in providing the opportunity to explore how a conceptual model could be implemented by neurons and synaptic connections. At the level of abstraction of most psychological models, and in the absence of data on the behaviour of neurons during memory tasks, this is not a tight constraint as the possible functional characteristics of large assemblies of neurons cover such a wide range. However, a soft constraint is still provided by avoiding mechanisms that are biologically implausible, such as modelling learning by error back-propagation.

Our specific goal in modelling the phonological loop was to overcome the limitations of the conceptual model by explaining a greater range of empirical phenomena, and so provide more insight into its underlying mechanisms. The first issue we encountered was deciding what data to model. Clearly, the larger task of simulating all known aspects of immediate serial recall must be tackled by starting with a tractable subproblem. For obvious reasons, we took it as of primary importance to be able to simulate effects that are already well described by the conceptual model. We took these as principally the effects of word length, phonemic similarity, and articulatory suppression. Given, further, that we had identified the absence of a serial ordering mechanism as a major omission from the conceptual model, we wanted our computational model to generate serial output, and to do so in such a way as to generate realistic patterns of error in the output. This led us to include, for our initial modelling (Burgess & Hitch, 1992), the sigmoidal function relating probability of list recall to list length, the bow-shape of the serial position curve, and characteristic patterns of transposition errors as additional goals of the simulation.

In an attempt to keep the complexity of the model within manageable proportions we deliberately chose not to address effects associated with learning and long-term memory in our initial work. We did this by simply building-in such effects, in the form of pre-learned connections linking words to their constituent phonemes, on the assumption that these associations could easily be made flexible (i.e. learnable) in subsequent development of the model.

As a check on the success or otherwise of the modelling, we adopted the tactic of seeing whether it would reproduce details of human data beyond the principal phenomena that were built in to its specification. One such effect, which has also attracted the interest of other modellers (Henson, Norris, Page, & Baddeley, in press), is the characteristic zig-zag serial position curves obtained in recalling lists in which alternate items are phonemically similar to one another (e.g. items at even positions in the sequence XBJGWDHC). Baddeley (1968) showed that errors tend to fall on, rather than after, the similar items. This is interesting because it seems to tell us something about the way phonological and serial order information combine with one another in memory. Indeed, Baddeley (1968) interpreted the zig-zag as evidence against models in which serial order information is stored via chaining associations between phonological representations of successive items (see e.g. Wickelgren, 1965).

Although connectionist modelling provides many additional constraints on ideas about mental processes, the problem of how to evaluate such models is as hard to determine as for any other type of model. As is clear, any model must address the experimental data. However, we do not regard providing a close statistical fit to any specific set of results as being particularly useful in itself. Given present knowledge, we are more interested in providing a qualitative fit to patterns of data over a wide range of phenomena with a minimal set of assumptions. Similarly, although it is evident that the more parsimonious of two accounts is generally to be preferred, parsimony is clearly not an end in itself. For example, a model that cannot be mapped onto a conceptual understanding of the processes giving rise to behaviour is useless. Finally, a model that makes a new contribution to our understanding should provide a novel interpretation of existing findings, and should suggest new directions for future research.

MODELLING BACKGROUND

Most commonly used connectionist models showing serial behaviour rely on some form of chaining mechanism which associates previous states to successive states. These models may use delayed connections propagating activation from previous time steps from output or hidden layers back to the input (Elman, 1990; Jordan, 1986), within the same layer (Kleinfeld, 1986; Sompolinsky & Kanter, 1986), or a more general holographic associative chaining as in the TODAM model (Lewandowsky & Murdock, 1989). However, a striking feature of human serial recall is that a sequence ABCDEF is much more likely to be mis-recalled as ACBDEF than as ACDEF_. Thus, as noted by Burgess and Hitch (1992), chaining of item or phoneme representations tends to generate errors that are incompatible with human behaviour. This point is emphasised by Henson et al. (in press) with specific respect to the recall of lists of alternating phonemically similar and dissimilar items.

Another striking feature of serial recall is that, although an item has a high probability of being recalled at or near to its serial position at presentation, if it has already been recalled at an earlier position, the probability of its recall falls to near zero for the next few serial positions. Thus for lists containing no repeated items, repeats in recall (where one of the items is incorrect) tend only to occur at longer lags (Conrad, 1965). Similarly, when lists contain a repeated item, there is a tendency for the second occurrence to be omitted in recall, known as the Ranschburg Effect, and this effect is weaker for widely separated repetitions (Jahnke, 1969). These effects point to a selection process at recall in which items compete to be chosen, are then immediately suppressed, and slowly recover. The "competitive queueing" (CQ) mechanism (see Houghton, 1990, Houghton, Hartley, & Glasspool this volume) is a simple instantiation of this basic process, which appears to be fundamental to serially ordered behaviour in general. It is interesting to note here that the serial behaviour of TODAM owes as much to the calculation of the probability of correct recall implicitly suppressing recalled items (Lewandowsky &

Murdock, 1989, p.33) as it does to the "theory of distributed associative memory" after which it is named.

Thus a minimal requirement for a model of immediate serial recall is CQ among items at presentation, and once more during recall. Given that items are suppressed in the order in which they are presented, and recover from suppression in the same order, such a mechanism would ensure recall of items in the correct order. Of course, to model human errors, the mechanism should also lead to mistakes. However, as we have argued previously (Burgess & Hitch, 1992), errors should not be completely determined, as humans do not always make precisely the same mistakes. Rather, given that the neuronal substrates responsible for the system's behaviour are non-deterministic, we should examine how the model performs in the face of random noise or unreliability in its components.

Such a minimal model would obviously be insufficient, and the model described in Burgess and Hitch (1992) assumes that two further components are necessary: a phonological store and a repeatable time-varying signal. The former is indicated by the phonemic similarity effect (Baddeley, 1966) and the latter by serial order intrusions (Conrad, 1960). Thus the core postulate of the model is that the characteristics of short-term memory for serially ordered items arise from the way that timing and phonemic information combine to prompt the competitive selection of each item.

MODEL DEVELOPMENT

The Initial Model (Burgess & Hitch, 1992)

To reiterate briefly, our initial model addressed the immediate recall of lists of familiar items and included no long-term learning mechanism. It attempted to simulate memory span, effects of phonemic similarity and word length, the shape of the serial position curve, and patterns of order error.

Figure 3.1B illustrates the architecture of the model, consisting of layers of artificial neurons. One layer provides a time-varying context signal, other layers correspond to input and output phonemes, and to a CQ system in which nodes representing items are closely connected to a "competitive filter" (Houghton, 1990). The serial order of a sequence of the presented items is learned in two ways: by associating the different context states to the items active at different times, and by associating the output phonemes of one item to the input phonemes of the next. The first of these corresponds to position–item associations, the second to chaining. The relative importance of these two types of order information is varied as the major free parameter of the model.

The operation of the model is given more fully in Burgess and Hitch (1992) and can be summarised as follows:

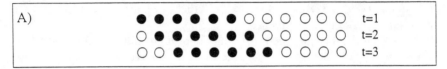

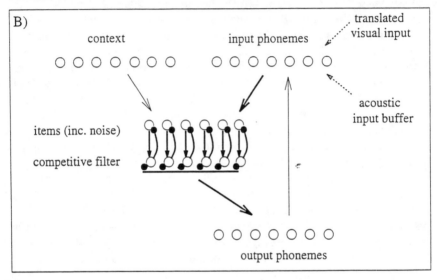

FIG. 3.1.   A. Context states as a function of serial position (t). Filled circles are active nodes, empty circles are inactive nodes. B. The architecture of the model, adapted from Burgess and Hitch (1992). Thin lines are connections with short-term plasticity; thick lines are fixed, pre-learned connections; inhibitory connections end in a filled circle rather than an arrow; dashed lines are routes by which information enters the model.

Presentation.   Presentation of an item activates the nodes in the input phoneme layer that correspond to the item's constituent phonemes. Activation feeds through to all items containing these phonemes via prelearned associations. The most active node in the item layer is then selected by the CQ system, and this item automatically activates its constituent output phonemes, before being suppressed. As each item is presented, the activations of the context nodes vary slowly in the form of a "moving window" (see Fig. 3.1A), modelling the presence of a timing signal external to the phonological loop. The connection weights supporting context–item and temporary chaining associations are strengthened by "one-shot" Hebbian learning (see Equation 1 later), and decay with time.

Recall.   At recall, the context states are reactivated in order, and for each item except the first, the input phonemes are activated by the output phonemes for the previous item (the first item is activated separately).

Activation feeds from the context and input phoneme layers to the item layer, the most active item node is selected (using CQ), output, and then suppressed. Errors occur in the selection process due to the noise in the activations of item nodes. They occur when there are many items with activation levels that differ by amounts similar to the size of the noise. This becomes more likely as the temporary connection weights decay and activation values approach zero. Under these conditions, items tend to be selected in the wrong order.

The model simulates the limited immediate memory span and the sigmoidal decline in the probability of list recall with increasing list length. The crucial factor here is that longer lists allow more time for decay. It also reproduces the phonemic similarity effect, and the tendency for errors to share phonemes with correct items. These effects occur straightforwardly because items sharing phonemes tend to have similar activation levels at recall and are therefore more affected by noise. The model also reproduces the word length effect and the linear relationship between recall and articulation rate. These effects occur because slower articulation increases the time interval and hence amount of decay between presentation of an item and its recall. Interestingly, they occur in the absence of subvocal rehearsal (which is simulated by repeated recalls in the model), consistent with recent empirical evidence implicating output delays in the word length effect (Henry, 1991; Cowan et al., 1992). The model also produces a bowed serial position curve, and the majority of errors are order errors. Order errors show the human pattern of tending to involve adjacent paired transpositions, but only when the model is driven almost entirely by the context–item associations with minimal chaining. This pattern of order errors arises because the context signals for any pair of items are more similar the more closely the items occurred in the input.

The model is clearly reasonably successful in meeting its original specification, i.e. exhibiting the principal phenomena that we identified at the outset, and remaining interpretable within the conceptual framework of the phonological loop. However, a more detailed inspection of both the model and the data reveal some important limitations. For example, the model successfully shows the phonemic similarity effect and the tendency for order errors to involve adjacent or nearby items, but does not reproduce the zig-zag serial position curve for lists of alternating phonemically similar and dissimilar items. Instead of showing a zig-zag, the serial position curve is smooth. The underlying problem is revealed by more detailed consideration of the workings of the model, as follows.

On the one hand, presentation of an item causes both activation of that item's node, and co-activation of nodes for phonemically similar items. Thus context states become associated not only to the correct item, but also to phonemically similar items, which leads to the phonemic similarity effect. On the other hand, each context state is also partially associated to items near the serial position of the correct one, due to the similarity of successive context states. This leads to order errors involving items at similar serial positions. However, these two effects interact when lists contain items of varying phonemic similarity, e.g. in a list of alternating phonemically similar and phonemically distinct items, similar items tend to be erroneously recalled in the place of dissimilar items much more frequently than is the case in experimental data. Clearly, the mechanisms of phonemic similarity and serial ordering are required to be more separate. Another, related limitation arises from the finding that chaining associations cannot account for order errors, as removing these associations from the model also raises the question of how the phonemic composition of items affects their recall.

Further limitations arise from deliberate omissions from the model, such as the absence of a long-term learning mechanism. Thus if the model is presented with a series of non-words, for which item–phoneme associations have not been pre-learned, it is difficult to see how selection of an item at recall can lead to production of the correct sound (i.e. activation of the correct output phoneme nodes). Relatedly, the model fails to address effects of word frequency, as it treats all the words it knows as equally familiar. Finally, the implementation of CQ was simplistic in the sense that items selected at presentation were suppressed uniformly until recall. That is, they were not allowed to recover after selection.

In light of these limitations, none of which seemed damaging to the central thrust of the model, it was decided to explore a revised and extended version.

The Current Model (Burgess, 1995)

The current model (see Fig. 3.2) addresses the limitations of the Burgess and Hitch (1992) model and extends it to cope with non-words, learning, and long-term memory. The new model retains the main features of a set of item nodes receiving input from both context and phoneme nodes, along with selection and subsequent suppression of the most active item using competitive queueing. However, it incorporates the following modifications, in rough order of importance:

1. The phoneme–item, item–phoneme, and context–item associations are implemented by connection weights with both short- and long-term Hebbian plasticity. This is biologically plausible given experiments showing simultaneous short- and long-term potentiation of synaptic pathways (see e.g. Bliss & Collingridge, 1993; Racine & deJong, 1988), and has been used previously in applications to memory (Gardner-Medwin, 1989, Hinton & Plaut, 1987).

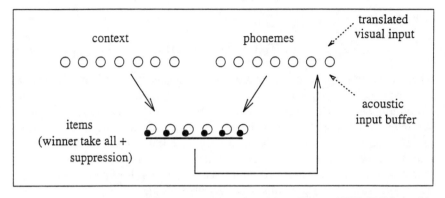

FIG. 3.2. The architecture of the current model, adapted from Burgess (1995). Full lines with arrows are excitatory connections with short- and long-term plasticity; the full line with the filled circles is the "winner take all" inhibitory interaction; dashed lines are routes by which information enters the model.

2. There are no chaining connections between input and output phoneme layers; a single layer is used to represent phonemes at both input and output.

3. The selection of an item at recall involves reactivation of its phonemic representation which in turn affects which item is output. Noisy activation values, leading to errors, are used only during the output process.

4. The "winner take all" component of CQ is implemented directly on the items, there is no extra "competitive filter" layer.

5. Items recover from suppression due to a decaying inhibition process.

In more detail, the modifications and their effects are as follows:

1. Each connection has a slowly incremental "long-term component", $W^l_{ij}(t)$, and a short-term component $W^s_{ij}(t)$, where t refers to the time-step and i & j identify the connected nodes. The short-term component is capable of large increases, but decays rapidly. The net weight of the connection is simply the arithmetical sum of the two components: $W_{ij}(t) = W^l_{ij}(t) + W^s_{ij}(t)$.

Hebbian learning occurs according to the following pairs of equations:

$$W^s_{ij}(t + 1) = c_j(t)a_i(t) \qquad \text{if } c_j(t)a_i(t) > W_{ij}(t);$$

otherwise

$$W^s_{ij}(t + 1) = W^s_{ij}(t) \qquad (1)$$

$$W^l_{ij}(t + 1) = W^l_{ij}(t) + \varepsilon c_j(t)a_i(t) \qquad \text{if } c_j(t)a_i(t) > 0;$$

otherwise

$$W^1_{ij}(t + 1) = W^1_{ij}(t) \qquad (2)$$

where $c_j(t)$ and $a_i(t)$ are the pre- and post-connection activations, and ε decreases with $|W^1_{ij}(t)|$ so that the long-term component saturates at some maximum value. These modifiable connection weights are always excitatory. As items only become active if selected by CQ, only weights to these items are ever increased. The presence of a long-term component in the context–item association and the way context varies with serial position means that if the same list is presented more than once its recall will improve, and serial order intrusions from previous lists may also occur.

2. As there is a single layer coding both input and output phonemes, selection of an item at presentation causes learning to occur in both the phoneme–item and item–phoneme links. An item's familiarity is reflected by the size of the long-term components of these connection weights, which increase with each (error free) presentation or recall of the item. For lists of novel nonwords, the item nodes are completely interchangeable, having only the short-term connections to phoneme nodes that are learned at presentation. It therefore does not matter which node is selected to represent a particular nonword. By comparison, presentation of a familiar item leads to the selection of a particular item node (due to the weights W^1_{ij}) and, during output, this item will activate its phonemes more strongly due to the additional effect of the long-term connection weights it has to its constituent phonemes. Unfamiliar items that are phonemically similar to a familiar item will tend to be represented by the familiar item node, and can take advantage of its long-term item–phoneme weights. However, the model does not address the problem of keeping distinct representations of nonwords as they become words.

3. At recall, the item initially selected automatically reactivates its phoneme nodes which in turn feed activation back to the item layer. Thus the item that is finally selected may be different, and is the one with the greatest net input from the context and phoneme nodes. This arrangement constrains output to be an item from the experimental vocabulary. The output selection process is taken to be noisy, corresponding to the psychological insight that errors tend to occur at retrieval.

4. The modification of the CQ mechanism is such that the "winner take all" interaction occurs within the item layer rather than in a separate competitive filter. This means that the selected item has activation 1 and all other items have activation 0, so that only the winning item is associated to the context and phoneme nodes.

5. The decaying inhibition that follows an item's selection increases the locality of errors, i.e. if item i + 1 replaces item i, then item i is most likely to

replace item i + 1 in turn (rather than e.g. item i + 2, which has had less time to recover from inhibition).

OPERATION OF THE EXTENDED MODEL

The details of the model, and an approximate mathematical analysis are given in Burgess (1995). We give only a brief outline here. Like the original, the model operates in time steps with duration equal to the time taken to present or recall an item (i.e. its spoken word length wl). The index t increases by 1 per time step, and refers to both time and serial position. Short-term connection weights and the inhibition applied to previously selected items decay by a factor Δ per second ($\Delta < 1$), and so Δ^{wl} per time step. The model does not address differences in rates of presentation and recall.

Parameters were set so that, with a realistic articulation rate of $wl = 0.3$ seconds per item, digit span was approximately 7 items. This was achieved by setting $\Delta = 0.75$ and introducing Gaussian noise with mean 0.0 and $\sigma = 0.5$.

Presentation. As in the original model, presentation of an item activates nodes in the phoneme layer and phoneme–item associations feed this activation through to the item layer. The most active item node is then selected by the CQ system, and all others are set to zero. At this point context–item, phoneme–item, and item–phoneme associations involving the selected item are learned according to equations (1) and (2). The short-term component of all connection weights then decays according to the duration of the time step (wl). Finally, the selected item is suppressed by increasing its inhibitory input. The context signal is then updated and the cycle is repeated, as each further list item is presented.

Recall. At recall, phoneme activations are set to zero and the context state for the first list item is reset to its original pattern. Activation feeds from the context layer to the item layer via the context–item associations, and the most active item node is selected. Next, the phoneme layer is fed activation via item–phoneme associations and in turn feeds back to the item layer via the phoneme–item links. The most strongly activated item in the presence of noise is selected for output. Next, there is learning (i.e. modification of connection weights), decay (of short-term connection weights, and of the inhibition felt by suppressed items), and then suppression of the selected item as at presentation. Finally, the context is updated and the cycle is repeated until recall of the list is complete. As in the original model, rehearsals of the list are treated as repeated recalls.

PERFORMANCE

Selected aspects of the model's performance are illustrated in Figs. 3.3–3.6 (for further details see Burgess, 1995). Figure 3.3 shows serial position curves for recall of a list of seven digits after different numbers of list rehearsals (i.e. repeated recalls following list presentation). Notice that recall declines with each rehearsal, as it does during an unfilled retention interval for supraspan lists. However, as in human data (Heffernan, 1991) there is stability after a small number of rehearsals, i.e. no further errors are committed. This is because of the increase in the long-term component of context–item connections during rehearsal. Notice also that the serial position curves exhibit primacy and recency. This is primarily due to the use of overlapping context states for adjacent items, which has the consequence that beginning and end items receive less interference from this source.

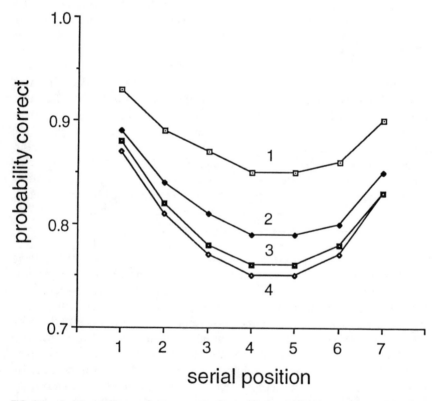

FIG. 3.3.   Serial position curves showing the effect of rehearsal, modelled as four consecutive recalls of a list of seven digits (labelled 1–4). Word length (wl) is 0.3 seconds. (Adapted from Burgess, 1995.)

Figure 3.4 shows serial position curves for lists of phonemically similar letters, phonemically dissimilar letters, and lists of alternating similar and dissimilar letters. As expected, the model exhibits poorer recall of phonemically similar items. More interestingly, it reproduces the zig-zag serial position curves characteristic of lists of alternating similar and dissimilar items (Baddeley, 1968). This is primarily because of the modification of the CQ mechanism so that only the winning item at each time step is associated to the currently active context and phoneme nodes, phonemically similar items are not.

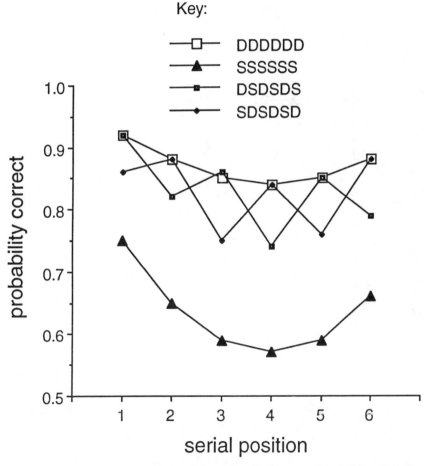

FIG. 3.4. Serial position curves for lists of letters that are phonemically dissimilar (DDDDDD), phonemically similar (SSSSSS), or alternating similar and dissimilar (either DSDSDS or SDSDSD). Each letter contains two phonemes; word length (wl) is 0.4 seconds; similar letters have one phoneme in common. (Adapted from Burgess, 1995.)

Figure 3.5 illustrates the probability of correctly recalling a list as a function of list length for familiar items (digits) and nonwords matched for spoken duration. Experimental data on memory for digits is also shown (Guildford & Dallenbach, 1925). The curve has the correct sigmoidal shape, and is lower for unfamiliar items, reflecting the absence of pre-learned phoneme–item and item–phoneme weights.

Figure 3.6 shows plots of span as a function of articulation rate. Experimental data for lists of words and non-words is also shown (Hulme et

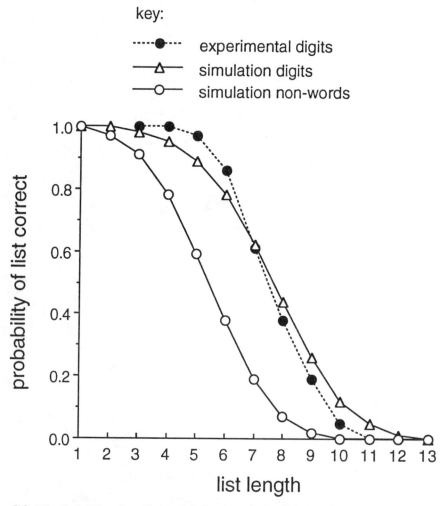

FIG. 3.5.   Probability of recalling a whole list versus list length (adapted from Burgess, 1995). Model curves are for digits (wl = 0.3 seconds) and for unfamiliar items of the same length. Experimental data on digits are adapted from Guildford and Dallenbach (1925).

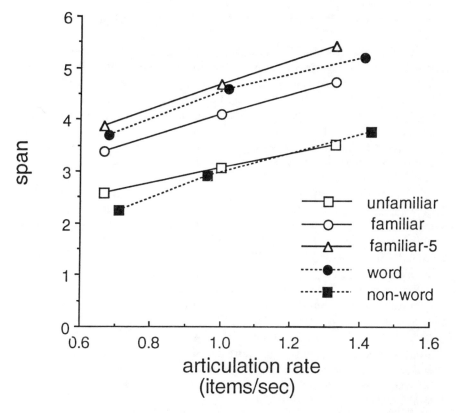

FIG. 3.6.   Span versus articulation rate for novel lists of familiar and unfamiliar words, and lists of familiar words after five repetitions (adapted from Burgess, 1995). Articulation rate was 1/wl with wl = 0.75, 1.0, and 1.5 seconds. Experimental data on recall of words and nonwords are also shown, adapted from Hulme, Maughan, and Brown (1991).

al., 1991). It can be seen that the model generates a linear relationship between span and articulation rate, with slope similar to the human data. This arises because of decay of the short-term weights and the extra time taken presenting and recalling lists of longer items. The figure also shows that for unfamiliar items the model generates a linear function with similar slope but lower intercept, consistent with the human data. This arises straightforwardly because the long-term item–phoneme and phoneme–item weights are, by definition, unaffected by decay. Finally, the figure shows recall of lists of familiar words following five repetitions of the list. As in the Hebb Effect, repetition improves recall. This is due to the gradual learning of long-term context–item weights. Repetition affects the intercept of the function relating span and articulation rate because the long-term context–

item weights are also unaffected by decay. This is a novel prediction of the model.

Even at the conceptual level, the construction of the model involved many simplifying approximations, and the avoidance of several crucial questions. Foremost among the approximations is the representation of time. For example, we have considered the long-term connection weights to be static, relative to the timescale over which short-term connection weights change. However it is clear that they too must decay over some longer timescale because, after a long gap without repetition, newly learned words become less pronounceable and serial order intrusions from a previous list become less common. We also made the "context" timing signal vary with serial position; reflecting the rhythm of presentation rather than absolute time—indeed the effect of temporal grouping can be modelled by modifying the context representation to reflect the presence of pauses during presentation (Hitch, Burgess, Towse, & Culpin, in press). For this reason, we have not yet examined the effect of varying presentation and recall rates independently.

The most obvious remaining questions include: (i) how to select an item node to form the long-term representation of a new item, without taking over existing item nodes; and (ii) how to learn the correct order of the phonemes within an item, taking into account the constraint of pronounce-ability—a possible extension to address this problem is presented in Hartley and Houghton (1995, see also Houghton et al., this volume); and (iii) why the recency effect should depend on the modality of presentation (Conrad & Hull, 1968). A possible extension to address the modality effect is presented in Neumann (1994). Answers to (i) and (ii) may help to overcome a further limitation of the model, namely its prediction that for mixed lists of words and nonwords, recall should be dominated by words. This is reminiscent of the difficulty the original Burgess and Hitch (1992) model had with mixed lists containing phonemically similar and dissimilar items, and may have similarly far-reaching implications.

DISCUSSION

The extended model maintains the strengths of the original model in generating basic phenomena such as span, effects of phonemic similarity, and word length, and patterns of error such as the serial position effect. This is so chiefly because its architecture maintains the core features of a CQ selection mechanism, a time-varying contextual signal, and item and phoneme layers, together with the operating principles of decaying temporary connections in a noisy system. In addition, the new model is successful in overcoming some of the limitations of the original model. Thus, it succeeds in reproducing the zig-zag serial position curve for lists of alternating phonetically similar and dissimilar items. The extended model also includes a simple mechanism for long-term learning based on non-decaying connection weights which reproduces human data on item familiarity, list repetition, and repeated rehearsal. Though not covered here, the extended model is also able to simulate patterns of order error more successfully than the original. For example, it produces serial order intrusions from prior lists due to the long-term component of context–item associations, and characteristic error patterns in lists containing repeated items due to decay in the inhibition given to selected items (see Burgess, 1995). We see, therefore, that the extended model reproduces a wide range of human data using a fairly simple mechanism. Furthermore, it is important to note that the simulations of different effects are obtained, as should be the case, without making any alterations to the basic parameters of the system.

In terms of the original concept of the phonological loop, both the extended and initial computational models have a straightforward interpretation. Thus the selection mechanism corresponds to the control process of articulation, and the phoneme layer corresponds to the phonological store. However, both models predict that there is a third, previously unsuspected, component of the loop, namely the context timing signal. The need for some such component arises from satisfying the constraints of simulation, and is also indicated by the presence of serial order intrusions. This is perhaps the most important theoretical prediction to emerge. It is possible to test this idea experimentally, and recent investigations have confirmed predictions from it (Hitch et al., 1995).

It is also interesting to note that the selection mechanism is sufficient to store serial order in itself, as items recover from suppression in the same order in which they were selected at presentation. This is consistent with it being a general-purpose serial ordering mechanism, with other applications besides the phonological loop (Houghton, 1990).

Finally, we must evaluate the usefulness of the model in terms of the criteria we set out at the beginning of this chapter. We consider the model to be successful in the following two respects: (i) it extends the explanatory power of current ideas, that is, the model provides an explanatory account of the occurrence of errors in immediate serial recall, beyond the simple prediction of capacity or span provided by the phonological loop idea. In particular it addresses the shape of the serial position curve, the effects of list length, word length, phonemic similarity, temporal grouping, and serial order intrusions. It is proposed as the starting point for a model of the effects of item familiarity and the role of rehearsal in vocabulary acquisition. (ii) It makes predictions. Many of the predicted error probabilities have not yet been checked experimentally: they are predictions. However, the major prediction of this model, and of

Burgess and Hitch (1992), is that, in addition to a short-term store of phonological information and a process of sub-vocal rehearsal, STM for ordered lists of verbal items involves a third component which provides a repeatable time-varying signal reflecting the rhythm of the items' presentation. Future work will look at modelling the "context" signal in more detail, and will try to relate it to more general work on timing signals (see e.g. Treisman, Cook, Naish, & McCrone, 1994).

ACKNOWLEDGEMENTS

NB was supported by a Royal Society University Research Fellowship. GJH was supported by a grant from the Joint Research Council Initiative on Human Computer Interaction and Cognitive Science.

REFERENCES

Aaronson, D. (1968). Temporal course of perception in an immediate recall task. *Journal of Experimental Psychology, 76*, 129–140.

Baddeley, A.D. (1966). Short-term memory for word sequences as a function of acoustic, semantic and formal similarity. *Quarterly Journal of Experimental Psychology, 18*, 362–365.

Baddeley, A.D. (1968). How does acoustic similarity influence short-term memory? *Quarterly Journal of Experimental Psychology, 20*, 249–264.

Baddeley, A.D. (1986). *Working memory*. Oxford: Clarendon Press.

Baddeley, A.D., & Hitch, G.J. (1974). Working memory. In G. Bower (Ed.), *The psychology of learning and motivation, vol. 8*, (pp. 47–90). New York: Academic Press.

Baddeley, A.D., Lewis, V.J., & Vallar, G. (1984). Exploring the articulatory loop. *Quarterly Journal of Experimental Psychology, 36*, 233–252.

Baddeley, A.D., Thomson, N., & Buchanan, M. (1975). Word length and the structure of short-term memory. *Journal of Verbal Learning & Verbal Behavior, 14*, 575–589.

Bjork, E.L., & Healy, A.F. (1974). Short-term order and item retention. *Journal of Verbal Learning and Verbal Behavior, 13*, 80–97.

Bliss, T.V.P., & Collingridge, G.L. (1993). A synaptic model of memory: Long-term potentiation in the hippocampus, *Nature, 361*, 31–39.

Burgess, N. (1995). A solvable connectionist model of immediate recall of ordered lists. In G. Tesauro, D. Touretzky, & T.K. Leen, (Eds.), *Neural information processing systems, 7*. Cambridge, MA: MIT Press.

Burgess, N., & Hitch, G.J. (1992). Towards a network model of the articulatory loop. *Journal of Memory and Language, 31*, 429–460.

Conrad, R. (1960). Serial order intrusions in immediate memory. *British Journal of Psychology, 51*, 45–48.

Conrad, R. (1964). Acoustic confusions in immediate memory. *British Journal of Psychology, 55*, 75–84.

Conrad, R. (1965). Order error in immediate recall of sequences. *Journal of Verbal Learning and Verbal Behavior, 4*, 161–169.

Conrad, R., & Hull, A.J. (1968). Input modality and the serial position curve in short-term memory. *Psychonomic Science, 10*, 135–136.

Cowan, N., Day, L., Saults, J.S., Keller, T.A., Johnson, T., & Flores, L. (1992). The role of verbal output time in the effects of word length on immediate memory. *Journal of Memory and Language, 31*, 1–17.

Crowder, R.G. (1972). Visual and auditory memory. In J.F. Kavanagh & I.G. Mattingly (Eds.), *Language by ear and by eye*, (pp. 251–276). Cambridge MA: MIT Press.

Ellis, N.C., & Hennelly, R.A. (1980). A bilingual word length effect: Implications for intelligence testing and the ease of mental calculations in Welsh and English. *British Journal of Psychology*, *71*, 43–51.

Elman, J.L. (1990). Finding structure in time. *Cognitive Science*, *14*, 179–211.

Gardner-Medwin, A.R. (1989). 'Doubly modifiable syapses: A model of short and long term auto-associative memory'. *Proceedings of the Royal Society London*, *B238*, 137–154.

Gathercole, S.E., & Baddeley, A.D. (1993). *Working memory and language*. Hove, UK: Lawrence Erlbaum Associates Ltd.

Guildford, J.P., & Dallenbach, K.M. (1925). The determination of memory span by the method of constant stimuli. *American Journal of Psychology*, *36*, 621–628.

Hartley, T., & Houghton, G. (1995). A linguistically-constrained model of short-term memory for nonwords. *Journal of Memory and Language*.

Healy, A.F. (1974). Separating item from order information in short-term memory. *Journal of Verbal Learning and Verbal Behavior*, *13*, 644–655.

Hebb, D.O. (1961). Distinctive features of learning in the higher animals. In J.F. Delafresnaye (Ed.), *Brain mechanisms and learning*. New York: Oxford University Press.

Heffernan, T.O. (1991). *The measurement of working memory capacity in children*. Unpublished PhD thesis. Department of Psychology, University of Manchester.

Henry, L.A. (1991). The effects of word length and phonemic similarity in young children's short-term memory. *Quarterly Journal of Experimental Psychology*, *43A*, 35–52.

Henson, R., Norris, D., Page, M., & Baddeley, A.D. (in press). Unchained memory: Error patterns rule out chaining models of immediate serial recall. *Quarterly Journal of Experimental Psychology*.

Hinton, G.E., & Plaut, D.C. (1987). Using fast weights to deblur old memories. In *Proceedings of the 9th Annual Conference of the Cognitive Science Society*, (pp. 177–186). Hillsdale, NJ: Lawrence Erlbaum Associations Inc.

Hitch, G.J., Burgess, N., Shapiro, J., Culpin, V., & Malloch, M. (1995). *Evidence for a timing signal in verbal short-term memory*. Paper presented to Experimental Psychology Society, Birmingham.

Hitch, G.J., Burgess, N., Towse, J., & Culpin, V. (in press). Grouping and immediate recall: A working memory analysis. *Quarterly Journal of Experimental Psychology*.

Hitch, G.J., & Halliday, M.S. (1983). Working memory in children. *Philosophical Transactions of the Royal Society London*, *B 302*, 324–340.

Houghton, G. (1990). The problem of serial order: a neural network model of sequence learning and recall. In R. Dale, C. Mellish, & M. Zock (Eds.), *Current research in Natural Language Generation*, (pp. 287–319). London: Academic Press.

Houghton, G. (1993). Inhibitory control of neurodynamics: Opponent mechanisms in sequencing and selective attention. In M. Oaksford & G.D.A. Brown (Eds.), *Neurodynamics and psychology*. London: Academic Press.

Hulme, C., Maughan, S., & Brown, G.D.A. (1991). Memory for familiar and unfamiliar words: Evidence for a long-term memory contribution to short-term memory span. *Journal of Memory and Language*, *30*, 685–701.

Hulme, C., Thompson, N., Muir, C., & Lawrence, A. (1984). Speech rate and the development of short-term memory span. *Journal of Experimental Child Psychology*, *38*, 241–253.

Jahnke, J.C. (1969). The Ranschburg effect. *Psychological Review*, *76*, 592–605.

Jones, D.M., & Macken, W.J. (1993). Irrelevant tones produce an irrelevant speech effect: Implications for phonological coding in working memory. *Journal of Experimental Psychology: Learning, Memory and Cognition*, *19*, 369–381.

Jordan, M.I. (1986). *Serial order: A parallel distributed approach*. ICI report 8604. Institute for Cognitive Science, University of California, San Diego, La Jolla, CA.

Kleinfield, D. (1986). Sequential state generation by model neural networks. *Proceedings of the National Academy of Science USA, 83,* 9469–9473.

Lewandowsky, S., & Murdoch, B.B. Jr. (1989). Memory for serial order. *Psychological Review, 96,* 15–57.

Miller, G.A. (1956). The magical number seven, plus or minus two: Some limits on our capacity for processing information. *Psychological Review, 63,* 81–97.

Neumann, C. (1994). *A feature-based approach to serial recall effects in immediate memory.* Unpublished MSc. Thesis, Department of Psychology, Purdue University, Indiana, USA.

Paulesu, E., Frith, C.D., & Frackowiak, R.S.J. (1993). The neural correlates of the verbal component of working memory. *Nature, 362,* 342–344.

Racine, R.J., & deJong, M. (1988). Temporal association in asymmetric neural networks. *Physical Review Letters, 57,* 2861.

Salamé, P., & Baddeley, A.D. (1982). Disruption of memory by unattended speech: Implications for the structure of working memory. *Journal of Verbal Learning & Verbal Behavior, 21,* 150–164.

Shallice, T. (1988). *From neuropsychology to mental structure.* Cambridge: Cambridge University Press.

Sompolinsky, H. & Kanter, I. (1986). Temporal association in asymmetric neural networks. *Physical Review Letters, 57,* 2861.

Treisman, M., Cook, N., Naish, P.L.N., & McCrone, J.K. (1994). The internal clock: Electroencephalographic evidence for oscillatory processes underlying time perception. *Quarterly Journal of Experimental Psychology, 47A,* 241–289.

Wickelgren, W.A. (1965). Short-term memory for repeated and non-repeated items. *Quarterly Journal of Experimental Psychology, 17,* 14–25.

4 Interactive processes in phonological memory

Susan E. Gathercole and Amanda J. Martin
University of Bristol, UK

Our aim in this chapter is to present a new theoretical perspective on phonological short-term memory (PSTM). The term PSTM is used here to refer to the well-documented capacities of both children and adults to retain sequences of verbal material over short periods of time. In recent years, there has been growing evidence that the model of the phonological loop component of working memory introduced originally by Baddeley and Hitch (1974) and later elaborated by Baddeley (1986) does not provide a complete account of phonological working memory. In this chapter, we take the opportunity to draw together findings from experimental, developmental, and neuropsychological studies of both short-term memory and language processing, with the aim of providing a more comprehensive account of phonological short-term memory function. It will be argued first that the capacity for temporary storage of verbal material develops as a byproduct of the speech input processing system, second that there is a highly interactive relationship between existing long-term knowledge and this pseudo-memory system, and third that this capacity is critical in language learning.

Before outlining this perspective in more detail, a brief summary of some of the recent developments in short-term memory research that have identified significant limitations to current models of PSTM is provided.

SPEECH PRODUCTION PROCESSES IN PSTM: THE CASE OF REHEARSAL

The role of speech production processes in PSTM, and specifically of articulatory rehearsal, is the major issue to have dominated short-term memory research during the past two decades. Baddeley and Hitch (1974) suggested that there is a specialised verbal component of short-term memory, which they termed the articulatory loop, and which consists of a process of covert articulation that serves to maintain representations of memory items in a speech-based form. Experimental evidence indicated that the articulatory loop was limited in capacity to approximately the amount of verbal material that can be articulated within a couple of seconds (Baddeley, Thomson, & Buchanan, 1975). Its operation was likened to that of a tape loop in which information that could not be recycled in articulatory form within two seconds was lost. Further experimental work by Baddeley and colleagues in the following years (e.g. Salamé & Baddeley, 1982; Vallar & Baddeley, 1984) led to a revised and elaborated model of this system, which following Baddeley (1990) is now termed the phonological loop. The revised loop system comprises two components: a phonological short-term store which holds phonological representations of memory items that decay over time, and an articulatory rehearsal process which serves to refresh fading representations in the phonological store by re-activating them in a serial, time-based manner. In the revised model too, therefore, speech production mechanisms maintained an important role in the temporary maintenance of verbal material.

The two-component phonological loop model has proved successful at embracing much of short-term memory research stimulated by the working memory approach, reviewed by Baddeley (this volume). For the present chapter, the most important findings relate to the functioning and nature of the rehearsal process, which has been very much tied to the execution of processes intrinsic to explicit speech production. Two phenomena in particular have been attributed to the rehearsal component of the phonological loop. The word length effect is the poorer recall of lists of long words (banana, elephant, telephone, etc.) than short words (cat, sun, egg, etc.). This phenomenon was first reported by Baddeley et al. (1975), and is attributed to the greater time taken to subvocally rehearse items of a longer articulatory duration; as a consequence, the representations in the phonological store of these items will be subject to lengthier periods between successive rehearsals and thus will be more likely to be lost due to decay.

The articulatory suppression effect is the equally well-established disruptive effect of subjects engaging in irrelevant articulation (for example, repeatedly saying hiya, hiya) while trying to remember a verbal memory sequence (e.g. Murray, 1967). The effect of articulatory suppression is claimed to be to suppress the operation of the articulatory rehearsal process, leading once again to loss of information from the phonological store due to decay. And consistent with this view, the effects of articulatory suppression and word length are found to be interactive: as long as presentation of the verbal memory list is visual, the word length effect is eliminated under conditions of articulatory suppression during the presentation of the memory list (Baddeley et al., 1975). Thus when rehearsal is prevented by suppression, variations in efficiency of rehearsal due to differences in articulatory duration of the lists of short and long words no longer influence recall accuracy. It should however be noted that with auditory presentation of memory lists, suppression needs to extend throughout presentation and recall to eliminate the word length effect (Baddeley, Lewis, & Vallar, 1984).

Converging findings from these and other paradigms (see Baddeley, this volume) led to the view that whereas auditory speech material gains automatic access to the phonological store, verbal material presented in other modes (such as pictures or written words) has to be converted into phonological form via the articulatory rehearsal process. Preventing rehearsal will therefore stop any inputs other than auditory speech-based material from reaching the phonological store.

This two-component model of the phonological loop also provided a coherent framework in accounting for long-observed developmental changes in PSTM (see Cowan & Kail, this volume, for a detailed account). Briefly, it appeared that the improvement in PSTM observed over the early and middle childhood years could readily be accounted for in terms of two processes. First, it was claimed that memory span improves with age as a consequence of the developmental improvement in the rate of spoken articulation which leads to faster subvocal rehearsal and so less opportunity for decay in the phonological store (Hulme, Thomson, Muir, & Lawrence, 1984; Nicolson, 1981). Second, Hitch and colleagues proposed that although children as young as 4 years of age can rehearse, they only do so spontaneously for auditory speech inputs that gain automatic access to the phonological store; when memory items were sequences of pictures of nameable objects, children below about 8 years of age seem to use visual memory rather than the phonological loop to mediate recall (e.g. Hitch & Halliday, 1983; Hitch, Halliday, Schaafstal, & Schraagen, 1988).

A number of significant problems have now emerged for accounts of both experimental data on adults and developmental findings that are based on the phonological loop model (see Gathercole & Hitch, 1993, and Cowan & Kail, this volume, for more detailed discussion). One problem is that the articulatory rehearsal process does not appear to be "articulatory" in any obvious sense. This conclusion arises from studies of the verbal memory abilities of individuals unable to speak for physical reasons, due either to acquired brain damage following a normal history of language development up to adulthood (Baddeley & Wilson, 1985) or to brain dysfunction already present at birth (Bishop & Robson, 1989). If these individuals cannot speak, can they rehearse? In both cases, normal word length effects in immediate recall were shown even when memory stimuli were presented in pictorial form, so the answer would appear to be yes. This pattern of findings indicates that rehearsal can occur both in individuals who cannot now speak and in those who have never been able to speak, and clearly challenge the view that rehearsal is a process of covert articulation, providing the basis for Baddeley's (1990) shift to using the term "phonological" rather than "articulatory" loop. Instead, it has been argued that the rehearsal process may correspond to a high level of activation of representations of articulatory gestures which may be based on the processes developed for the perception of speech (see Gathercole & Hitch, 1993, for discussion).

Other research has identified more serious shortcomings of the body of evidence linking the word length effect to the operation of the rehearsal process, irrespective of its detailed mechanical nature. First, it has become apparent that the differential delays involved in orally recalling sequences of short and long words can explain at least part of the word length effect (Avons, Wright & Pammer, 1994; Cowan et al., 1992). Indeed, Brown and Hulme (1995) have neatly demonstrated that a simple mathematical model of a trace decay function with no capacity for rehearsal can amply simulate the word length effect in recall as well as a number of other core short-term memory phenomena. Note, however, that decay during output does not itself provide a single adequate account of the word length data obtained with normal adults: findings of the disappearance of the word length effect under conditions of articulatory suppression while the output demands are held constant (e.g. Baddeley et al., 1975, 1984) remain plausibly accommodated by a rehearsal explanation of the word length effect. Nonetheless, the implications of studies that rely solely on the word length effect as an index of rehearsal must now be viewed as at best ambiguous.

Second, there is increasing doubt as to whether the presence of a word length effect in young children's recall of spoken word lists reflects subvocal rehearsal. When a spatial rather than a spoken recall procedure is used, Henry (1991) has demonstrated that the word length effect in recall of spoken word lists disappears for 5-year-old children, implicating once more an output rather than rehearsal locus to the length effect.

Other findings too suggest that the presence of a word length effect in young children's recall of auditory lists does not arise from rehearsal. Gathercole, Adams, and Hitch (1994) found that there was no significant correlation between the rates of explicit articulation and memory span for a large sample of 4-year-old children. Significant correlations between articulation rate and span were, however, found for a group of adults. These results indicate that 4-year-old children do not normally rehearse auditory material in span tasks, whereas adults do. Studying the same sample of children one year later, Gathercole and Adams (1994) reported the presence of significant word length effects in the memory span of the children who were now 5 years of age. Once again, however, the children's articulation rates and span for the short and long words were independent of one another, suggesting no use of articulatory rehearsal. The findings from these studies converge on the view that young children cannot rehearse.

In summary, the available data on children's PSTM now align more closely with the traditional view of developmental psychologists that covert rehearsal does not emerge until 7 or 8 years of age (e.g. Flavell, Beach, & Chinsky, 1966), than the original view emerging from the application of the working memory approach that children can rehearse at a much younger age, given speech-based inputs. As with the adult data, the more general implication of this work for the model of the phonological loop is that the word length effect may have multiple sources, and should not be taken as a sole index of rehearsal activity.

SPEECH PERCEPTION, NOT SPEECH PRODUCTION, CONSTRAINS PSTM

The preceding section summarises some of the theoretical problems arising from the long-standing emphasis by short-term memory researchers on the role of articulatory rehearsal processes in immediate memory. Our contention in this chapter is that the capacity to retain verbal material over short periods of time is indeed an integral part of the speech processing system, but that it depends much more closely on the processes and products of speech perception than speech production.

Specifically, we propose that the processes of speech perception result in the temporary activation of phonological representations of incoming speech, and that these representations form the basis for performance in immediate memory tasks. The precise nature of these representations or the system for representation is not critical for the present purposes, but could readily correspond to patterns of activation across a network of phonological units (McClelland & Elman, 1986). By the present view, the activated phonological representations correspond to the contents of the phonological store component of the phonological loop model; *there is no separate temporary memory system*. As well as mediating speech perception and performance on PSTM tasks, these phonological representations form the basis for performance on any tasks demanding judgments of sound structure; these will include both tests traditionally classified as "perceptual", such as minimal pairs discrimination (in which subjects judge whether pairs of spoken stimuli differing in one phonetic feature only are the same or different) and phoneme detection (where subjects have to detect a target phoneme in an incoming speech stream). The same representations will also underpin performance in tests of "phonological awareness" such as the detection of rhyme (Bradley & Bryant, 1983), phoneme segmentation (Liberman, Shankweiler, Fischer, & Carter, 1974), and phoneme deletion (Morais, Cary, Alegria, & Bertelson, 1979).

Although by this account a common substrate of activated phonological representations resulting from the speech perception process is suggested to underpin performance on both immediate memory tasks and measures of phonological processing, the demands of the different tasks tapping the common phonological representations arising from the processes of speech perception will inevitably vary. The different levels of explicit and analytic knowledge of the sound structure of language needed to perform the wide range of tasks classed as tapping "phonological awareness" have already been considered in detail by the Brussels group (e.g. Morais, Alegria, & Content, 1987; Morais & Mousty, 1992). We suggest that, in contrast, tests of immediate memory may provide particularly sensitive tests of the quality of the representations arising from speech perception because they do not require complex analytic comparisons of different parts of the incoming memory sequence. Immediate memory tasks simply require access to and ordered output of the activated phonological specification.

Speech perception does not consist simply of a passive analysis of the incoming acoustic information; it is a highly interactive process in which sensory analysis is aided by at least two different sources of knowledge about the phonological structure of the language. One type of knowledge concerns the statistical properties of its phonological structure: this includes both its phonetic repertoire and phonotactic structure (e.g. Cole & Jakimik, 1980; Frauenfelder, Baayen, Hellwig, & Schreuder, 1993). Another source of knowledge concerns the phonological characteristics of words known by the listener: the mental lexicon (Lahiri & Marslen-Wilson, 1991; Marslen-Wilson & Tyler, 1980). It follows from this that by tapping the products of the speech perception process, tasks of short-term memory will inevitably be influenced by the perceiver's knowledge of their language in a complex and highly interactive manner.

Recent research on PSTM has identified specific experimental phenomena which may well reflect these two knowledge-based influences on speech perception. These phenomena, and their accounts in terms of the interactive approach proposed here, will now be considered.

The Lexicality Effect in Immediate Memory

The lexicality effect refers to the robust finding that subjects are much better at recalling lists of familiar words than lists of the same length that contain either English-sounding nonwords such as "maffow", "taffost", and "crepog", or unfamiliar Italian words such as "lago", "prete", and "dite" (Hulme, Maughan, & Brown, 1991). Across a series of studies, this research team has made important advances in understanding the psychological processes underpinning this advantage to words over nonwords. They have provided convincing evidence that it is the subjects' familiarity with the phonological structure of the words, and not with nonphonological features such as their semantic attributes, that gives rise to the lexicality effect.

Hulme, Roodenrys, Brown, and Mercer (1995) manipulated phonological familiarity with nonwords by measuring subjects' memory span for English and Italian words on two occasions: first, at the beginning of the first experimental session, and second, after exposure to the phonological forms of the Italian words but not their English translations. The results were clear: span for the Italian words was significantly increased by providing phonological familiarisation. Thus, at least one source of the lexicality effect appears to be the contribution to immediate memory performance of stored knowledge of phonological structures, even in the absence of associated semantic attributes. Brown and Hulme (1995; see also Schweikert, 1993) use the term "redintegration" to describe this process by which incomplete temporary memory representations are restored by phonological specifications in long-term memory.

This view that stored phonological lexical representations contribute to immediate memory performance can be readily accommodated by the interactive perceptual approach advanced in this chapter. Lexical influences on the analysis of the incoming sensory signal have been extensively researched by psycholinguists in the past 20 years, and the nature of these influences is now well understood. According to the cohort model of word recognition, for example, the phonological structure of incoming speech is analysed and used to activate consistent stored phonological representations in the mental lexicon, on an on-line basis (Marslen-Wilson, 1987). The TRACE model of McClelland and Elman (1986) allows the activation of such lexical representations to boost consistent phonological representations, constituting an interactive activation system at the phoneme and word levels of representation. The result is that, all other things being equal, the patterns of activation of phonological elements will be stronger for familiar than unfamiliar words. From our perspective, it follows directly that immediate memory performance will therefore be better for words than for nonwords.

By this account, the locus of the lexicality effect is the system of bidirectional excitatory associations between phonological representations and stored knowledge of the phonological structure of words. In the next section, a similar PSTM phenomenon is described whose origins may reside at a second level of contribution of phonological knowledge to speech perception: the phonotactic level.

The Wordlikeness Effect in Nonword Repetition

In recent years, there has been increasing use in immediate memory tasks of nonwords rather than words as the memory stimuli (e.g. Gathercole & Baddeley, 1989; Hulme et al., 1991; Roodenrys, Hulme, & Brown, 1993). As nonwords are by definition unfamiliar, and so do not correspond directly to any representation in the mental lexicon, it has been argued that memory measures using nonwords as the experimental stimuli will be more sensitive to the capacities of the phonological loop component of working memory than tests using words. More specifically, the proposal is that when nonwords are employed as memory items, there is less opportunity for recall to be mediated by the activation of stored knowledge rather than temporary phonological representations.

It was this view that nonword memory measures provide "purer" measures of PSTM capacities that led us to develop the Children's Test of Nonword Repetition (CNRep) as a means of providing a sensitive measure of phonological memory skills in young children (Gathercole, Willis, Baddeley, & Emslie, 1994). In this test, the child is required to repeat a spoken nonword as soon as it is heard, and the accuracy of the repetition attempt is scored. This procedure is repeated for 40 nonwords, which vary in length from two to five syllables. The test is suitable for use with normal children up to about 8 years of age, and yields a measure that is highly correlated with auditory digit span.

It has become increasingly apparent, however, that the view that nonwords are not influenced by the subject's pre-existing knowledge of the language is oversimplistic. Across several studies, we have been concerned to identify the consequences for immediate memory of varying the degree of "wordlikeness" of nonwords. To obtain measures of wordlikeness, adult subjects were asked to judge, using a 5-point scale, to what degree each nonword in the CNRep would pass for a real word in the English language (Gathercole, Willis, Emslie, & Baddeley, 1991). Mean wordlikeness ratings were calculated for each item.

We then investigated the relationship between children's accuracy of repeating individual words in the CNRep and the wordlikeness ratings. For children aged 4, 5, and 6, rated wordlikeness was significantly correlated with repetition accuracy, due to higher repetition accuracy for the more wordlike nonwords. This phenomenon is termed the *wordlikeness effect*.

More recently, children's repetition accuracy for sets of nonwords of high wordlikeness (e.g. "defermication") and low wordlikeness (e.g. "loddernapish") were compared; the two sets of stimuli were matched for number of phonemes and syllables. Mean repetition accuracy scores on the low- and high-wordlike stimuli were calculated for groups of 4-year-old and 5-year-old children. The results are summarised in Fig. 4.1.

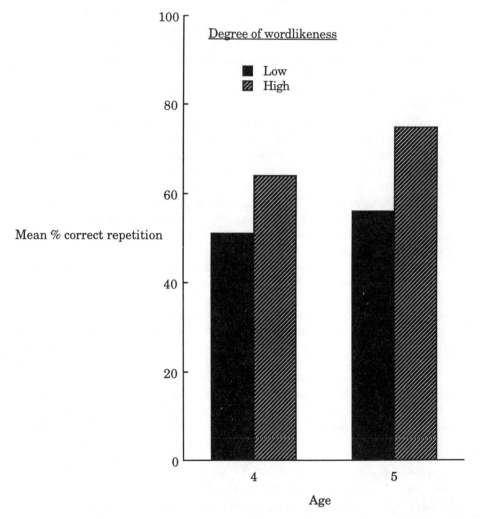

FIG. 4.1.   Mean percentage accuracy of nonword repetition, as a function of age and degree of wordlikeness of the nonwords (Gathercole, 1995).

Repetition accuracy was once again significantly greater for the high-than low-wordlike stimuli, and the wordlikeness effect was significantly greater for the older children. These results indicate that immediate memory for at least some nonwords is influenced by knowledge about the structure of the language to a degree that increases with age. A corresponding sensitivity to the wordlikeness of nonwords has recently been demonstrated in adults, too. Gathercole, Martin, and Hitch (in preparation) presented pairs of nonwords to adult subjects for immediate repetition; items in the pair were of either low wordlikeness (e.g. "empliforvent, woogalamic") or high wordlikeness (e.g. "adnesteric, corbealyon"). Mean repetition accuracy was significantly greater for the high-wordlike pairs (78%) than for the low-wordlike pairs (66%). So in adults as well as children, immediate recall of nonwords is influenced by the degree of wordlikeness of the nonword stimuli.

As a means of analysing the mechanisms underpinning the wordlikeness effect in nonword repetition, we have recently completed a study investigating the phonological characteristics of nonwords of differing degrees of wordlikeness (Martin & Gathercole, in preparation). Of particular interest were the phonological neighbourhood characteristics of low- and high-wordlike nonwords: in particular, we wanted to know whether the phonological neighbourhoods containing real words of high-wordlike nonwords were more densely populated than the neighbourhoods of low-wordlike nonwords. To address this issue, data were obtained on the distributions of familiar words which subjects generated as being similar to particular nonwords.

A corpus of 140 nonwords was obtained from a variety of published and unpublished sources. Subjects heard each spoken nonword, and were required to make two responses. First, they rated the wordlikeness of the item on a 5-point scale ranging from 1 (very unlike a real word) to 5 (very like a real word). Following this, they were given a period of 12 seconds to say aloud any real words that the nonword brought to mind, and the experimenter recorded these items.

There were two reasons why we chose to obtain estimates of the lexical density of the phonological space occupied by the nonwords (in other words, of their phonological neighbourhoods) based on subjects' generation of phonological neighbours, rather than relying on more "objective" dictionary-based phonological specifications of lexical items. First, dictionary-based estimates of close phonological neighbours inevitably involve selecting arbitrary criteria to define phonological neighbours: for example, by including only words that differ by one phoneme from the target word, providing a phonological n-count analogous to the orthographic n-count (Coltheart, Davelaar, Jonasson, & Besner, 1977). Such a criterion is certainly problematic when the nonwords vary in length, as in the present corpus where they range from 1 to 5 syllables. It seems implausible that a word differing by one phoneme from a nonword is equivalently similar in psychological terms to a short word containing only three phonemes as to a multisyllabic word containing 12 phonemes. By obtaining subjective data on the words "brought to mind" by the individual nonwords, we aimed to avoid such problems raised by the selection of arbitrary "objective" criteria. Second, dictionary-based estimates give equal weight to neighbours satisfying the search criteria irrespective of their frequency of usage and hence familiarity to the subject. Given the ubiquity of the influences of frequency on word recognition (see Garnham, 1985, for review), this frequency-independence seems psychologically implausible. By asking subjects to generate the words themselves, however, we were able to obtain a measure of neighbourhood density that had an implicit frequency-weighting, as subjects were more likely to generate lexical neighbours to nonwords that have higher frequencies of occurrence.

Mean wordlikeness values for each nonword were obtained by averaging across the 35 subjects who heard each item. Several different measures were derived from the words generated for each nonword:

1. *Phonological n-count.* This measure was the number of different words generated across all subjects which differed from the nonword by only one phoneme.

2. *Weighted phonological n-count.* The total number of words produced by subjects differing by only one phoneme from the target was calculated, thus giving multiple credits to words generated by more than one subject.

3. *Word count.* The number of different words (irrespective of their degree of phonological deviation from the nonword) generated in response to each nonword was calculated.

4. *Weighted word count.* The total number of words generated by all subjects for each nonword was scored.

Wordlikeness was found to be related to (in descending order of strength of association): weighted word count (21% of unique variance), word count (6%), and phonological n-count (2%). Each of these neighbourhood measures accounted for significant portions of unique variance, although phonological n-count accounted for a very small portion. Weighted phonological n-count failed to account for significant portions of unique variance in the wordlikeness measure (1%).

These findings indicate that wordlikeness judgements are indeed based, either directly or indirectly, on the lexical density of the phonological space occupied by the nonwords. The rated wordlikeness for a particular word is more strongly related to the total number of lexical neighbours generated than to the number of neighbours differing by a phoneme only, suggesting that in psychological terms, neighbourhoods can extend across several phonemes in phonological space. It is also notable that wordlikeness was much better predicted by the weighted word count, in which credit is given for the number of different subjects who generate a particular neighbour, than the pure word count. The implication is that there is a strong word-frequency-based component in the processes by which subjects estimate rated wordlikeness such that nonwords sharing phonological neighbour-hoods with high-frequency words are perceived as being more densely populated than those nonwords with low-frequency lexical neighbours.

This study has supplied useful detailed information on the basis of which wordlikeness judgements are made, confirming the importance of phonological neighbourhood density in estimations of wordlikeness. The precise source of the wordlikeness effect in tasks involving the recall of nonwords, however, has yet to be investigated directly.

The account of the wordlikeness effect in nonword repetition that we currently favour is that the wordlikeness effect reflects the influence of knowledge about the phonotactic properties of the language on the perception of the phonological structure of the nonword. Phonotactic properties are the constraints on the possible sequencing and positions of phonetic segments allowed in words. Although we have not as yet measured phonotactic probabilities directly in our nonword corpus, it is well established that high probability phonotactic patterns are associated with dense lexical neighbourhoods (Landauer & Streeter, 1973; Luce, Pisoni, & Goldinger, 1990). Given the strong positive association between the wordlikeness of nonwords and the size of their phonological neighbour-hoods (Martin & Gathercole, in preparation), it is almost certainly the case that highly wordlike nonwords are indeed composed of phonological sequences with high phonotactic probabilities.

There is a large body of evidence that adults do make use of phonotactic probabilities in recognising spoken words (e.g. Massaro & Cohen, 1983; McClelland & Elman, 1986). In terms of the theoretical framework presented in this chapter, the influence of phonotactic knowledge could readily be located in the representations resulting from speech perception. In a distributed memory system, this knowledge could readily be embodied in the connections between adjacent elements at the phoneme level, with phoneme sequences that are relatively common in the language having stronger excitatory connections than rarer phoneme sequences. Thus an unfamiliar spoken word containing phoneme combinations with high transitional probabilities within the language will be more readily (e.g. with less sensory information and with higher signal-to-noise ratios) represented as a pattern of activation across the set of phoneme units than items with low phoneme transition probabilities. If, as we argue in this chapter, PSTM is based on the representations resulting from the perceptual analysis process, the better quality of perceptual representation resulting from spoken nonwords of high degrees of phonotactic regularity will result directly in increased probability of correct output and hence recall.

Evidence that the wordlikeness effect in nonword repetition originates in the products of speech perception is provided by a recent study in our laboratory of the nonword repetition abilities of English–French bilingual children (Gathercole & Thorn, 1995). The children, aged between 4 and 8 years of age, were classified as either simultaneous bilinguals (having acquired both English and French simultaneously at the normal age) or sequential bilinguals (having acquiring French after having either partly or completely acquired English as a native language). The vocabulary skills of these two groups of bilinguals endorsed this classification, which was based on questionnaires completed by the parents. The mean vocabulary standardised scores were close to 100 (i.e. average for their chronological age) for the simultaneous bilingual children in both English and French. In contrast, the sequential bilingual group had a mean standardised vocabulary score of about 113 for English and 75 for French. Thus both English and French appeared to have been acquired as native languages by the simultaneous bilinguals. In contrast, for the sequential children the native language was English and French constituted a second language.

Our main interest was in the influences of word-based knowledge on the nonword repetition capacities of the bilingual children in both English and French. We were fortunate in having access to a French test of nonword repetition developed by Grant, Karmiloff-Smith, Berthoud, and Christophe (unpublished) which was constructed in a way that closely resembles our CNRep test (Gathercole et al., 1994). Wordlikeness ratings were also available for the French nonword test, enabling us to construct sets of low- and high-wordlike French nonwords matched for numbers of phonemes and syllables.

The results were clear: wordlikeness effects were only present in nonword repetition when the nonword stimuli were in the child's "native" language. The simultaneous bilingual group showed superior repetition of high- than low-wordlike nonwords in both English and French; in contrast, the sequential bilinguals (who acquired French later than English) showed a wordlikeness effect in the repetition of English but not French nonwords.

These findings indicate that sensitivity to the wordlikeness of nonwords in a repetition paradigm is restricted to the native language. We suggest that the reason for this is that the wordlikeness effect in nonword memory is an emergent property of the speech perception system. The analytic processes that serve to process incoming speech become specialised and attuned to the sound structures of the language at an early stage in language acquisition. The phonological network that represents the product of these processes will be similarly framed by the specialised phonological structure of the language.

This process of language-specific specialisation is typically detected before 12 months of age in normal infants, and has been found for a variety of structural properties of the native language (e.g. Jusczyk, Cutler, & Redanz, 1993; Jusczyk et al., 1992 ; Werker & Tees, 1984). In particular, Jusczyk, Luce, and Charles-Luce (1994) have recently demonstrated that infants' preference for unfamiliar speech stimuli (in other words, nonwords) that incorporate phonotactic patterns of high probability (such as "riss") over low probability patterns (such as "youdge") emerges between 6 and 9 months of age.

The early specialisation of the analytic processes underpinning speech perception processes for the native language will place significant limits on the ability of older children and adults to discriminate the phonological structure of non-native languages. The phonological and phonotactic characteristics of all languages differ significantly from one another, and the presence of already developed perceptual processes for analysing the sound structure of one's native language are likely to limit the acquisition of a second language, at the phonological level at least. It is this factor that presumably underpins the diminishing capacity to acquire the phonology of a second language with increasing age which is often termed a "critical period" for phonology (e.g. Long, 1990).

Children learning another language after the native tongue has already been partly acquired therefore fail to develop the specialised perceptual procedures for analysing the sound structure of the second language. Instead, sequential bilinguals may simply apply to spoken inputs in the second language the perceptual processes developed for the first language (see also Cutler, Mehler, Norris, & Segui, 1989). Thus, the sequential English–French bilinguals "perceive" French stimuli as though they were English nonwords. We argued earlier that the perceptual processes and their outputs are the source of wordlikeness effects in nonword repetition, as a consequence of their implicit use of phonotactic knowledge for the native language. By this argument, English–French sequential bilinguals would indeed not be expected to show wordlikeness effects in French, because there is no reason why nonwords varying in wordlikeness to a native French speaker should vary in wordlikeness in the same way to a native English speaker. Simultaneous bilinguals, in contrast, presumably develop parallel repertoires of perceptual processes specialised for each language, and so will perceive incoming stimuli in an appropriate language-specific manner that will result in wordlikeness effects in either tongue.

Evidence from Special Populations

We have suggested that PSTM performance is mediated not by a specialised phonological memory system, but instead by access to the products of a speech perceptual system in which perceptual analyses of incoming speech sounds and stored knowledge about the native language interact in a complex manner designed to maximise rapid and accurate speech recognition. This perspective provides straightforward accounts of phenomena such as lexicality effects in immediate memory and wordlikeness effects in nonword repetition. It is also argued that the phonological network can be activated in a top-down fashion to mediate memory for nonauditory inputs such as pictures of nameable objects and printed words. In this way, the factors limiting the normal development of perceptual analytic processes and the phonological network will influence memory for nonauditory as well as auditory inputs.

This account of PSTM phenomena in terms of speech perceptual processes unites much of the work on the perceptual and PSTM abilities of individuals from special populations. In this section we provide a brief overview of the extent to which perceptual and PSTM capacities are bound together.

Individuals Who Cannot Speak. Individuals who are unable to produce speech following brain damage nonetheless show apparently normal PSTM characteristics, as discussed earlier (Baddeley & Wilson, 1985; Bishop & Robson, 1989). Whereas these findings raise significant theoretical problems for theories that invoke speech production mechanisms in the specialised phonological memory system, they can readily be accommodated by the present framework which unites speech perception with PSTM. Provided that subjects have normal speech perceptual abilities—and the evidence is that even congenital anarthrics do (MacNeilage, Rootes, & Chase, 1967; see also Liberman & Mattingley, 1985)—there should be normal functioning in tasks requiring access to the products of the speech perception system. The reason for this is that performance on PSTM tasks is believed to reflect access to the products of the speech perception process, and is largely independent of speech production.

This perspective provides an account of why the basic phonological representations underpinning performance on PSTM tasks are normal in individuals who cannot produce speech. It does not, however, deliver an explanation of how the activation levels of phonological representations can be maintained over longer periods of time, which replaces the concept of articulatory rehearsal. The issue of what psychological processes do underpin strategic rehearsal is beyond the scope of the present framework, which focuses instead on the basic system for representing phonological inputs.

Individuals Who Cannot Hear. Whereas impaired or absent speech production abilities should not impair PSTM according to the present approach, the consequences of partial or profound deafness should be very considerable. Degraded perceptual inputs during the early childhood period would be expected to hamper or indeed prevent the development of specialised analytic procedures for recognising the sound structure of the native language, leaving deaf individuals with little possibility for using phonological representations resulting from perceptual experience to mediate their immediate memory performance.

At a gross level, the predicted profile of profound deafness being accompanied by an apparent inability to use the sound-based features of nonauditory events such as pictures or printed words is upheld. Studies of immediate memory function in groups of deaf people almost invariably reveal poor performance and a reduced sensitivity to the sound-based characteristics of the labels of the memory stimuli (e.g. Campbell & Wright, 1990; Olsson & Furth, 1966; Pintner & Paterson, 1917).

Comprehensive analyses of memory function in samples of individuals with hearing impairments, however, have yielded a more complex picture. In an influential study, Conrad (1979) reported findings from a study of many aspects of cognitive and language functioning of 359 deaf schoolchildren aged 15–16 years. It was found that at least some deaf children appeared to be capable of using "internal speech" to mediate short-term memory for nameable visual events, where internal speech was indexed by a sensitivity to the sound-based structure of the memory sequence. Consistent with the present hypothesis that PSTM performance is mediated by access to the products of the speech perception process, Conrad reported a significant association between the degree of hearing impairment and the proportion of children showing evidence for internal speech. If it is assumed that increasing degrees of deafness result in the development of less effective processes for discriminating sounds in the language, then this relationship is one we would predict. However, the presence of internal speech was even more strongly linked with the degree of intelligibility of the individual's spoken language, leading Conrad to propose a causal model in which two factors—intelligibility of speech and nonverbal intelligence—governed the development of internal speech in deaf children.

Conrad's (1979) conclusions, like the body of evidence reviewed earlier in this chapter which arose from the working memory approach, therefore identified the speech production mechanisms as critical contributors to the normal operation of the verbal short-term memory system. There is, however, at least one other possible interpretation of Conrad's data. Speech intelligibility may itself provide an indirect index of the degree to which the deaf child has been able to develop a functioning speech perception system, because accurate representations of phonological form are required to guide the child in the articulatory gestures required to produce discriminable speech. Consistent with this view, degree of speech intelligibility is related both to degree of hearing impairment and to nonverbal intelligence

(Conrad, 1979). Thus the close links between speech intelligibility and use of internal speech in memory tasks could reflect a common influence on both measures of the child's ability to develop adequate perceptual analytic processes, resulting in a phonological network that is sufficiently well elaborated both to guide speech output and to mediate immediate recall.

The studies reviewed here investigated memory functioning in individuals who were either deaf from birth or acquired their hearing impairment very early in life. A more common source of hearing impairment in childhood is the intermittent conductive hearing loss known as *otitis media*. Otitis media is defined as recurrent episodes of middle-ear effusion which occur at least four times in a period of six months, and is quite common in infancy and early childhood. Individual episodes result in temporary hearing loss averaging 30dB, with the mean duration of an episode of about 30 days (Klein & Rapin, 1993).

Thus the typical child suffering otitis media will experience significant hearing loss for about 50% of the time during the first few years of life. As this is the critical period at which the native language is being acquired, it is not surprising that otitis media has come to be associated with poor language development. There is now evidence that the child's ability to discriminate native speech sounds shows persistent impairments as a consequence of their intermittent conductive loss. Eimas and Clarkson (1986) recently demonstrated that children with a history of otitis media have impaired phonological discrimination skills even when they are clear of middle-ear effusion at test. The implication of this finding is that these children have failed to develop the specialised processes for analysing the sound structure of their own language that would be expected on the basis of their chronological age. In terms of the present theoretical approach, their problems would result in impaired development of both the analytic processes that act on incoming speech and the phonological network that represent the outputs of these perceptual processes. We would therefore expect poor performance on tests of PSTM in children who have experienced otitis media for long periods during the preschool years: an inadequate speech perceptual system will result in poor phonological representations to form the basis for PSTM performance.

Individuals With Specific Language Impairment.   Children who fail to develop language at a normal rate in the absence of any obvious aetiology such as low intelligence, sensory deficits, or social deprivation are often classified as having a specific language impairment (SLI). Many language-related deficits in SLI children have been documented (see Bishop, 1992, for review); these range from failures to acquire grammatical morphemes (Gopnik & Crago, 1991) and problems in hierarchical structuring (Cromer, 1978) to highly specific deficits in processing the transitional information constituting the speech signal (e.g. Tallal & Piercy, 1975; Tallal, Stark, & Mellits, 1985).

There has recently been considerable interest in whether SLI children have selective impairments of PSTM. Gathercole and Baddeley (1990a) assessed the performance of a group of SLI children (mean age 8 years) on a range of verbal tasks. This group were compared with younger control children of matched verbal abilities (mean age 6 years). The task that best discriminated the two groups was nonword repetition (see also Kamhi & Catts, 1986; Taylor, Lean, & Schwartz, 1989). Similar findings have recently been reported by Bishop, North, and Donlan (in press), in a study of pairs of monozygotic and dizygotic twins in which one twin was classified as SLI. Nonword repetition ability, and in particular the CNRep task (Gathercole et al., 1994), was once again found to be significantly impaired in SLI children, and also appeared to have a strong heritability component. The strength of the association between CNRep scores and developmental language disorders have led Bishop and colleagues to propose that the nonword repetition task provides an effective phenotypic marker for SLI.

The present concern is with the nature of the nonword repetition deficit in children with disordered language development. Do such children have deficits with the perceptual analysis of the speech signal that results in poor phonological representations? There is certainly some evidence in support of this view. Tallal and colleagues have argued strongly that the causal basis of the whole range of language learning problems experienced by SLI children is that they have difficulties in processing rapid transitional information that characterises speech inputs (e.g. Tallal et al., 1985). Other researchers have argued more generally that these children have impaired phonological systems (e.g. Leonard, 1982). Perhaps, then, one of the primary causes of SLI is an impaired ability to develop the perceptual analytic procedures specialised for the native language, and it is this impairment that lies at the root of their poor nonword repetition ability. According to this view, the poor perceptual analytic skills of SLI children will result in a profile of language learning difficulties that are similar in nature, although weaker in magnitude, to children who are deaf.

LONG-TERM LEARNING

The view developed so far in this chapter is that performance on tests of immediate verbal memory is not served by access to an independent specialised temporary memory system, but instead is mediated by the phonological representations resulting from speech perception. The perception of speech consists of more than just sensory analysis, being influenced both by knowledge of the structures of familiar words within the mental lexicon and of the phonotactic properties of the language. Speech perception therefore arises from the operation of a set of highly interactive processes. It follows directly from our analysis that performance on immediate verbal memory tasks will similarly reflect the contributions of stored knowledge of the language as well as sensory analysis procedures.

In this final section, we propose a further level of interactivity to this system. There is now compelling evidence that learning the phonological forms of new words is limited by the same factors that constrain performance on PSTM tasks. Four lines of enquiry support this conclusion. First, experimental studies using learning paradigms designed to simulate the learning of new words have shown that long-term phonological learning is influenced by the same variables (such as word length, phonological similarity, and articulatory suppression) as tests of PSTM (Papagno & Vallar, 1992; Papagno, Valentine, & Baddeley, 1992). Second, children's scores on tests of PSTM such as nonword repetition provide excellent predictors of their natural vocabulary knowledge (Gathercole & Baddeley, 1989; Gathercole, Willis, Emslie, & Baddeley, 1992; Michas & Henry, 1994), of their abilities to acquire a foreign language (Service, 1992), and their speed of learning new phonological forms in an experimental task (Gathercole & Baddeley, 1990b; Gathercole, Hitch, Service, & Martin, submitted; Michas & Henry, 1994). Third, individuals with very poor PSTM function as a result of either acquired brain damage or a developmental disorder have been shown to have highly specific deficits in long-term phonological learning (Baddeley, Papagno, & Vallar, 1988; Baddeley & Wilson, 1993). A final source of evidence linking phonological memory function to word learning is provided by Papagno and Vallar (1995), who found that adult subjects with a particular facility for acquiring foreign languages had superior performance on tests of PSTM than matched non-polyglot subjects. Thus, unusually good skills at acquiring new vocabularies appear to be accompanied by excellent immediate verbal memory skills, mirroring findings of poor nonword learning in individuals with impaired immediate memory skills (Baddeley, 1993; Baddeley et al., 1988; Baddeley & Wilson, 1993).

These findings have led to the suggestion that one of the primary functions of PSTM is to support word learning in the native language. Baddeley, Gathercole, Papagno, and Bishop (in preparation) argue that the temporary phonological representations tapped in PSTM tasks form the basis for the construction of more permanent representations of phonological structure, in the lexicon. Integrating this view with the present proposal that PSTM performance arises from access to the phonological system specialised for representing the outputs of the speech perception process, our claim here is that patterns of activation within this phonological system are used to build permanent knowledge structures.

The framework is represented schematically in Fig. 4.2, and can be summarised as follows. Temporary phonological representations of incoming speech are constructed in the basis of the perceptual analytic processes developed for the native language in early childhood. The "representations" may be conceived as patterns of activation across a phonological network (although it is not critical for the present framework, which is pre-computational, to do so). The strength of the activation patterns associated with particular inputs will depend, in addition to the outputs of the perceptual analytic processes, both on pre-existing strengths of association between adjacent phonological elements (reflecting the

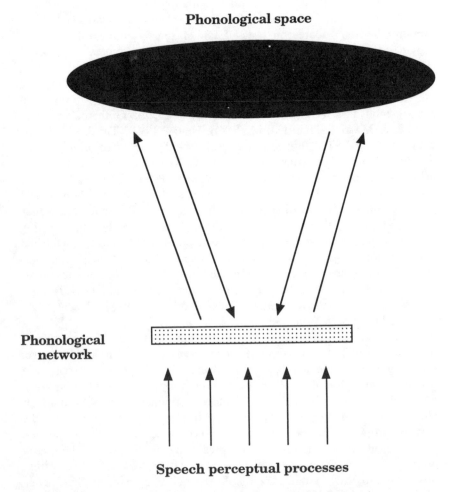

FIG. 4.2.   Schematic representation of the perceptual–phonological framework.

phonotactic properties of the language) and on excitatory links arising from activation of lexical representations of known phonological sequences. Access to the phonological network for nonspeech inputs is achieved via this lexical pathway.

The phonological specifications of new words are based, according to this framework, on the temporary patterns of activation in the phonological network. The precise nature of this process by which patterns of activation in the phonological network result in permanent phonological specifications remains to be identified. One possibility is that the lexical phonological representations are organised in phonological space, where phonological space is framed by the phonological parameters of the existing lexicon. By this view, phonological space consists of histories of occurrence of phonological events, with high levels of activation associated with familiar words that have been encountered on many occasions. When an unfamiliar phonological structure is presented, it results in an increase in the activation level (which may previously have been zero) of its unique coordinates in phonological space. Activation may also spread to adjacent locations in space.

When a previously experienced phonological form is once again encountered, the activation of its coordinate may provide a degree of top-down excitation of its component phonological features in the phonological network which is directly related to its previous history of occurrence. Frequent words will therefore excite their component phonemes in the phonological network in this downwards fashion more strongly than a word encountered only once before, for example. The re-occurrence of a particular phonological form in both cases will also increment the level of activation of its coordinates in phonological space, as well as transmitting activation back down to the phonological network.

It follows from this model that any factors or processes that influence the quality of the representations (or patterns of activation) in the phonological network will also affect the degree of activity in the relevant area of phonological space. We have recently obtained some evidence in support of this claim, in a study in which adult subjects learned sets of word–nonword pairs (Gathercole, Martin, & Hitch, in preparation). The nonwords in each pair were either of low wordlikeness (e.g. "kipser") or of high wordlikeness (e.g. "stirple"). Highly wordlike nonwords were learned significantly faster than low-wordlike nonwords; by the final learning trial subjects could accurately recall to the cue word 73% of the wordlike nonwords, but only 60% of the low-wordlike stimuli.

So, wordlikeness appears to exert a common influence on both immediate memory and long-term learning. We suggest that in both types of paradigm, the beneficial effect of high degrees of wordlikeness arises from the higher levels of pre-existing activation between phoneme combinations that occur more frequently in the language, leading to stronger patterns of activation within the phonological network. The quality of these phonological specifications will influence both performance on immediate memory tasks, which is mediated by access to the phonological network, and the speed of building long-term specifications of the phonological content of new words. It is proposed that there is a direct link between their degree of activation of elements both within the phonological network and their corresponding coordinates in phonological space.

It should be noted that the present framework identifies another possible source for the wordlikeness effect in nonword memory to the effects of phoneme transition probabilities operating in the interconnections between elements in the phonological network. According to this account, even unfamiliar phonological structures contact their unique coordinates in phonological space and there will be some spread of activation to adjacent coordinates. We have already shown that highly wordlike nonwords have more close phonological neighbours than nonwords of low wordlikeness (Martin & Gathercole, in preparation). Therefore the spread of activation across phonological space will reach more words for the highly wordlike stimuli. As a consequence, the representations of highly wordlike nonwords in the phonological network will reach more top-down activation from lexical items. As yet, there are no data to distinguish between this explanation of the wordlikeness effect and the account considered earlier in terms of phonotactic influences on connections between elements in the phonological network.

In summary, the incorporation of a learning process in this perceptually based framework provides a coherent account of the close empirical links established between PSTM performance and long-term phonological learning. The high degree of interactivity between the phonological network that holds incoming perceptual forms and phonological space in which familiar words are represented readily accounts both for influences of lexical and sublexical knowledge on immediate memory performance, and influences of factors influencing the perceptual process on long-term learning.

COMPUTATIONAL MODELS OF PSTM

The theoretical framework presented in this chapter has been phrased in quasi-computational terms, with many of these terms and many aspects of this structure corresponding to the parallel distributed processing approach developed by McClelland, Rumelhart, and associates (1986), and implemented more specifically in the TRACE model of speech perception (McClelland & Elman, 1986). Despite shared terminology with TRACE in particular, our framework is expressible at present only in verbal and not in computational form, for a number of reasons. First, although a distributed memory approach has been shown to be successfully applied to the perception of single words from a limited vocabulary as in the case of TRACE, immediate memory tasks typically involve either lists of words or phonologically unfamiliar stimuli. The serial nature of both the memory inputs and phonological output raises serious problems for modellers, particularly when common phonological elements such as phonemes recur in different combinations in the memory sequence (see Houghton, Hartley, & Glasspool, this volume, and Burgess & Hitch, this volume, for detailed discussions of this and other related problems). Second, the concept of phonological space also does not align readily with the relatively simple unit-based architecture of TRACE. Third, TRACE is not a learning system, and it does not have any capacity for learning new phoneme patterns of words. The range of the present framework is therefore very different from the detailed computational specification of the perception of single words alone.

There are also significant differences between the scope of the theoretical framework advanced in this chapter and those of current computational models of verbal short-term memory. One of the most significant developments in short-term memory research in recent years has been the implementation of computational models of the phonological short-term memory system, as attested by the contributions in the present volume of Murdock, Schweikert, Hayt, Hersberger, and Geuntert; Burgess and Hitch; Brown and Hulme; and Houghton et al. The goal of these research teams has been to test specific computational models derived from verbal theories against relevant empirical phenomena. Considerable success has already been achieved in developing more specific theoretical accounts of core experimental findings than has been afforded by verbal theories alone.

However, the implemented models of PSTM are designed to model detailed aspects of immediate memory performance such as the basic STM phenomena of word length, phonological similarity, and recency effects (Brown & Hulme, 1995, this volume; Burgess & Hitch, 1992, this volume) and memory for nonwords (Glasspool, 1995, and Hartley & Houghton, 1995; both described in Houghton et al., this volume). In contrast, the present approach aims to provide a general account of the phonological basis for immediate verbal memory performance which readily accommodates both recent findings of influences of long-term knowledge on immediate memory.

In summary, the present chapter provides an account of performance on test of phonological short-term memory in terms of the highly interactive processes specialised for the perception of speech and the learning of new words. This approach can readily accommodate influences of long-term knowledge on immediate memory performance, and can be extended to explain how the phonological forms of new words are learned. It is argued that this interactive framework provides a broad perspective on phonological short-term memory function which complements the exciting theoretical developments arising from the development of more specific computational accounts of immediate verbal memory.

REFERENCES

Avons, S.E., Wright, K.L., & Pammer, K. (1994). The word-length effect in probed and serial recall. *Quarterly Journal of Experimental Psychology, 47A*, 207–232.

Baddeley, A.D. (1986). *Working Memory*. Oxford: Clarendon Press.

Baddeley, A.D. (1990). *Human memory: Theory and practice*. Hove, UK: Lawrence Erlbaum Associates Ltd.

Baddeley, A.D. (1993). Short-term phonological memory and long-term learning: A single case study. *European Journal of Cognitive Psychology, 5*, 129–148.

Baddeley, A.D., Gathercole, S.E., Papagno, C., & Bishop, D.V.M. (in preparation). *The role of the phonological loop in vocabulary acquisition*.

Baddeley, A.D. & Hitch, G.J. (1974). Working memory. In G. Bower (Ed.), *The psychology of learning and motivation* Vol. 8, (pp. 47–90). New York: Academic Press.

Baddeley, A.D., Lewis, V.J., & Vallar, G. (1984). Exploring the articulatory loop. *Quarterly Journal of Experimental Psychology, 36*, 233–252.

Baddeley, A.D., Papagno, C., & Vallar, G. (1988). When long-term learning depends on short-term storage. *Journal of Memory & Language, 27*, 586–596.

Baddeley, A.D., Thomson, N., & Buchanan, M. (1975). Word length and the structure of short-term memory. *Journal of Verbal Learning & Verbal Behavior, 14*, 575–589.

Baddeley, A.D. & Wilson, B. (1985). Phonological coding and short-term memory in patients without speech. *Journal of Memory & Language, 24*, 490–502.

Baddeley, A.D. & Wilson, B. (1993). A developmental deficit in short-term phonological memory: Implications for language and reading. *Memory, 1*, 65–78.

Bishop, D.V.M. (1992). The underlying nature of specific language impairment. *Journal of Child Psychology and Child Psychiatry, 33*, 3–66.

Bishop, D.V.M., North, T., & Donlan, C. (in press). Nonword repetition as a phenotypic marker for inherited language impairment: Evidence from a twin study. *Journal of Child Psychology and Psychiatry*.

Bishop, D.V.M. & Robson, J. (1989). Unimpaired short-term memory and rhyme judgment in congenitally speechless individuals: Implications for the notion of "Articulatory Coding". *Quarterly Journal of Experimental Psychology, 41A*, 123–140.

Bradley, L. & Bryant, P.E. (1983). Categorizing sounds and learning to read—a causal connection. *Nature, 301*, 419–420.

Brown, G.D.A. & Hulme, C. (1995). Modelling item length effects in memory span: No rehearsal needed? *Journal of Memory and Language, 34*, 594–621.

Burgess, N. & Hitch, G.J. (1992). Toward a network model of the articulatory loop. *Journal of Memory and Language, 31*, 429–460.

Campbell, R. & Wright, H. (1990). Deafness and immediate memory for pictures: Dissociations between "inner speech" and "inner ear". *Journal of Experimental Child Psychology, 50*, 259–286.

Cole, R.A. & Jakimik, J. (1980). A model of speech perception. In R.A. Cole (Ed.), *Perception and production of fluent speech*, (pp.133–163). Hillsdale, NJ: Lawrence Erlbaum Associates Inc.

Coltheart, M., Davelaar, E., Jonasson, J.T., & Besner, D. (1977). Access to the internal lexicon. In S. Dornic (Ed.), *Attention and performance, VI*. New York: Academic Press.

Conrad, R. (1979). *The deaf schoolchild: Language and cognitive function.* London: Harper & Row.

Cowan, N., Day, L., Saults, J.S., Keller, T.A., Johnson, T., & Flores, L. (1992). The role of verbal output time in the effects of word length on immediate memory. *Journal of Memory & Language, 31,* 1–17.

Cromer, R.F. (1987). The basis of childhood dysphasia: A linguistic approach. In M. Wyke (Ed.), *Developmental dysphasia* (pp. 85–134). London: Academic Press.

Cutler, A., Mehler, J., Norris, D., & Segui, J. (1989). Limits on bilingualism. *Nature, 340,* 229–230.

Eimas, P.D. & Clarkson, R.L. (1986). Speech perception in children: Are there effects of otitis media? In J.F. Kavanagh (Ed.), *Otitis media and child development.* Maryland: York Press.

Flavell, J.H., Beach, D.R., & Chinsky, J.M. (1966). Spontaneous verbal rehearsal in a memory task as a function of age. *Child Development, 37,* 283–299.

Frauenfelder, U.H., Baayen, R.H., Hellwig, F.M., & Schreuder, R. (1993). Neighbourhood density and frequency across languages and modalities. *Journal of Memory & Language, 32,* 781–804.

Garnham, A. (1985). *Psycholinguistics: Central topics.* London: Methuen.

Gathercole, S.E. (1995). Is nonword repetition a test of phonological memory or long-term knowledge? It all depends on the nonwords. *Memory & Cognition, 23,* 83–94.

Gathercole, S.E. & Adams, A.-M. (1994). Children's phonological working memory: Contributions of long-term knowledge and rehearsal. *Journal of Memory & Language, 33,* 672–688.

Gathercole, S.E., Adams, A.-M., & Hitch, G.J. (1994). Do young children rehearse? An individual differences analysis. *Memory & Cognition, 22,* 201–207.

Gathercole, S.E. & Baddeley, A.D. (1989). Evaluation of the role of phonological STM in the development of vocabulary in children: A longitudinal study. *Journal of Memory & Language, 28,* 200–213.

Gathercole, S.E. & Baddeley, A.D. (1990a). Phonological memory deficits in language disordered children: Is there a causal connection? *Journal of Memory & Language, 29,* 336–360.

Gathercole, S.E. & Baddeley, A.D. (1990b). The role of phonological memory in vocabulary acquisition: A study of young children learning arbitrary names of toys. *British Journal of Psychology, 81,* 439–454.

Gathercole, S.E. & Hitch, G.J. (1993). Developmental changes in short-term memory: A revised working memory perspective. In A. Collins, S.E. Gathercole, M.A. Conway, & P.E. Morris (Eds.), *Theories of memory.* Hove, UK: Lawrence Erlbaum Associates Ltd.

Gathercole, S.E., Martin, A., & Hitch, G.J. (in preparation). *Wordlikeness effects in the immediate repetition and long-term learning of new words.*

Gathercole, S.E., Hitch, G.J., Service, E., & Martin, A.J. (submitted). *Short-term memory and long-term phonological learning in young children.*

Gathercole, S.E., & Thorn, A. (submitted). *Verbal short-term memory in bilingual and non-bilingual children: Long-term knowledge contributions are restricted to native languages.*

Gathercole, S.E., Willis, C.S., Baddeley, A., & Emslie, H. (1994). The Children's Test of Nonword Repetition: A test of phonological working memory. *Memory, 2,* 103–127.

Gathercole, S.E., Willis, C., Emslie, H., & Baddeley, A. (1991). The influences of number of syllables and word-likeness on children's repetition of nonwords. *Applied Psycholinguistics, 12,* 349–367.

Gathercole, S.E., Willis, C., Emslie, H., & Baddeley, A. (1992). Phonological memory and vocabulary development during the early school years: A longitudinal study. *Developmental Psychology, 28,* 887–898.

Glasspool, D.W. (1995). Competitive queuing and the articulatory loop: An extended network model. In J. Levy, D. Bairaktaris, J. Bullinaria, & D. Cairns (Eds.), *Connectionist models of memory and language*. London: UCL Press.

Gopnik, M. & Crago, M.B. (1991). Familial aggregation of a developmental language disorder. *Cognition, 39*, 1–50.

Grant, J., Karmiloff-Smith, A., Berthoud, C., & Christophe, A. (unpublished). French nonword repetition test.

Hartley, T. & Houghton, G. (1995). A linguistically constrained model of short-term memory for nonwords. *Journal of Memory and Language, 34*.

Henry, L.A. (1991). The effects of word length and phonemic similarity in young children's short-term memory. *Quarterly Journal of Experimental Psychology, 43A*, 35–52.

Hitch, G.J. & Halliday, M.S. (1983). Working memory in children. *Philosophical Transactions of the Royal Society, London, B302*, 324–340.

Hitch, G.J., Halliday, M.S., Schaafstal, A.M., & Schraagen, J.M.C. (1988). Visual working memory in young children. *Memory & Cognition, 16*, 120–132.

Hulme, C., Maughan, S., & Brown, G.D.A. (1991). Memory for familiar and unfamiliar words: Evidence for a long-term memory contribution to short-term memory span. *Journal of Memory & Language, 30*, 685–701.

Hulme, C., Roodenrys, S., Brown, G., & Mercer, R. (1995). The role of long-term memory mechanisms in memory span. *British Journal of Psychology, 86*, 527–536.

Hulme, C., Thomson, N., Muir, C., & Lawrence, A. (1984). Speech rate and the development of short-term memory span. *Journal of Experimental Child Psychology, 38*, 241–253.

Jusczyk, P.W., Cutler, A., & Redanz, N. (1993). Preference for the dominant stress patterns of English words. *Child Development, 64*, 675–687.

Jusczyk, P.W., Kemler Nelson, D.G., Hirsch-Pasek, K., Kennedy, L., Woodward, A., & Piwoz, J. (1992). Perception of acoustic correlates of major phrasal units by young infants. *Cognitive Psychology, 24*, 252–293.

Jusczyk, P.W., Luce, P.A., & Charles-Luce, J. (1994). Infants' sensitivity to phonotactic patterns in the native language. *Journal of Memory & Language, 33*, 630–645.

Kamhi, A.J. & Catts, H.W. (1986). Towards an understanding of developmental reading and language disorders. *Journal of Speech and Hearing Disorders, 51*, 337–347.

Klein, S.K. & Rapin, I. (1993). Intermittent conductive hearing loss and language development. In D. Bishop & K. Mogford (Eds.), *Language development in exceptional circumstances*. Hove, UK: Lawrence Erlbaum Associates Ltd.

Lahiri, A. & Marslen-Wilson, W. (1991). The mental representation of lexical form: A phonological approach to the recognition lexicon. *Cognition, 38*, 245–294.

Landauer, T.K. & Streeter, L. (1973). Structural differences between common and rare words: Failure of equivalence assumptions for theories of word recognition. *Journal of Verbal Learning and Verbal Behavior, 12*, 119–131.

Leonard, L.B. (1982). Phonological deficits in children with developmental language impairment. *Brain & Language, 16*, 73–86.

Liberman, A.M. & Mattingley, I.G. (1985). The motor theory of speech perception revisited. *Cognition, 21*, 1–36.

Liberman, I.Y., Shankweiler, D., Fischer, F.W., & Carter, B. (1974). Explicit syllable and phoneme segmentation in the young child. *Journal of Experimental Child Psychology, 18*, 201–212.

Long, M.H. (1990). Maturational constraints on language development. *Studies in Second Language Acquisition, 12*, 251–285.

Luce, P.A., Pisoni, D.B., & Goldinger, S.D. (1990). Similarity neighbourhoods of spoken words. In G.T.M. Altmann (Ed.), *Cognitive models of speech perception: Psycholinguistic and computational perspectives*. Cambridge, MA: MIT Press.

MacNeilage, P.F., Rootes, T.P., & Chase, R.A. (1967). Speech production and perception in a patient with severe impairment of somasthetic perception and motor control. *Journal of Speech and Hearing Research, 10*, 449–468.

Marslen-Wilson, W.D. (1987). Function and process in spoken word recognition. *Cognition, 25*, 71–102.

Marslen-Wilson, W.D. & Tyler, L.K. (1980). The temporal structure of spoken language understanding. *Cognition, 8*, 1–71.

Massaro, D.W. & Cohen, M.M. (1983). Phonological constraints in speech perception. *Perception & Psychophysics, 34*, 338–348.

Martin, A. & Gathercole, S.E. (in preparation). *Phonological neighbourhood and analysis of nonwords as a function of wordlikeness.*

McClelland, J.L. & Elman, J.L. (1986). The TRACE model of speech perception. *Cognitive Psychology, 18*, 1–86.

McClelland, J.L., Rumelhart, D.E. & the PDP Group. (1986). *Parallel distributed processing: Explorations of the microstructure of cognition, vol 2.* Cambridge, MA: Bradford Books.

Michas, I.C. & Henry, L.A. (1994). The link between phonological memory and vocabulary acquisition. *British Journal of Developmental Psychology, 12*, 147–164.

Morais, J., Alegria, J., & Content, A. (1987). The relationships between segmental analysis and alphabetic literacy: An interactive view. *Cahiers de Psychologie Cognitive, 7*, 462–464.

Morais, J., Cary, L., Alegria, J., & Bertelson, P. (1979). Does awareness of speech as a sequence of phones arise spontaneously? *Cognition, 7*, 323–331.

Morais, J. & Mousty, P. (1992). The causes of phonemic awareness. In J. Alegria, D. Holender, J.J. de Morais, & M. Radeau (Eds.), *Analytic approaches to human cognition.* Amsterdam: North Holland Press.

Murray, D.J. (1967). The role of speech responses in short-term memory. *Canadian Journal of Psychology, 21*, 263–276.

Nicolson, R. (1981). The relationship between memory span and processing speed. In M.Friedman, J.P. Das, & N. O'Connor (Eds.), *Intelligence and learning.* New York: Plenum Press.

Olsson, J.E. & Furth, H.G. (1966). Visual memory-span in the deaf. *American Journal of Psychology, 79*, 480–484.

Papagno, C. & Vallar, G. (1992). Phonological short-term memory and the learning of novel words: The effects of phonological similarity and item length. *Quarterly Journal of Experimental Psychology, 44A*, 46–67.

Papagno, C. & Vallar, G. (1995). Verbal short-term memory and vocabulary learning in polyglots. *Quarterly Journal of Experimental Psychology, 48A*, 98–107.

Papagno, C., Valentine, T., & Baddeley, A. (1992). Phonological short-term memory and foreign-language vocabulary learning. *Journal of Memory & Language, 30*, 331–347.

Pintner, R. & Paterson, D.G. (1917). A comparison of deaf and hearing children in visual memory for digits. *Journal of Experimental Psychology, 2*, 76–88.

Roodenrys, S., Hulme, C., & Brown, G. (1993). The development of short-term memory span: Separable effects of speech rate and long-term memory. *Journal of Experimental Child Psychology, 56*, 431–442.

Salamé, P. & Baddeley, A.D. (1982). Disruption of memory by unattended speech: Implications for the structure of working memory. *Journal of Verbal Learning & Verbal Behavior, 21*, 150–164.

Schweikert, R. (1993). A multinomial processing tree model for degradation and redintegration in immediate recall. *Memory & Cognition, 21*, 168–175.

Service, L. (1992). Phonology, working memory, and foreign-language learning. *Quarterly Journal of Experimental Psychology, 45A*, 21–50.

Tallal, P. & Piercy, M. (1975). Developmental aphasia: The perception of brief vowels and extended stop consonants. *Neuropsychologia, 13*, 69–74.

Tallal, P., Stark, R.E., & Mellitts, E.D. (1985). Identification of language-impaired children on the basis of rapid perception and production skills. *Brain & Language*, *25*, 314–322.

Taylor, H.G., Lean, D., & Schwartz, S. (1989). Pseudoword repetition ability in learning-disabled children. *Applied Psycholinguistics*, *10* 203–219.

Vallar, G. & Baddeley, A.D. (1984). Fractionation of working memory: Neuropsychological evidence for a short-term store. *Journal of Verbal Learning & Verbal Behavior*, *23*, 151–161.

Werker, J.F. & Tees, R.C. (1984). Cross-language speech perception: Evidence for perceptual reorganization during the first year of life. *Infant Behavior and Development*, *7*, 49–63.

5

The representation of words and nonwords in short-term memory: Serial order and syllable structure

George Houghton, Tom Hartley, and David W. Glasspool
University College London, UK

INTRODUCTION

It is possible that different forms of human memory are essentially specialised for remembering different kinds of things: e.g. semantic memory for interlinked systems of decontextualised "knowledge", episodic memory for one-off, temporally organised sequences of events, procedural memory for motor coordination etc. If this is so, then many of the characteristics of these memory systems will have evolved as solutions to the specific problems posed by (i) the conditions under which the target information must be learned, and (ii) the adaptive function of this information, i.e. how the learned information is put to use to guide action and thought. In this paper, we consider the implications of this position for verbal short-term memory.

With regard to the conditions of learning, spoken words, like auditory signals generally, are temporally distributed; all the information to be retained is never simultaneously present in the environment. This temporal dimension cannot be ignored, as the serial order of information in a verbal or auditory signal is typically crucial to its identity or meaning. Verbal stimuli are also transient: when a speaker has finished saying a word, no trace of it is left in the environment to be re-examined. Information about the structure of a verbal stimulus must therefore be encoded on-line in a single trial, before the stimulus vanishes. With respect to the issue of the use of the acquired information, the central feature of the verbal memory system in the "articulatory loop" model is that the code is speech based, i.e. the representations formed in memory are sufficient to enable spoken recall. We may conclude from this that single-trial verbal learning can generate the kind of representations that underlie normal speech production. This raises the issue of the different demands made on the memory system by novel and familiar words. If the input stimuli are familiar words, then recall can be supported by the long-term phonological representations of those words. If the stimuli are unfamiliar, then the appropriate representation must be constructed on-line, as the stimuli occur. Thus models that hope to address, say, nonword repetition must perforce address the question of how novel speech output representations can be formed so quickly.

In the following section, we discuss two particular aspects of phonological structure which concern us: first its inherently serial nature, and second, the role of syllable structure as understood by linguistics and studies of speech production. We then consider a number of recent computational models of verbal STM, focusing on the way in which they represent verbal stimuli, and the how they handle the difference between words and nonwords.

SERIAL ORDER AND PHONOLOGICAL STRUCTURE IN VERBAL MEMORY

The articulatory (or "phonological") loop (AL) component of the Baddeley and Hitch (1974) working memory model is postulated to be a special-purpose store for the short-term retention of verbal input which may be presented just once (Baddeley, this volume). Functions attributed to this system include roles in language comprehension, vocabulary acquisition and learning to read (Gathercole & Baddeley, 1993). Although the model has been highly influential in motivating a variety of revealing empirical studies (see Gathercole & Baddeley, 1993, for review), considered as a theoretical construct it is completely silent on a number of central issues. In particular, it provides no mechanism whereby the order of input items may be represented, and, though claimed to be a specifically verbal store, does not address the issue of the phonological representation of learned items. For the special case of nonwords, these two problems combine: Into what constituents (phonemes, syllables) does the system analyse nonwords and how does it rapidly learn the order of these constituents? Such questions are not theoretical niceties that experimenters can safely ignore. Indeed, the centrality of the problem of serial order is implicit in the analysis of order errors in serial recall tasks. Order errors are used as a measure of the degree of failure of the system, which presupposes that retention of serial order is one of its primary functions.

Serial order problems may arise at a number of levels. In a typical span task using familiar words, the order of the items is not predictable and hence must be represented *de novo* in a single trial. The form of the individual items however is already known, and it can be assumed that the problem of recalling the serial form of the words themselves is strongly supported by lexical representations in long-term memory (Glasspool, 1995; Hulme, Maughan, & Brown, 1991). However, when the to-be-recalled items are nonwords (as most words are to young children, or foreign language learners), their form must be learned at the same time as their order. Studies show that, compared to words, nonword stimuli lead to both more (Hulme et al., 1991) and different (Ellis, 1980; Treiman & Danis, 1988) errors. In particular, systematic errors occur in the recall of the forms of nonwords which are either absent or rare in the recall of familiar words. Furthermore, the nonword errors studied by Treiman and Danis (1988) indicate that the problem of recalling the serial order of phonemes within a syllable is constrained in a way in which the problem of recalling the order of words in a random, non-grammatical list is not. English-speaking subjects required to recall a grammatical sentence of English, although they may make mistakes, will most likely still produce a grammatical response, and not show, say, the paired transposition errors typical of digit span tasks. The structure of English words and syllables is similarly "grammatically constrained", and recall of nonword lists shows clear evidence of the operation of these constraints.

For serial recall tasks, the required representation of a stimulus, novel or familiar, is one that will support the correct spoken production of that stimulus. For familiar items, such a representation will already exist in the phonological lexicon. For nonwords it must be constructed on-line. We see no reason to suppose that the representation of a (phonologically legal) nonword will be qualitatively different to that of a known word (today's words were yesterday's nonwords). It is natural then to turn to theories of spontaneous speech production to provide constraints on the representation of verbal stimuli in STM.

Phonological Structure in Speech Production

Models of the representations and processes involved in speech production have been developed on the basis of both distributional cross-linguistic data and psycholinguistic studies, including naturally occurring speech errors. The conclusions of such work that concern us here are that (a) the syllable is a major component of linguistic representation and speech production, and (b) the syllable has significant internal structure, and cannot be reduced to a string of phonemes. Detailed review of the full range of evidence in support of these conclusions is beyond the scope of the current paper. For linguistic evidence see Fudge, 1969; Greenberg, 1978; Hogg and McCully, 1987; Selkirk, 1982, 1984. For psycholinguistic data see Goswami and Bryant,

1990; Levitt, Healy, and Fendrich, 1991; Treiman, 1986, in press; Treiman and Danis, 1988; Treiman, Straub, and Lavery, 1994.

Linguistic studies have shown that the syllable unit is essential to the concise expression of many phonological regularities found in languages. Across languages, the phonemes in a syllable appear to be organised serially according to the "sonority principle" (SP). Sonority is a somewhat abstract notion related to the acoustic energy in the speech signal. The peak of this energy is located in the vowel. If the vowel is accompanied by surrounding consonants, then those nearest the vowel will be more sonorous than those further away. Consonants with the lowest sonority are stops and fricatives followed by continuants, glides, and semivowels. Voiced consonants are more sonorous than unvoiced. Thus the low-sonority consonants occur first and last in syllables. Any continuants, glides etc, will appear between these consonants and the vowel. Even by itself, the SP provides quite strong constraints on syllable structure. For instance, it suffices to predict that /flunt/ would be a possible syllable, whereas /lfutn/ would not. However, it does not exhaust the phonotactic constraints found in particular languages. For instance, German allows the initial consonant cluster /shl/, whereas English does not, even though it permits both phonemes to occur in those positions otherwise (cf. *shrink*, *sleep*). Nevertheless, the SP provides a concise description of a pattern of universal applicability, so that, in considering a particular language, it is important to distinguish those phonotactic constraints that follow from it from those that are parochial.

Cutting across issues of the order of phonemes is the question of whether the syllable has internal boundaries. Much evidence supports a primary division of the syllable into onset and rhyme, the onset being the set of consonants (if any) that precede the vowel, and the rhyme comprising the vowel and any following consonants (Treiman, 1986). The rhyme may be thus divided into vowel and coda. An example is given in Fig. 5.1 of the organisation of the syllable *shrimp*, showing both the structure and sonority relations.

In the following section we look at a number of recent computational models of verbal STM and consider how they address the following issues: (1) the internal serial structure of the items to be remembered, (2) constraints on this internal structure, as discussed earlier, and (3) differences in the memory demands of words and nonwords. All three models discussed employ the "competitive queueing" approach to serial order (Houghton, 1990), whereby responses to be generated in sequence actually become activated in parallel (Lashley, 1951). These mechanisms avoid the use of associative chaining links between successive responses, such as are found in the convolution based models of Murdock and colleagues (known as TODAM, e.g. Lewandowsky & Murdock, 1989; Murdock, this volume)[1]. Chaining seems an unlikely model for serial

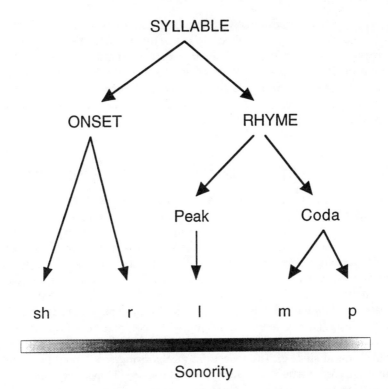

Sonority

FIG. 5.1. Syllable structure and sonority. Syllables have internal structure, with a primary division into onset and rhyme. The serial order of phonemes in a syllable conforms to the sonority principle—sonority increases towards the vowel, and decreases away from it. Most models of speech production assert the importance of such structure, for instance in constraining speech errors. If verbal STM is a speech-based memory system, capable of supporting speech production (e.g. nonword repetition), then it must produce such representations from the input in a single trial.

---

[1] TODAM is a model of associative memory based on the operation of vector convolution. This operation allows for two memory items, represented as points in some feature space, to be associated together in a distributed memory trace. Retrieval is effected by an (approximate) inverse operation, correlation. Lewandowsky and Murdock (1989) extend TODAM to serial order memory by representing words in a target list as (random) vectors, and then associating successive words (vectors) together using convolution. This method requires that each word is represented "in parallel", as a single vector, rather than as the temporal sequence of items (e.g. phonemes) that they actually are. Lewandowsky and Murdock (1989) thus ignore the serial structure of words and use representations that appear to have no systematic relationship to any aspect of phonological structure. In addition, the model has no lexicon and does not distinguish between words and nonwords. Its status as a model of *verbal* recall is therefore somewhat unclear. It may be taken as embodying an implicit claim that properties of spoken words such as those with which the present article is concerned are of no importance for understanding how these words are memorised or recalled.

behaviour generally (Chomsky, 1959; Gallistel, 1980; Lashley, 1951), and has frequently been specifically criticised in the domain of short-term recall (Burgess & Hitch, 1992; Henson, Page, Norris, & Baddeley, in press; Jensen & Rohwer, 1965; Mewhort, Popham, & James, 1994). Before describing the specific models, we briefly review the general properties of competitive queueing mechanisms (see e.g. Houghton & Hartley, in press, for a more detailed discussion).

COMPETITIVE QUEUEING AND SERIAL ORDER

Competitive queueing (CQ) models are parallel models of serial order based on temporally modulated response competition. In such models, a number of responses can be active in parallel, but with an activation gradient over them such that the sooner a response is to be generated the more active it is. All concurrently activated responses compete for control of output in a separate system known as a "competitive filter". This mechanism selects the most active response, and, after selection, inhibits it (cf. Estes, 1972; Grossberg, 1978; Rumelhart & Norman, 1982). This feedback inhibition allows the remaining activated responses to compete for the next output position, resulting in serial behaviour from a parallel system. (For more detailed discussion of the selection mechanism, see Houghton, 1994a; Houghton & Hartley, in press; Houghton & Tipper, in press). The postulation of a separation between a response preparation stage (with many responses active in parallel), and response selection (in which one response dominates), is consonant with the position developed by Lashley in his classic paper on serial order (Lashley, 1951; Houghton & Hartley, in press).

In recent CQ models, the information required to generate the appropriate activation gradient over responses is stored in the connections to the response nodes from another set of nodes constituting a time-varying "control" or "context" signal (Fig. 5.2). During learning, items in the target sequence activate corresponding response or output nodes. At the same time, the internally generated context signal is also active, but with its state varying over the course of list presentation. Response nodes activated by the input become associated with concurrently active states of the context by a simple "Hebbian" weight change rule (such rules can perform unsupervised, single-trial learning, which is clearly essential in the context of short-term memory). If the changing context signal is temporally correlated, i.e. is more similar to itself at nearer points in time, then items occurring near to each other in the input will be associated with similar states of the context. Recovery of the context signal during recall activates those response nodes that became associated with it during learning. Due to its temporally

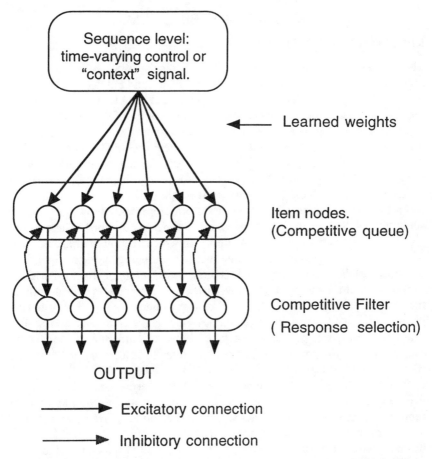

FIG. 5.2.   Basic architecture of competitive queueing models. Items are sequenced according to a dynamic activation gradient over to-be-generated responses (competitive queue). This gradient is produced by input from nodes at the sequence level through a set of learned weights. Activated responses compete for output at the competitive filter, which selects the most active response. Selected responses are then inhibited by one-to-one feedback from the competitive filter to the item nodes.

correlated nature, any state of the context will re-activate a number of responses in parallel, but with an activation gradient over them as described earlier. Ideally, the context state will most strongly activate that response which co-occurred with it during learning, and more weakly activate responses which occurred close by (Houghton, 1994b). In combination with the competitive filter selection mechanism described earlier, the time-varying response gradient induced by recovery of the context signal results in serial recall of the target sequence.

MODELS OF VERBAL STM

Burgess and Hitch (1992)

The Burgess and Hitch (B&H) model is a mechanistic realisation of the articulatory loop (AL) component of the Baddeley and Hitch (1974) memory model (Burgess & Hitch, 1992, this volume). The AL is a hypothetical memory system dedicated to the short-term retention of speech inputs. The basic AL model is theoretically lacking in a number of ways: in particular, it provides no learning algorithm by which the memories are formed and it has little to say about the way in which serial order information is represented or used in recall (Burgess & Hitch, 1992). To overcome these limitations, B&H develop a CQ model of short-term serial recall.

In the B&H model, the input items are represented by the *parallel* activation of sets of phoneme nodes, one set per input word. These nodes give rise to the activation of word nodes to which they are connected, and the word nodes become associated with a changing context signal, as described earlier (see Burgess & Hitch, this volume). In the original formulation of the model (Burgess & Hitch, 1992), recall was driven both by the CQ mechanism acting at the level of word nodes, and by the formation of inter-item associative links (chaining) among the phoneme nodes. The chaining mechanism proved problematic however, and Burgess and Hitch suggested it be dropped, as it has been in later formulations of the model (Burgess, 1995; Burgess & Hitch, this volume; Glasspool, 1995)[2].

Errors in the recall of the model are due to information loss, which has two sources: decay in the context-to-word weights, and a small amount of random noise in word node activations. The model performs well on a variety of data traditionally associated with the articulatory loop. For instance, without further assumptions, it shows limited span, effects of word length (reduction in span), phonemic similarity effects, and the predominance of order errors characteristic of human serial recall. More recent work with the model (Burgess, 1995; Burgess & Hitch, this volume) shows clear primacy and recency effects, and effects of rehearsal, and goes some way towards modelling effects of stimulus familiarity (word–nonword differences).

Burgess and Hitch make some attempt to model the specific nature of the verbal stimuli. There is a distinction between word and phoneme levels, with phonemes being explicitly represented and words being linked to their constituent phonemes. In principle, this architecture could distinguish

---

[2] Note that inter-item chaining between phonemic representations of words in the Burgess and Hitch model is really only feasible if words are represented as a parallel set of phonemes, i.e. if the serial nature of words is ignored (see Footnote 1). The use of inappropriate representations can thus fail to constrain other modelling choices in important ways.

between words and nonwords—input phoneme combinations not matching a stored representation would constitute a nonword, and would have to be encoded on-line (see the model of Glasspool, described next). However, the sound of a word is represented as a set of phonemes with no order defined over them, so that, for instance, /tap/, /pat/, and /apt/ would be represented identically. Thus the model does not produce serial recall below the word level, and cannot address the problem of the single-trial learning and recall of the serial structure of nonwords (the key feature of phonological vocabulary acquisition). Nonetheless, the fact that serial recall in the model occurs at the level of discrete whole items (words), means that once a word is selected for output by the competitive filter, a phonological sequencing mechanism could be responsible for generating the articulatory "plan" for that word. In conclusion, the B&H model succeeds in accounting for a variety of important word-level STM phenomena using a representation of the input items that captures at least the fact that verbal stimuli are hierarchically structured, and can be decomposed into phonemes.

Glasspool, 1995

Glasspool's model is an extension of the B&H model which treats input items (words and nonwords) as a sequence of phonemes, rather than as a parallel set. This model thus attempts to come to grips with the fact that verbal recall is serially ordered at more than just the word level. The model is also intended to handle nonwords as well as words. It is clearly important that models of verbal STM can learn nonwords, as this appears to be one of its crucial functions in language acquisition (Gathercole & Baddeley, 1989). In addition, a variety of data indicate that storing nonwords is more difficult than storing words (Bisiacchi, Cipolotti, & Denes, 1989; Hulme et al., 1991; Treiman & Danis, 1988).

In order to address the fact that words are themselves sequences of phonemes, the model operates at a finer temporal grain than the B&H model. The model's input and output thus consists of a series of individual phonemes, rather than the word-sized chunks that form the input and output for the B&H model. To model memory for nonwords, Glasspool proposes that a purely phonological trace is laid down in STM, in addition to a trace containing information about words appearing in the input. The phonological trace is assumed to be the primary resource used to recreate the input at recall. If a target list consists only of nonwords, then this phoneme-by-phoneme record is all that is available to support recall. However, if recognisable words appeared in the input list then lexical information will also be available *in addition* to the phonological trace. The model thus postulates two separate serial storage mechanisms operating in parallel on the same input (Fig. 5.3). Although separate, the two

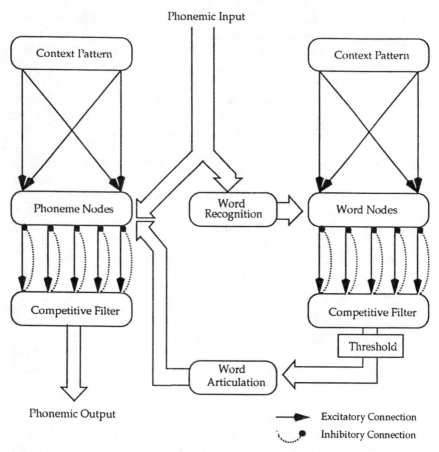

FIG. 5.3. Architecture of the Glasspool, 1995, articulatory loop model. The model learns both words and nonwords by maintaining two separate memory traces, one at the word level and one at the phoneme level. Words in the input are learned (and recalled) at both levels simultaneously. Nonwords are only represented at the phoneme level.

mechanisms work according to the same competitive queueing principles. Thus, words (and nonwords) are represented as strings of phonemes, and the sequencing of phonemes does not involve any mechanisms not found at the word level.

This arrangement has a number of attractions. First, the model makes no distinction at all in its dynamics between words and nonwords. The basic operation of the model is the same for either, although words are more robustly stored because a strong word-level trace is able to support recall. Nonwords will only leave traces at the lexical level if they are particularly similar to known words. Second, the memory processes are simplified compared with a system that, say, used only a single, word-level trace. In such a model, an "uncommitted" word node must be assigned to represent a nonword, ensuring that it does not interfere with other words or nonwords to be stored. This is likely to be quite a complex process. Glasspool's architecture lays down a single phonological trace for all items, word or nonword, as phonemes arrive, and only supplements it with lexical information as and when it becomes available.

The implementation of this model described in Glasspool (1995) uses a competitive queueing serial recall mechanism modelled after that of Burgess and Hitch described earlier. A set of "context" nodes carries an activation pattern which changes gradually during recall, each context state correlating well with immediately previous and subsequent states, and poorly with more distant states. A set of temporary weights encodes associations (using Hebbian learning) between the context pattern at each presentation step and the patterns of activation over sets of phoneme and word nodes (representing the current phoneme and the current word respectively). During recall the same sequence of context states is repeated, tending to drive the phoneme and word nodes through their original sequence of activations. Competitive filters select the most active phoneme and word nodes at each step, and subsequently inhibit the winning nodes.

The complete implementation is shown in Fig. 5.3. Because phonemes and words occur at different temporal grains, the context signals driving the word and phoneme nodes are separated, allowing the phoneme context signal to change more rapidly than the word signal. The phoneme context signal is updated as each phoneme is input (during learning) or output (during recall). The word context is only updated when a word is recognised or produced. This pattern thus changes once per word, and stays constant throughout presentation or recall of the word.

The word nodes are connected to both input (recognition) and output (articulation) phoneme nodes, as in the B&H model. However, unlike B&H, the activation of phoneme nodes occurs serially. The recognition component thus activates a word node following the arrival, in appropriate order, of its constituent phonemes. The articulation component produces an ordered series of phonemes during word recall. The output of the word level is added to any activation phoneme nodes may receive from the phonemic sequencing level. The output from the word level is thresholded, so that it only influences the phoneme units when a word node has been strongly activated. Partial activation of words can occur when a nonword has partially triggered the recognition system during presentation, causing a similar word to be partially learned in that list position.

Information loss in the model occurs in the same way as it does in the B&H model, through a mixture of decay and noise. The context-to-word and context-to-phoneme weights are allowed to decay with time, and random noise is added to phoneme and word node activations. The parameters of decay rate and noise are set to values that give human-like serial recall span. This degrading of information results in a performance pattern similar to that of the B&H model, but with an additional lexicality factor. For instance, the model produces the same human-like S-shaped curves of recall against list length as the B&H model. Recall is poorer for longer lists, whether of words or nonwords, due to the decay of the temporary weights with time. This effect is purely temporal, rather than being based on the number of items in the list, in agreement with psychological data (Baddeley, Thomson, & Buchanan, 1975; Ellis & Hennelly, 1980; Hulme et al., 1991). The model also shows phonemic similarity effects (more errors on lists of phonemically similar words) for both words and nonwords, and primacy and recency effects.

Most important are the differences in the behaviour of words and nonwords. The model's recall is better for lists of words than for nonwords (Hulme et al., 1991). The advantage found for words is due to the support they receive from their long-term memory representations. Nonwords can only be recalled by the model on a phoneme-by-phoneme basis using the phonological trace. Because in any target list there will be fewer words than phonemes, the word trace has to encode fewer items than the phoneme trace, and is thus more robust. As far as we are aware, Glasspool's work is the first STM model to be able to simulate such data.

Lexicality effects are also evident in the type as well as the number of errors the model makes. The model produces both item and order errors, although order errors predominate, as found in human data (Aaronson, 1968). The nonword lists however are more prone to phonemic misordering errors. This phenomenon has been observed in human nonword recall (Ellis, 1980; Treiman & Danis, 1988). Item errors at the word level tend to be intrusions of words phonemically similar to those in the target list. At the phonemic level, intrusions of phonemes from outside the stimulus list are uncommon. Thus nonword item errors are generally the result of the misordering of phonemes. The competitive queueing mechanism produces many order errors under the influence of noise, so that phonemic transpositions and exchanges are common. In lists of words, errors affect whole words, rather than their individual phonemes, due to the strength of the influence from the word system (long-term memory) on the phonemic output.

Glasspool's proposal of two competitive queues operating in parallel clearly represents an increase in complexity over the original B&H model. However, this is offset by its handling of nonwords and by the relative simplicity of the storage mechanism, when compared with what might be required by alternatives, such as assigning new temporary word nodes for nonwords. It also seems intuitively satisfying that a phonological trace of the input should exist in the absence of word or nonword representations. Interestingly, the somewhat similar idea of a composite context signal, incorporating elements entrained to high- and low-frequency components of the stimulus (as with the phoneme and word contexts in this model) is suggested by Burgess and Hitch (this volume) in connection with grouping effects.

Hartley and Houghton, in press

The Hartley and Houghton (in press) model also adopts the CQ approach to verbal STM pioneered by Burgess and Hitch (1992, this volume). Like the Glasspool model, it aims to handle nonwords and to produce serial recall at the subword level. In line with Glasspool, the model proposes that sequencing must be effected at the word and subword levels by separate mechanisms. It departs from Glasspool's work however by proposing that the phonemic sequencing mechanism is not identical to that used for sequencing random lists of words, because, as noted, syllables are not constructed from random sequences of phonemes. Phonemic sequencing errors rarely (if ever) consist of the local transposition errors characteristic of unadorned CQ mechanisms (and which are found at the word level in span tasks). Hartley and Houghton therefore develop linguistically motivated subword sequencing principles based on data of the kind reviewed earlier ("Serial order and phonological structure in verbal memory"). In the area of spontaneous speech production, studies of error data (such as spoonerisms, e.g. barn door → darn bore) have led to the development of models such as those of Shattuck-Hufnagel (1979), and Dell (1986, 1988). Although these models differ in many important respects, they share the central features that (i) syllables are a fundamental unit of speech planning, and (ii) the structure and content of syllables are separately represented. The content of a syllable can be represented as a set of phonemes. The structure might be something like that shown in Fig. 5.1 for the word *shrimp*. The very same structure would be assigned to a phonemically quite distinct syllable, e.g. *blunt*. In Fig. 5.1, it is the syllable structure (a tree in this case) that defines the order of the phonemes, by associating each with a distinct terminal slot.

Structures such as that shown in Fig. 5.1 are static objects, and to be translated into behaviour some process must be able to interpret them, to read off the order of phonemes. Computational models of this sort are of the symbolic variety, typically directly implementing such structures (e.g. as embedded ordered sets) and using the recursive capacities of computer programming languages to interpret them (e.g. Houghton & Pearson, 1988). They thus maintain a clear distinction between competence and performance, or data and algorithm (the "von Neumann" architecture). Neural network models such as those discussed earlier do not recognise such a division. Network structures are not read and interpreted by independent algorithms. If they are to perform dynamically, the dynamics must emerge through the interaction of the network's parts, using the fundamental processes of excitation and inhibition. Thus, although implementing complex structural constraints is simple using the symbolic computational paradigm, they are altogether more difficult to comprehend from a connectionist standpoint.

Nonetheless, the strength of the evidence for the importance of such structure in speech production is such that attempts have been made to incorporate it into connectionist models, for instance by Dell (1986, 1988). Dell's models separate syllabic structure and content by containing nodes that stand for positions or slots in a syllable, for instance initial consonant, vowel, final consonant etc. When such a "slot node" is active, it sends activation to all those phoneme nodes which can occur in that slot, e.g. just vowels nodes in the vowel slot. A given syllabic structure can be represented by chaining a sequence of such slot nodes together. Production of a syllable then involves both direct, parallel, activation of its constituent phonemes by a "content pathway", and sequential activation of a set of slot nodes. The combination of these two inputs leads to sequential selection of the most active phoneme node at each slot. Phonemes thus compete for output according to activation level, as in CQ models, but the use of syllabic slot nodes essentially restricts competition at any position to those phonemes which can occupy that position. This scheme reduces the potential for error in a CQ ordering system by reducing the number of effective competitors at each position (given that all the phonemes in a syllable are accessed in parallel). It also has the consequence that any errors that do occur will tend to conform to the structure of the target syllable. If the serial order of phonemes is defined by the ordering of slots that those phonemes can fill, then there is no need for any associative links between successive phonemes. Many different orders of the same elements can therefore be stored.

Dell's models are concerned with spontaneous speech production (recall from long-term memory) and account for a variety of relevant findings, particularly concerning phonemic speech errors. Treiman and Danis (1988) present data showing that errors in the immediate serial recall of nonwords are constrained in precisely the same way, indicating that the structural constraints on the production of speech from long-term phonological memory are operative in short-term memory. The fact that they are found with nonwords shows that the kinds of internal representation responsible for constraining speech errors can be constructed in a single trial. It follows then that models of serial recall below the word level should employ the same sequencing principles as have been found to apply in spontaneous speech.

Hartley and Houghton's model is the first attempt to incorporate substantive theoretical insights from speech production into verbal STM. Following Dell and others, they propose that spoken inputs are parsed into syllables, and that syllabic representations are separated into (interacting) content and structure pathways. In particular:

1. *The content pathway.* Syllables are divided into onset and rhyme constituents. The onset and rhyme nodes of a given syllable have direct connections to the phonemes comprising them.
2. *The structure pathway.* Individual phonemes are associated with slots in a "syllabic template". This is a cyclical structure which passes through one cycle every syllable, providing a representation of "syllabic phase". Points in the cycle are related to sonority, in that only certain phonemes can be associated with any point in the cycle. Low sonority phonemes are associated with the beginning and end points of the cycle, higher sonority phonemes with central points. Connections from onset and rhyme nodes to the template encode those positions that are used in a given syllable.

These components and links between them are shown in Fig. 5.4.

The behaviour of the model is heavily dependent on the use of the sonority-based syllable template (Fig. 5.4). It is implemented using five nodes, each node representing a "slot" or syllable position (Fudge, 1969). Each slot is associated with only a subset of the phonemes of English, coded in long-term weights connecting the phoneme and slot nodes (Fig. 5.4). Activation of the template proceeds cyclically, starting at slot 1 and moving round the cycle to slot 5. Any slot can be omitted if the target syllable contains no corresponding phoneme (which slots are used is specified by the "structure pathway"). Each time activation crosses the "syllable boundary" a new syllable is started. Given a string of input phonemes, the model is able to use these resources to parse them into syllables. For instance, given the input /rumelhartandnorman/, it produces the syllables rum, el, hart, and, nor, man.

The template can represent most legal syllables of English (syllables with fewer than five phonemes simply involve fewer slots), but does not capture detailed phonotactic constraints. It essentially acts to enforce the sonority constraint, outlawing syllables such as *vskisr*, *lfutn* etc. but allowing, for instance, *shlop* as an English syllable. Intuitively, syllables that break the sonority constraint appear more bizarre than those that merely offend against parochial English phonotactics. If syllable structure constraints in a given language are mixture of the universal and particular, it is important to assess how much behavioural data can be explained by reference to each independently.

The behaviour of the model in simulating serial recall data can be divided into learning and recall phases.

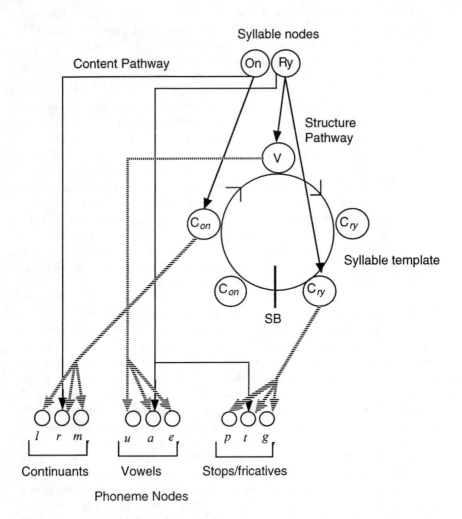

FIG. 5.4. Phonological representation of a syllable (/rat/) in the Hartley and Houghton (1995) model. Not all connections or nodes are shown. Strings of input phonemes are divided up into syllables (syllable group). Syllables are represented in terms of their phonemic content (phoneme group) and the "slots" they use in a generalised syllable template. Syllable group nodes are composed of pairs of onset and rhyme nodes. The solid lines represent temporary weights, formed during rapid learning (short-term memory). The dashed lines are permanent connections (long-term memory). Syllable structure and content are separately represented, but interact during recall. Key: On = onset, Ry = rhyme, C = consonant, V = vowel, SB = syllable boundary.

116

Learning. When a syllable is learned, its constituent phonemes are presented to the model serially. This input activates the appropriate phoneme nodes in sequence, and also leads to activation of the syllable template. Starting at slot 1, each phoneme activates the next available template node with which it is compatible. At the same time an uncommitted onset/rhyme node pair is activated. Until a vowel occurs only the onset node is active. Occurrence of a vowel triggers activation of the rhyme node. *Temporary* links are formed (by Hebbian weight change rules) between onset/rhyme nodes (Syllable group, Fig. 5.4) and (i) nodes representing its constituent phonemes (Phoneme group), and (ii) its syllabic structure (Syllable template). Unlike the permanent pathways linking the syllable template to phoneme nodes, these temporary links are subject to weight decay.

The internal representation of a syllable is thus distributed, crucially involving a separation between its phonemic content and structure. When the model encodes a sequence of syllables, each syllable is assigned a separate representation at the syllable group level (each syllable is represented "orthogonally" by its own onset/rhyme node pair), but uses the same phoneme nodes and the same syllable template. The serial order of the syllables themselves is separately learned and represented, and is assumed to be due to a mechanism with properties like those of the Burgess and Hitch model (i.e. non-chaining, with a parallel response gradient over to-be-recalled items). No links of any kind are formed between successive syllables.

Recall. During recall, activation of syllable group nodes is postulated to be under the control of a CQ sequencing mechanism, as described by Burgess and Hitch (1992), and Burgess (1995). This leads to the parallel activation of a number of syllable nodes, but with the usual activation gradient over them, such that the sooner a syllable is to be produced the more active it is. Activation spreads in parallel from all activated syllable (onset/rhyme) nodes to both the phoneme nodes and the syllable template. This parallel activation of syllables leads to a number of phoneme nodes being primed in parallel, giving rise to a degree of response competition. Clearly, however, the phonemes associated with the currently most active syllable will receive the greatest amount of priming. At the same time, activation spreads from syllable group nodes to slot nodes in the syllable template. This activation primes those slots that were activated when the syllable was presented. Recall of the syllable consists of cyclic reactivation of the syllable template. If recall is correct, those template nodes that are being primed by input from the syllable group will be activated sequentially. As a template node becomes active, it sends activation along its permanent links to the set of phoneme nodes that can occur at that position. Phoneme nodes can thus receive input along temporary links from the syllable group, and along permanent links from the template. Ideally, however, for any syllable slot, one phoneme node which can occur in that slot will be receiving most input by the content pathway—the one associated with the currently most active onset or rhyme node. This phoneme will be selected for output. Note that the primary competitors for output at any position will not be the phonemes that are to occur next within the syllable, but *those that occur at the same position in upcoming syllables*, i.e. those compatible with the current syllabic position. The existence of these competitors from later syllables is due to the competitive queuing sequencing mechanism operating at the syllable level.

Data on nonword recall (Treiman & Danis, 1988; Treiman, in press) shows that subjects required to repeat strings of six phonologically legal monosyllabic nonsense syllables make errors on about 50% of items. This error rate is considerably higher than is found in, say, digit span tasks. The data show that this impaired performance is not accounted for by subjects making more ordering errors on nonwords, i.e. the deficit is not at the level of the ordering of items dealt with by Burgess and Hitch. Rather, the nonwords themselves are incorrectly recalled. Most importantly though, the nonword errors are far from random, and provide clear evidence for the operation in short-term memory of the same kinds of constraints found in spontaneous speech. To take a specific example, Treiman and Danis (1988) required subjects to repeat back lists of six monosyllabic nonwords. In each list all the items had the same consonant–vowel serial order; CVC for instance. As noted earlier, subjects made errors on about half of all items. However, 96% of the errors on CVC lists had CVC structure. A similar pattern was found for lists of CCV and VCC items. As the structure of the target items was maintained, it follows that most of the errors were phonemic substitutions. Errors leading to structural changes (insertions and deletions) were rare. Such data show that, in lists of similarly structured items, the syllabic form of the targets is being retained better than the phonemic content. This would appear to be impossible if syllabic structure and content were not separately represented.

Hartley and Houghton (in press) simulated this experiment with the model described earlier, using the same stimulus lists that Treiman and Danis used. The lists were presented to the model in the manner described and the model was required to recall them. The temporary weights formed during learning were subject to decay, and activations in the network subject to a degree of noise (the same "information loss" manipulations used by Burgess & Hitch and by Glasspool). The decay and noise parameters were set so that the model had human-like nonword span (Hulme et al., 1991) and made about 50% errors on such lists (i.e. 50% of the nonwords recalled were wrong in some way). For CVC lists, Hartley and Houghton found that about 90% of the model's errors conformed to the CVC structure of the target words. As with the human data, it follows that most of the model's errors were phoneme substitutions. The reason for this finding in the model is that the "information loss" manipulations are causing phonemes that should be produced at a particular point in the list to suffer a debilitating degree of competition from co-activated phonemes. These competitors are sometimes winning, leading to errors. However, the syllabic form of the target items is being retained more successfully, as all target syllables are CVC and hence reinforce each other. Because phoneme selection involves input along the template-to-phoneme connections, competition remains largely restricted to those phonemic competitors associated with the target slot. Thus errors have the following characteristics:

1. They are largely phoneme substitutions.
2. The substituting phonemes generally occur elsewhere in the target list.
3. Phoneme substitutions maintain syllabic structure, as must substitutions are "like-with-like". For instance, vowels hardly ever swap with consonants.

The model thus shows the basic characteristics of nonword serial recall errors in normal adults (Ellis, 1980; Treiman, in press; Treiman & Danis, 1988), and can model error distributions at quite fine grains of analysis (see Hartley & Houghton, in press, for further examples). In addition, the same type of errors predominate when patients with acquired deficits in nonword repetition repeat polysyllabic nonwords (Bisiacchi et al., 1989; Caramazza, Miceli, & Villa, 1986). Hartley and Houghton model such deficits by increasing the rate of temporary weight decay. Recall becomes impaired, but the impairment affects phonemic content more than syllable structure. It is difficult to see how results such as these would be possible without the use of the syllable template to control phoneme sequencing.

DISCUSSION

The work discussed here covers a wide range of data on short-term verbal recall in some detail. These attempts to expand the breadth and depth of short-term memory theory have led to the fairly rapid development of models with highly articulated internal structure. These models employ a variety of complex, interacting processes (time-varying contexts, competitive filters, feedback inhibition, syllable templates etc.) which are hardly anticipated in more traditional verbal or diagrammatic models. We believe the development of this machinery is justified by the detailed qualitative and quantitative modelling that it permits. We finish this chapter by reviewing the issues addressed at the outset (phonological structure, and the word–nonword distinction) in the light of these models.

Phonological Structural Constraints in STM

The idea that there are constraints on phoneme sequencing within syllables simply means that fewer orders of phonemes occur in attested syllables than would in principle be possible (say, by random sequencing). This point can be illustrated by an example from Greenberg (1978) concerning the number of possible initial consonant clusters in English. The maximum initial cluster length is three. English has 22 consonants, of which about 20 can occur as sole initial consonants. Omitting phoneme duplications, there exist $22 \times 21 = 642$ different ordered pairs of these phonemes, of which 28 actually occur as initial clusters. Again omitting repeats, there exist $22 \times 21 \times 20 = 12,840$ possible ordered triples, of which 8 are found. Taken in total, only 0.43% (55/13,504) of the *a priori* possible clusters actually occur. Even this small set is further constrained by regularities such as Hjelmslev's (1936) "resolvability" principle, which states that longer consonant sequences in a language only contain subsequences (including singletons) that also occur in the same syllable position. For instance, the English initial cluster /str/ contains subsequences /st/ /tr/ /s/ /t/ and /r/, all of which are legal onsets.

Once one divides phonemes into groups by articulatory criteria, and uses these groups to define syllable positions, then one finds that the number of possible syllable structures falls even further. Some speech production models such as Dell (1988) postulate the existence of a small number of competing syllabic frames. Hartley and Houghton (in press) take this "data compression" process to the extreme by postulating the existence of a single dynamic template, whose cyclical operation can be "reconfigured" on-line by inputs from separate onset/rhyme nodes. Despite this, it might still be objected that the resulting model is rather complex. Given that children are not born with mature articulatory skills, and can learn language-specific phonotactic constraints, the question arises of how such a structurally complex system could develop. One approach is to reiterate that the basic articulatory and acoustic properties of human language are universal. The vast majority of sounds that the human vocal tract is capable of making never occur as linguistically significant units in any language. No languages are known that are not constructed from a small number of vowels and a somewhat larger number of consonants. All languages form basic syllables around vowels, and syllable structure generally follows the sonority constraint (Selkirk, 1984). In general, languages prefer simple syllable structures (CV, CVC) over complex ones (Greenberg, 1978). The result is that previously unheard languages are recognisable as human speech.

Such cross-linguistic evidence supports the idea that speech is as much an evolved, species-specific communication system as is, say, bird song (Marler, 1991). Song birds such as the swamp sparrow have a fairly elaborate, characteristic song. Marler and colleagues have shown that a swamp sparrow reared in isolation and exposed to the song of its own species interspersed with the song of another, closely related, species preferentially learns its conspecific song. Deprived of access to the song of its own species, it spontaneously generates a degraded form. Song is therefore learned, but learning is based on an innate template. This template may provide both a "leg up" in the learning process, and also act as a filter on environmental input, directing the bird's attention towards conspecific signals and filtering out noise. Although not wishing to stretch this analogy with the human case too far, it does provide a conclusive demonstration that there is nothing biologically implausible about the suggestion that vocal communication systems can be based on quite elaborate and detailed innate constraints. Thus the development of structures of the type employed by Hartley and Houghton may depend on the maturation of universal endogenous factors as much as on environmental input[3].

It is instructive in this regard to compare this model with an attempt to learn syllabic constraints without the explicit representation of structural information. Dell, Juliano, and Govindjee (1993) trained a sequential network of the type developed by Jordan (1986) and Elman (1990) on sets of three phoneme words, and looked for evidence in the performance of the model for the extraction of structural regularities. This type of model may be (approximately) considered as a chaining model of serial order, in that the current output of the network is cued by some internally maintained history of its previous states. This history includes a sequence-specific component (referred to as the "plan") which initiates recall of a sequence and remains constant throughout it. This allows the network to know which sequence to produce, and also supplies a different "context" for each word, so that different orders of the same items can be encoded (always a problem in chaining models). Apart from the weights from plan units, all sequences learned by such a network must use the same sets of recurrent connections. Given that the model is basically sequencing by chaining, this will lead on the one hand to sequences containing identical sub-sequences supporting each other, and sequences containing different orders of the same items interfering with each other. In short, the model is sensitive to transition probabilities (including high-order ones) in its stimulus set and will exploit redundancies. Dell et al. set out to see whether such a network, trained on a corpus of legal English syllables, would come to (implicitly) embody syllabic structure as a by-product of learning specific sequences. If so, there might be no need to postulate the existence of explicit structural information. It

---

[3] Hartley and Houghton (1995, appendix 2) show that the template in their model can be trained to act as a syllabic parser on the basis of exposure to a representative sample of English words.

would simply be an artifact of the extraction of the transitional statistics of phonemes in syllables.

The claims Dell et al. make for their model are quite far reaching, stating for instance that "...much of the psychological data that is thought to support the phonological structure-content distinction in production can be explained by a mechanism in which no such distinction is explicitly present." (Dell et al., 1993, p.151). It is unfortunately beyond the scope of the current chapter to examine these claims in any detail with respect to spontaneous speech production. Clearly though, if they were to prove well founded then they would seriously undermine Hartley and Houghton's argument that the need for explicit representation of syllable structure in short-term memory is independently motivated by the fact it is an inevitable property of speech production models. However, one can turn this argument on its head. Instead of STM models taking their lead from studies of spontaneous speech, might not results from STM studies be used to inform theories of speech production from long-term memory? This is precisely the logic behind the studies of Rebecca Treiman and colleagues (Treiman & Danis, 1988; Treiman et al., 1994) on nonword serial recall. Treiman's primary interest in this work is not in the properties of short-term memory *per se*, but in the representations underlying speech production. Nonword recall is used because subjects make many more phonological errors with nonwords than with words, and the constraints on the form of these errors is taken to be revealing with respect to the structures involved in *all* speech production. The crucial property of immediate nonword recall is that, whatever the representations used, *they must be formed in a single trial.* Hartley and Houghton show how this is possible using an explicit model of syllable structure to parse the input and assign individual phonemes to syllabic positions. The model of Dell et al. discussed earlier is inherently incapable of encoding a sequence of nonwords in a single trial, as it requires the use of hidden units[4] and associated complex error-correcting learning algorithms. One exposure to each of a set of novel words would be quite insufficient to permit the network to learn them. As far as we can see, any network capable of forming *implicit* representations of syllable structure, as an artifact of learning high-order transition probabilities among phonemes, is likely to have much the same learning limitations as the Dell et al. model. We therefore suggest that short-term memory data can constrain models of speech production from long-term memory. In particular, models that cannot form appropriate representations of nonwords in a single trial may

---

[4] Hidden units are essential to the model to allow it to cope with sequences containing different orders of the same items. It is also the hidden units that extract an implicit representation of the grammar of the target sequences (Elman, 1990), i.e. to the extent that the network does develop an implicit model of syllable structure, it needs hidden units to do it.

be using the wrong representation. The reciprocally constraining nature of insights into normal speech production and short-term memory are further emphasised in the next section.

Long-term Memory and Nonword Recall

Recent experimental investigations of verbal short-term memory have increasingly used nonword recall tasks in preference to or in combination with tasks using words (Bisiacchi et al., 1989; Ellis, 1980; Gathercole & Baddeley, 1989; Gathercole, Willis, Emslie, & Baddeley, 1991; Hulme et al., 1991; Treiman & Danis, 1988; Treiman et al., 1994). Gathercole and Baddeley (1993, p.48) argue that "[P]erformance on immediate memory tasks can reflect the contribution of long-term memory knowledge as well as short-term memory processes... We therefore expect to gain a more sensitive measure of phonological memory skills by using memory items for which there are no long-term lexical representations, because subjects will be less able to use lexical knowledge to supplement phonological short-term memory." This position begs the question of what (precisely) phonological short-term memory consists of, what it represents and how, and how lexical knowledge interacts with it. The models discussed earlier provide some initial answers to these questions.

Glasspool, 1995, is probably the best-developed model capable of handling both words and nonwords. In this model, the phonological representation is simply a stream of phonemes, and a (non-lexical) "phonological memory" system produces a pure phonemic representation of all the input, irrespective of its lexical status. Another (lexical) component looks for known words in the input stream. Any phoneme sequence constituting a word becomes represented twice, once as a sequence of phonemes, once as a word. Nonword sequences are represented at the phoneme level only. During recall, the two components interact so that phoneme-level recall is supplemented by word-level information when available, leading to improved recall of words over nonwords. For the model to work, it is clearly essential that the two subsystems represent the phonological content of the input in precisely the same way. Note then that the "phonological" (non-lexical) memory system uses nodes representing known phonemes, i.e. long-term phonological knowledge (presumably acquired, in part, through learning words).

Glasspool's model sequences phonemes with the same type of mechanism that sequences whole words. However, phonemic error data indicate that phonemic sequencing is not achieved in precisely this manner (Treiman & Danis, 1988). Thus, a finer-grained understanding of the interaction between lexical and phonological knowledge in short-term memory will require that a more realistic view of phonology be developed. A first step in this direction is taken in the Hartley and Houghton (in press) model by postulating that the sublexical serial recall process is not simply a finer-grained copy of that operating at the word level. In this model, although competitive activation-based selection processes are still used at the phonemic level, they are supplemented by the syllabic template, which biases output competition at any point in favour of that *class* of responses associated with the current state of the template. Addition of specific lexical input to the Hartley and Houghton model would clearly be via this template. For known words, connections from syllable-group nodes to the template and phoneme nodes would not be subject to the weight decay used in modelling the short-term memory data. Thus if words were recognised in the input stream, then these long-term connections could be used during recall. This should reduce phonemic sequencing errors occurring as a result of weight decay.

Thus, although the model has not yet been extended to incorporate specific lexical input, it does use long-term phonological knowledge in the representation of nonwords. This knowledge is likely to be a component of any model hoping to deal with "wordlikeness" effects (Gathercole et al., 1991), as wordlike-nonwords must contain acceptable syllables. As noted earlier, this knowledge must be to some degree acquired, presumably as a part of lexical learning. Thus, it may be maintained that in the Hartley and Houghton model "phonological short-term memory" is never entirely free of (indirect) lexical influences.

To summarise, phonological short-term memory in these models consists of the rapid and temporary binding of familiar phonological elements into possibly novel combinations. Where familiar patterns are found in the input they are used, and use of these long-term representations is more robust than those constructed in a single trial[5]. This assimilation of the novel to the familiar probably occurs up to the "highest level" possible, so that if a "random" string of words just happens to form a sentence, it will be better recalled than if it did not. Verbal short-term memory, like most biological memory, therefore seems to be essentially concerned with assimilating the new to the old. As suggested at the outset, many of its idiosyncratic features may simply reflect the serially ordered, speech-based nature of the stimuli to be encoded.

CONCLUSION.

Recent theoretical work in verbal short-term memory has taken advantage of the development of neural network models of serial order which can learn rapidly and are naturally prone to the same kinds of limitations and errors

---

[5] Houghton, Glasspool, and Shallice (1994) apply precisely this logic to the modelling of quantitative differences in the spelling of words and nonwords by certain neurologically impaired subjects.

in serial recall as human subjects (Burgess & Hitch, 1992; Houghton, 1990). As well as providing solutions to such central problems as the representation of serial order, these models have achieved a much finer-grained fit to the data than is possible using the intuitive verbal models that inspired the accumulation of that data. In particular, recent work has begun to incorporate long-term knowledge into short-term memory processes. The integration of theories of speech production with short-term memory models means that the theory of "phonological" short-term memory finally has some genuine phonology in it.

The experimental study of short-term verbal memory has recently been reinvigorated by seminal discoveries regarding its functional significance in a number of domains (Gathercole & Baddeley, 1993). The new wave of theoretical work covered in part in the current chapter complements these studies, as well as raising problems and questions of its own. It seems reasonable to anticipate that the continuing interaction between theory and experiment in this field will eventually yield a picture of short-term memory of considerable richness and depth.

REFERENCES

Aaronson, D. (1968). Temporal course of perception in an immediate recall task. *Journal of Experimental Psychology*, 76, 129–140.

Baddeley, A.D. & Hitch, G. (1974). Working memory. In G. Bower (Ed.), *The psychology of learning and motivation, Vol. 8*. New York: Academic Press.

Baddeley, A.D., Thomson, N., & Buchanan, M. (1975). Word length and the structure of short-term memory. *Journal of Verbal Learning and Verbal Behavior*, 14, 575–589.

Bisiacchi, P.S., Cipolotti, L., & Denes, G. (1989). Impairments in processing meaningless verbal material in several modalities: The relationship between short-term memory and phonological skills. *Quarterly Journal of Experimental Psychology*, 41A, 292–320.

Burgess, N. (1995). A solvable connectionist model of immediate recall of ordered lists. In G. Tesauro, D. Touretzky, & T.K. Leen (Eds.), *Neural information processing systems, 7*. Cambridge, MA: MIT Press.

Burgess, N. & Hitch, G.J. (1992). Towards a network model of the articulatory loop. *Journal of Memory and Language*, 31, 429–460.

Caramazza, A., Miceli, G., & Villa, G. (1986). The role of (output) phonology in reading, writing and repetition. *Cognitive Neuropsychology*, 3, 37–76.

Chomsky, N. (1959). A review of B.F. Skinner's *Verbal Behavior*. *Language*, 35, 26–58.

Dell, G.S. (1986). A spreading activation theory of retrieval in sentence production. *Psychological Review*, 93, 283–321.

Dell, G.S. (1988). The retrieval of phonological forms in production: Tests of predictions from a connectionist model. *Journal of Memory and Language*, 25, 124–142.

Dell, G.S., Juliano, C., & Govindjee, A. (1993). Structure and content in language production: A theory of frame constraints in phonological errors. *Cognitive Science*, 17, 149–195.

Ellis, A.W. (1980). Errors in speech and short term memory: The effects of phonemic similarity and syllable position. *Journal of Verbal Learning and Verbal Behavior*, 19, 624–634.

Ellis, N.C. & Hennelly, R.A. (1980). A bilingual word-length effect: Implications for intelligence testing and the relative ease of mental calculation in Welsh and English. *British Journal of Psychology*, 71, 43–51.

Elman, J.L. (1990). Finding structure in time. *Cognitive Science, 14*, 179–211.

Estes, W.K. (1972). An associative basis for coding and organisation in memory. In A.W. Melton & E. Martin (Eds.), *Coding process in human memory*. Washington, DC: Winston.

Fudge, E.C. (1969). Syllables. *Journal of Linguistics, 5*, 193–320.

Gallistel, C.R. (1980). *The organisation of action*. Cambridge, MA: MIT Press.

Gathercole, S., & Baddeley, A. (1989). Evaluation of the role of phonological STM in the development of vocabulary in children: A longitudinal study. *Journal of Memory and Language, 28*, 200–213.

Gathercole, S.E. & Baddeley, A.D. (1993). *Working memory and language*. Hove, UK: Lawrence Erlbaum & Associates Ltd.

Gathercole, S.E., Willis, C.S., Emslie, H., & Baddeley, A. (1991). The influences of number of syllables and wordlikeness on children's repetition of nonwords. *Applied Psycholinguistics, 12*, 349–367.

Glasspool, D.W. (1995). Competitive queuing and the articulatory loop: An extended network model. In J. Levy, D. Bairaktaris, J. Bullinaria, & D. Cairns (Eds.), *Connectionist models of memory and language*. London: UCL Press.

Goswami, U., & Bryant, P.E. (1990). *Phonological skills and learning to read*. Hove, UK: Lawrence Erlbaum Associates Ltd.

Greenberg, J.H. (1978). Some generalizations concerning initial and final consonant clusters. In J.H. Greenberg (Ed.), *Universals of human language, Vol. 2: Phonology*. Stanford, CA: Stanford University Press.

Grossberg, S. (1978). Behavioral contrast in short term memory: Serial binary memory models or parallel continuous memory models? *Journal of Mathematical Psychology, 17*, 199–219.

Hartley, T., & Houghton, G. (in press). A linguistically constrained model of short-term memory for nonwords. *Journal of Memory and Language*.

Henson, R., Page, M., Norris, D., & Baddeley, A. (in press). Unchained memory. *Quarterly Journal of Experimental Psychology*.

Hogg, R. & McCully, C.B. (1987). *Metrical phonology: A coursebook*. Cambridge: Cambridge University Press.

Houghton, G. (1990). The problem of serial order: A neural network model of sequence learning and recall. In R. Dale, C. Mellish, & M. Zock (Eds.), *Current research in natural language generation*. London: Academic Press.

Houghton, G. (1994a). Inhibitory control of neurodynamics: Opponent mechanisms in sequencing and selective attention. In M. Oaksford & G.D.A. Brown (Eds.), *Neurodynamics and psychology*. London: Academic Press.

Houghton, G. (1994b). *Some formal variations on the theme of competitive queuing*. Tech. rep. UCL-PSY-CQ1. Department of Psychology, University College, London.

Houghton, G., Glasspool, D.W., & Shallice, T. (1994). Spelling and serial recall: Insights from a competitive queuing model. In. G.D.A. Brown & N.C. Ellis (Eds.), *Handbook of spelling: Theory, process and intervention*. Chichester: Wiley.

Houghton, G. & Hartley, T. (in press). *Parallel models of serial behaviour: Lashley revisited*. *Psyche*.

Houghton, G. & Pearson, M. (1988). The production of spoken dialogue. In M. Zock & G. Sabah (Eds.), *Advances in natural language generation, Vol. 1*. London: Pinter.

Houghton, G. & Tipper, S.P. (in press). Inhibitory mechanisms of neural and cognitive control: Applications to selective attention and sequential action. *Brain and Cognition*.

Hjelmslev, L. (1936). On the principles of phonematics. *Proceedings of the 2nd International Congress of Phonetic Sciences*, (pp. 49–54). [Cited in Greenberg, 1978.]

Hulme, C., Maughan, S., & Brown, G.D.A. (1991). Memory for familiar and unfamiliar words: Evidence for a long-term memory contribution to short-term span. *Journal of Memory and Language, 30*, 685–701.

Jensen, A.R. & Rohwer, W.D. (1965). What is learned in serial learning? *Journal of Verbal Learning and Verbal Behavior, 4*, 62–72.

Jordan, M.I. (1986). *Serial order: A parallel distributed approach.* ICI report 8604, Institute for Cognitive Science, University of California, San Diego.

Lashley, K.S. (1951). The problem of serial order in behavior. In L.A. Jeffress (Ed.), *Cerebral mechanisms in behavior.* New York: Wiley.

Levitt, A., Healy, A.F., & Fendrich, D.W. (1991). Syllable-internal structure and the sonority hierarchy: Differential evidence from lexical decision, naming and reading. *Journal of Psycholinguistic Research, 20*, 337–363.

Lewandowsky, S., & Murdock, B.B. (1989). Memory for serial order. *Psychological Review, 96*, 25–57.

Marler, P. (1991). The instinct to learn. In S. Carey & R. Gelman (Eds.) *The epigenesis of mind: Essays on biology and cognition.* Hillsdale, NJ: Lawrence Erlbaum Associates Inc. [Reprinted in M.H. Johnson (Ed.) 1993). *Brain development and cognition: A reader.* Oxford: Blackwell.]

Mewhort, D.J.K., Popham, D., & James, G. (1994). On serial recall: A critique of chaining in the theory of distributed associative memory. *Psychological Review, 101*, 534–538.

Rumelhart, D.E. & Norman, D.A. (1982). Simulating a skilled typist: A study of skilled cognitive-motor performance. *Cognitive Science, 6*, 1–36.

Selkirk, E. (1982). The syllable. In H.D. van der Hulst, & N. Smith (Eds.), *The structure of phonological representations. Part II.* Dordrecht: Foris.

Selkirk, E. (1984). On the major class features and syllable theory. In M. Aronoff & R.T. Oehrle (Eds.), *Language sound structure: Studies in phonology presented to Morris Halle by his teacher and students.* Cambridge, MA: MIT Press.

Shattuck-Hufnagel, S. (1979). Speech errors as evidence for a serial-ordering mechanism in sentence production. In W.E. Cooper & E.C.T. Walker (Eds.), *Sentence processing: Psycholinguistic studies presented to Merrill Garret.* Hillsdale, NJ: Lawrence Erlbaum Associates Inc.

Treiman, R. (1986). The division between onsets and rhymes in English syllables. *Journal of Memory and Language, 25*, 476–491.

Treiman, R. (in press). *Errors in short-term memory for speech: A developmental study.*

Treiman, R., & Danis, C. (1988). Short-term memory errors for spoken syllables are affected by the linguistic structure of the syllables. *Journal of Experimental Psychology: Learning, Memory and Cognition, 14*, 145–152.

Treiman, R., Straub, K., & Lavery, P. (1994). Syllabification of bisyllabic nonwords: Evidence from short-term memory processes. *Language and Speech, 37*, 45–60.

6

Nonword repetition, STM, and word age-of-acquisition: A computational model

Gordon D.A. Brown
University of Warwick, UK

Charles Hulme
University of York, UK

INTRODUCTION

As the chapters in this book testify, there has been much recent progress towards a computational-level understanding of the mechanisms that underlie human short-term memory performance. Indeed, there are encouraging signs of a convergence towards a vocabulary of common terminology and the development of a "toolbox" of different mechanisms that can be invoked to explain, at a computational level, many of the phenomena of human short-term memory. However, a wide gap between models and data remains in many areas.

We will review some of the computational insights that have emerged concerning the possible function of having an episodic memory system that is separate from long-term semantic, structured memory. We also consider recent psychological research on the role and function of human short-term memory (STM), suggesting for example that one important role of STM may be its involvement in the acquisition of new vocabulary items by young children.

Our aim in the present chapter is to bring together these psychological and computational traditions. We proceed in the following manner. First of all, we review some computational evidence (from the work of McClelland and O'Keefe) that points to one possible functional advantage of having an episodic memory that is separate from a long-term store. The suggestion here is that it may be computationally efficient to have a separate memory store in which episodic information is represented quickly but in an unstructured way. This can be seen as functioning in a way that is complementary to a separate long-term store. In the long-term store, information is registered more slowly, after many exposures to each item, and the gradual registration of new information allows for the construction of a more efficient, semantically structured memory system. Thus we will see that the computational evidence points very directly to a possible role of a fast-learning episodic store in the efficient acquisition of long-term information. Second, we describe a recent tradition of psychological research, showing that in the early stages of children's development there is a strong correlation between children's phonological skill (as assessed by nonword repetition ability) and their subsequent vocabulary knowledge (i.e. the vocabulary score a year or so later; see Gathercole & Baddeley, 1993, for a review). This line of research, in some respects similarly to the computational work alluded to earlier, has been taken as evidence for a functional role of short-term memory in long-term storage of information.

Thus both computational and psychological research are consistent with the idea that the representation of information in a short-term of episodic storage system may be causally involved in the subsequent efficient long-term representation of that information. In the remainder of this chapter, we explore this issue computationally, in the context of an implemented model of phonological short-term memory that we have recently developed to account for phenomena such as lexicality effects and word length effects in memory span tasks (Brown & Hulme, 1995). After describing this model in some detail, we then show that it gives rise to the prediction that any limitations on phonological short-term memory capacity should be particularly pertinent to the permanent acquisition of long words—because the short-term memory storage of a long unfamiliar word is, according to the model, more short-lived and temporary than storage for shorter unfamiliar words, and so there is less time to transfer the representation of an unfamiliar item into long-term memory. It is predicted, therefore, that long words will be acquired by children at a later age than short words, even when the words are of the same frequency.

Finally, we show that this prediction can be confirmed in an analysis of the age-of-acquisition of long and short words.

COMPUTATIONAL ADVANTAGES OF A SEPARATE SHORT-TERM MEMORY

We now describe some computational insights that have recently emerged regarding the functional relationship between different memory systems in the brain, specialised to store information in different organisational forms and with different time-scales of learning. The basic framework we describe may be found in McClelland, McNaughton, and O'Reilly (1994), while its detailed relationship to the neuroanatomy of the hippocampus is discussed more fully in O'Reilly and McClelland (1994).

A central assumption, which is common to many models of hippocampal memory function, is that the neocortex maintains long-term, relatively stable, and structured representations of the world, in which similar events are represented close to one another in the memory space, while the hioppocampus stores "episodic" memories in such a way that similar events can have distinct representations. Thus the hippocampus must perform "pattern separation" (at the time of initial storage) and also pattern completion (in order that a representation may be reinstated from a partial cue).

There are two types of requirement on a complete memory system. First of all, the long-term store, or semantic memory, must represent information in an economical way and in a structured manner that allows appropriate generalisations to be readily made. As McClelland et al. (1994) point out, we now know from many connectionist studies that this kind of representation can best be achieved by gradual, low, gradient-descent learning with interleaved presentation of items. For present purposes, the crucial point is that only small changes to the weights in the connectionist network are made following each presentation of an item or association to be represented. This means that the weights in the network come to represent in an efficient fashion what is common to different patterns—the hidden units in the network gradually come to encode similarities between different patterns, with the result that efficient storage and generalisation is achieved. Because only small changes to the network can result from each presentation, no one instance (which might be atypical of the general structure of the world to be represented) can have too great an influence on the organisation of the network. Hinton (1989) and others have shown how a connectionist network, using interleaved learning and making only small changes to the network during learning, can come to learn and represent the semantic structure that is implicit in a set of patterns.

To summarise: an efficient long-term memory must learn and represent the underlying structure of the world, in such a way that similar patterns are assigned similar representations in the network, and this is best achieved via slow incremental learning procedures. This general type of memory functioning is assigned by McClelland et al. to the neocortex, broadly defined. However, it is also necessary for the organism to have the ability to represent information quickly and episodically—so that a pattern does not need to be presented many times before it can be stored. Furthermore, similar patterns may need to be given quite separate representations (so that similar patterns do not get confused). This function—of episodic memory and pattern separation—is assigned to the hippocampus, where it is assumed that faster network changes can be achieved on the basis of a single or a small number of presentations

A crucial assumption made by McClelland et al. (1994) is that patterns can be reinstated in the hippocampus, and then "re-presented" (as in rehearsal) to the neocortex over a period of time. This is the process of "consolidation"—it allows episodically stored patterns to be presented many times to the neocortex, over a timescale of hours, days, weeks, or even many years—thus allowing for the slow, interleaved gradient-descent learning, that will allow the stable extraction of underlying structure, as described earlier. Thus the two systems together provide for both fast episodic learning and the slower creation of a usefully structured long-term memory.

McClelland et al. show how such an account can explain phenomena such as retrograde amnesia (whereby recent memories are not fully consolidated in the neocortex, and can therefore be lost with higher probability than older memories) and preserved implicit learning in amnesia (this can result from the gradual small changes that ARE made to neocortical representations over repeated presentations of the material to be learned).

To conclude this section: recent computational research has provided valuable insights into why two separate memory systems might be valuable, and into what the relationship between them might be. One "episodic" memory system is responsible for the rapid, episodic representation of new information—and a second "long-term memory" learns more slowly, but extracts the underlying similarity structure among items. Idiosyncratic information, which is only characteristic of particular episodes, will be lost. There is a reciprocal relation between these, because the episodic store can be used to achieve multiple presentations of a pattern (that has in fact only been experienced once) to the long-term memory system.

SHORT-TERM MEMORY AND
VOCABULARY ACQUISITION

We now turn to some psychological research on the relationship between short-term memory and long-term learning. We focus particularly on work by Gathercole and Baddeley (e.g. 1990a, 1993) which has demonstrated a strong relationship between children's nonword repetition ability and the size of their vocabularies.

In 1984, Vallar and Baddeley described a patient (PV) who appeared to have a severely impaired phonological short-term memory store. Baddeley, Papagno, and Vallar (1988) showed that the lack of a phonological short-term memory store in this patient produced difficulty in long-term learning. PV was virtually unable to learn new associations involving unfamiliar items, although associations between familiar items could be learned. Thus PV (whose native language was Italian) could learn associations between arbitrary pairs of familiar Italian words, but could not learn associations between familiar Italian words and Russian words (the latter being effectively nonwords for PV). This result points very clearly to a relation between phonological short-term memory and long-term learning.

More recently, Gathercole and Baddeley (1993, for a review) have shown that there is a strong correlation between nonword repetition ability and vocabulary size in children. The suggestion here is that children's ability to represent novel items temporarily, in a phonological STM, will be related to their ability to form long-term memory representations of these items. A crucial result consistent with this is that in 4-, 5-, and 6-year-old children there was a high correlation between nonword repetition score and vocabulary size. However correlation does not prove causality, and so Gathercole, Willis, Emslie, and Baddeley (1992) analysed their data longitudinally, using cross-lagged correlations. This analysis found that nonword repetition at age 4 predicted vocabulary size at age 5, but not vice versa, when other relevant variables were partialled out. At later ages—from age 5 to age 6, and age 6 to age 8—the pattern was reversed; vocabulary size predicted subsequent nonword repetition score.

These results clearly suggest a possible causal relationship between children's ability to create a temporary representation of an unfamiliar spoken item and their ability to acquire vocabulary knowledge. As Gathercole and Baddeley (1993) point out, this is perhaps in a sense unsurprising—if information cannot be maintained temporarily, then it cannot be registered in a longer-term store. However, we need an account of why separate systems need to be involved—why cannot new vocabulary items be stored directly in long-term memory, if they can be registered at all? The computational work of McClelland and his colleagues that we described earlier is concerned with processes happening over very different timescales to those likely to be involved in phonological short-term memory and acquisition of vocabulary items. Some of the same principles may nevertheless apply—especially when the degraded nature of speech input is taken into consideration. Thus we suggest that a more efficient vocabulary may be constructed if potential new vocabulary items are not directly added into the system. Rather, it makes computational sense to represent a first instance of a new item in temporary form. This representation can then interact with existing vocabulary information, to "clean up" the new representation, and bring it into a representational format that is consistent with the organisation of the existing lexicon. This will be necessary because no two tokens of the same spoken word will be identical, and it would clearly be undesirable to create a new vocabulary entry for each heard token of a particular word. It may also be necessary to check that the new item is really not simply a distorted exemplar of a word that is already known. Furthermore, even the temporary storage of the new item in phonological short-term memory may allow a time window over which the item can become efficiently stored in long-term memory, via some form of gradient-descent learning, in such a way that it is stored in the appropriate part of memory space, close to representations of other similar vocabulary items. This may be possible over a much shorter timescale than is necessary for the general consolidation of episodic memories into long-term structured memory as discussed by McClelland et al., because of the relatively constrained structure of spoken English words. Thus even short-term temporary storage may allow for multiple presentations of a novel item to a long-term memory store, allowing structural information to be incorporated.

Our suggestion is, then, that the relationship between phonological short-term memory and long-term memory for vocabulary items is in computational respects akin to the relationship between the hippocampus and the neocortex proposed by McClelland and his colleagues. The timescales over which the processes operate are however clearly different.

Here we report a computational investigation of the idea that short-term memory limitations may be a limiting factor for long words in particular. First, however, we need to examine the relation between short-term memory capacity and vocabulary acquisition in more detail. One possibility is that the high correlations between short-term memory capacity (as assessed by nonword repetition) and vocabulary size in fact represent the opposite direction of causality to that discussed by Gathercole and Baddeley—the correlations could reflect the fact that long-term memory can be used to support performance in a short-term memory task. If possession of a larger vocabulary leads to superior nonword repetition performance, the direction of causality would be from vocabulary size to nonword repetition performance, rather than the reverse. This possibility was suggested by Snowling, Chiat, and Hulme (1991). It is certainly the case that there is a long-term memory contribution to memory span tasks under many circumstances (e.g. Hulme, Maughan, & Brown, 1991; Brown & Hulme, 1992). Thus the presence of within-age correlations between nonword repetition and vocabulary size is indeed consistent with the possibility that children with larger vocabularies are more able to use long-term lexical knowledge to improve performance to the nonword repetition task.

However the crossed-lagged correlational evidence described by Gathercole et al. (1992) is consistent with the idea that, at least for the young children (4 and 5 years old) the direction of causality is from nonword repetition ability to vocabulary size, rather than the other way round. For older children, the reverse is observed—vocabulary size independently predicts nonword repetition ability. Further evidence in support of a causal relationship between phonological STM and vocabulary comes from a study by Gathercole (1995) which found that unwordlike nonwords were better predictors of subsequent vocabulary size than more wordlike nonwords. This could be taken to suggest that the correlation between nonword repetition and vocabulary size does not reflect a lexical contribution to nonword repetition, because the more wordlike nonwords would presumably benefit more from the existence of supporting lexical representations. This evidence is perhaps not definitive, however, because it is possible that the less wordlike nonwords, being more difficult, might provide a more "sensitive" measure of the underlying lexical contribution to STM performance.

An alternative possibility is that the quality of sublexical phonological representations is driven by vocabulary growth, and that nonword repetition performance is in turn causally determined by the availability of good-quality sublexical representations. Metsala and Stanovich (1995) discuss this possibility, and present some evidence in support of it. A central assumption here is that the requirement to represent an increasing number of similar lexical items in phonological long-term memory is what drives the development of segmentalised lexical representations, leading ultimately to superior performance on sound awareness tasks (see e.g. Metsala, in press; Snowling & Hulme, 1994; Walley, 1993). The greater the number of words that must be represented in memory, the greater the need to represent fine-grain distinctions between them (at, for example, a phonemic level). Impaired phonemic awareness can arise if this segmental restructuring does not take place in the normal fashion, leading to developmental reading problems (this is the "Lexical Restructuring Deficit Hypothesis"—Metsala, submitted). So, it is possible that vocabulary size will be causally related to the availability of underlying phonemic representations. However, the presence of such phonemic representations will also lead to improved performance on a variety of phonological tasks including conventional measures of memory span and also word and nonword repetition tasks. This is because it will only be possible to maintain short-term representations of unfamiliar items if the representations can be created in the first place—for nonwords, it is plausible that low-level segmental representations will be necessary for this. Therefore, Metsala and Stanovich (1995) suggest that the correlations that have been found between nonword repetition scores and vocabulary size are in fact a reflection of the mediating influence of phonemic representations. It is suggested that vocabulary growth leads to better phonemic representations, which leads to better nonword repetition performance.

This suggestion has the merit of explaining the stronger relation between vocabulary size and nonword repetition when the nonwords are un-wordlike (Gathercole, 1995). In support of their suggestion, Metsala and Stanovich directly compare nonword repetition score and phoneme awareness ("isolating initial phoneme") scores as predictors of vocabulary size (with age partialled out). They find that phonemic awareness predicts unique vocabulary size variance even when both age and nonword repetition score (for unwordlike nonwords) is partialled out. The reverse is not the case, however—inclusion of the phoneme awareness measure completely removes the relation between nonword repetition and vocabulary size.

These data, although only cross-sectional to date, are clearly consistent with the suggestion that vocabulary growth is the driving factor leading to the development of phonemic representations, which in turn leads to improved nonword repetition performance.

More definitive evidence will emerge when longitudinal data are available from this and other ongoing studies. There is a further difficulty, in that direct comparisons between predictors cannot always be straightforwardly interpreted, because different tasks might not be equally good indices of the relevant underlying psychological capacities. Suppose, for example, that performance on a phoneme segmentation task turned out not to be a very good or direct measure of the underlying phonemic representations assumed to be necessary for task performance, and nonword repetition turned out to be a much better, more direct measure of underlying phonological STM capacity. It would then be possible for nonword repetition scores to show the strongest statistical correlation with vocabulary scores, even if the underlying causality were that vocabulary size determined phonemic representations which in turn determined nonword repetition score.

Given this problem, and the absence of longitudinal data concerning the relations over time of phoneme awareness, nonword repetition scores, and vocabulary size, the most plausible conclusion seems to be that there are reciprocal relations between these, as suggested by Gathercole et al. (1992). We know of no data inconsistent with this possibility.

We further assume that vocabulary growth is indeed a driving force behind the development of segmental lexical representations. The process of learning to spell in an alphabetic language is also a factor that may be causally related to improved performance or phoneme awareness tasks (Ellis & Cataldo, 1990; Frith, 1985). The availability of underlying phoneme-level representations will inevitably allow better representation and temporary storage of nonwords, just as the provision of phoneme-level representations can be shown computationally to lead to selectively improved performance on nonword compared with word reading (Brown, in press).

The better temporary storage of unfamiliar items that results from the existence of more segmental, phoneme-level representations will in turn lead to improved ability to acquire new vocabulary items. This in turn will lead to the development of better segmental representations, which will lead to superior nonword STM, and easier vocabulary acquisition. This is thus a classic case of "the rich getting richer" (Stanovich, 1986). We represent this symbiotic causality in Fig. 6.1.

Of course the relative contribution of the different causal pathways may change over developmental time, and indeed the results of several longitudinal studies suggest that this is the case. However, for present purposes the important conclusion is that the ability to maintain temporary representations of unfamiliar items is causally related to the ability subsequently to form a long-term memory representations of those items, whether or not this is mediated by the underlying quality of phonemic representations (which may in turn themselves be mediated by vocabulary size).

We now return to the issue we introduced earlier: the relation between the temporary storage of unfamiliar items, and the creation of permanent representations of items in long-term memory.

A TRACE DECAY MODEL OF PHONOLOGICAL SHORT-TERM MEMORY

There are by now many connectionist models of memory that in some way incorporate separate short-term and long-term storage (see Levy & Bairaktaris, 1995, for a review). In addition, there are now good network models of phonological short-term memory (e.g. Burgess & Hitch, 1992, this volume) including memory for nonwords (Glasspool, in press; Hartley & Houghton, in press; Houghton, Hartley, & Glasspool, this volume). However, in this section we describe a rather different approach that we

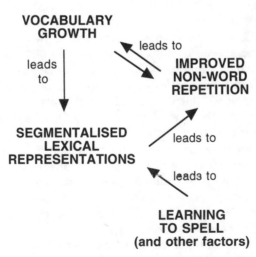

FIG. 6.1. Assumed causal relations between vocabulary size, nonword repetition ability, and other factors.

have taken; an approach that does not focus on the low-level mechanisms that support short-term memory, but, rather, examines the general characteristics of models of STM that could give rise to the empirically observed properties of the system. The full model is described in Brown and Hulme (1995), and explores the ability of a trace decay model of memory, operating without a rehearsal process, to account for basic memory span data.

Brown and Hulme were primarily concerned with two basic empirical phenomena in memory span: item length effects, and lexicality effects. The fact that memory span is greater for words than for nonwords (Hulme et al., 1991) is just one piece of evidence that long-term memory representations contribute to memory span. For present purposes, we are more concerned with the widely observed linear relationship between memory span and the speed with which the items to be remembered may be rehearsed.

A linear relationship between articulation rate and span has been found across many different populations of subjects and item types. The relationship has been observed in children of different ages (Hulme & Muir, 1985; Hulme, Thomson, Muir, & Lawrence, 1984; Nicolson, 1981) and in adults (e.g. Baddeley, Thomson, & Buchanan, 1975). Cross-linguistic differences in memory span can also be partly explained in terms of the differences in articulation rate for items in different languages (Ellis & Hennelly, 1980; Naveh-Benjamin & Ayres, 1986; Standing, Bond, Smith, & Isely, 1980; Stigler, Lee, & Stevenson, 1986). Finally, memory span (when defined as the number of items that can be correctly recalled) is larger for short words than for longer words in the same language (Baddeley et al., 1975, where "length" is measured in terms of articulatory duration. For present purposes, it is important to note that this linear relationship is generally observed to hold for both words and nonwords. Hulme et al., (1991) measured memory span for short, medium, and long words, and also short, medium, and long nonwords. They assumed that any lexicality effects would reflect a long-term memory contribution to span, and that the slope of the speech rate/recall function would reflect the rehearsal procedures' contribution to span. The trend of results of a range of similar experiments is illustrated schematically in Fig. 6.2.

It can be seen that the span–speech-rate function has a relatively steep slope and a near-zero intercept for unfamiliar nonwords; a shallow slope and moderate intercept for "trained" (more familiar) nonwords or low-frequency words, and a higher intercept for highly familiar words. It can also be seen that a linear function related speech rate to memory span for both words and nonwords. Memory span was reduced for the nonwords relative to the words, but the slope of the speech rate/recall function was the same for both words and nonwords. Only the intercepts of the speech rate/span functions differed between words and nonwords. Although the precise

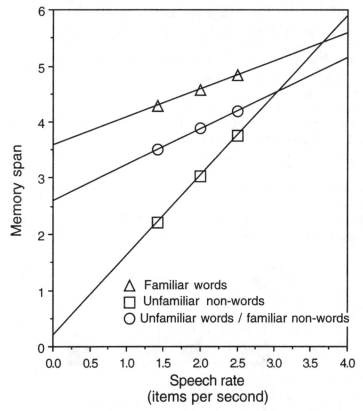

FIG. 6.2.   Schematic illustration of the speech rate/recall relationship observed in several experiments using different materials.

pattern of results (especially the steeper slope and near-zero intercept observed for unfamiliar nonwords) is not exactly the same in every experiment, the general pattern illustrated in Fig. 6.2, and the linear relationship, has been replicated many times (see Brown & Hulme, 1995).

This linear relationship rate between speech rate and span has generally been taken as evidence for verbal trace decay models (e.g. Baddeley, 1986; Schweickert & Boruff, 1986). These models assume that a phonological trace is normally created when each item is encoded, and that this trace decays over time. If the subvocal rehearsal procedure is available, it can be used to refresh the decaying trace, and so as many item memories can be maintained in the store as can be rehearsed within the time taken for the stored information to decay. Thus items that are longer (in terms of how long they take to articular) take longer to rehearse, and so fewer of them can be maintained in the time the trace takes to decay. However Brown and

Hulme (1995) argued that this linear relationship between span and speech rate could be explained without assuming the existence of a rehearsal process. They illustrated this with a simple model in which the only source of information loss was trace decay, and in which no rehearsal process was implemented. The model provided a good account of the data illustrated in Fig. 6.2, and other data.

The model represents the memory trace as a series of 0.1-second time slices, to approximate continuous time. These 0.1-second segments are treated as the basic units in the model. The strength of each segment of the trace may vary between 0 and 1, and its value is updated on every 0.1-second cycle. The strength associated with each segment can be viewed as a measure of memory trace strength at any point in time. Each incoming segment of an item is assumed to be registered correctly in the trace with a fixed strength (usually 0.95). The basic model is illustrated in Fig. 6.3, which illustrates the passage of time in 0.1-second segments for both presentation and recall of a

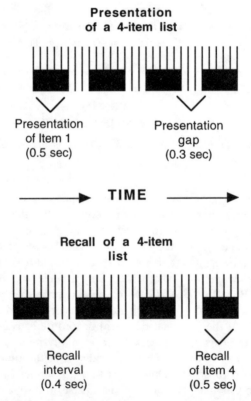

FIG. 6.3.   Presentation and recall of a list of four items over a series of 0.1-second time slices.

list of four items. The filled segments represent intervals of time in which a segment of an item is represented, and the unfilled segments between the filled segments represent intervals of time between presentation or recall of individual items. In the figure, each item is assumed to take 0.5 seconds to articulate, and therefore occupies 5 of the 0.1-second segments. The gap between presentation of each item is set at 0.3 seconds, and the gap between recall of each item is set at 0.4 seconds.

During the input of a list of items to be remembered, each segment's strength is assumed to decay by a small proportion in each 0.1-second time slice. Thus decay accumulates exponentially—segments that are near the beginning on the input stream will have more time to decay. Decay occurs over time during output as well. The probability of correctly recalling an entire nonword is then assumed to be the product of the recall probabilities for each segment of the word (note the short items will benefit in this process, simply because they are represented over fewer 0.1-second time segments).

Finally, the probability of an item's recall is then incremented by an amount designed to reflect the possibility of long-term memory influences during recall. As such influences are assumed to be minimal during the recall of unwordlike nonwords, of the type used in the experiments discussed earlier, we do not discuss this "redintegrative" processing stage further, although it is the primary source of lexicality effects in the full model.

In summary, Brown and Hulme demonstrated that a simple trace decay model of this type, operating without a rehearsal process, can give rise to item length effects due to opposing effects of decay and redintegration, and lexicality effects that occur only during redintegration. Further simulations demonstrated that item length effects can also be obtained when forgetting in due to interference or imperfect trace registration instead of trace decay. The model gives a good fit, for example, to the data illustrated in Fig. 6.2.

Rather than review the range of data that the model is able to account for, we now describe some new simulation results that assess the ability of the model to maintain representations of single nonwords of different lengths, as would be required for the permanent acquisition of new vocabulary items.

MEMORY FOR NONWORDS: THE "LONG MEANS LATE" HYPOTHESIS

The model described earlier gives a good account of the data concerning memory span for different lengths of both words and nonwords. We therefore used it to examine the hypothesis that short-term memory limitations would be more of a limiting factor in the acquisition of long vocabulary items than for short ones.

To summarise, the complete hypothesis is follows. We term this the "long means late" hypothesis, because it predicts that, all other things (such as word frequency) being equal, long words will be later acquired than short words.

1. The quality of the long-term representation that can be produced for an item using a standard gradient-descent learning algorithm (back-propagation, in the simulations to follow) will be dependent on the amount of time that a temporary representation of the item can be maintained in phonological short-term memory. This is simply because more repeated presentations will be possible over a longer length of time.

2. A short-term representation will be available for an unfamiliar item for a longer amount of time if the item (nonword) is short rather than long in temporal duration.

3. Therefore, all other things being equal, it should be hard to form long-term memory representations of long words than of short ones.

To investigate this, the first step was to examine the length of time for which representations of long (three-syllable) medium length (two-syllable), and short (one-syllable) nonwords could be maintained in temporary phonological storage.

We therefore ran a version of the trace decay model described earlier and (at more length) in Brown and Hulme (1995), using the same parameters that had been shown in the original version of the model to give rise to a good fit to the empirical data on memory span for nonwords. However in this new simulation the model was given just one item to remember—this was either a short, a medium, or a long nonword. For "short" items we assumed a spoken duration of 0.4 seconds (speech rate: 2.5 items per second); "medium" nonwords were 0.5 seconds long (2 items per second), and "long" nonwords were 0.7 seconds long (1.43 items per second). We then simply noted the number of time cycles that elapsed before the representation of the item could not be recalled with a probability of 50% or greater. The results are shown in Fig. 6.4.

It can readily be seen that, not surprisingly, the length of time for which an unfamiliar item can be retained by the model depends on the length of the item, being nearly three times as long for the short item as for the long item.

Long-term Learning as a Function of Short-term Retention Time

It is clearly the case that this should lead to a better opportunity for long-term learning of the shorter item. Although this is intuitively obvious, we nevertheless illustrated it with a simple backpropagation network (representing each item as a random 5-element vector, using a network

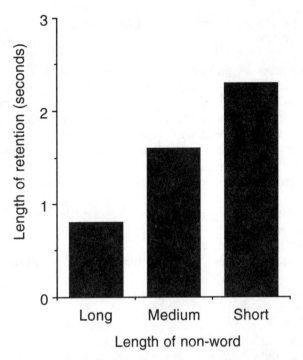

FIG. 6.4.   Durations for which representations of long (3-syllable), medium (2-syllable), and short (1-syllable) items could be maintained in the trace decay model of phonological short-term memory.

with 5 input units, 5 output units, 3 hidden units, and a learning rate of 0.001). The task of the network was simply to reproduce each item that was presented on its input units, on its output units.

We assumed that each cycle of learning takes 0.01 seconds. This allows for 80 trials of learning for the long nonword, 160 for the medium, and 230 for the short. Not surprisingly, a lower error score was obtained for the short item than for the long item, after the differential amounts of learning. The precise error scores were: short items: 0.01; medium items: 0.03; long items: 0.07. Thus the long items were much less well represented in long-term memory, because they were available for less time in the short-term store.

In psychological terms, we take these simple simulation results as confirmation of our intuitive "long means late" hypothesis: that long nonwords would be less easily registered into a long-term store, because they can be maintained for a shorter length of time in temporary phonological memory.

Psychological Evidence for the "Long Means Late" Hypothesis

We have predicted, on the basis of computational/functional considerations, that long words will be acquired by children at a later age than short ones, even if other factors are constant. In this final section, we briefly describe an analysis we have carried out which confirms that this is indeed the case. To do this, we used the Oxford Psycholinguistic Database (Quinlan, 1992). This is a computerised dictionary with information on many word characteristics, such as word length (in both letters and number of syllables), word frequency, and the rated age-of-acquisition of many of the words. We used this database to examine the relation between word frequency and rated age-of-acquisition for long and short words separately. The prediction to be tested was that the function relating word frequency and age-of-acquisition would be different for long and short words, such that long words of a given frequency would be later acquired than shorter words of equivalent frequency.

The word frequency values were those from Kucera and Francis (1967), and the age-of-acquisition ratings were taken from Gilhooly and Logie (1980). There is considerable evidence that age-of-acquisition ratings are both reliable and valid indicators of the age at which words are actually acquired by children. Word length was defined in terms of the number of syllables contained in the word; the ideal analysis would look at the actual spoken duration of each item, as this is the factor that is assumed to limit the amount of time for which the item can be preserved in phonological short-term memory. However for present purposes it was assumed that syllable length would provide an adequate approximation to spoken duration, given the number of items available.

The results of this simple analysis can be seen in Fig. 6.5. The numbers of the graph represent the number of words giving rise to each data point. Only four items were available in the "short but late acquired category" and this datum has therefore not been included.

It can readily be seen that for the vast majority of words for which the relevant data were available (546 short words and 230 long words) the prediction was confirmed. In general, the long words were rated as being acquired at least a year later than short words of equivalent frequency. There is one data point that does not conform to this trend; the small number of words (14) that were long yet rated as early-acquired although low in Kucera–Francis word frequency. This data point appears to be inconsistent with the "long means late" hypothesis under consideration. However, inspection of the actual items that give rise to this data point reveals that most of the items were words such as "grandmother", "grandfather" etc., which have common abbreviations ("gran", "nana"

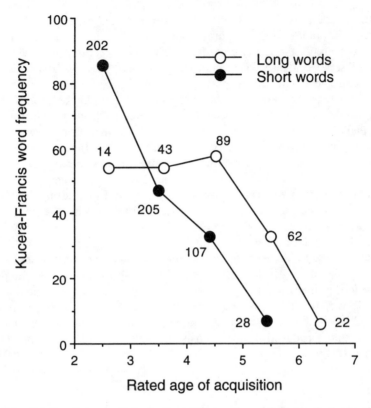

FIG. 6.5.   Relations between rated age of acquisition and word frequency for long and short words.

etc.) that tend to be used by children. Furthermore, the functional frequency of these words would be likely to be higher for children than would be indicated by their value on the Kucera–Francis word frequency count. The shortening of these words by and for children is, of course, exactly what one would expect if the limited phonological short-term memory capacity of children was a limiting factor on their acquisition of long vocabulary items.

We therefore take the data in Fig. 6.5 as at least consistent with the "long means late" hypothesis, and indeed they may perhaps be seen as tentative support for it.

SUMMARY

We began by considering some computational ideas that point to a possible functional reason for having a separate memory store in which information could be represented quickly but in a manner that did not encode the structural relations between stored patterns. This can then function efficiently in tandem with a separate long-term store, in which information comes to be represented more gradually but in a structured way. We then reviewed some evidence from children's vocabulary acquisition; evidence that is consistent with the suggestion that the length of time for which a potential new vocabulary item can be represented in a phonological STM is related to the probability of it becoming registered in long-term memory for vocabulary. We do not wish to overstate the parallels between the computational studies and the experimental evidence—they are concerned with different processes happening over quite different timescales. Nevertheless, we do believe that the computational results are suggestive of the general relationship between "episodic" memory and long-term, structured memory. A similar relationship, albeit over a different timescale, may hold between phonological STM and vocabulary. Such a relationship may hold even if the correlation between nonword repetition scores and vocabulary size is mediated by the level of underlying phonemic representations.

We explored some consequences of this approach for vocabulary acquisition, in the context of our own "trace delay" model of phonological STM. It was predicted on the basis of this that long words should be acquired later than short words of the same frequency, and we reported an analysis that produced results consistent with this "long means late" hypothesis.

ACKNOWLEDGEMENTS

This work was supported by a grant from the Economic and Social Research Council (UK) to both authors. We are grateful to Susan E. Gathercole and Jamie L. Metsala for helpful discussions and comments.

REFERENCES

Baddeley, A.D. (1986). *Working memory*. Oxford: Oxford University Press.

Baddeley, A.D., Papagno, C., & Vallar, G. (1988). When long-term learning depends on short-term storage. *Journal of Memory and Language, 27*, 586–596.

Baddeley, A.D., Thomson, N., & Buchanan, M. (1975). Word length and the structure of short-term memory. *Journal of Verbal Learning and Verbal Behavior, 14*, 575–589.

Brown, G.D.A. (in press). Developmental and acquired dyslexia: A connectionist comparison. *Brain and Language*.

Brown, G.D.A. & Hulme, C. (1992). Cognitive psychology and second language processing: The role of short-term memory. In R.J. Harris (Ed.), *Cognitive approaches to bilingualism*, (pp. 105–122). North Holland: Elsevier Science Publishers.

Brown, G.D.A. & Hulme, C. (1995). Modelling item length effects in memory span: No rehearsal needed? *Journal of Memory and Language, 34*, 594–621.

Burgess, N., & Hitch, G.J. (1992). Towards a network model of the articulatory loop. *Journal of Memory and Language, 31(4)*, 429–460.

Ellis, N.C., & Cataldo, S. (1990). The role of spelling in learning to read. *Language and Education, 1,* 1–28.

Ellis, N.C. & Hennelly, R.A. (1980). A bilingual word-length effect: Implications for intelligence testing and the relative ease of mental calculation in Welsh and English. *British Journal of Psychology, 71,* 43–51.

Frith, U. (1985). Beneath the surface of developmental dyslexia. In K.E. Patterson, J.C. Marshall, & M. Coltheart (Eds.), *Surface dyslexia.* Hillsdale, NJ: Lawrence Erlbaum Associates Inc.

Gathercole, S.E. (1995). Is nonword repetition a test of phonological memory or long-term knowledge? It all depends on the nonwords. *Memory & Cognition, 23*(1), 83–94.

Gathercole, S.E., & Baddeley, A.D. (1990a). Phonological memory deficits in language disordered children: Is there a causal connection? *Journal of Memory and Language, 29,* 336–360.

Gathercole, S.E., & Baddeley, A.D. (1990b). The role of phonological memory in vocabulary acquisition: A study of young children learning arbitrary names of toys. *British Journal of Psychology, 81,* 439–454.

Gathercole, S.E., & Baddeley, A.D. (1993). *Working memory and language.* Hove, UK: Lawrence Erlbaum Associates Ltd.

Gathercole, S.E., Willis, C.S., Emslie, H., & Baddeley, A.D. (1992). Phonological memory and vocabulary development during the early school years: A longitudinal study. *Developmental Psychology, 5,* 887–898.

Gilhooly, K.J., & Logie, R.H. (1980). Age of acquisition, imagery, concreteness, familiarity, and ambiguity measures for 1944 words. *Behavior Research Methods and Instrumentation, 12,* 395–427.

Glasspool, D. (in press). Competitive queueing and the articulatory loop. In J. Levy, D. Hairaktaris, J. Bullinaria, & D. Cairns (Eds.), *Connectionist models of memory and language.* London: UCL Press.

Hartley, T., & Houghton, G. (in press). A linguistically constrained model of short-term memory for nonwords. *Journal of Memory and Language.*

Hinton, G.E. (1989). Learning distributed representations of concepts. In R.G.M. Morris (Ed.), *Parallel distributed processing: Implications for psychology and neurobiology.* Oxford, Oxford University Press.

Hulme, C., Maughan, S., & Brown, G.D.A. (1991). Memory for words and nonwords: Evidence for a long-term memory contribution to short-term memory tasks. *Journal of Memory and Language, 30,* 685–701.

Hulme, C. & Muir, C. (1985). Developmental changes in speech rate and memory span: A causal relationship? *British Journal of Developmental Psychology, 3,* 175–181.

Hulme, C., Thomson, N., Muir, C., & Lawrence, A. (1984). Speech rate and the development of short-term memory span. *Journal of Experimental Child Psychology, 38,* 241–253.

Kucera, H., & Francis, W.N. (1967). *A computational analysis of present-day American English.* Providence, RI: Brown University.

Levy, J.P., & Bairaktaris, D. (1995). Connectionist dual-weight architectures. *Language and Cognitive Processes, 10,* 265–283.

McClelland, J.L., McNaughton, B.L., & O'Reilly, R.C. (1994). *Why are there complementary learning systems in the hippocampus and neocortex: Insights from the successes and failures of connectionist models of learning and memory.* Technical Report PDP.CNS.94.1, Carnegie Mellon University.

Metsala, J.L. (in press). An examination of word frequency and neighborhood density in the development of spoken word recognition. *Memory and Cognition.*

Metsala, J.L. (submitted). *The development of phonemic representations in reading disabilities: A test of the lexical restructuring deficit hypothesis.*

Metsala, J.L. & Stanovich, K.E. (1995, April). *An examination of young children's phonological processing as a function of lexical development.* Paper presented at the Annual American Educational Research Association, San Francisco, California.

Naveh-Benjamin, M. & Ayres, T.J. (1986). Digit span, reading rate, and linguistic relativity. *Quarterly Journal of Experimental Psychology, 38A,* 739–751.

Nicolson, R. (1981). The relationship between memory span and processing speed. In M. Friedman, J.P. Das, & N. O'Connor (Eds.), *Intelligence and learning.* New York: Plenum Press.

O'Reilly, R.C., & McClelland, J.L. (1994). *Hippocampal conjunctive encoding, storage and recall: Avoiding a tradeoff.* Technical Report PDP.CNS.94.4, Carnegie Mellon University.

Quinlan, P.T. (1992). *The Oxford Psycholinguistic Database.* Oxford: Oxford University Press.

Schweickert, R., & Boruff, B. (1986). Short-term memory capacity: Magic number or magic spell? *Journal of Experimental Psychology: Learning, Memory and Cognition, 12*(3), 419–425.

Snowling, M., Chiat, S., & Hulme, C. (1991). Words, nonwords and phonological process: Some comments on Gathercole, Willis, Emslie and Baddeley. *Applied Psycholinguistics, 12,* 369–373.

Snowling, M., & Hulme, C. (1994). The development of phonological skills. *Philosophical transactions of the Royal Society of London, Series B, 346,* 21–27.

Standing, L., Bond, B., Smith. P., & Isely, C. (1980). Is the immediate memory span determined by subvocalisation rate? *British Journal of Psychology, 71,* 525–539.

Stanovich, K.E. (1986). Matthew effects in reading: Some consequences of individual differences in the acquisition of literacy. *Reading Research Quarterly, 21,* 306–407.

Stigler, J.W., Lee, S-Y., & Stevenson, H.W. (1986). Digit memory in Chinese and English: Evidence for a temporally limited store. *Cognition, 23,* 1–20.

Vallar, G., & Baddeley, A.D. (1984). Fractionation of working memory: Neuropsychological evidence for a short-term store. *Cognitive Neuropsychology, 1,* 121–141.

Walley, A.C. (1993). The role of vocabulary development in children's spoken word recognition and segmentation ability. *Developmental Review, 13,* 286–350.

7

Associations and dissociations between language impairment and list recall: Implications for models of STM

Randi C. Martin and Mary F. Lesch
Rice University, Texas, USA

INTRODUCTION

Some of our most basic daily activities require the ability to retain serial order information in working memory. For example, auditory word perception depends on retaining the order in which phonemes occurred until the appropriate lexical entry has been activated. Experimentally, the retention of serially ordered verbal information has been examined by determining the effect of various factors on memory span—the length of a word or nonword list that can be immediately recalled in correct order 50% of the time. A large body of evidence supports the role of phonological codes in memory span performance. For example, memory span is smaller for phonologically similar than for phonologically dissimilar items (Conrad & Hull, 1964; Hintzman, 1965; Luce, Feustel, & Pisoni, 1983; Sperling & Speelman, 1970; Wickelgren, 1966) and is smaller for items taking longer to pronounce (Baddeley, Thomson, & Buchanan, 1975; Mackworth, 1963; Schweickert & Boruff, 1986). Some theories have postulated a short-term store specifically dedicated to the retention of phonological information (e.g. Baddeley, 1986; Cowan et al., 1992; Schweickert & Boruff, 1986). Other evidence, however, supports a contribution from lexical and semantic factors in verbal serial recall. For example, span performance is greater for words than for nonwords, suggesting that the lexical information provided by words is represented in short-term memory (Brener, 1940; Crowder, 1978; Hulme, Maughan, &

149

Brown, 1991). Saffran and N. Martin (1990) have observed effects of two other lexical variables, imageability and frequency, on span performance. Theorists noting these non-phonological contributions have emphasised the relation between the codes and processes involved in language processing and those involved in word list recall (e.g. R. Martin, Shelton, & Yaffee, 1994; N. Martin & Saffran, 1992a,b). In the present research, two theories taking the latter approach are examined for their adequacy in accounting for the relations between language processing and list recall for three aphasic patients.

In previous work in our laboratory, Martin, Shelton, and Yaffee (1994) obtained evidence for separate phonological and semantic capacities in STM in a study of two aphasic patients with very reduced memory span. One of these, patient EA, did not show the standard effects of phonological variables on span, indicating reduced capacity for the retention of phonological information. She did, however, recall word lists better than nonword lists and performed better on a probe recognition task that required the retention of semantic information than on a probe recognition task requiring the retention of phonological information. The other patient, AB, showed a reverse pattern, as he showed normal effects of phonological variables on span but little difference between word and nonword span. In addition he performed worse than EA on the semantic probe task but better than her on the phonological probe task.

Martin et al. (1994) interpreted these findings within a model of short-term memory in which there is a close connection between the types of representations involved in word recognition and production and the representations retained in STM (see also, Martin & Breedin, 1992). In the view of R. Martin and colleagues, verbal STM is a limited-capacity buffer for retaining all of these representations, where the phonological, lexical, and semantic representations for the same word are linked. Although the output of language processing constitutes the representations stored in this buffer, the quality of language processing and the capacity of the buffer are not viewed as identical. That is, capacity of the buffer (or decay rate) may be affected by brain damage, although single word processing remains intact (Martin, 1993; Martin & Breedin, 1992).

N. Martin and Saffran (1992a,b) have put forward a proposal that is similar in suggesting a close relation between language processing and short-term memory. These researchers have framed their model in an interactive-activation framework, based closely on Dell and O'Seaghdha's (1992) model of language production. In their model, which we will refer to as the interactive activation model of retrieval and repetition (IARR), auditory input activates phonological nodes in a phonological network which then activate lexical nodes (See Fig. 7.1). The target lexical node, as well as phonologically similar lexical nodes, are activated by the phonological nodes. Activation then spreads forward from the activated lexical nodes to

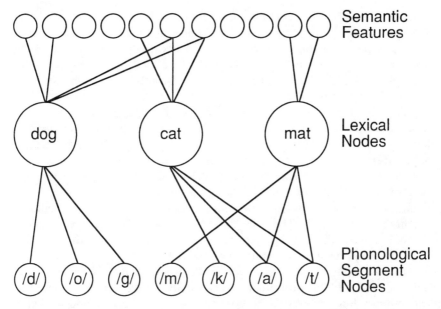

FIG. 7.1. Diagram of the N. Martin and Saffran (1992a) model of retrieval and repetition, which is based closely on Dell and O'Seaghdha's (1992) model of language production.

semantic (feature) nodes and backward from the lexical nodes to the decaying phonological nodes. Finally, the target-lexical and the phonologically related lexical nodes receive feedback from the activated phonological nodes and semantic nodes.

According to this approach, the activation of nodes resulting from spreading activation and feedback between different levels should predict the influence of various factors on short-term recall. Consistent with the IARR approach, Watkins and Watkins (1977) have observed an effect of frequency on the recall of supraspan lists at all but the last two serial positions. This suggests that frequency aids in the recall of items for which the phonological trace has decayed. Saffran and N. Martin (1990) also found that effects of frequency were limited to longer list lengths, suggesting that the phonological activation available for items in shorter lists is sufficent for retrieval whereas retention of items in longer lists requires lexical support. The repetition performance of patients with deficits of phonological retention should reveal effects of word frequency (which are assumed to reflect lexical processes at the level of the phonological word form) and imageability (which is assumed to reflect the "richness" of a semantic representation in terms of multiple connections among multiple semantic nodes) as the patient's performance will rely more on the activation of lexical and semantic representations in the face of a rapidly decaying phonological trace.

Saffran and N. Martin (1990) have used this language-based model of short-term memory to form predictions concerning the effects of frequency and imageability on the serial recall of patients with different types of STM impairment (e.g. a semantic, phonological, or global deficit). They have also attempted to account for naming performance within this model (N. Martin, Dell, Saffran, & Schwartz, 1994). Indeed, as indicated earlier, their model is based on a model of production that is essentially run in reverse in order to deal with comprehension (or, rather, the reception and retention of language). Saffran and N. Martin's appeal to representations and processes active during language comprehension and production to predict and explain performance on span tasks implies a close relationship between span performance and performance on tasks assumed to reflect the integrity of linguistic representations or processes (e.g. lexical decision, naming, comprehension tasks). Thus, in the IARR approach there is a closer linkage between the quality of word processing and short-term retention than in the approach of R. Martin and colleagues.

The two approaches also differ in their specificity—N. Martin and Saffran (1992a, b) have formulated very specific predictions concerning the activation of linguistic representations (phonological, lexical, and semantic) at various list positions during serial recall. Later, we will outline their predictions concerning effects of frequency (which is assumed to reflect lexical activation) and imageability (which is assumed to reflect semantic activation) as a function of serial position. We will present data from our patients on the repetition of word lists varied on frequency and imageability in order to evaluate these predictions. These repetition tasks as well as the auditory discrimination, auditory lexical decision, the Philadelphia Naming Test, and position probe tasks were supplied by Saffran and N. Martin (these tests form part of The Philadelphia Comprehension Battery; Saffran et al., 1989). Where appropriate, we will suggest modifications of the IARR approach that are necessary for it to cope with our results.

According to the IARR approach, a selective semantic impairment (which is assumed to affect connections between semantic and lexical nodes) should differentially affect retention of items at early list positions. This is because, in recall, the phonological traces for the list-initial items have faded with the passage of time associated with the processing of items intervening between their presentation and their recall, forcing a reliance on lexical representations. For later list items, the phonological trace has not decayed and is available to support recall (however, this would hold true only if subjects cannot recall early list items, or if they do not recall the items in order). If span is stressed, there should be a reduced primacy effect (which is assumed to be due to semantic processes) and an imageability effect at early list positions (as the patient will, nonetheless, rely on semantic activation to support recall of these items, even if this activation is degraded). The loss of semantic support, in the form of reduced feedback from semantic nodes to lexical nodes, should result in the production of phonologically related word and nonword errors, particularly at early list positions. The production of semantic errors is unlikely, as the reduced activation of lexical nodes from semantic nodes reduces the probability that semantically related lexical nodes will be activated.

According to the IARR approach, a selective phonological impairment should result in the reduction of the recency effect, as the basis for this effect is assumed to be a persisting phonological trace for list-final items. It is assumed that a phonological impairment reflects the insufficent spreading or maintenance of activation between lexical and phonological nodes. The performance of patients with a phonological deficit would be expected to rely on semantic information and would be expected to show effects of imageability and frequency, particularly at later list positions.

On the basis of memory span data, the three patients who are presented here showed a deficient contribution from semantic information on list recall, as all showed little or no advantage of word list over nonword list recall. Two of these patients, AB and ML, show evidence of a deficit in the retention of semantic information (see N. Martin et al., 1994, for previous evidence on patient AB). The third patient, MS, is believed to have an impairment in retrieving phonology from semantics (Bartha, Lesch, & Martin, 1994). For each patient, we will first present data on standard span tasks and several other tasks relevant to determining the nature of the patient's deficit. We will then present data on word-list repetition and probe tasks in which frequency and imageability of the items were varied. The study of N. Martin et al. (1994) used span tasks that varied, for example, phonological similarity, word length, and lexical status to examine the patients' ability to retain phonological and semantic information. In contrast, the research of N. Martin and Saffran (1992a, b) has emphasised the effects of frequency, imageability, and serial position on list repetition in assessing retention deficits for semantic and phonological information. It is of considerable theoretical and methodological interest to determine whether patterns implicating the same deficit are obtained for both types of materials.

PATIENT AB

Patient Description

AB is a 76-year-old right-handed male who suffered a left hemisphere cerebral vascular accident (CVA) in 1979. At the time of his CVA, AB had been a practising lawyer. A CT scan revealed low-density regions in the posterolateral aspect of the left frontal lobe and the adjacent anterior parietal lobe.

As reported by R. Martin et al. (1994), AB suffers from an impairment in the retention of semantic information. This impairment was evident in his performance on span tasks, a category probe task, and attribute questions. We will review these data here. However, it should be noted that some of the data presented here represent a more recent testing of AB than that reported by R. Martin et al. (1994).

Span Tasks

AB's performance on memory span tasks revealed normal effects of phonologically related variables: better performance for nonrhyming than rhyming items and better performance on auditory than visual presentation (R. Martin et al., 1994) (Table 7.1 presents span data for AB, ML, and MS). AB's performance on a rhyme probe task also suggested a fairly well preserved ability to maintain phonological representations. In the rhyme probe task, patients judged whether a probed word rhymed with any item in a preceding list. Lists varied from one to seven items in length. For each list length, half of the trials were rhyme-present and half rhyme-absent. On rhyme-present trials, each serial position was probed equally often. AB's estimated span (75% correct) on the rhyme probe task was 4.62 items, suggesting that his ability to retain phonological information is relatively unimpaired because, although reported by R. Martin et al. (1994) as falling outside the range of normals, his performance on this task was significantly better than another patient (EA) shown to have a phonological impairment. In a category probe task, in which patients judged whether a probe word was in the same category as any of the items in a preceding list, AB obtained an estimated span of 2.19 items, indicating an impairment in retaining semantic information. Also consistent with a semantic impairment was the only slight advantage for word lists (see Table 7.1).

Auditory Discrimination

In a test of auditory discrimination, patients were presented with 80 word (e.g. gist–just) and 80 nonword (e.g. fud–fid) minimal pairs and were asked whether the items in each pair were the same or different. Imageability (abstract vs. concrete) as well as the position of the difference were varied. There were three presentation conditions: (1) no delay, (2) unfilled delay, and (3) filled delay. In the no delay condition, presentation of the second item immediately followed presentation of the first. This condition assesses the patient's ability to perceive the presence or absence of similarity in auditorily presented stimuli. The unfilled delay condition, in which the stimuli to be compared were presented five seconds apart, assesses the ability to hold on to a phonological representation. In the filled delay

TABLE 7.1
Serial Recall Performance as a Function of Stimulus Type:
Percentage of Lists Correct

	Auditory Presentation			Visual Presentation		
	2	3	Mean	2	3	Mean
Phonologically Similar and Dissimilar Word Lists						
AB						
Dissimilar	90	40	65	55	25	40
Similar	60	0	30	15	20	18
ML						
Dissimilar	80	40	60	60	10	35
Similar	70	0	35	40	50	45
MS						
Data Unavailable						
Word and Nonword Lists						
AB						
Word	73	27	50			
Nonword	77	13	45			
ML						
Word	70	10	40			
Nonword	60	10	35			
MS						
Word	100	50	75			
Nonword	90	80	85			

condition, the first stimulus was presented, then the tester and the patient counted out loud from one to five, and then the second stimulus was presented. It was assumed that the act of counting out loud would prevent rehearsal of the initial item during the delay and, therefore, a comparison of the filled and unfilled delay conditions would allow for the determination of whether the patient was able to make use of rehearsal processes to benefit performance.

AB made 10% errors overall in the auditory discrimination task with poorer performance in the filled delay (15% errors) than in the unfilled delay (9% errors) or the no delay condition (6% errors). The 6% difference between the filled delay and the unfilled delay conditions suggests that AB may have been able to benefit from rehearsal of the initial item in the unfilled delay condition. AB was slightly more likely to make errors when the stimuli to be compared were nonwords (12% errors) than when they were words (8% errors) suggesting that lexical phonology aids retention. The 6% errors that AB made in the no delay condition is also consistent with an impairment in phonetic processing. His relatively good performance overall suggests that his phonetic perception deficit is mild, consistent with findings on minimal pair CV discrimination reported in R. Martin et al. (1994).

Auditory Lexical Decision

In the lexical decision task there were 80 word and 80 nonword stimuli. The words varied on number of syllables, imageability, and frequency. The nonwords were derived from the word stimuli by changing one or two phonemes. AB fairly reliably rejected nonwords (4% errors). However, he classified 12.5% of the words as nonwords. There was an effect of number of syllables such that AB classified 33% of one-syllable words as nonwords, 5% of two-syllable words as nonwords, and 0% of three-syllable words as nonwords. There was little effect of imageability (AB made 12.5% errors on high-imageability words and 12.5% errors on low-imageability words), or frequency (10% errors for high-frequency words and 15% errors for low-frequency words) of the stimuli which suggests that lexical-semantic factors are not at work. AB's errors on word stimuli suggest that he may have some impairment in gaining access to lexical entries via phonological input. Also consistent with this suggestion is the observation of a syllable effect—AB was more likely to classify short words (words with more phonological neighbours) as nonwords. Finally, we should note that the three nonwords that AB classified as words all differed from real words by only one phoneme. This result is also consistent with a phonetic impairment (i.e. if AB cannot discriminate /ba–pa/ 100% of the time, he may say "bickle" is a word).

Attribute Questions

In this task, patients were asked questions concerning the attributes of objects. Questions were in the form "Which is soft, cotton or sandpaper?". Successful performance on this task requires retention of the attribute in question (soft) and the attributes of both objects until a decision is made, and is thus assumed to reflect the ability to retain semantic information. AB performed poorly on this task, obtaining only 50% correct. That his poor performance reflects an inability to retain semantic information, and not a lack of knowledge about objects and their attributes, is suggested by his perfect performance with untimed visual presentation of the questions and his much improved performance (83% correct) with auditory presentation when the format of the questions was changed so that he only had to consider one object (e.g. Is sandpaper soft?).

Naming

As reported by R. Martin et al. (1994), AB demonstrated normal naming on the Boston Naming Test (Kaplan, Goodglass, & Weintraub, 1976) as he scored 76/84 correct (mean = 70.8, SD = 11.7 for normal subjects).

As part of the current investigation, AB was tested on the Philadelphia Naming Test which consists of 175 items with names varying on number of syllables and frequency. AB made 20/175 (11%) errors. 2/20 of these errors were phonologically related words (e.g. wagon → viking). 17/20 errors were semantically related. There were three types of semantic errors: seven responses were scored as errors because they were "too specific" (e.g. mountain → the Alps, king → King Tut), nine other responses were associatively or semantically related (house → school), and one response was a description (bench → "shelf, slats, I can't think of it"). Errors occurred more often with names consisting of one (11% errors) or two syllables (16% errors) than with three-syllable names (5% errors). There was no effect of frequency. Finally, it should be noted that for 7/20 (35%) of the responses scored as errors, AB eventually came up with the correct name (e.g. pipe → smoking → pipe). For six of these errors the initial response was a semantically related word and for the other error the initial response was a phonologically related nonword.

List Repetition

For all of the list repetition tasks, half of the lists were composed of high-imageability words and half of low-imageability words. Within each level of imageability, half of the lists were composed of high-frequency words and half of low-frequency words. The single word repetition task consisted of 240 words. AB performed at a high level making only 2% errors. AB was also presented with 240 pairs of words (in two sets with the second set reversing the order of the words within each pair) for repetition. On these lists, performance dropped to 60% lists correct. In his recall, AB omitted about 7% of the items. His poor performance reflects his tendency to report the last item first and the first item last (on 30% of the trials repetition was initiated with the second list item) rather than a failure to report the item correctly (86% of the items were reported). When an error was due to an incorrect response and not due to an omission or a reversal of items, they were generally (15/28) phonologically related words (e.g. metal → meadow) indicating the retention of phonological information. Occasionally (2/28), AB reported a phonologically related nonword (e.g. obsession → subsession). 11/28 error responses were intrusions from previous lists.

For the repetition of three-word lists, AB was presented with 80 lists that were varied on frequency and imageability. AB failed to repeat a single list correctly. However, he recalled 65% of the items. AB insisted on reporting the last list item first (recall was initiated with the list-final item 80% of the time). As shown in Fig. 7.2 (which indicates whether an item was recalled, but not whether it was recalled in its correct position), there was an effect of imageability on performance, with AB reporting 14% more high-imageability words than low-imageability words. Furthermore, the difference was greatest for items occurring in the first list position (23%) and smallest for items occuring in the last list position (10% for the second list position and 7% for the last list position). AB was also slightly more likely to report high-frequency than low-frequency words (5% more high-frequency words were reported). There was an effect of recency such that 96% of items occurring in the final list position were recalled compared to 46% of items occurring in the initial position and 53% recall for items

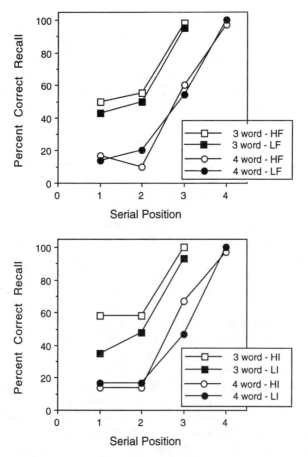

FIG. 7.2. Frequency and imageability effects as a function of serial position—patient AB.

occurring in the middle list position. Although most of AB's errors were errors of omission (30% of the items were omitted), actual error responses tended to be phonologically related words (6/8). There was one intrusion from a previous list and one phonologically related nonword response.

For the repetition of four-word lists, AB was presented with 60 lists varied on frequency and imageability. AB again obtained 0% lists correct and again insisted on reporting the last list item first (92% of trials). Overall, 46% of the items were recalled, with percentage recall for the first through fourth serial position being 15%, 15%, 57%, and 98%. AB omitted 51% of the items. Errors again tended to be phonologically related words (4/5 error responses) however, unlike performance on the three-word lists, imageability had little effect on whether AB reported an item correctly (3%). However, although there was no effect of imageability overall, there was a 20% advantage for high-imageability items at the third list position. It is interesting to note that the observation of effects of imageability and frequency seem to be related to list length and overall levels of recall. This is an issue that we will return to later. There was no effect of word frequency.

Position Probe Task

AB showed a recency effect, but a much reduced primacy effect, in a position probe task when recall was cued by an item's position in a three- or four-word list. In this task, AB was presented with 66 lists of three-word strings and 120 lists of four-word strings. This task was used in order to determine whether a report strategy could explain AB's failure to report list-initial items (See Saffran & N. Martin, 1990). AB recalled 51% of probed items with three-word lists and 38% of probed items with four-word lists. For three-word strings AB recalled 86% of items occurring in the final list position versus 36% and 29% of items in the first and second serial positions, respectively. Performance was similar for four-word strings: AB recalled 90% of list-final items and 17%, 10%, and 34% of items in the first, second, and third serial positions, respectively. AB's performance on this task suggests that his poor performance on early list items in serial repetition tasks could not be attributed to decay of early items resulting from a strategy of recalling list-final items first.

Discussion of AB

AB's performance on span tasks suggests that his ability to retain phonological information is good relative to his ability to retain semantic information. A semantic retention deficit was particularly evident in his performance on the attribute questions where performance was near chance.

However, it is worth noting that, although AB seems to have a deficit in the retention of semantic information, comprehension appears to be intact.

For example, AB performed fairly well on the attribute questions when the memory load was reduced—when only one object needed to be considered AB obtained 83% correct and he scored 100% correct when the questions were presented visually (with unlimited viewing time). R. Martin et al. (1994) also found that, with untimed presentation, AB performed perfectly on a category judgement task in which subjects judged whether an exemplar was a member of a category. On the Peabody Picture–Vocabulary Test (PPVT; Dunn & Dunn, 1981), a standardised test of word–picture matching, AB obtained a standard score of 110 when scored against the norms for 40-year-old subjects (m = 100, s = 15).

AB's performance on the repetition of lists varied on frequency and imageability is consistent with the predictions of the IARR approach for a patient with a semantic retention deficit. AB's insistence on reporting the last list item first, particularly evident with the longer list lengths, suggests that recency of input and, hence, phonological processes are critical for retrieval.

The effect of imageability observed in AB's recall is consistent with the suggestion that the primacy effect is due to semantic variables—AB showed the largest effect of imageability in the first list position, suggesting that it is these items that require semantic support for recall. However, it is critical to note that, although there was an effect of imageability on the recall of early list items, AB's recall of these items was extremely poor. AB showed a reduced primacy effect, an effect of imageability at early list positions, and errors at these list positions were primarily phonologically related words. The presence of phonologically related errors suggests the availability of phonological information and indicates that there is a reduction in the semantic activation that feeds back to the lexical and phonological levels of representation.

Consistent with N. Martin and Saffran's assumption that STM operates over representations normally active during language comprehension and production, AB shows some difficulties in the processing of single words. Although AB's pattern of performance may not indicate a severe impairment, he failed to show a normal level of performance on any of the tasks relevant to single word processing (e.g. auditory lexical decision, auditory discrimination, and naming). It should be noted, however, that even though AB's performance on these tasks is not perfect, it is not clear how his relatively good performance on these tasks translates into very poor performance on repetition tasks.

Of the patients reported by N. Martin and Saffran (1992b), VP's pattern of performance on list repetition seems most similar to that of AB. Both AB and VP performed fairly well on single word repetition obtaining 98% and 92% correct, respectively. Both patients showed recency, a loss of primacy, and effects of imageability at early list positions. Their patterns of performance were also similar on some of the language processing tasks, suggesting preserved phonological abilities and disrupted semantic abilities. Both AB and VP peformed relatively well on the auditory discrimination task obtaining about 90% correct overall. On the auditory lexical decision task, AB made about 8% errors overall as compared to 9% errors overall for VP. However, although AB tended to make more errors on word stimuli (about 13% errors on words compared to 4% errors on nonwords), VP seemed slightly more likely to make errors on nonwords (11% errors on nonwords compared to 7% on words). A semantic deficit was suggested by VP's performance on a word-to-picture matching task (with a target picture and three distractors)—VP obtained 100% correct in the across-category condition as compared to 88% correct in the within-category condition. AB's semantic deficit was most obvious in his performance on the attribute questions.

Despite these similarities, a striking discrepancy between AB and VP was evident in their performance on the naming task. AB exhibited only a slight impairment, making 11% errors on this task, whereas VP made about 72% errors, indicating a severe naming impairment. Most of VP's naming errors consisted of "no responses" (about 20% of the errors) and descriptions (about 18% of the errors). However, he also produced a large number of formal paraphasias (about 15% of the errors) and perseverations (about 13% of the errors).

In fact, all three of the patients reported by Martin and Saffran (1992b) demonstrated fairly severe impairments in single word processing (particularly in naming). The data from the Martin and Saffran (1992b) patients is consistent with the suggestion that a severe impairment in processing single words translates into a severe short-term memory impairment. However, our patient AB, who performs relatively well on single word processing tasks but poorly on STM tasks, provides a dissociation between the two types of processes. Although we will defer further discussion of this issue until later, it is interesting to note that the next patient we will discuss, ML, demonstrates an even more striking discrepancy between performance on single word processing tasks and span tasks.

Although the IARR approach predicts a recency effect and no primacy effect associated with a semantic deficit, it is not obvious why AB insisted on reporting the last list item first on a great majority of the trials in list repetition (even though he was instructed to begin recall with the first list item). For a large proportion of the lists, recalling the last item first could not be attributed to a loss of the memory trace for the first list item. For example, on three-word lists, AB initiated recall with the list-final item on 80% of the lists even though he was later able to report 46% of list-initial items. To account for this pattern within the IARR approach, one might hypothesise that AB begins recall with items having the highest level of activation, perhaps realising that those items may be lost if their recall is deferred while earlier list items are produced. An alternative possibility is that AB's output order pattern results from excessive retroactive interference between list items. His ability to recall the first item later might be attributed to a reduction in this interference over time or a reduction that somehow results from recall of the first list item. Consequently, recall of the early items is superior in list recall, where this recall is delayed, than in the probed recall where the recall of early items occurs immediately after the end of the list. This interpretation is consistent with models of short-term memory that suggest interference rather than decay as the mechanism for forgetting. For example, Nairne (1990) suggested that traces of later list items can overwrite feature values that they share with traces of earlier list items.[1] We should also note at this point that the observation of intrusion errors (11/28 error responses on two-word lists) is also consistent with the idea that the failure to recall certain items is not due to the complete loss (through decay) of trace information, but rather to "competition" among traces. That is, it would be hard to explain how an item from a previous list supplanted one from a current list if the patient's deficit were attributed to overly rapid decay at various levels. It should be noted, though, that proactive rather than retroactive interference would have to be invoked to account for intrusions.

PATIENT ML

Patient Description

ML is a 55-year-old right-handed male who suffered a left hemisphere CVA in 1990. He had completed two years of college and had been employed as a draftsman prior to his CVA. CT scan revealed an infarction involving the left frontal and parietal operculum. Atrophy in the left temporal operculum was noted, as was mild diffuse atrophy.

Span Tasks

On the span tasks ML showed normal effects of phonological similarity. As can be seen in Table 7.1, ML recalled more phonologically dissimilar than phonologically similar (word and letter) lists. He also showed a slight advantage for auditory presentation over visual presentation. ML's rhyme probe span was 2.28 items. ML showed little advantage for word lists over nonword lists (see Table 7.1) suggesting that his span performance does not

---

[1] Nairne (1990) suggests the possibility that the overwriting process does not permanently erase feature values. If not, then it would be possible that an item that could not be recalled at one moment, could later be accurately recalled.

benefit from the semantic information provided by word stimuli. A further indication of an impairment in the retention of semantic information is ML's category probe span of only 1.5 items.

Auditory Discrimination

ML performed at a high level on the auditory discrimination task making only 3% errors overall. ML was more likely to make errors to nonword stimuli (5%) than to word stimuli (< 1%). This high level of performance suggests that ML's perception of auditory stimuli is intact, as is his ability to retain a phonological representation over a short period (the five-second delay between stimuli in the delay conditions).

Auditory Lexical Decision

ML's performance on the lexical decision task was excellent (1% errors). Clearly, ML is able to access lexical representations via phonology.

Attribute Questions

ML obtained 65% correct on the attribute questions when they were in the form "Which is red, a cherry or an onion?" suggesting a deficit in retaining semantic information. As was the case with AB, performance improved when only one object needed to be considered (88% correct) suggesting that ML still has access to semantic information regarding objects and their attributes, but has difficulty retaining that information in short-term memory when considering more than one object.

Naming

ML only made 2% errors (4/175) on the naming test. 2/4 of these errors were semantic descriptions (e.g. scale → "measurement of weight") and 2/4 were semantically related (e.g. train → railroad). On 3/4 of these trials ML eventually responded with the correct name (e.g. cowboy → man ... outlaw ... westerner ... cowboy).

List Repetition

On single word repetition, ML repeated 96% of the words correctly. His error responses (i.e. errors that were not errors of omission) were all phonologically related words (2/6) (e.g. leader → reader) or phonologically related nonwords (5/6) (tendency → tendent). ML also made omissions on three low-frequency–low-imageability items. ML obtained 94% correct on two-word lists and omitted fewer than 1% of the items. 3/9 errors were phonologically related words while 2/9 were phonologically related nonwords. Four errors consisted of intrusions from previous trials. On three trials, ML failed to make any response for the second list item (two of these trials were low-frequency–low-imageability and the third was high-frequency–high-imageability).

ML obtained 29% lists correct on three-word lists. He recalled 76% of the items and omitted 14%. Out of 14 error responses, one was a phonologically related error, 12 were intrusions from previous lists, and on one trial ML repeated the same item twice. The overall effect of imageability was 12%. Imageability had the greatest effect on recall of items in the second list position (33% more high-imageability words were recalled than low-imageability words). The overall effect of frequency was 8%, with the largest effect at the third serial position (15%) (see Fig. 7.3).

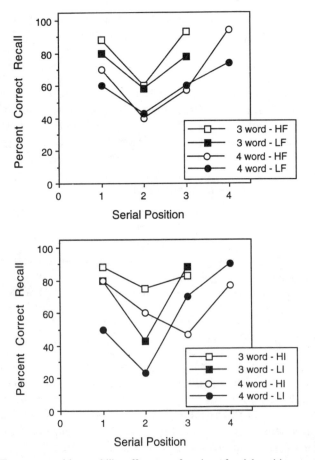

FIG. 7.3. Frequency and imageability effects as a function of serial position—patient ML.

ML obtained 10% lists correct on four-item lists. He recalled 63% of the items and omitted 36%. ML tended to report the first list item first and then the last list item. Most of ML's errors were errors of omission. Of six error responses, four were phonologically related words, two were intrusions from a previous list. One of these intrusions was semantically related to the target item (e.g. river → valley). Overall, there was little effect of imageability (an 8% advantage for high-imageability items) or frequency (10% advantage for high-frequency items). However, there was a large advantage (30% and 37%) for high-imageability items occurring in the first and second list positions, respectively. In list repetition, ML tended to show both primacy and recency effects. He tended to initiate recall with the list-initial items (96%, 81%, and 42% of trials were initiated with recall of the initial item for two-, three-, and four-word lists, respectively) which was then followed by recall of the list-final item.

Position Probe Task

ML showed a clear recency effect for both three-word and four-word strings (95% correct for items occurring in the list-final position in three-word strings and 100% correct for four-word strings). There was some indication of a reduced primacy effect with three-word strings (50%, 36%, and 95% items recalled for the the first, second, and third serial positions, respectively), and no sign of a primacy effect with four-word strings (30%, 30%, 40%, and 100% correct recall across serial positions).

Discussion of ML

ML's performance was similar to AB's on the span tasks showing effects of phonologically related variables, but little advantage for word over nonword stimuli. Like AB, he performed poorly on the attribute questions. This pattern of performance suggests a semantic retention deficit. Other evidence suggests that ML has at most a mild deficit in his knowledge of semantic information. On the PPVT (Dunn & Dunn, 1981), he obtained a standard score of 113. On a task in which the subject sees a picture of one object and is asked to pick the object that is most closely related to it from a pair of objects (e.g. which is most closely related to a *desk*, a *table*, or a *bureau*?) ML obtained 88% correct. He also performed well on the attribute questions when the memory load was reduced, suggesting that it was the memory load, and not poor comprehension, that resulted in his poor performance.

Consistent with the predictions of the IARR, and consistent with the pattern found for AB, imageability had a strong effect on the recall of earlier list items (for the four-item lists, 30% and 37% advantage for high-imageability words in the first two list positions, respectively). Most of ML's errors were errors of omission. However, when he did make erroneous responses, they were usually phonologically related words or nonwords, which is also consistent with the suggestion that ML has a problem retaining semantic information, but has some ability to retain phonological information. A third finding consistent with a semantic deficit was some indication of a reduced primacy effect, particularly in the position probe task with four-word lists.

Although ML's performance on the list repetition tasks resembled AB's in some respects, it differed from AB's in that he was much better able to report the list-initial item first. Perhaps this difference might be explained on the grounds that ML, although very impaired, had somewhat better ability to retain semantic information than AB. ML did show a higher level of recall than AB in terms of lists and items correct on the list repetition tasks, and he performed somewhat better than AB on the attribute question task. Going against this notion, however, is ML's worse performance on the category probe task and the fact that his span advantage for words over nonwords was no larger than AB's.

In terms of the interference hypothesis introduced in connection with the serial report pattern of AB, it might be hypothesised that ML experienced greater retroactive interference than normal, but less than AB. As a consequence he showed a primacy effect with both list recall and the probe task for the three-item lists, but no primacy effect on either task for the four-item lists. The absence of the primacy effect with four-item lists could be explained on the grounds that the longer list length caused greater retroactive interference. Also, the large number of intrusions (12/14 error responses) on ML's recall of three-word lists would be more consistent with an interference effect than a decay account. However, as noted with respect to similar errors from AB, intrusions would result from proactive rather than retroactive interference.

The most surprising aspect of ML's performance was the discrepancy between his performance on span tasks relative to performance on language processing tasks (as indicated earlier, AB shows this same discrepancy to a lesser extent). ML has a very reduced span, but performs at very high levels on most other tasks. We will return later to a discussion of the implications that this pattern of performance has for specifying the relationship between language processing and STM.

PATIENT MS

Patient Description

MS is a 26-year-old right-handed male. He contracted herpes encephalitis in 1993 which resulted in an impairment of his language abilities while sparing most other cognitive abilities. He has had two years of college education. An EEG recording suggested left temporal damage.

Span Tasks

On a digit span task, MS's performance was excellent as he obtained 80% correct on serial recall of seven-item lists. He also performed well on the rhyme probe task (83% correct with six-item lists). MS's span performance showed a slight advantage for nonword lists (4.5 items = 75% correct performance) over word lists (3.8 items = 75% performance). MS's performance on the nonword lists was actually within normal range; however, his poorer performance with word than nonword lists is the reverse of the normal pattern (see Table 7.1). Excellent performance on the digit and rhyme probe span tasks suggests a good ability to retain phonological information, whereas the poorer performance with word stimuli as compared to nonword stimuli suggests that MS's recall does not benefit from the semantic information provided by words. Thus, MS's pattern on the span tasks is somewhat similar to AB's and ML's except that his retention of phonological information appears to be entirely normal. MS's normal performance with digits but subnormal performance on span tasks containing words other than digits might be related to the frequency of the items, given that digits are high-frequency words. As will be documented later, frequency had a large effect on MS's performance on a number of tasks.

Naming

MS's performance on the naming test was very poor (76/175 pictures named correctly). There was an effect of frequency such that 87% of high-frequency items were named correctly as compared to 20% of low-frequency items. 95% of MS's errors were semantic descriptions (i.e. circumlocutions. For example, for *chimney*: "I think this one starts with a 'c'. It's the stuff that are on the top of a house that you put, if you, if it gets real cold you can put a, uh, you can cut a tree down and catch it on fire inside your house. But, they, uh, the heat comes in, but the, the bad smelling stuff that can knock you out and kill you goes outside your house."

List Repetition

In single word repetition, MS made two errors, obtaining 98% correct. Both error responses were phonologically related nonwords (e.g. exclusion → explusion). On repetition of word pairs, MS obtained 93% lists correct. Occasionally, MS reported the items in the reverse order; however, when erroneous items were produced, they were phonologically related (four out of five of these errors were phonologically related nonwords while the other error was a phonologically related word).

On three-word repetition, MS obtained 83% lists correct. His performance suggested a somewhat reduced recency effect as he obtained 95%, 94%, and 86% correct for the three serial positions. His performance revealed an effect of frequency such that 15% more high-frequency words were recalled. The effect of frequency was the greatest at the final list position with a 28% benefit of high-frequency words in the third list position as compared to 10% and 7.5% for the first two list positions. In the IARR approach, a reduced recency effect is taken to imply a phonological deficit, as recency is assumed to be due to a persisting phonological trace of the final list items. Thus, this pattern contrasts with the conclusion from the span tasks which was indicative of a semantic deficit. The observation of a frequency effect at the final list position suggests that recall of final list items relies on lexical activation.

Out of 20 error responses on the three-word lists (there was one omission), 45% (9/20) were phonologically related nonwords and two of these responses included a semantic description of the item. For example, for the list *lobster*, *castle*, and *bagpipe*, MS responded: "losser—the thing you eat, the place the kings go in" and "it comes from the place where men wear the same things as women" (mimics use). 25% (5/20) were phonologically related words and one of these responses included a semantic description. Another 25% (5/20) of the error responses consisted of semantic descriptions without the production of a phonologically related word or nonword. The semantic descriptions occurred predominantly on low-frequency, but high-imageability items. The fact that 8/20 of MS's error responses included a semantic description suggests that MS often retained the semantic information about a word that he could not produce correctly (see Fig. 7.4)

In recall of four-word lists, MS's performance again showed a reduced recency effect. He recalled 97%, 82%, 75%, and 68% of the items across the four serial positions. He recalled 23% more high-frequency items than low-frequency items and 17% more high-imageability than low-imageability items. The effect of imageability was greatest at the second (24%) and fourth list positions (23%) whereas the effect of frequency was largest at the third list position (36%).

MS omitted only nine items in recall of the four-item lists. His errors were predominantly phonologically related to the target (13/47 errors were phonologically related words and 17/47 errors were phonologically related nonwords). All but three of the 30 phonologically related errors occurred on low-frequency items. Six of his 47 errors were semantic descriptions, and an additional two were substitutions of semantically related words. Seven out of these eight semantically related errors occurred on low-frequency items, and six of the eight occurred on high-imageability items.

Position Probe Task

MS's performance on the position probe task did not mirror his performance on the list repetition tasks in that recall of list-final items was 100% correct for both three-word and four-word strings. Also, his

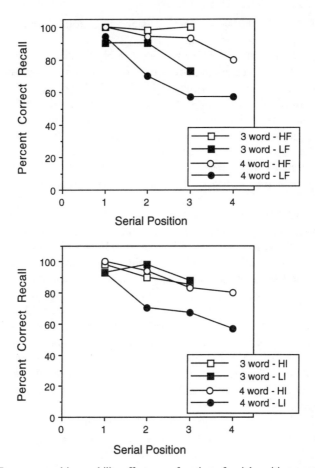

FIG. 7.4.   Frequency and imageability effects as a function of serial position—patient MS.

overall level of performance was very high as he scored 94% correct on the three-item lists and 93% correct on the four-item lists.

Discussion of MS

MS's pattern of performance on the span tasks and the materials from the Philadelphia Battery suggested contradictory conclusions about the nature of his STM deficit. MS's performance on the rhyme probe and digit span tasks and on the word vs. nonword span tasks suggested a normal ability to retain phonological information, but a reduced ability to retain semantic information. In contrast, the observation of a reduced recency effect on the list repetition tasks would imply a phonological retention deficit, according to the IARR model. However, there was no indication of a reduced recency effect in the position probe task.

We believe that these seemingly contradictory findings can be reconciled by assuming that in language processing and short-term memory there is a separation between input and output phonological codes (see Bartha et al., 1994; Howard & Franklin, 1990; Monsell, 1987; Romani, 1992). It appears that MS has difficulty retrieving an output phonological code from semantics, although he is able to access semantics from an input phonological code. That is, although MS demonstrated a severe impairment in naming (which involves accessing an output phonological code from semantics), he shows at most a mild impairment in comprehension (which involves accessing a semantic representation from an input phonological code). On the PPVT (Dunn & Dunn, 1981), MS obtained a standard score of 86, which places him in the low–normal range. On the "which is most closely related?" task described in regard to ML, MS obtained 81% correct. In another task, pictures of animals, vehicles, clothing, and edible plants were presented by category and MS was asked five questions about each pictured object. For example, for the animal category, MS was asked: Does it have fur? Does it eat other animals? Is it found in water? Is it domestic? and Is it dangerous? Therefore, good performance on this task requires relatively detailed semantic knowledge. MS obtained 94% correct overall. Thus, it appears that MS's severe naming deficit could not be attributed to a semantic deficit. The fact that the circumlocutions he produced in naming were often detailed and accurate descriptions of the object is also supportive of this conclusion.

In addition to his ability to use input phonological codes to access semantics, MS appears to have a normal ability to retain input phonological representations, as evidenced by his performance on the rhyme probe task, which does not require output of the list. He can also translate these input phonological codes into an output phonological code for list repetition, as indicated by his good performance on nonword recall. MS's naming and list repetition performance suggest that his ability to access phonology from semantics is highly related to frequency, with preserved access only for the highest-frequency items. For normal subjects, the link between semantics and output phonology can support word recall, making it superior to nonword recall. For MS, this support is not available to aid word recall, particularly for low-frequency items.

Thus, we are arguing that MS retains an input phonological representation and a semantic representation of the items in a list, but lacks the link to output phonological codes. The semantic descriptions and semantic substitutions that were evident in MS's list recall support this conclusion. The fact that these semantic descriptions occurred predominantly on low-frequency items is consistent with the predominance of semantic descriptions in his naming responses for low-frequency items.

The serial position effects that were found for MS can be accounted for on the grounds that MS retains input phonological codes very well, and by the end of the short lists that were presented for repetition, has sufficient phonological information to produce the early list items correctly. However, as list recall proceeds, the phonological information is decaying, and without support from the semantic level to output phonology, there is insufficient phonological information remaining for accurate recall of later list items. (In order to account for greater decay for late than for early list items, one would have to assume that MS recalls the list more slowly than it is presented, or that recall of early list items provides some type of interference in the phonological retrieval of later list items.)

Thus, although MS's performance on the list repetition tasks indicates a phonological deficit, other aspects of performance argue strongly against a general loss of activation of phonological representations. Instead, a separation between the retention of input and output phonological codes needs to be postulated. MS shows a normal ability to retain input phonological codes. However, he shows a decrement in the retention of output phonological codes due to damage to the interconnections between semantics and output phonology.

GENERAL DISCUSSION

A Methodological Issue

For AB and ML, the pattern of performance with respect to the variables of imageability and frequency was consistent with that predicted by the IARR approach for a semantic retention deficit. For MS, the pattern with respect to these variables was consistent with that predicted for a phonological retention deficit (although, as we have noted, only when output phonology was involved). Thus, in accordance with the IARR approach, a selective semantic impairment resulted in reduced primacy and an imageability effect at early list positions. A selective phonological impairment resulted in the reduction of the recency effect and effects of imageability and frequency particularly at later list positions. Thus, these predictions imply that variables (frequency and imageability) affect performance even though the variable is associated with a code that the patient presumably has trouble retaining. For example, patients with semantic deficits show effects of imageability on recall. Although these predictions may seem counterintuitive, there is a fair amount of evidence from the present study and the prior work of Martin and Saffran (1992a,b; Saffran & Martin, 1990) supporting these claims. However, the use of repetition tasks may be somewhat problematic in examining effects of imageability and frequency as a function of serial position.

The problem in using repetition tasks to assess phonological and semantic activation is that it is only possible to observe effects in this task when levels of recall are moderate (i.e. when recall is at ceiling or close to floor, there is little room for observing effects of frequency or imageability). We observed this pattern in our patients. As we noted earlier, it was of interest that AB showed an overall imageability effect on recall of three-word lists, but not on recall of four-word lists. On four-word lists AB's performance dropped substantially from that on three-word lists and, even though there was no effect of imageability overall, *or* at serial positions one, two, or four (where level of recall was at 15%, 15%, and 98%, for the three positions), there was a 20% advantage for high-imageability words at the third list position (where level of recall was at 57%). It should be noted that an imageability effect at this list position would not be predicted by N. Martin and Saffran. It also seemed to be the case for both ML and MS that the observation of frequency and imageability effects was related to level of recall. Although this suggests that the repetition task is not ideally suited to examining phonological and semantic activation, we are not arguing that the patterns observed by N. Martin and Saffran and by ourselves are not meaningful (for example, it is not the case that BOTH frequency and imageability effects emerge with certain levels of recall irrespective of the patient's deficit). However, it would seem important to theoretically motivate the relationship between level of recall and the observation of frequency and imageability effects. Also, tasks utilising other measures (such as priming) may provide a more accurate view of phonological and semantic activation as a function of serial position (as it seems that, in repetition tasks, effects could be hidden by high levels of recall).

Dissociations Between Single Word Processing and List Retention

N. Martin and Saffran (1992b) presented data from several patients that were consistent with their predictions concerning the relationship between language impairment and the observation of effects of frequency and imageability in list repetition. That is, they obtained evidence consistent with the suggestion that a semantic impairment results in reduced primacy and large effects of imageability on the recall of list-initial items. Their model also fared well in its predictions for a phonological impairment—a phonological deficit resulted in decreased recency and large effects of frequency on the recall of list-final items. Furthermore, their data were consistent with the suggestion of a close relationship between quality of language processing and quality of STM processing, in that all their patients displayed severe deficits in single word processing (particularly in naming) and correspondingly severe deficits in STM processing. However, the relatively narrow range of language impairment displayed by their patients made it difficult to examine how language and STM abilities covary. Our data, taken together with Martin and Saffran's data, represent a much wider range of language abilities and permit a more intensive investigation of the relationship between language and short-term memory.

As indicated previously, R. Martin et al. (1994) argued that the capacity of STM is, to some degree, independent of the quality of language processing. In their view, the output of language processes constitute the representations that are stored in short-term memory. If these representations are degraded, then short-term recall will be adversely affected.[2] However, factors other than the quality of language processing may also affect capacity. Capacity for the retention of phonological or semantic codes may be reduced even though processing in these domains is well preserved. In the IARR approach, on the other hand, language and STM processes are viewed as operating over the same set of representational units in an interactive-activation network. This model suggests that short-term memory performance is predicted by the activation and decay parameters that are needed to account for single word processing. However, N. Martin and Saffran (e.g. Saffran, 1990) have acknowledged the need for factors other than quality of language processing, particularly in accounting for the maintenance of order information. None the less, their work has focused on the relationship of language deficits to STM deficits.

Although N. Martin and Saffran's (1992b) data are consistent with their model, the data we have presented provides evidence for dissociations between single word processing and short-term memory. For ML, there was a large discrepancy between performance on span tasks and performance on language processing tasks (as indicated earlier, AB shows this same discrepancy to a lesser extent). ML has a very reduced span but performs at very high levels on single word tasks. These results with AB and ML indicate that a severe language impairment is not necessary to produce a severe STM impairment. Consequently, these results support R. Martin et al.'s contention that factors other than the quality of single word processing affect STM capacity.

On the other hand, striking correspondences between single word processing and short-term memory were observed for MS and for patients reported by N. Martin and Saffran (1992a,b). For MS, the semantic descriptions and word frequency effects that were noted in his picture

---

[2] Martin and Breedin (1992) found that some patients with mild deficits in speech perception nonetheless showed a normal level of STM performance and normal effects of phonological variables. They argued that top-down effects from lexical representations might serve to fill in imperfect perceptual representations, particularly when, as in that study, the words in the memory lists were repeatedly sampled from a small set.

naming were also evident in his list recall. For the patients reported by N. Martin and Saffran (1992b: NC, EMC, & DB) the types of errors that were made in auditory lexical decision and in naming could be used to predict the types of errors and serial position effects that would be observed in list recall. These correspondences provide strong support for the contention that the language codes and links between codes that are involved in single word processing are the representations that are maintained in STM. When these codes are defective or when the association between codes (e.g. between semantics and phonology) are decreased in strength, the effects of these impairments will be revealed in list recall. As discussed previously, the results from MS support the further conclusion that a separation between input and output phonology must be postulated to explain both his single word and STM deficits.

Assuming that the codes maintained in short-term memory are those derived from language processing at all levels, the question then arises as to what other factors must be postulated to account for very restricted STM capacity for patients showing good single word processing. In the earlier discussion of the results for AB and ML, we raised the possibility that an increase in inter-item interference might provide a basis for a dissociation between single word processing and list retention. In the IARR approach, the processing of every word in a list is carried out in the same network. However, because the same network is involved, processing of a subsequent word should wipe out the activation that was present for the previous word. Some type of buffered maintenance of prior list items would seem to be a requirement. With the assumption of buffered maintenance comes the possibility that the representations for the different words maintained in this buffer may interfere with each other. One line of evidence in support of an interference effect was the observation of intrusion errors in the recall of both AB and ML. For AB, we also observed difficulty in initiating recall with list-initial items even though it was found that these items were sometimes still available (which was evidenced by their eventual recall). This suggested that later list items were somehow interfering with recall of earlier list items. Therefore, it seems that failures of recall result from the interaction of two factors: (1) degraded trace representation due to damage to particular levels of the word processing system, and (2) "competition" among traces. Presumably, the nature of the competition process will change as a function of the type of STM impairment involved.

As indicated earlier, Nairne (1990) has proposed a feature model of STM that includes inter-item interference as the mechanism of forgetting. In this model, a list item is simultaneously encoded in primary and secondary memory as traces consisting of modality-dependent (aspects of the stimulus related to the mode of its presentation) and modality-independent (e.g. the meaning of the stimulus remains the same regardless of mode of presentation) features. Primary memory refers to immediate (short-term) memory while secondary memory corresponds to LTM. Recall is based on a matching process in which trace information in primary memory is compared to a relevant set of traces in secondary memory (the search set). Selection of a trace for recall is made on the basis of trace similarity. Although in many models decay is the mechanism of forgetting, the overwriting of trace features is the mechanism proposed by Nairne. If trace $n + 1$ shares a feature value with trace n, then there is some probability that the feature in trace n will be overwritten by the feature in trace $n + 1$. However, it is important to note that trace overwriting will result in a decreased likelihood of correct recall *only* if the overwriting results in increased similarity between this trace and other traces. Furthermore, Nairne suggests that modality-dependent information can interfere only with modality-dependent information, and that modality-independent information can only interfere with modality-independent information. Nairne has shown that a quantitative model incorporating these assumptions can account for an impressive number of findings in the short-term memory literature such as the modality effect, suffix effects, the phonological similarity effect, and grouping effects. Recently, Neath and Nairne (in press) have extended the model to account for the word length effect.

In order to extend Nairne's account to the data presented here, additional assumptions would have to be made. Some distinction would have to be drawn between phonological and semantic features (both of which would be considered modality-independent features) in order to accommodate findings suggesting that some patients appear to lose semantic information but retain phonological information whereas some patients show the reverse. It is undoubtably the case that for word lists composed of randomly selected words, the degree of phonological similarity between items would be higher than the degree of semantic similarity between items. Perhaps this fact would go some way in accounting for differences in the retention of these different codes. Also, some means for realising proactive interference would be needed to account for intrusions from previous lists.[3] Finally, it would have to be assumed that, by some unknown mechanism, brain damage could increase the degree of retroactive and proactive interference between items. It remains to be seen whether all of these assumptions could be incorporated into a quantitative model such as Nairne's, which would produce predictions that fit the patient data. Nonetheless, it is important to point out that an interference-based model of short-term memory exists that accounts for a wide range of data. Further investigation appears warranted

---

[3] Nairne (personal communication) has indicated that one means of predicting proactive interference in his model would be to assume that the long-term memory search set increases as the number of lists presented increases. In Nairne (1990), the long-term memory search set included only those items presented on that trial.

to determine whether such an approach could account for short-term memory deficits for patients who show accurate single word processing.

CONCLUSION

We have compared two approaches to studying short-term memory—that of R. Martin and colleagues and that of N. Martin and Saffran. In the approach used by R. Martin (e.g. R. Martin et al., 1994) evidence for a semantic retention deficit came in the form of the observation of effects of phonologically related variables (e.g. smaller span for phonologically similar than for phonologically dissimiliar word lists), but no effect of lexicality (e.g. little benefit in recall for word over nonword lists). Evidence for a phonological deficit came in the form of the opposite pattern of results. N. Martin and Saffran (1992a,b) have taken a somewhat different approach— they have examined the effects of frequency (presumably reflecting lexical activation) and imageability (presumably reflecting semantic activation) as a function of serial position in list recall. Reduced primacy and effects of imageability at early list positions are taken to be indicative of a semantic impairment, whereas reduced recency and effects of frequency at later list positions are taken to be indicative of a phonological impairment. They have also looked at error responses as a means of assessing the integrity of different levels of representation (phonological, lexical, semantic). We have obtained somewhat converging results in using both of these approaches to examine the nature of STM impairment in two of the three patients reported here: AB, ML. In order to reconcile the results from the two types of materials for patient MS it was necessary to make a distinction between input and output phonological codes. Even more problematic for the IARR model was the observation of very poor STM performance for patients with good single word processing. We view the relationship between language processing and STM performance as more indirect than that proposed by N. Martin and Saffran. Both approaches assume that the codes maintained in STM are those derived from language processing at all levels. However, based on the data reported here, we believe that models of STM must further assume that these representations are held in a buffer prior to recall and that recall proceeds on the basis of a competitive process that results from the interplay between quality of codes at different levels and competition among traces.

ACKNOWLEDGEMENTS

This research was supported by NIH grant no. DC00218 to Randi C. Martin at Rice University. The authors would like to thank Michael Bartha for his help in testing patient MS and Trisha Burton for her assistance in organising the data.

REFERENCES

Baddeley, A.D. (1986). *Working memory.* Oxford: Clarendon Press.

Baddeley, A.D., Thomson, N., & Buchanan, M. (1975). Word length and the structure of short-term memory. *Journal of Verbal Learning and Verbal Behavior, 14,* 575–589.

Bartha, M.C., Lesch, M.F., & Martin, R.C. (1994). Meaning without names: Picture-naming and word-list repetition in anomic aphasia. *Brain and Language, 47,* 332–335.

Brener, R. (1940). An experimental investigation of memory span. *Journal of Experimental Psychology, 26,* 467–482.

Conrad, R. & Hull, A.J. (1964). Information, acoustic confusion, and memory span. *British Journal of Psychology, 55,* 429–432.

Cowan, N., Day, L., Saults, J.S., Keller, T.A., Johnson, T., & Flores, L. (1992). The role of verbal output time in the effects of word length on immediate memory. *Journal of Memory and Language, 31,* 1–17.

Crowder, R.G. (1978). Memory for phonologically uniform lists. *Journal of Verbal Learning and Verbal Behavior, 17,* 73–89.

Dell, G.S. & O'Seaghdha, P.G. (1992). Stages of lexical access in language production. *Cognition, 42,* 287–314.

Dunn, L.M. & Dunn, L.M. (1981). *Peabody Picture Vocabulary Test—Revised.* Circle Pines, MN: American Guidance Service.

Hintzman, D.L. (1965). Classification and aural coding in short-term memory. *Psychonomic Science, 3,* 161–162.

Howard, D., & Franklin, S. (1990). Memory without rehearsal. In G. Vallar & T. Shallice (Eds.), *Neuropsychological impairments of short-term memory,* (pp. 287–318). Cambridge, UK: Cambridge University Press.

Hulme, C., Maughan, S., & Brown, G.D.A. (1991). Memory for familiar and unfamiliar words: Evidence for a long-term memory contribution to short-term span. *Journal of Memory and Language, 30,* 685–701.

Kaplan, E., Goodglass, H., & Weintraub, S. (1976). *Boston Naming Test.* Philadelphia: Lea & Febiger.

Luce, P.A., Feustel, T.C., & Pisoni, D.B. (1983). Capacity demands in short-term memory for synthetic and natural speech. *Human Factors, 25,* 17–32.

Mackworth, J.F. (1963). The duration of the visual image. *Canadian Journal of Psychology, 17,* 62–81.

Martin, N., Dell, G.S., Saffran, E.M., & Schwartz, M.F. (1994). Origins of paraphasias in deep dysphasia. Testing the consequences of a decay impairment to an interactive spreading activation model of lexical retrieval. *Brain and Language, 47,* 609–660.

Martin, N., & Saffran, E.M. (1992a). A computational account of deep dysphasia: Evidence from a single case study. *Brain and Language, 43,* 240–274.

Martin, N., & Saffran, E.M. (1992b). *Temporal effects on repetition: Evidence for common processes mediating lexical retrieval and verbal STM.* Paper presented at the Academy of Aphasia, Toronto, October.

Martin, R.C. (1993). Short term memory and sentence processing: Evidence from neuropsychology. *Memory and Cognition, 21,* 176–183.

Martin, R.C., & Breedin, S. (1992). Dissociations between speech perception and phonological short-term memory deficits. *Cognitive Neuropsychology, 9*(6), 509–534.

Martin, R.C., Shelton, J., & Yaffee, L.S. (1994). Language processing and working memory: Neuropsychological evidence for separate phonological and semantic capacities. *Journal of Memory and Language, 33,* 83–111.

Monsell, S. (1987). On the relation between lexical input and output pathways for speech. In A. Allport, C. MacKay, W. Prinz, & E. Scheerer (Eds.), *Language perception and production:*

Relationships between listening, speaking, reading and writing, (pp. 273–311). Orlando, FL: Academic Press.

Nairne, J.S. (1990). A feature model of immediate memory. *Memory & Cognition, 18*, 251–269.

Neath, I., & Nairne, J.S. (in press.). Word-length effects in immediate memory: Overwriting trace decay theory. *Psychonomic Bulletin & Review.*

Romani, C. (1992). Are there distinct output buffers? Evidence from a patient with an impaired output buffer. *Journal of Language and Cognitive Processes, 7*, 131–162.

Saffran, E.M. (1990). Short-term memory impairment and language processing. In A. Caramazza (Ed.), *Cognitive neuropsychology and neurolinguistics: Advances in models of cognitive function and impairment* (pp. 137–168). Hillsdale, NJ: Lawrence Erlbaum Associates Inc.

Saffran, E.M., & Martin, N. (1990). Neuropsychological evidence for lexical involvement in short-term memory. In G. Vallar & T. Shallice (Eds.), *Neuropsychological impairments of short-term memory*, (pp. 428–447). London: Cambridge University Press.

Saffran, E.M., Schwartz, M.F., Linebarger, M., & Bochetto, P. (1989). *The Philadelphia Comprehension Battery*, [unpublished].

Schweickert, R. & Boruff, B. (1986). Short-term memory capacity: Magic number or magic spell? *Journal of Experimental Psychology: Learning, Memory, and Cognition, 12*, 419–425.

Sperling, G., & Speelman, R.G. (1970). Acoustic similarity and auditory short-term memory. In D.A. Norman (Ed.), *Models of human memory*, (pp. 151–202). New York: Academic Press.

Watkins, O.C., & Watkins, M.J. (1977). Serial recall and the modality effect. *Journal of Experimental Psychology: Human Learning and Memory, 3*, 712–718.

Wickelgren, W.A. (1966). Distinctive features and errors in short-term memory for English consonants. *Journal of the Acoustical Society of America, 39*, 388–398.

8

Auditory short-term memory and the perception of speech

Clive Frankish
University of Bristol, UK

INTRODUCTION

In recent years, a great deal of progress has been made in understanding the relationship between short-term memory functions and language processing. It has become apparent that both are highly dependent on the creation, organisation, and maintenance of phonological representations. In children, the ability to perform STM tasks that require phonological skills are good predictors of language development, as indexed by vocabulary scores or reading ability (Gathercole & Baddeley, 1993). Neuropsychological evidence also underlines this linkage, with many reported cases in which impairment of language functions are associated with STM deficits.

The working memory model proposed by Baddeley and Hitch (1974) includes a dedicated subsystem which is responsible for maintaining phonological information in STM. Most of the evidence for the existence and characteristics of this "phonological loop" has come from experiments using the serial recall paradigm. The ability to reproduce a sequence of unrelated words immediately after presentation is heavily dependent on the operation of the phonological loop. If this system is effectively disabled by articulatory suppression, or by using words with highly confusable phonological representations, recall performance is severely curtailed.

Within this framework, it is often tacitly assumed that a common phonological code is used for the representation of both spoken and written language in STM. When a word is read or an object named, the

179

corresponding phonological code is activated and under normal circumstances can be entered into the phonological store. For spoken words,
Baddeley, Lewis, and Vallar (1984) argued that phonological codes are
directly created during the perception of speech, and that access of these
codes to the phonological store is direct and obligatory. Once it is
established in the phonological store, there are no characteristics of the
resulting memory representation that are source-dependent. This does not
exclude the possibility that there are *additional* memory systems associated
with particular sensory channels. There is no reason why the working
memory model should not be extended to include modality-specific sensory
stores. However, the role of these systems has largely been overlooked or
marginalised in this theoretical analysis of short-term memory and language
functions.

In this chapter I shall review the some of the evidence that modality-
specific auditory storage makes an important contribution to the perception
and immediate recall of spoken language. Two themes will be developed.
The first and major theme is that there is an auditory memory subsystem
that is specifically involved in the storage of speechlike stimuli. Within this
system, speech sounds are represented in terms of acoustic features, rather
than modality-independent phonological codes. The second theme concerns
the way in which short-term memory function is influenced by suprasegmental features of the speech signal. These are the variations in pitch and
timing that make up the intonation patterns of natural speech; features that
have no direct visual equivalent in written language. It is now apparent that
these acoustic cues are very effective in supporting immediate memory for
sequences of spoken words. Taken together, these two lines of evidence
indicate the extent to which modality-specific auditory memory might be
involved in the interpretation of spoken language.

ECHOIC STORAGE

Divided Attention Studies

The existence of a relatively peripheral auditory store was initially suggested
by Broadbent (1958), to account for data from studies of selective listening
and dichotic memory. These studies provided strong evidence that the
perception of spoken messages is mediated by a perceptual system that is only
capable of handling one message at a time. However, it was also apparent that
if two short messages were presented simultaneously, responses could be
made to both. Broadbent argued that a serial processing mechanism can deal
with two simultaneously presented spoken messages by first attending to one,
and then subsequently retrieving the other from a preattentive auditory store.
Access to this store was seen to be obligatory; i.e. all auditory inputs are
initially registered at this level, regardless of attentional bias.

Broadbent's account of dichotic memory performance has not been substantially revised or improved on, and subsequent multistore models of memory (e.g. Atkinson & Shiffrin, 1968) retained the notion of "sensory registers" in which information from the senses is briefly preserved. Neisser (1967) used the term "echoic memory" to describe the auditory register. This is a term that nicely captures people's subjective experience of auditory persistence, and for this reason will be used in the current discussion.

The dichotic memory paradigm is a useful tool for investigating echoic storage. When subjects are instructed to attend to a sequence of words arriving at a specified ear and to recall them first, these items are perceived and recalled in much the same way as a single sequence. Memory performance is based on the post-perceptual short-term memory systems described in the working memory model. As the sequences are short, they can generally be recalled with very few errors. In contrast, memory for unattended items is much poorer. The fact that these items can be recalled at all is evidence for the existence of echoic memory, but the low level of performance suggests that this system is relatively inefficient. Memory for the unattended sequence is also strongly dependent on serial position. Subjects almost always report the last item correctly, but there is a steep decline in performance at earlier positions (e.g. Bryden, 1971). This pattern of performance seems to be a fundamental characteristic of echoic memory. A similar recall advantage for the final item in the attended sequence can also be explained by supposing that memory performance is based on the combination of information from echoic traces and from working memory.

The distinction between echoic storage and post-perceptual memory systems can also be demonstrated by changing the order in which items are recalled. In the working memory model, it is supposed that information in the phonological store decays rapidly, but can be refreshed via the articulatory loop. This process can be inhibited by requiring subjects to engage in some irrelevant articulatory activity, such as reciting "the the the..." This pre-emptive use of the articulatory loop severely impairs immediate recall performance (Baddeley & Hitch, 1974). A related process presumably occurs during the recall phase of the serial recall task. "Output interference" occurs when the process of writing or speaking early list items prevents maintenance of information in the phonological store. All other things being equal, items appearing later in the recall attempt are therefore less likely to be correct.

In the dichotic memory paradigm, this pattern of results is found for attended items. Bryden (1971) instructed subjects to attend to items on one ear, and then to report either the attended or unattended items first. Attended items were reported more accurately if they were recalled first, showing clear effects of output interference. However, unattended items were recalled equally well, whether reported first or second. This is precisely what we would expect if these items are retrieved from echoic storage, and are thus unaffected by processes occurring within the phonological subsystems of working memory.

Modality and Suffix Effects in Serial Recall

Echoic memory can make a significant contribution to immediate memory performance in the dichotic memory task. However, this is a rather artificial situation in which working memory is deliberately overloaded. Immediate memory is more usually tested by asking subjects to reproduce a single, much longer sequence of items in strict serial order. When presentation rates are close to the rates of relaxed natural speech, subjects are able to attend fully to the stimulus items, and the resources of working memory can be fully utilised. Echoic memory makes only a limited contribution to memory performance, although that contribution is clearly marked. In serial recall, error rates tend to increase over successive serial positions, regardless of presentation modality. However, subjects can almost always recall the final item in a spoken list; a phenomenon that is conveniently described as "auditory recency". The corresponding recency effect for visually presented lists is small or non-existent (Conrad & Hull, 1968).

Crowder and Morton (1969) interpreted the modality effect in serial recall in terms that are largely consistent with the analysis offered here. They began with the assumption that for verbal stimuli, auditory and visual inputs converge at the lexical level. Recognition of a written or spoken word affords access to a common set of phonological features, thus providing a basis for representation in postcategorical memory systems. As this representation is modality-independent, it follows that the advantage for auditory as compared with visual stimuli must reflect processes occurring at an earlier stage in perception. The simplest interpretation of the evidence then available was that auditory recency reflects the operation of a limited-capacity peripheral auditory store, which Crowder and Morton (1969) termed "precategorical acoustic storage" (PAS).

If memory functions are described purely in terms of a storage metaphor, then PAS can be regarded as an auditory input buffer. In a sequence of spoken words, each word enters the buffer, and in so doing overwrites any existing traces in this store. At the end of the sequence, all except the final item have been overwritten in this way. Auditory recency is explained if these PAS traces of the final item survive long enough for the information to be used in immediate recall. PAS also provided a straightforward account of the stimulus suffix effect. This is the finding that auditory recency is largely eliminated if the stimulus sequence is immediately followed by a single redundant word or syllable that subjects are instructed to ignore (Crowder,

1967). Because access to PAS is obligatory, the suffix automatically overwrites traces of the final list item that would normally give rise to auditory recency.

Summary: Pre- and Postcategorical Representations of Speech in STM

Although there are important differences in matters of detail, these accounts of auditory short-term memory have a great deal in common with each other, and with more recent models of working memory. There is general agreement that verbal stimuli can be represented in post-perceptual short-term memory in a phonological code that is independent of input modality. At the same time, there is also good evidence for retrieval of auditory information from an echoic store. However, it is unclear how a system that makes such an apparently localised and limited contribution to immediate memory could play a significant role in language processing. We might thus conclude, as Haber (1983) did in the case of iconic memory, that this is a laboratory curiosity which is of no more than marginal significance. If so, there would be little point in extending current models of working memory to take account of echoic storage. To do so would divert attention from the areas in which this model has been most successful, without extending its explanatory power in any significant way. One aim of the present chapter is to present some evidence that indicates that such a conclusion would be premature.

LINKS BETWEEN ECHOIC MEMORY AND SPEECH PERCEPTION

The idea that immediate recall of auditory sequences is partly supported by retrieval from an acoustic buffer has not gone unchallenged. Subsequent research has revealed that auditory recency is a more complex phenomenon than was originally suggested by Crowder and Morton (1969). There are two major difficulties for the PAS model. The first is that some non-auditory stimuli can produce strong recency effects in serial recall. This is particularly true of lip-read speech, which as a purely visual stimulus should not gain access to an acoustic store. The second is that some auditory stimuli produce strong recency effects, while others do not. For example, vowel sounds seem to be better represented in echoic memory than either consonants or nonspeech sounds. However, although these findings cannot be explained in terms of a simple acoustic buffer store, they do not provide any compelling reason to abandon the central hypothesis that auditory recency reflects the availability of information in a functionally distinct memory system. By exploring the boundary conditions for auditory recency, we can begin to understand the nature of this system, and its relationship to other aspects of auditory perception. On the whole, the evidence seems to point to a close link with processes involved in speech perception.

Recency Effects for Lip-read and Mouthed Speech

One reason for supposing that the phenomenon of auditory recency is theoretically significant is that it allows us to distinguish between two types of speech-related code in short-term memory. As we have seen, there is ample evidence that immediate serial recall of verbal sequences is mediated by phonological codes, regardless of whether the initial presentation is auditory or visual. However, there is no evidence that at the end of a sequence, the last phonological code to be created has any special status. Even when subjects are encouraged to generate vivid auditory images of visually presented items being read in a familiar voice, there is no sign of auditory recency (Nairne & Pusen, 1984). Unsuccessful attempts have also been made to produce enhanced recency by increasing the visual distinctiveness of the final list item by changes in colour, location, or temporal characteristics (e.g. Crowder, 1986; McDowd & Madigan, 1991; LeCompte, 1992). Finally, auditory recency is not diminished when a spoken list is followed by a visual suffix, even when subjects are required to respond to it by writing or by generating an auditory image (Morton & Holloway, 1970; Nairne & Pusen, 1984). All these findings reinforce the view that perception of a spoken word creates a memory representation with attributes that cannot be reproduced as a result of reading a written word, or through auditory imagery. According to the PAS hypothesis, the critical difference is that the sounds of speech are additionally held in an acoustic buffer store.

One major difficulty for this view is that strong recency effects are also obtained in experiments where hearing subjects are required to lip-read items from a silent video of a speakers face (Campbell & Dodd, 1980; Greene & Crowder, 1984; de Gelder & Vroomen, 1992). Lip-read and auditory recency apparently share a common basis, as auditory recency is reduced by a lip-read suffix, and vice versa. This contrasts with the situation for spoken and written stimuli, where cross-modal effects are not found. Results similar to those for lip-reading are also obtained when list items are presented in written form, but subjects are instructed to mouthe each item silently as it is presented (Greene & Crowder, 1984; Nairne & Walters, 1983; Turner et al., 1987). Once again, cross-modal suffix effects indicate a common basis for recency in memory for heard and mouthed stimuli.

Although we are not yet in a position to give a full account of the relationship between listening, lip-reading, and mouthing, there is an emerging consensus that they are all linked in some way to the processes involved in perceiving speech (e.g. Campbell, 1990; Crowder, 1983; de

Gelder & Vroomen, 1992, 1994; Greene & Crowder, 1984). The data from short-term memory experiments fit well with theories of speech processing that distinguish between auditory and phonetic modes of perceiving auditory events. The motor theory of speech perception proposes that perception in the "speech mode" is closely linked to the processes involved in speech production (Liberman & Mattingly, 1985). Identification of speech sounds is achieved by a specialised phonetic processor which interprets acoustic features as cues that signal articulatory gestures made by the speaker. One piece of evidence that supports this theory is the fact that speech perception can be influenced by direct visual perception of articulatory gestures through lip-reading. The effects of combining visual and auditory cues can be seen both in improved perception of degraded speech (Breeuwer & Plomp, 1984), and in the perceptual distortions that occur when auditory and visual cues conflict (McDonald & McGurk, 1978).

If the "auditory" recency obtained with speech stimuli is identified with processes occurring in a phonetic module, the results from lip-read and mouthed stimuli no longer seem quite so problematic. The explicit link to perceptual mechanisms is also more in keeping with a process view of memory (Crowder, 1993). In its original version, the PAS hypothesis could be regarded as a way of modelling the persistence of activation in perceptual mechanisms involved in the processing of auditory events. The evidence from lip-reading and mouthing compels us to take a rather broader view of auditory perception, but the explanation of recency phenomena in serial recall remains essentially the same. Recency is a consequence of perceptual processes occurring in a system that is not involved in the derivation of phonology from print.

AUDITORY RECENCY AND THE SPEECH/ NONSPEECH DISTINCTION

The second major problem for theories of acoustic buffer storage is that strong recency is not always a feature of memory for sequences of auditory stimuli. If there is an acoustic buffer store, we might expect that it would retain information about any type of auditory event. This turns out not to be the case; auditory recency is very much dependent on the nature of the items being remembered. If anything, the strong recency effect found with spoken digit lists is an exception, rather than a general rule. Some types of stimuli give rise to intermediate levels of recency, whereas for others, serial position curves resemble those normally obtained with visual presentation. Two distinctions are important in determining whether sounds are retained in echoic memory. For speech, it seems that echoic traces are much stronger for vowels than for consonants. However, the overriding distinction is between speech and nonspeech sounds; there is no evidence for strong auditory recency in recall of sounds other than speech. Taken together, these observations provide further evidence of a relationship between echoic memory and the phonetic processor.

Vowels vs. Consonants in Echoic Memory

One reason for postulating the existence of a separate phonetic processor is that many speech sounds are categorically perceived. This is particularly true of stop consonants, such as /b/, /d/, and /g/. For these sounds, there are critical acoustic variations which listeners are unable to detect unless they cause a shift in phonemic classification. This is an essential characteristic of speech perception which enables us to disregard allophonic variation; i.e. changes in the acoustic realisation of a particular phoneme according to the articulatory context in which it is produced. In fact, for speech sounds that are categorically perceived, it seems that listeners *cannot* discriminate these within-category changes in acoustic parameters. Liberman and Mattingly (1985) have interpreted these findings as evidence that the perceptual response of the speech processor is purely phonemic.

There are correspondences between speech perception and serial recall performance that can be neatly explained in terms of the characteristics of echoic memory. Categorical perception has been demonstrated for stop consonants, but not for vowel sounds (Fry, Abramson, Eimas, & Liberman, 1962) unless these are very brief (Pisoni, 1971). When immediate memory is tested with sequences of CV syllables distinguished only in terms of stop consonants (e.g. /ba/, /da/, /ga/), modality and suffix effects are absent. However, when lists consist of items differing in vowel sounds (e.g. /ba/, /bi/, /bu/) both auditory recency and suffix effects are found (Cole, 1973; Crowder, 1971; de Gelder & Vroomen, 1994). Both of these effects are stronger for long than for short vowels (Crowder, 1973).

These correspondences are not surprising. The ABX procedure used for investigating categorical perception of speech sounds is one that relies heavily on short-term memory. On each trial, subjects hear a sequence of three sounds; A and B are the stimuli whose discriminability is being tested, and X is a probe that subjects must identify as either A or B. Categorical perception is demonstrated when subjects' ability to do this is apparently based entirely on the phonetic labels they assign to the test pair. We can explain why this should happen for consonants but not for vowels in terms of differences in short-term memory functions. In the ABX procedure, perception of the test pair results in the creation of both an echoic trace and a phonological code. If consonants are poorly represented in echoic memory, as the serial recall studies indicate, then discrimination must be based on phonological codes. For test pairs that are identically categorised, there is no longer any basis for discrimination.

However, if two extended vowel sounds are identically categorised, discrimination can still be achieved by referring to a relatively intact echoic trace. According to this analysis, differences in the discrimination functions for consonants and vowels are the result of differences in the extent to which acoustic cues underlying the perception of these speech sounds are preserved in an echoic store.

Although this account has been presented in terms of a vowel/consonant contrast, there is no evidence that the linguistic dimension is intrinsically significant. It seems more plausible that these results should be explained in terms of acoustic distinctiveness. This was the position taken by Darwin and Baddeley (1974), who found modest auditory recency in an immediate recall task when list items contained highly discriminable consonants (*ag, am, ash*). They also showed that the amount of recency obtained for vowel-varying lists depends on their acoustic similarity, defined in terms of differences in first and second formant frequencies. Larger recency and suffix effects were obtained for lists composed of vowels that were widely separated in the F1/F2 vowel space than for those that were closer together. This is what we would expect if auditory recency is based on a somewhat degraded representation in an echoic store. If the stimulus set consists of highly discriminable items, correct identification will be possible even when some of the acoustic detail has been lost.

In general, it is likely that features other than formant characteristics will contribute to acoustic distinctiveness. In most of the memory studies using CV or VC syllables, serial position data have showed only modest recency effects. This might be a consequence of the unfamiliar stimuli used, or the limited vocabulary size (three items in most cases). However, another characteristic of these studies is that most have used synthesised speech stimuli. This has the advantage of improving experimental control, but also has the effect of eliminating much of the acoustic variability present in natural utterances. This includes differences in duration, envelope characteristics, vocal instability, and so on. This variability contributes to the acoustic distinctiveness of naturally spoken lists of words or digits, but is largely absent from most of the synthesised utterances used in serial recall experiments.

Speech vs. Nonspeech in Echoic Memory

There is as yet no evidence for strong auditory recency in serial recall of nonspeech sounds. For example, when subjects recall a sequence of familiar environmental sounds such as a siren or a ringing telephone, recency is much less pronounced than when the stimuli are the corresponding spoken labels *siren, telephone,* etc. (Rowe & Cake, 1977; Rowe & Rowe, 1976). More recently, the contrast between speech and nonspeech stimuli has been thoroughly explored in a series of experiments by Surprenant, Pitt, and Crowder (1993). One hypothesis specifically tested in this study was that recency might be determined by the familiarity or discriminability of the stimulus items. This hypothesis was not supported; there was no sign of strong recency for a variety of nonspeech sounds that should have been both familiar and discriminable. In one experiment, lists were constructed from severely degraded tokens of the digits one to four that subjects were trained to label either as the appropriate digits, or as environmental sounds. In neither condition was there a substantial recency effect. These sounds were so degraded that they could no longer be identified as speech, and the attachment of speech or nonspeech labels made little difference to memory performance. Nor was there a substantial recency effect when musically trained subjects recalled sequences of piano notes, even when these were restricted to a small subset of widely spaced, highly discriminable pitches. In another experiment, both meaningfulness and discriminability were further enhanced by using notes played on a violin or piano, providing contrasts in timbre as well as pitch. Despite this, recency was no stronger when musically trained subjects recalled the sequences in terms of the names of the instruments.

In sharp contrast to these results, Surprenant et al. (1993) did find strong auditory recency effects when spoken digits were used as list items. When each list included digits recorded in the voices of four different speakers, serial position data were almost identical for conditions in which subjects recalled the sequence of digits, or the sequence of voices. Both showed the strong auditory recency that is typical of digit recall. One surprising finding was that when subjects recalled the sequence of voices, there was also a strong recency effect for lists that consisted solely of the digit "one" spoken in the four different voices.

Some of these results have been replicated and extended in experiments conducted by myself and a student, Julia Bishop. The first of these was designed to clarify the status of the speech/nonspeech distinction. We were particularly intrigued by the fact that Surprenant et al. (1993) reported strong recency when subjects recalled the sequence of voices when lists consisted of phonemically identical items, but not when they recalled sequences of musical pitches. In the former experiment, two of the speakers were male, and two were female. Although we have no further information about differences in vocal characteristics of these speakers, it is likely that voice pitch would be a reliable discriminative cue. On the other hand, the experiments with musical stimuli suggest that pitch information is not retained in echoic memory. There is a possible conflict here that might be resolved if echoic traces are established only for stimuli that are perceived as speech. For these sounds there may well be a memory representation that preserves acoustic parameters of the speech signal, including pitch. If so, we might find strong recency in memory for pitch sequences, provided that the stimulus items are perceived as speech.

To test this hypothesis we used a speech synthesiser to generate lists of phonemically identical syllables, spoken at four clearly discriminable pitches (65, 87, 117, and 156Hz.) This is a range of just over an octave, corresponding to the notes C, F, **Bb**, and Eb. Two sets of stimuli were generated; one consisting of the vowel sound "ah", the other of the syllable "dah". One reason for this was that pure vowel sounds generated by the synthesiser could be interpreted either as speech or nonspeech. However, the formant transitions in the "dah" sound gave it an unambiguously speechlike quality. These stimuli were used to generate six-item lists, in which two pitches occurred once and two occurred twice. Within a list, all the items were phonemically identical, and there were equal numbers of "ah" and "dah" lists. The presentation rate was one second/item.

Fourteen subjects were trained to label the four pitches with the numbers 1–4, with 1 representing the lowest pitch. Training with individually presented stimulus items was continued until a test criterion of correct identification of 10 consecutive stimuli was achieved. This was followed by a series of 12 practice trials with the immediate recall task, and then 36 experimental trials. Recall was written, using the digit codes to record the pitch sequence.

The results of this experiment were quite clear; there were no recency effects for either type of stimulus item (Fig. 8.1a). The overall level of performance was the same for "ah" and "dah" lists [$F(1,13) = 0.02$]. There was a significant interaction of stimulus type with serial position [$F(5,65) = 2.54$, $P < 0.05$], but it would be difficult to interpret this as a difference in recency. If recency is defined in relative terms as the difference in error rates at serial positions 5 and 6, then neither condition showed any recency at all; there were no significant differences in errors at these two positions, either for the "ah" [$t(13) = 0.12$] or "dah" [$t(13) = 0.55$] stimuli. Nor was there a significant difference when these measures were compared across conditions [$t(13) = 0.46$].

The results obtained by Surprenant et al. (1993) when subjects recalled speaker identities cannot therefore be explained in terms of retention of information about voice pitch. Recall of pitch sequences does not give rise to auditory recency, even when the stimuli are perceived as speech. However, there is still one procedural difference to be explored. In the original experiment, the stimuli were words; the digit "one" in each of the four voices, whereas we used single vowel sounds and CV syllables. We therefore conducted a second experiment to see whether we could reproduce the original result with these simpler, non-lexical items.

Digitised recordings were made of four speakers saying the syllable "dah". Two were male, and two female, and the mean pitches of the voices

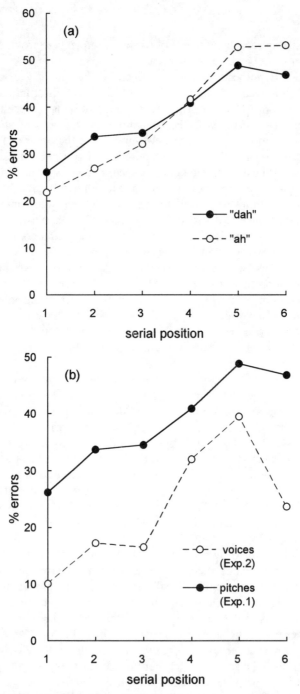

FIG. 8.1. Serial position data, (a) for recall of pitch sequences, and (b) comparing recall of voice and pitch sequences.

were measured at 85, 111, 185, and 225Hz. Training and test procedures were essentially the same as for the first experiment, with speakers numbered 1–4 for response purposes. Nineteen subjects each recalled a total of 36 experimental lists, with items presented at a rate of one per second.

Serial position data from this experiment are shown in Fig. 8.1b, together with the data from the "dah" condition from the previous experiment. For the naturally spoken "dah" stimuli, there is a modest but unmistakable recency effect, with a significant difference in error rates at positions 5 and 6 [$t(18) = 3.14$, $P < 0.01$]. Overall memory performance was also better for the naturally spoken than for the synthesised "dah" sequences [$t(31) = 3.23$, $P < 0.01$].

We were thus able to reproduce the findings reported by Surprenant et al. (1993), but with a more specific contrast between the conditions in which subjects recalled either pitches or voices of spoken items. The data shown in Fig. 8.1b were obtained using stimuli that were phonemically identical within and between conditions. Differences in memory performance must therefore be a direct consequence of differences in the acoustic rather than phonetic cues that distinguished items within the two stimulus sets. In terms of perceptual classification, both sets of stimuli were highly discriminable; subjects had little difficulty in learning to label them correctly, although the acoustic cues on which this labelling was based were different in the two cases. Closer examination of these acoustic differences suggests that these findings are quite consistent with the view that speech is represented in echoic memory primarily in terms of the acoustic features used for phonetic classification.

A THEORETICAL INTERPRETATION: ECHOIC MEMORY AND THE EXTRACTION OF SPEECH CUES

The results of these experiments with speech and nonspeech stimuli are important because they clearly define some of the boundary conditions for echoic memory. There is no evidence of strong auditory recency effects in serial recall of nonspeech sounds, even for stimuli that are meaningful, familiar, and distinctive. Robust recency effects are normally found when the stimuli are spoken words. Within the category of speech sounds, vowels are better represented in echoic memory than consonants, although these differences should perhaps be identified with differences in acoustic distinctiveness rather than phonemic category. The importance of acoustic rather than phonemic properties is further supported by data that show moderate recency effects when subjects recall the sequence of speakers who utter a series of phonemically identical stimuli. However, distinctiveness of acoustic cues is not a sufficient condition for effective retrieval from echoic memory. There is no evidence that echoic storage contributes to immediate recall of phonemically identical items synthesised at clearly discriminable pitches.

This rather complex set of results falls into a pattern that clearly identifies echoic memory with processes occurring during the early stages of speech processing. One essential prerequisite for the identification of phonetic segments is a perceptual mechanism capable of analysing spectral characteristics of the speech signal. Steady-state vowels can be identified by determining the frequencies of the first two or three formants, which appear as peaks in the spectral envelope. The acoustic cues for transients such as stop consonants are less well understood, but may include features derived from the overall shape of the spectrum (Stevens & Blumstein, 1981). Whatever the exact details, it is clear that interpretation of the speech signal requires a perceptual mechanism that is capable of a relatively complex acoustic analysis that includes the identification of critical spectral features.

The phonetic processor itself can be modelled as a neural network in which the output layer corresponds to the set of phonemes in the listener's language. The input layer would consist of a set of feature units, some of which are activated by the outputs of lower-level auditory processes that derive spectral features. There will also be units at this level that respond to other acoustic properties of the speech signal which contribute to the identification of phonetic segments. These include, for example, features of the amplitude envelope, which can help distinguish between voiced and unvoiced consonants. Other input units might be activated by speech-related perceptual processes, such as visual or proprioceptive tracking of articulatory movements.

This general outline is consistent with our current understanding of the development of speech perception in infancy. The basic requirements for a phonetic processor seem to be present more or less at birth. Studies of speech perception in very young infants (and also animals; e.g. Kuhl & Miller, 1978) have demonstrated that the auditory system naturally functions in a way that causes speech sounds to be partitioned into categories (Eimas, Siqueland, Jusczyk, & Vigorito, 1971; Jusczyk, 1985). This partitioning is initially based on a preliminary analysis of the acoustic signal during which various parameters, including spectral characteristics, are derived. In children, the perceptual response is modified as a result of early exposure to the child's native language, until it becomes sensitive only to those combinations of features that are linguistically significant (Werker & Tees, 1984). In terms of the network model, it is presumably at this stage that the final mappings between input and output layers are established. When this happens, the infant still responds to the same acoustic information, but this is now being processed in a way that takes into account the phonological structure of the language that is being learned.

Within this framework, we can model the representation of speech sounds in echoic memory in terms of patterns of activation in the input layer of the phonetic processor. This interpretation would account for the restriction of echoic memory phenomena to stimuli that are perceived as speech. It would also account for the failure to find echoic memory for voice pitch. In the frequency analysis of acoustic stimuli, the critical information for phoneme identification consists of features in the spectral envelope, such as the peaks that correspond to formant frequencies. If the echoic trace records only these broad-band spectral characteristics, this would account for the fact that vowel identity is recoverable, but fundamental frequency (i.e. pitch) is not.

This point is illustrated in Fig. 8.2, which shows idealised frequency spectra for two different vowel sounds, spoken at two pitches. A listener would have no difficulty in discriminating between any two of these sounds

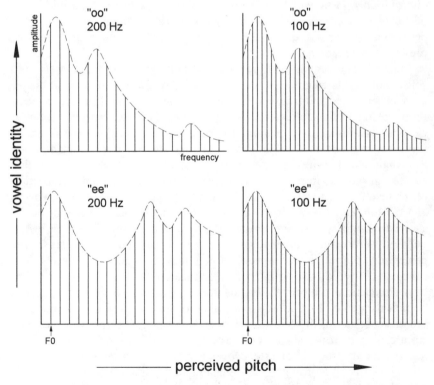

FIG. 8.2. Speech spectograms illustrating vowel sounds that differ either in fundamental frequency or spectral envelope.

on the basis of pitch, or vowel identity, or both. However, these two types of discrimination are based on quite different perceptual processes. In the spectrum of a steady-state vowel sound, the pitch of the speaker's voice determines the harmonic spacing, but not the shape of the spectral envelope. For perceptual units tuned to respond to spectral features, pitch is therefore not a salient characteristic. So far as the phonetic processor is concerned, the input vectors for the syllable "dah" spoken at two clearly discriminable pitches could be identical. On the other hand, speaker identity will be signalled by changes in a range of acoustic parameters, including spectral characteristics. Input vectors for the same syllable uttered by two different speakers could therefore be significantly different. Our experiments with synthesised and naturally spoken syllables support the hypothesis that echoic memory reflects these perceptual distinctions. This analysis also highlights the deficiencies of theories that explain auditory recency in terms of the distinctiveness or discriminability of the stimuli (e.g. Glenberg & Swanson, 1986; Nairne, 1988). Effective retrieval from memory clearly requires that memory representations of stimulus items should be discriminable. However, we cannot necessarily predict the discriminability of items in memory on the basis of physical distinctiveness, or even perceptual performance, as the relevant perceptual cues may not be preserved in the memory trace.

Finally, there is the difference in echoic memory for vowels and consonants. This might be more appropriately described as a difference between sustained and transient stimuli, as it can again be explained in terms of purely acoustic characteristics. The generally poor representation of consonants implies that memory for patterns of activity in the phonetic processor is determined by the length of time for which a particular input was maintained. Although the network may be capable of producing perceptual outputs in response to transient events, the temporal resolution of the resulting memory trace may be limited. The contrast between vowels and consonants also confirms that although echoic memory is specifically associated with speech perception, it is a record of input activity in the phonetic processor, rather than the perceptual output. Because the perceptual output is a sequence of phonetic segments, vowels and consonants should have equal status at this level.

A connectionist approach that incorporates these general principles has been developed by McClelland and Elman (1986). In the TRACE model of speech recognition, there is a layer of input units that respond to acoustic features of the speech signal. One crucial aspect of the model is that these input units are traces that extend over periods of time that might include several words. According to McClelland and Elman (1986, p.167), this means that "the distinction between perception and (primary) memory is completely blurred since the percept is unfolding in the same structures that serve as working memory". The model thus incorporates a model of echoic memory, albeit one based on a set of acoustic features that may not have a well established psychoacoustic basis. The TRACE model also assumes that activity in feature-level units can be modified by feedback from the phoneme level, implying that an incomplete echoic trace could be enhanced as a result of top-down activation. However, this seems less likely in the light of evidence from the following series of experiments, which suggests that the quality of the echoic trace is entirely determined by the acoustic properties of the sensory input.

DIRECT EVIDENCE FOR ACOUSTIC CODING IN ECHOIC MEMORY

The view taken here is that for heard speech the echoic trace is derived directly from acoustic characteristics of the speech signal which are used for identifying phonemes. Although there is now a substantial amount of evidence to support this theoretical analysis, much of this evidence is indirect. It would perhaps be more convincing if we could demonstrate directly that the perceptual attributes of a spoken word are reproduced in the echoic trace. I believe that this has now been demonstrated in some of our recent experiments with degraded speech stimuli.

One of the original aims of these experiments was to draw a distinction between speech-like representations that are constructed in a postcategorical phonological store, and those that are fully determined by the sensory input. The distinction can be phenomenologically unclear in situations where speech perception is aided by top-down processing. One example is the phoneme restoration effect, where listeners are unable to identify precisely which segment of a spoken sentence has been deleted and replaced with an extraneous sound (Warren, 1970). This is a perceptual illusion that occurs because subjects are unable to make correct source attributions for individual phonemes. A similar illusion has been reported for cases in which a degraded speech signal is presented simultaneously with the corresponding written form. Frost, Repp, and Katz (1989) found that when severely degraded speech was accompanied by printed versions of the spoken words, subjects reported that the speech was quite intelligible. However, when the printed word was also degraded, subjects commented that they could not hear any speech at all in the auditory input. Subjects' erroneous judgements of speech intelligibility in the first case again seem to be due to a failure in source monitoring.

These findings suggest a simple experiment. If the addition of a printed text allows subjects to "hear" a spoken word that is presented in severely degraded form, will the echoic trace reflect the acoustic reality or the subjective experience? The former would be consistent with the notion of an acoustic buffer, whereas the latter would at the very least suggest a processing stage that involves some top-down activation.

In one such experiment, subjects recalled nine-digit lists with synchronised presentation of each item as a spoken word and as a visual display of the corresponding Arabic numeral. Both visual and auditory signals were computer-controlled to ensure exact synchronisation. The spoken digits were recorded by a female speaker, at a mean pitch of 210Hz, and in one condition these were presented in undegraded form. In a second condition, the digits were degraded by band-pass filtering at 250Hz. For each condition, a total of 20 subjects recalled a total of 36 digit sequences, presented at a rate of 0.6 second/item, using written recall. The digit sequences were constructed from Latin squares, so that for each condition, each digit appeared equally often in each serial position. The order of conditions was randomised within the experimental session. The final part of the session consisted of an intelligibility test, in which the degraded speech stimuli were presented one at a time without the written forms, at a rate of 2 seconds/item. Subjects were asked to write down each digit as it was presented.

Serial position data for the memory task are shown in Fig. 8.3a. Degrading the speech signal had a substantial impact on recency; there were 17.6% more errors at the final position in the filtered than in the unfiltered condition. This value is remarkably close to the mean error rate of 17.9% in the intelligibility test for filtered digits.

We can explore the relationship between perceptual discrimination and memory performance further by looking at the intelligibility of individual digits. Each subject recalled a total of 36 lists in the filtered speech condition, and within these lists, each digit appeared in each serial position exactly four times. If we pool the memory data over all 20 subjects, this means that for each of the digits 1–9, there are 80 trials in which that digit appeared in the final list position. For each digit, it is therefore possible to calculate the number of times it was incorrectly recalled when it appeared in this position. We can also derive a measure of intelligibility for each digit, by counting the mean number of identification errors in the intelligibility test If the echoic trace preserves those acoustic features that are used in speech recognition, we might expect to find a relationship between recall and intelligibility scores. This is precisely what happened. The correlation between these scores for the final serial position was 0.93, with a slope of 0.84 (Fig. 8.3b). Even with only nine data points, this is a highly significant correlation ($P < 0.01$).

These data strongly suggest that recall of the final item in a spoken list is based on a memory representation that has the same perceptual characteristics as the original speech sound. Analysis of confusion matrices for memory and perceptual errors lends further weight to this interpretation.

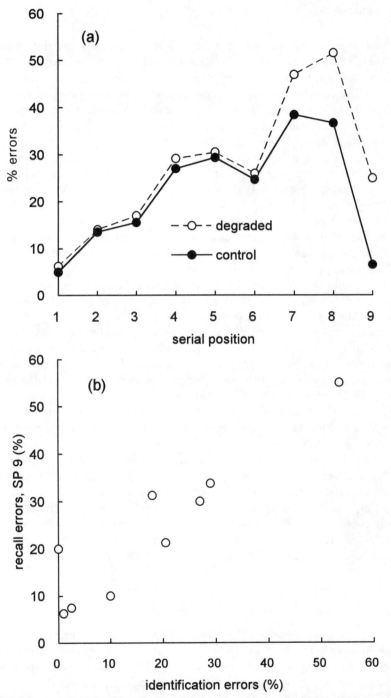

FIG. 8.3. (a) Serial position data for recall of band-pass filtered digits, and unfiltered control, (b) recall accuracy for filtered digits at the final position in the list, plotted against intelligibility.

For the memory and intelligibility data, 9 × 9 confusion matrices were constructed by recording for each error the item that was presented, and the item recalled or identified. Correct responses were excluded from this analysis. The correlation between these confusion matrices was again very high, at 0.74. This means that subjects' ability to identify the degraded speech in a perceptual task predicted not only the level of memory errors, but also the pattern of substitutions when errors occurred.

By extending this analysis to earlier serial positions, we can establish the extent to which the echoic trace contributes to recall of earlier items in the memory sequence. Figure 8.4a shows the correlations between memory and intelligibility data, calculated for overall error rates. The critical value of r for nine paired values is 0.67 ($P < 0.05$); this value is exceeded for positions 7–9. Figure 8.4b shows the slope calculated for the linear regression. Again, this confirms that recall of items at the end of the list is strongly determined by the accuracy of perceptual identification.

Finally, although these correlations are apparently very strong, there may be some unease about the reliability of relationships based on a small sample of items. The experiment was therefore repeated with two levels of speech degradation, achieved by band-pass filtering at either 200 or 300Hz. This resulted in mean error rates in the intelligibility test of 29% and 11%, respectively. Although both sets of stimuli were derived from the same utterances, the correlation between intelligibility scores for digits at the two levels of filtering were not particularly high ($r = 0.46$). For this sample of 18 items differing in intelligibility, there was still a strong relationship between intelligibility scores and memory errors for items at the final serial position ($r = 0.85$, $P < 0.01$).

In these data we have direct evidence that terminal list items in a spoken list are recovered from a memory representation that has the same perceptual characteristics as the original acoustic events. This does not mean that echoic memory is a tape recording of the acoustic signal—the experiments reviewed and reported here have shown that the encoding of acoustic features is highly selective. However, it does appear that these selected features are faithfully copied into the echoic trace.

CONCLUSION: ECHOIC MEMORY *IS* AN ACOUSTIC RECORD

What can we now say about the acoustic features that are represented in echoic memory? There is good evidence that spectral characteristics are encoded, but pitch (harmonic spacing) is not. Furthermore, spectral characteristics are encoded with a relatively low temporal resolution, so that the rapid transitions associated with stop consonants are lost. A suggestion made earlier was that the amplitude envelope of the speech signal

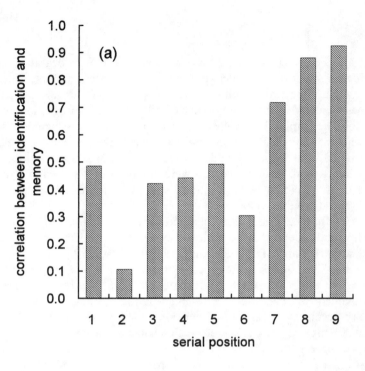

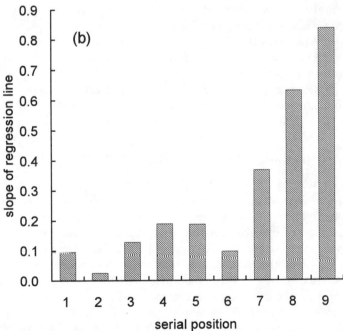

FIG. 8.4.   Relationship between item intelligibility and recall performance at all list positions: (a) correlation coefficients, (b) slope of regression line.

might also be preserved. The data from experiments with degraded speech lend further support to this idea. In this case the speech signal was processed by a low-pass filter with a roll-off of 24dB per octave. This severely reduces the cues available in the spectral envelope, but voicing information and the time-domain amplitude envelope are well preserved. Intelligibility scores were only maintained at a reasonably high level because the digits constitute a restricted and highly familiar vocabulary. For these stimuli, both intelligibility and memory scores were highest for "six" and "seven", which are the two digits with the most distinctive amplitude envelopes (short vowel, and disyllable, respectively).

It is useful to consider these characteristics in relation to the nature of speech sounds. Continuous speech consists of an extended vocal signal (i.e. vowel sound), whose amplitude and spectral characteristics are modulated over time. This signal is periodically interrupted by partial or complete closures in the vocal tract, and some of these interruptions are also accompanied by the addition of high-frequency noise bursts. Echoic memory seems to be an episodic record of these signal characteristics, although temporal integration means that some of the detail is lost. Current evidence suggests that this record is created during the interpretation of the acoustic signal by a dedicated phonetic processor. If we think of this system as a neural network, then echoic memory might be characterised as a continuous record of the input vector; i.e. the pattern of activation in units located in the input layer. Despite the loss of detail, there is sufficient information in this trace to support lexical matching, particularly in situations where there are strong contextual cues. This matching process will be heavily dependent on features that are well preserved in the echoic trace. These are generally features that provide information about characteristics such as vowel identity and syllabic stress.

ECHOIC MEMORY AND PROSODIC STRUCTURE

We are left with two puzzles. Why is echoic memory effectively restricted to the last few segments of speech, and why is pitch information so poorly represented? The conventional answer to the first is that capacity is limited by overwriting or interference. The reason for the second remains obscure. It is obvious that we are sensitive to the pitch of a speaker's voice—whether in singing, or in the variations in pitch that we perceive as intonation patterns. My own view has been that these two issues are closely related, and bound up with the suprasegmental structure of speech.

The first point to note is that echoic memory is not normally restricted to the last few segments of speech. This is true only under conditions that are seldom encountered outside the psychological laboratory; i.e. when we ask someone to recall a sequence of items that are spoken in a monotone at a constant tempo. Investigations of echoic memory have conventionally been undertaken using speech stimuli from which many of the characteristics that uniquely distinguish spoken from written language have been rigorously excluded. Natural utterances are characterised by frequent adjustments in pitch and timing, which together make up the prosodic structure of speech. These prosodic cues serve a number of linguistic functions, acting as syntactic and semantic markers, or signalling the speaker's intent. But as well as this, prosodic structure can greatly increase the effective capacity of echoic memory (Frankish 1985, 1989, 1995).

Speakers generally use the patterns of conventional speech even for semantically unstructured materials such as lists of digits. When asked for my telephone number, I am unlikely to begin reciting "zero … one … one … seven …" in a perfectly regular monotone. Memory for long, unstructured sequences can be improved by breaking them into smaller groups, and we show an intuitive awareness of this when we convey information to others. The simplest way to achieve this in a spoken sequence is by pausing briefly between successive groups of items. Recall of spoken lists improves substantially when they are grouped in this way (Ryan, 1969). However, temporal or spatial grouping of visually presented lists has very little effect on performance, provided that subjects are already using an appropriate grouping strategy. This means that for temporally structured lists there is an advantage of auditory over visual presentation at all serial positions, rather than at the end of the list (Frankish, 1985). For a nine-item auditory list grouped in threes, there is strong recency effect for each group, and this can be eliminated by the addition of a spoken suffix to each group (Frankish, 1985). In this and other ways, the advantage for grouped auditory lists shows all the hallmarks of an echoic memory trace that extends over the entire sequence.

Grouping effects in recall of spoken sequences can be produced not only by inserting pauses, but also by having alternate groups uttered by male and female speakers, or presented to left or right ears (Frankish, 1989). This again reinforces the theoretical links with conventional studies of echoic memory and PAS; when the same physical cues are used to distinguish between a suffix and the preceding list items, the magnitude of the suffix effect is decreased (Morton, Crowder & Prussin, 1971).

The connection between these grouping manipulations and prosodic structure was originally made on *a priori* grounds. Both seem to involve the development of structures based on variations in timing and voice quality. More recently, this relationship has been directly demonstrated, using sequences generated using a speech synthesiser, programmed to mimic the pitch contour of a naturally spoken utterance (Frankish, 1995). In this case, the 3–3–3 grouping pattern was defined solely by pitch modulation—all item durations were identical, and there were no lengthened pauses between groups (see Fig. 8.5). For these lists, there was again a grouping advantage which extended over all serial positions. In contrast, when digit lists were synthesised with pitches corresponding to the melody for the first line of *My bonnie lies over the ocean*, recall was no better than for lists spoken in a monotone.

These results complement the new data presented in this chapter. The rationale behind the *My bonnie* experiment was that if pitch were represented as an item attribute in echoic memory, then subjects could use this information to locate items in their correct serial positions. As this did not happen, we cannot explain the effects of the natural intonation contour in these terms either. This supports the earlier conclusion that pitch is not directly encoded in echoic memory, but leaves us with the problem of explaining why pitch *changes* are so effective. The most likely explanation seems to be that there is a perceptual mechanism that parses the speech input on the basis of pitch and timing cues. When subjects listen to a digit sequence spoken with the intonation contour shown in Fig. 8.5, they *hear* it as three groups of three. In other words, a structural parser identifies some of these pitch movements as discontinuities or boundaries. If anything is copied into the echoic trace, it is likely to be a record of these structural features, rather than the pitch information from which they are derived.

We have now identified two types of information that are extracted from the speech signal; one is the set of acoustic features that can be used to identify phonetic segments, and the other specifies the suprasegmental structure. It is still unclear how these interact, although there is strong empirical support for the idea that items associated with an "end" marker are more likely to be retrieved from echoic memory. It is difficult to see how such a process could work unless these markers were directly represented in the echoic trace.

IMPLICATIONS FOR SHORT-TERM MEMORY RESEARCH

At the beginning of this chapter I drew attention to the fact that current models of short-term memory implicitly assume that the phonological codes established during reading and listening are largely source-independent. It is certainly theoretically convenient to suppose that some linguistic representations in working memory are based on abstract phonological specifications. However, there is also very strong evidence for additional, modality-specific representations in short-term memory that are the direct consequence of processes occurring during perceptual analysis of the speech signal. I have argued first that these echoic traces are not at all like abstract phonological representations, and second, that they may play a significant role in supporting immediate ordered recall of naturally spoken sequences.

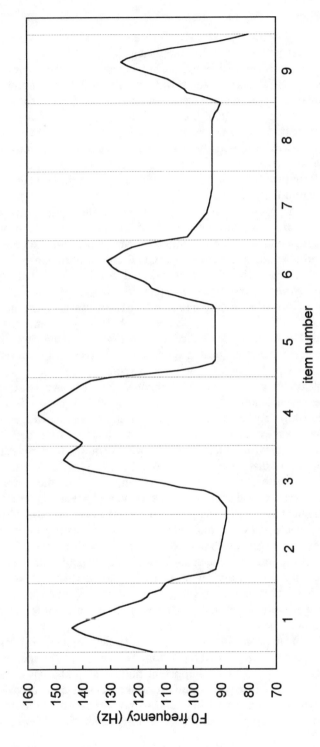

FIG. 8.5. "Natural" intonation contour for nine-digit lists, grouped in threes (Frankish, 1995).

These are sufficient grounds for supposing that echoic memory is more than a laboratory curiosity. Although we still have very little direct evidence, it is more than likely that this system will play a part in the comprehension of continuous speech, particularly where immediate on-line interpretation is made difficult by poor signal quality or syntactic complexity. In the laboratory context, we should be cautious in interpreting the results of studies that involve contrasts between immediate recall of spoken and written verbal sequences. And on a more technical note, it is important to be aware of the extent to which short-term recall of spoken material is sensitive to suprasegmental features.

We can illustrate these points by considering their implications for studies of language development, and the theoretical interpretation of relationships between language and working memory. For the young child, speech is the sole medium for language development. Children are particularly sensitive to prosodic cues in speech, and this is reflected in the exaggerated prosody found in speech used by caregivers (e.g. Snow, 1972). One common characteristic of adults' speech to children is that the most important words in an utterance are emphasised by accented pitch. It is significant that in the immediate recall task, performance is substantially enhanced by the insertion of pitch accents at group boundaries (Frankish, 1995). In ongoing studies of memory performance in 5- and 6-year-old children, we have found that span measures are substantially increased if lists are read with a strongly grouped intonation.

The relationship between speech perception and phonological processing in children has been extensively discussed in the chapter by Gathercole and Martin. The analysis presented here fits well with their approach. For example, failure to distinguish between different types of speech-based representations in short-term memory has contributed to the uncertainty about whether very young children rehearse when spoken presentation is used. Phonological and echoic representations are associated with different stages of language processing, and represent different attributes of speech. However, they do necessarily share many common characteristics. Both will be influenced by parameters such as item similarity and word-length. If children's memory performance is influenced by these variables we cannot therefore conclude that they are using abstract phonological codes. In fact it now seems much more likely that in young children these influences reflect their use of echoic memory.

One of the most promising areas for future development in this area seems to be the study of nonword repetition. The nature of the speech input in this task makes it particularly important that we should analyse the role of echoic memory. Because the stimuli are spoken as single (or occasionally paired) polysyllabic utterances, they tend to possess some of the prosodic structure that characterises natural speech. In English, this is based at the word level on alternating patterns of strong/weak syllables, with further distinctions between primary and secondary stress. This rich prosodic structure is likely to maximise the effectiveness of the echoic trace. Conformity with this pattern, or lack of it, might well be a factor in the wordlikeness effect for nonword repetition (as in the contrast between *defermication*, and *loddernapish*). More generally, it may be the case that children who find this task difficult do not necessarily have difficulty in registering the stimulus in echoic memory, although this may be true for some with specific language impairments. The difficulty for many may be in the translation from acoustic to phonological representation, and in buffering the corresponding articulatory specification in order to produce a spoken response.

REFERENCES

Atkinson, R.C., & Shiffrin, R.M. (1968). Human memory; A proposed system and its control processes. In K.W. Spence & J.T. Spence (Eds.), *The psychology of learning and motivation, Vol. 2.* New York: Academic Press.

Baddeley, A.D., & Hitch, G. (1974). Working memory. In G. Bower (Ed.), *The psychology of learning and motivation,* (pp. 47–90). New York: Academic Press.

Baddeley, A.D., Lewis, V.J., & Vallar, G. (1984). Exploring the articulatory loop. *Quarterly Journal of Experimental Psychology, 36,* 233–252.

Breeuwer, M., & Plomp, R. (1984). Speechreading supplemented with frequency-selective sound-pressure information. *Journal of the Acoustical Society of America, 76,* 686–691.

Broadbent, D.E. (1958). *Perception and communication.* London: Pergamon Press.

Bryden, M.P. (1971). Attentional strategies and short-term memory in dichotic listening. *Cognitive Psychology, 2,* 99–116.

Campbell, R. (1990). Lipreading, neuropsychology, and immediate memory. In G. Vallar & T. Shallice (Eds.), *Neuropsychological impairments of short-term memory.* Cambridge: Cambridge University Press.

Campbell, R., & Dodd, B. (1980). Hearing by eye. *Quarterly Journal of Experimental Psychology, 32,* 85–89.

Cole. R.A. (1973). Different memory functions for consonants and vowels. *Cognitive Psychology, 4,* 39–54.

Conrad, R., & Hull, A.J. (1968). Input modality and the serial position curve in short-term memory. *Psychonomic Science, 10,* 135–136.

Crowder, R.G. (1967). Prefix effects in immediate memory. *Canadian Journal of Psychology, 21,* 450–461.

Crowder, R.G. (1971). The sound of vowels and consonants in immediate memory. *Journal of Verbal Learning and Verbal Behavior, 10,* 587–596.

Crowder, R.G. (1973). Precategorical storage for vowels of long and short duration. *Perception and Psychophysics, 13,* 502–506.

Crowder, R.G. (1983). The purity of auditory memory. *Philosophical Transactions of the Royal Society London, B302,* 251–265.

Crowder, R.G. (1986). Auditory and temporal factors in the modality effect. *Journal of Experimental Psychology: Learning, Memory and Cognition, 12,* 268–278.

Crowder, R.G. (1993). Systems and principles in memory theory: Another critique of pure memory. In A.F. Collins, S.E. Gathercole, M.A. Conway, & P.E. Morris (Eds.), *Theories of memory.* Hillsdale NJ: Lawrence Erlbaum Associates Inc.

Crowder, R.G., & Morton, J. (1969). Precategorical acoustic storage (PAS). *Perception and Psychophysics, 5,* 365–373.

Darwin, C.J., & Baddeley, A.D. (1974). Acoustic memory and the perception of speech. *Cognitive Psychology, 6,* 41–60.

de Gelder, B., & Vroomen, J. (1992). Abstract versus modality-specific memory representations in processing auditory and visual speech. *Memory and Cognition, 20,* 533–538.

de Gelder, B., & Vroomen, J. (1994). Memory for consonants versus vowels in heard and lipread speech. *Journal of Memory and Language, 33,* 737–756.

Eimas, P.D., Siqueland, E.R., Jusczyk, P., & Vigorito, J. (1971). Speech perception in infants. *Science, 171,* 303–306.

Frankish, C. (1985). Modality-specific grouping effects in short-term memory. *Journal of Memory and Language, 24,* 200–209.

Frankish, C. (1989). Perceptual organization and PAS. *Journal of Experimental Psychology: Human Learning and Memory, 15,* 469–479.

Frankish, C. (1995). Intonation and auditory grouping in immediate serial recall. *Applied Cognitive Psychology, 9,* S5–S22.

Frost, R., Repp, B.H., & Katz, L. (1989). *Can speech perception be influenced by simultaneous presentation of print?* Status Report on Speech Research SR-97/98. New York: Haskins Laboratories.

Fry, D.B., Abramson, A.S., Eimas, P.D., & Liberman, A.M. (1962). The identification and discrimination of synthetic vowels. *Language and Speech, 5,* 171–189.

Gathercole, S.E., & Baddeley, A.D. (1993). *Working memory and language.* Hillsdale, NJ: Lawrence Erlbaum Associates Inc.

Glenberg, A.M., & Swanson, N.G. (1986). A temporal distinctiveness theory of recency and modality effects. *Journal of Experimental Psychology: Learning, Memory and Cognition, 12,* 3–15.

Greene, R.L., & Crowder, R.G. (1984). Modality and suffix effects in the absence of auditory stimulation. *Journal of Verbal Learning and Verbal Behavior, 23,* 371–382.

Haber, R.N. (1983). The impending demise of the icon: A critique of the concept of iconic storage in visual information processing. *The Behavioral and Brain Sciences, 6,* 1–54.

Jusczyk, P. (1985). Auditory versus phonetic coding of speech signals during infancy. In J. Mehler, M. Garrett, & E. Walker (Eds.), *Perspectives on mental representation: Experimental and theoretical studies of cognitive processes and capacities.* Hillsdale, NJ: Lawrence Erlbaum Associates Inc.

Kuhl, P.K., & Miller, J.D. (1978). Speech perception by the chinchilla: Identification functions for synthetic VOT stimuli. *Journal of the Acoustical Society of America, 63,* 905–917.

LeCompte, D.C. (1992). In search of a strong visual recency effect. *Memory and Cognition, 20,* 563–572.

McDowd, J., & Madigan, S. (1991). Ineffectiveness of visual distinctiveness in enhancing immediate recall. *Memory and Cognition, 19,* 371–377.

Liberman, A.M., & Mattingly, I.G. (1985). The motor theory of speech perception revised. *Cognition, 21,* 1–36.

McClelland, J.L., & Elman, J.L. (1986). The TRACE model of speech perception. *Cognitive Psychology, 18,* 1–86.

McDonald, J., & McGurk, H. (1978). Visual influences on speech perception processes. *Perception and Psychophysics, 24,* 253–257.

Morton, J., Crowder, R.G., & Prussin, H.A. (1971). Experiments with the stimulus suffix effect. *Journal of Experimental Psychology, 91,* 169–190.

Morton, J., & Holloway, C.M. (1970). Absence of a cross-modal 'suffix effect' in short-term memory. *Quarterly Journal of Experimental Psychology, 22,* 167–176.

Nairne, J.S. (1988). A framework for interpreting recency effects in immediate serial recall. *Memory and Cognition, 16,* 343–352.

Nairne, J.S., & Pusen, C. (1984). Serial recall of imagined voices. *Journal of Verbal Learning and Verbal Behavior, 23,* 331–342.

Nairne, J.S., & Walters, V.L. (1983) Silent mouthing produces modality- and suffix-like effects. *Journal of Verbal Learning and Verbal Behavior, 22,* 475–483.

Neisser, U. (1967). *Cognitive psychology.* New York: Appleton–Century–Crofts.

Pisoni, D.G. (1971). *On the nature of categorical perception of speech sounds.* Supplement to Status Report on Speech Research. New York: Haskins Laboratories.

Rowe, E.J., & Cake, L.J. (1977). Retention of order information for sounds and words. *Canadian Journal of Psychology, 31,* 14–23.

Rowe, E.J., & Rowe, W.G. (1976). Stimulus suffix effects with speech and nonspeech sounds. *Memory and Cognition, 4,* 128–131.

Ryan, J. (1969). Temporal grouping, rehearsal, and short-term memory. *Quarterly Journal of Experimental Psychology, 21,* 148–155.

Snow, C. (1972). Mothers' speech to children learning language. *Child Development, 43,* 549–565.

Stevens, K.N., & Blumstein, S.E. (1981). The search for invariant acoustic correlates of phonetic features. In P.D. Eimas & J.L. Miller (Eds.), *Perspectives on the study of speech.* Hillsdale, NJ: Lawrence Erlbaum Associates Inc.

Surprenant, A.M., Pitt, M.A. & Crowder, R.G. (1993). Auditory recency in immediate memory. *Quarterly Journal of Experimental Psychology, 46A,* 193–223.

Turner, M.L., LaPointe, L.B., Cantor, J., Reeves, C.H., Griffeth, R.H., & Engle, R.W. (1987). Recency and suffix effects found with auditory presentation and with mouthed visual presentation: They're not the same thing. *Journal of Memory and Language, 26,* 138–164.

Warren, R.G. (1970). Perceptual restoration of missing speech sounds. *Science, 167,* 392–393.

Werker, J.F., & Tees, R.C. (1984). Cross-language speech perception: Evidence for perceptual reorganization during the first year of life. *Infant Behavior and Development, 7,* 49–63.

9

The object-oriented episodic record model

Dylan M. Jones, Philip Beaman, and William J. Macken
University of Cardiff, UK

Advances in the understanding of memory over the past few decades have typically incorporated the notion of storage in terms of functionally distinct but interconnected stores which are seen to underpin the phenomena of remembering. Each of these stores, or modules, has associated with it a distinct form of representation that constrains the way in which material within a module may be addressed, retrieved, or interfered with. Limitations on the storage and processing capacity of such modules is also usually specified. Implicit or explicit within many of these modular approaches is the notion of a fractionation between storage and perceptual processes (see e.g. Atkinson & Shiffrin, 1968; Baddeley & Hitch, 1974). Thus, stores may be long-term or short-term, they may be associated with each of the senses, or more abstractly, may be devoted to verbal or spatial information that transcends the senses. The concepts described in this chapter are contrary to this tradition and involve an approach to understanding memory as a set of procedures or operations taking place within a unitary rather than a modular system, many of which are intrinsically connected to what are usually considered to be more peripheral perceptual processes.

The model described in this chapter is referred to as the Object-Oriented Episodic Record (O-OER) model. The model eschews the modularity assumptions of many traditional models, and instead proposes a single unitary representational space within which the basic units are objects: amodal, abstract representations of items and events. The processes whereby the objects are formed and organised in memory are not seen as being distinct from processes of perception and attention.

Typically, evidence of the functional characteristics of representations or modules is drawn from experiments in which performance is measured under a range of interfering conditions. The reasoning behind this approach is that different interfering stimuli produce effects on distinct components of performance, so that the pattern of performance under a range of interfering conditions reveals the functional identity of the components underpinning that performance. Thus, the approach typically taken assumes that certain stimuli interfere with the operation of some modules, but not others, and thereby the modular fractionation of cognition may be established. This is an approach adopted in the development of the working memory model (see Baddeley & Hitch, 1974; Gathercole & Baddeley, 1993) and is extended here, but with rather different conclusions.

In this chapter, we describe the evolution of the O-OER model, beginning with an examination of some aspects of the role of auditory attention in short-term verbal memory, and moving on to the effects of articulatory processes, and the nature of spatial memory. It was not the original intention to fashion a general model of memory; however, despite this, the model emerged in a more or less compelling way from a long series of experiments, that then suggested further generalities. The model still requires a good deal of refinement, but even in its inchoate form, we would claim it has proved to be useful in suggesting a range of simple but novel propositions.

THE IRRELEVANT SPEECH EFFECT AND THE CHANGING-STATE HYPOTHESIS

The detrimental effect of irrelevant speech on serial recall is well documented (Colle, 1980; Colle & Welsh, 1976; Jones & Morris, 1992a; Salamé & Baddeley, 1982). It is an extremely robust experimental finding, typically reducing the level of recall accuracy by about 30%. A sequence of digits, letters, or words is presented to the subject, usually visually and at a constant rate. There is a retention interval, in the region of 10–30 seconds. Following the retention interval the subject recalls the items in the order in which they were presented. Items are scored as correct only if they appear in the correct position in the sequence. Speech or noise may be presented at any point during the experiment, but subjects are forewarned not to attend to it, and are assured that they will not be tested on its contents. A typical pattern of results is shown in Fig. 9.1 in which the effect of different types of auditory material has been contrasted.

The justification for using the irrelevant speech and immediate serial recall paradigm as a measurement of short-term recall has been elaborated

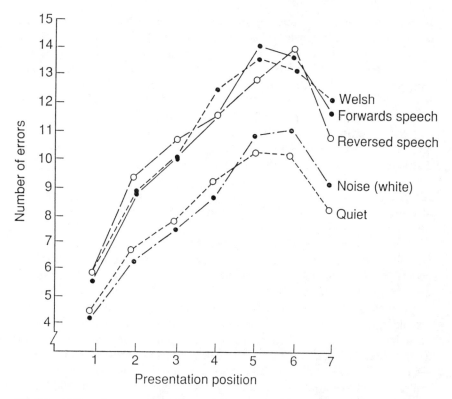

FIG. 9.1. Effects of a range of sounds on serial errors in short-term recall. Forward speech is a narrative passage spoken in English, and the reversed condition is the same material played backwards. A comparable narrative passage was used for Welsh speech. White noise was continuous. Results from Jones, Miles, and Page (1990).

on in detail elsewhere (e.g. Baddeley, 1986). Briefly, the effects of irrelevant speech are believed to shed light on the processes involved in attentional control of immediate memory. By selectively disrupting certain aspects of the process that share some important characteristics with the representational format of the task-irrelevant material, it is hoped that processes involved in memory can be identified. Thus, the introduction of irrelevant material should reveal the interactions between processing of the to-be-remembered material and the processes involved in the supposed automatic processing of irrelevant speech

A number of factors are known to influence the disruptive capabilities of irrelevant auditory material on short-term serial recall of visually presented material. Some results have helped to rule out a number of competing explanations. An initially surprising result is that neither intensity of background noise, nor meaning of irrelevant speech have any effect. The lack of an effect of intensity rules out the likelihood of the finding being the result of change in the subject's level of physiological arousal (Colle, 1980), in the range of up to about 75dB (A) that has so far been explored. The equivalent level of disruption caused by speech in an unknown language (Colle, 1980; Colle & Welsh, 1976; Salamé & Baddeley, 1982), or in the subject's own language played backwards (Jones, Miles & Page, 1990; see Fig. 9.1) likewise suggests that meaning has no effect. Importantly, these results suggest that subjects are not simply (contrary to instructions) being distracted by a more interesting series of irrelevant stimuli. In passing, it is worth noting that this latter result also tends to suggest that pattern-recognition procedures specialised to the phonetic structure of speech are also unlikely to be involved, as arguably reversed speech does not contain familiar acoustic/phonetic sequences.

Such aspects of the disruptive effect of irrelevant speech on recall of visually presented verbal material have led to the suggestion that the effect occurs at a postcategorical structural or phonological level of verbal processing. The effect, according to this view, is one of phonological confusion between the irrelevant auditory input, and the to-be-remembered visually presented material. Nonspeech sound such as continuous white noise has no such detrimental effect on recall (Colle, 1980, see also Fig. 9.1). Therefore it has been argued that obligatory access to a short-term memory system used for short-term recall of verbal material is granted to sounds that are registered as speech or "speech-like", and the irrelevant material has its disruptive effect in this store by a corruptive process related to the similarity between the memory items and the irrelevant speech (Salamé & Baddeley, 1982).

However, further evidence casts doubt on this view of the disruptive process. Critically, Jones, Madden, and Miles (1992) showed that the presence of irrelevant speech *per se* is not sufficient to produce the irrelevant speech effect. They found no disruption of memory for sounds comprising a single repeated utterance or a digitally extended continuous utterance (stimuli that we refer to as steady-state). However, the usual disruption was found with sequences of different syllables, even with a set as small as four syllables repeated in the same order. This effect was referred to as the *changing-state* effect and represents one of the foundation stones in the development of the O-OER model. This effect points to a temporal dimension in the irrelevant speech effect, namely that some sort of perceptual shift over time is required, and this temporal component may be viewed as conveying the serial ordering of discrete items or events (Jones et al., 1992). If changing state is the critical factor in determining disruption by irrelevant speech, the question as to whether the effect is restricted to speech sounds is raised.

THE FUNCTIONAL EQUIVALENCE OF SPEECH AND NONSPEECH IN MEMORY

It is possible from a modular point of view of mental organisation (e.g. Fodor, 1983) that the results obtained with irrelevant speech reflect the functioning of a short-term memory system specialised for the processing of verbal material. One possible mechanism as suggested by Salamé and Baddeley (1982, 1989) is a filter that allows speech obligatory access to the short-term memory system, disrupting the mnemonic processes operating on the representations of the to-be-remembered material. At a second stage, once the speech has passed through the filter, representations in memory are somehow interfered with, possibly as a result of the similarity of the two types of information, one from the deliberate rehearsal of a list, and the other from irrelevant speech, entering memory uninvited via the filter. There is a logical objection to such a system, however, because if a hypothetical speech-filter which acts to prevent the access of white noise and other nonspeech sounds to the system categorises auditory representations as "speech-like" or otherwise, it would already have taken some account of the degree of similarity between auditory material and speech. Thus, claiming that only phonologically similar material causes disruption to recall from the system—a property of the second stage of processing—involves an unnecessary duplication of function.

Additionally, experimental evidence goes against the notion of a "speech-only" filter system. The fact that reversed speech seems to produce effects roughly equivalent to those of normal speech suggests that if there is such a filter, it passes some rather unusual forms of the signal (Jones et al., 1990). More compelling is evidence that irrelevant tones can also display an irrelevant "speech" effect (Jones & Macken, 1993). In line with the changing-state hypothesis, which makes no distinction between speech and nonspeech sounds, it was predicted that a sequence of discrete tones that changed in pitch should significantly disrupt serial recall. As shown in Fig. 9.2, depicting the results of Jones and Macken (1993, Experiment 5), this prediction was confirmed, and furthermore the disruption was at a level equivalent to that of irrelevant speech sounds, in this case syllables varying in pitch by the same degree as the tones. The lack of an effect with steady-state sounds also held for nonspeech with auditory material comprised of a repeated tone producing no disruption of serial recall (Jones & Macken, 1993, Experiment 4)

The irrelevant speech effect obtained using tones was achieved using nonspeech sounds that changed abruptly in pitch to produce a changing-state effect. Convergent evidence then tends to suggest a process that operates on representations of the stimuli based on their acoustic parameters, rather than any abstract phonological level of analysis. Narrative speech is full of sudden physical alterations in the speech signal

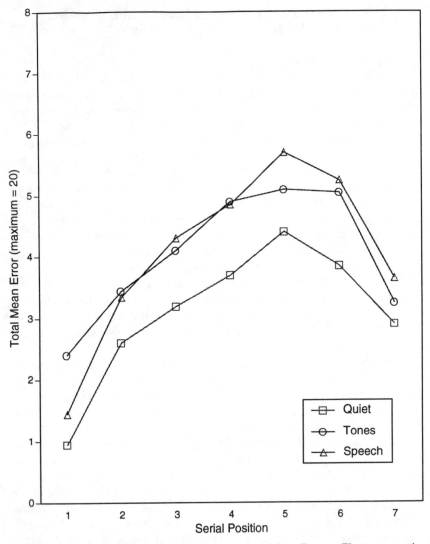

FIG. 9.2.   Effects of syllables and tones on short-term serial recall errors. The tones were in a random sequence of four different pitches. In the syllable condition the same syllable was repeated but at one of four different pitches (changes comparable in magnitude to those of the tones). Data from Jones and Macken (1993).

but obviously such changes are not unique to speech signals. Previous suggestions that the effect was speech-specific seem to have been based on contrasting the effects of speech material with white noise or other steady-state nonspeech sounds (Salamé & Baddeley, 1982, 1989).

Further evidence for the functional equivalence of speech and nonspeech in short-term memory comes from studies concerning children's development of language (Gathercole & Baddeley, 1990). Children with a language disorder who exhibit impaired digit spans, thus suffering from a quantifiable deficit in short-term memory for speech, also have problems in echoing back an unfamiliar sound. Recall of a list of speech sounds is related in these cases to repetition of nonspeech, suggesting a central deficit concerned with the perception and recall of meaningless (hence unfamiliar) digit strings, and unfamiliar sounds. Clearly, caution is needed when applying a modular model of information processing. Such models generally presuppose separate forms of input representations for each module, but it is unclear given these results what the differences between functional units for speech and nonspeech modules are likely to be, or why the use of one module should be affected by the functioning of another. There are a number of advantages that accrue to such models (see e.g. Shallice, 1988, for a discussion), but it will be argued that it is unreasonable to expect that all of the brain's functioning is modular in structure (Fodor, 1983).

The common feature of those conditions that produce appreciable disruption within the irrelevant speech paradigm is that the auditory stream contains discrete units, each of which is different in some critical way to the one that preceded it.

HOW IS THE CHANGING-STATE EFFECT RELATED TO HABITUATION?

One possible way to explain the effects of changing state is to think of it in terms of habituation of the orienting response, a reduction in vigour, and likelihood of an attentional switch to a novel stimulus as a result of repeated presentation. This explanation suggests that presentation of an irrelevant auditory stimulus sequence, and changes in state within that sequence, elicit an orienting response from the subject, and it is this response, which reflects a switch of attentional resources away from the to-be-remembered material, that disrupts serial recall. Changing-state irrelevant material regularly provides a novel stimulus, and so triggers an involuntary orienting response. Steady-state auditory material, on the other hand, is rapidly habituated because it involves regular presentation of the same auditory object, the orienting response thus declines, and consequently there is no further disruptive effect on attending to the to-be-remembered material (Jones & Morris, 1992b; Näätänen, 1990; Öhman, 1979).

However, the changing-state effect cannot be ascribed simply to the habituation of the orienting response for a number of reasons; first, if habituation is considered to be the reason for the lack of an irrelevant speech effect with steady-state material, then changing-state material should not continue to produce a strong effect if subjects are pre-exposed to the material for a sufficient length of time to derive expectations regarding the irrelevant input. In this case, assuming habituation to occur post-categorically, or at a supra-segmental level of analysis, it would also be expected that the orienting response would diminish. Subjects exposed to contrasting sets of letter-names that were repeated throughout the sequence ("CHJU", "CHJU", etc.) did not show any reduction in the degree of disruption, suggesting that the predictability of the changes in state, which is likely to be implicated in any explanation based on habituation, had no effect (Jones et al., 1992). Second, there is the question of why the locus of the effect seems to be in memory rather than in encoding (Hanley & Broadbent, 1987; Miles, Jones & Madden, 1991; Salamé & Baddeley, 1982). Changing state shows impairments of equal magnitude at both input and rehearsal stages of a serial recall task. Assuming that a distinction between encoding and memory can be sustained, this suggests that the speech is exerting an effect at only one of these stages. A plausible explanation, therefore, is that the effect occurs during the subjects' rehearsal procedure, which occurs both when the subject is being presented with the list, and during a period allocated to rote rehearsal. That is, subjects rehearse the lists as they are presented, as well as after presentation has ceased. Thus if the orienting response were responsible for the effect, it appears, implausibly, only to affect performance during rehearsal, not input or recall. This need not rely on the assumption that habituation is a peripheral process (see Hall, 1980, for a review), as it is equally consistent with a "central" view of habituation that it should also occur at encoding or recall.

Third, and most compellingly, why should the effect appear only in certain tasks—those that involve a serial order component—and not in tasks with a lesser reliance on the serial order component? In tasks where the list of to-be-remembered material is represented to the subject, and the subject is required to recall the identity of the item that has not been represented (the missing item task; Jones & Macken, 1993; Macken & Jones, 1995) no changing-state effect is found. This task arguably has no inherent serial order component, as only the identity of the missing item has to be recalled. There is no differential effect of task difficulty, as control and steady-state conditions do not differ significantly between memory tasks when the overall probability of an item being in error is calculated (Macken & Jones, 1995, Experiment 4). While acknowledging the central role of serial recall, it is important to acknowledge that a range of tasks, not nominally regarded as serial recall, do involve preservation of serial order information. Even when a subject is presented with a paired associate task, therefore, the links between pairs will be subject to disruption by irrelevant speech (LeCompte, 1994).

In the light of the foregoing findings it seems unlikely that a simplistic solution to the changing-state effect based on existing theories of habituation to novel stimuli is plausible. Accordingly, the O-OER model was devised to account for the effects of changing-state auditory material on short-term serial recall.

THE NATURE OF "CHANGING STATE"

For changing state to be registered, we may propose that some sort of segmentation of a signal into component units must first occur, as a change in state implies a difference between an attribute of the auditory stream at a particular point in time and the corresponding attribute at a subsequent point in time, such that temporally distinct units may be contrasted. The changing-state effect may be characterised as a series of reactions within short-term memory to changes in the auditorily presented irrelevant input which lead to the disruption of memory for a sequence of events. Thus, a good deal more needs to be understood of the processes that segment the auditory input into its constituent units, and the way that those units are sequentially compared need to be established.

Clearly, the fact that meaning only plays a minor role in the irrelevant speech effect means that segmentation of the auditory input on the basis of meaningful units (e.g. words or phrases) is not the critical factor. With words, strong cues to segmentation are available at the boundaries in the form of sharp changes in energy, both in frequency and amplitude. That these might serve as the basis for segmenting irrelevant speech is suggested by a range of studies in which slow randomly varying pitch glides were used as irrelevant material instead of speech. If the glides were continuous, there was little disruption. If the same glides were interrupted suddenly and regularly by quiet, thereby introducing sudden transitions of energy, there was once again appreciable disruption of short-term serial recall (Jones, Macken, & Murray, 1993). Figure 9.3a illustrates both the continuous pitch glides (upper panel) and schematically the frequency with which the glides were then interrupted by quiet (shown by solid vertical lines in the lower panel). Performance effects are shown in Fig. 9.3b in which the interrupted glide is more disruptive than the continuous glide.

That segmentation of the auditory input on the basis of abrupt energy transitions is a crucial initial stage in establishing changing state is also illustrated by the effects of auditory babble. If instead of a single voice a number of voices are mixed to create a "babble" of irrelevant speech stimuli then the propositions relating to segmentation in the changing-state hypothesis suggest that the relation between the degree of disruption and the number of voices is non-monotonic. That is, as the number of voices increases to about three the dose of words will increase, thereby increasing the amount of changing-state information within the auditory stream (see Bridges & Jones, in press, for a discussion about dose). Above that number,

Time

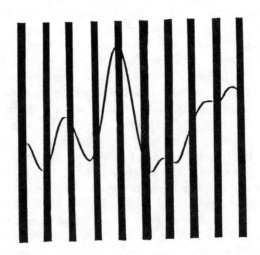

FIG. 9.3a.

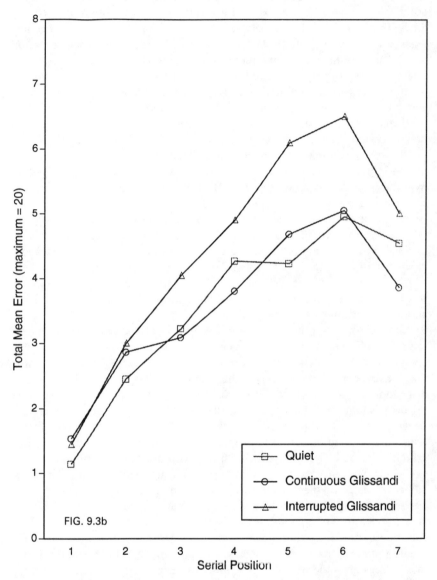

FIG. 9.3. The effects of pitch glides on short-term serial recall errors. Figure 9.3a shows the different types of stimuli. The upper panel shows in schematic form the changing frequency of the glide over time and the lower panel shows how the glides were interrupted with silence (shown by the solid bars). Figure 9.3b shows the effects of the two types of glide on performance, compared to quiet. Data from Jones et al. (1993).

the disruptive effect of speech will diminish. This will be because as the number of voices increases beyond a certain level, it becomes increasingly likely that the boundaries between words of one speaker will become masked by the words of another. In other words, the basis of segmentation will be undermined with greater numbers of speakers (see Hellbrück & Kilcher, 1993). In practice, once the babble contains more than a few voices, disruption begins to diminish (Jones & Macken, 1995a,b). It is not safe to generalise too widely about the exact number in view of the likely effect of particular characteristics of a mix of voices, however. In some types of babble certain voices will be more distinctive by virtue of their pitch or loudness, for example, but the rule in its general form, that the relation is non-monotonic, seems to be a safe one to adopt. The changing-state hypothesis further suggests that the effect of masking peaks and troughs of signal strength should be also modified by processes of auditory streaming (see Jones & Macken, 1995a). Even with as many as six voices, by assigning each voice to a particular location in space, so that each voice comes from a distinct position, disruption is once again restored to a level markedly greater than if all the voices come from a single locus (Jones & Macken, 1995b). Clearly, it is not the mere presence of sound that is important, it is the power of the nervous system to organise it, even though the sound is, to all intents and purposes, unattended.

Although we are not yet in a position to specify the exact way in which sequences of segmented objects are compared, and how the products of this comparison wield their disruptive power, there is ample evidence to show that the distinctiveness of items in the auditory stream predicts the degree of disruption of short-term memory. It follows directly from the changing-state hypothesis that the similarity within streams, rather than similarity between streams (in this case, between the irrelevant speech and the to-be-remembered stimuli) is the primary determinant of disruption. For example, if the effect of irrelevant speech containing a rhyming sequence (e.g. door, war, more, etc.) is compared with a non-rhyming sequence (e.g. hat, cow, nest, etc.) then this second relatively more distinct type of sequence has a greater effect on performance (Jones & Macken, 1995c; see Fig. 9.4). One implication of these findings is that there might be some kind of continuous function relating the degree of correlation between successive events and the disruption of memory. Another important implication is that the findings go some way towards ruling out explanations of the irrelevant speech effect based on the phonological similarity of the speech to the items being rehearsed in memory (Salamé & Baddeley, 1982, 1989). It is tempting to conclude that this successive comparison yields information about the ordinal associations between items in the auditory stream, and that this order information is the critical aspect of changing-state auditory streams which gives rise to their disruptive power.

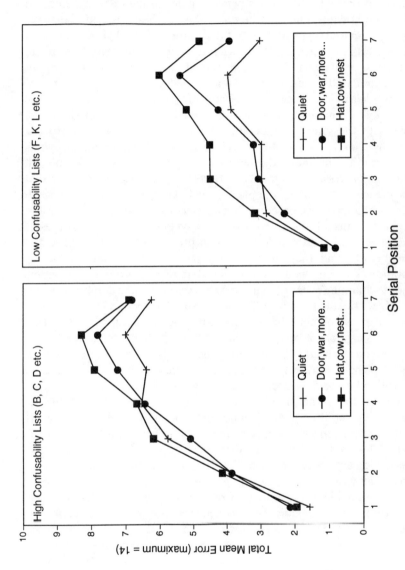

FIG. 9.4. Effects of similarity within the auditory stream on short-term serial recall. Rhyming sequences (door, war, more, etc.) show significantly more disruption than non-rhyming sequences (hat, cow, nest, etc.). Data from Jones and Macken (1995c). The disruptive effect is more pronounced when the items in the to-be-remembered list are phonologically different (right-hand panel).

Because of the particular susceptibility of tasks in which order of items has to be preserved, one inference that may be drawn from these experiments is that the interfering quality of the irrelevant speech works at the level of ordinal associations between items in the to-be-remembered and irrelevant streams. One way in which this can be envisaged is that the process of perceptual segmentation of the auditory material yields a series of auditory objects[1], defined by changing state, held together by linkages to form streams, and assembled within a field representing some form of working memory "thoroughfare" (Allport, 1989). These linkages are the source of disruption between objects of auditory origin that are automatically organised on this field, and objects of visual origin which gain access to the same representational space via the rehearsal process. Analogically, this space can be conceived of as a blackboard, on which objects from different knowledge sources or modalities may be assembled. The rehearsal process, it is suggested, reflects the preservation of material at the episodic level of analysis; the phenomenal experience of serial rehearsal strategies is of a repetitive process of mental reconstruction of the order and the physical forms of the items to be remembered. Semantic processes operate convergently on the object at a conceptually deeper level ("beneath" the blackboard), and they may possibly redefine the initial product of segmentation, but only as a result of deploying some forms of mnemonic strategies ("chunking", or reassembling the object/linkage combinations).

The object-oriented form of organisation overcomes the "binding problem" that is inherent to modular approaches (Allport, 1989). If a single event is capable of being represented in more than one module then a modular account should specify how the two representations interact. Illusory or dismembered conjunctions are exceptionally rare, which suggests a powerful and error-free mechanism is at work, but modular approaches hardly ever address the issue of binding (see Jones, 1993, for further discussion). A non-modular architecture views the convergence of information from different senses from the same distal entity as "object-oriented". This contrasts with the "dismembered" architecture of modular theories, which are frequently forced to rely on executive components to coordinate activities between separate sensory modalities. Streams concerned with each stimulus are formed by a process akin to auditory scene analysis. These streams require the prior parallel activation of a number of perceptual processing units, and thus fit with the theory of synchronised neural activity ("temporal binding") which has been suggested within the

---

[1] The term "objects" rather than events is used to emphasise the amodal, propositional form of the representation. The term is not unique to the O-OER model, having been used previously by Whitfield (1979) in a similar context. It should also be noted for purposes of clarity that the term "changing state" was used by Campbell and Dodd (1980) to describe a different effect.

fields of neuroscience and artificial neural networks as a possible way of overcoming the binding problem within a single sensory modality (Hummel & Biederman, 1992; Knudsen, duLac, & Esterly, 1987). Stream formation reflects such processes of association by spatiotemporal synchrony that can, in principle, be described by a set of production rules specifying the conditions under which streams are formed, although these rules have yet to be specified clearly.

Thus, the O-OER model embodies a prime tenet of the changing-state hypothesis; that changing-state irrelevant speech possesses some property that steady-state input does not possess. This is explained within the model by the assumption that changing-state irrelevant speech has inter-item associations that provide an episodic record of recent items/events, but that these inter-item associations do not exist for steady-state material. Steady-state material, because of the lack of any discernible physical change from one segmentable entity to the next, has no need for multiple representations. Thus, what is lost in irrelevant speech interference tasks, as suggested by previous theorists as the prime general cause of forgetting in serial short-term memory, is primarily the order component of the items (Estes, 1972; Wickelgren, 1965) contained within the inter-item associations which provide cues to serial order, and associative links to later items. This then prevents the accurate cueing of later items within a series. It has been demonstrated that a model dependent on prior item cueing (a chaining model) can produce many of the observable effects of serial order recall, provided that approximate cueing from an earlier, misrecalled item, is possible (Lewandowsky & Murdock, 1989). Chaining models of this sort effectively represent a Markov process of state transitions (movement from a state representing a to-be-remembered item to the next item in a series that is serially ordered, each with an associated probability—see Minsky, 1968). Given that memory for order must be a system *a priori* that evolves over time, then a finite set of state variables that determine the state of the system at a given time, and a set of evolution equations that describe the changing values of this system over time, are capable of describing a set of these movements along this state transition network stochastically as a Markov chain.

A geometric model of the set of all possible states of the system represents the state space of the system. Given the conditions for change and some initial conditions sufficient to uniquely specify a point in the state space, subsequent changes in the system can then be plotted as a curve or trajectory of the system, referred to in the O-OER model as the episodic trajectory. Thus far this is a characterisation of a fairly standard connectionist representation as a distributed pattern of unit activations. Typically, however, connectionist models are unconcerned with the trajectory, the semantic interpretation of their outputs depending on arrival at only one point attractor for each input (coded as a vector of activation values) which represents the system in a stable or "relaxed" state (Smolensky, 1986). Within O-OER, tracing the episodic trajectory, which is equivalent to the phenomenal experience of rehearsing the material using a serial order strategy, involves passing through transient attractors which represent (or contain representations of) the to-be-remembered material. If more than one stream is present, attractors irrelevant to the rehearsed stream, which underlie the serial order component of any changing-state stream, exert an effect. This has the result that if two streams of changing-state material X and Y are present, then stream X is capable of perturbing stream Y away from the episodic trajectory, such that tracing the trajectory, maintenance rehearsal, is impaired, and the result is clearly detrimental to serial recall. The strength of this effect is dependent on the coherence of stream X, the number of changes in state that exist within the stream to act as distractors. Rehearsal is required to maintain the coherent shape of the episodic trajectory, which, dependent on internal system variables, decays over time (see Fig. 9.5).

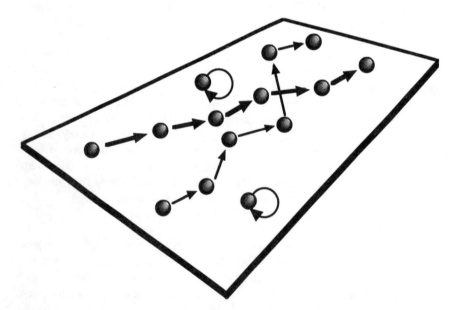

FIG. 9.5. Schematic representation of the O-OER model. The arrangement of items ("objects") is shown on a virtual surface. The objects are joined by links tracing out two trajectories that traverse the surface. One might be from a changing-state irrelevant speech source and the other might be from a to-be-remembered list of syllables. Two objects are self-referential, illustrating the representation of steady-state streams of irrelevant activity.

HOW GENERAL IS THE NOTION OF CHANGING STATE?

A theoretical consideration based on the preliminary sketches for the unitary model presented earlier is the extent to which the "unitary" nature of the model extends. The model is dependent on the idea that visually presented verbal material can be translated into a form that is isomorphic with auditorily presented non-verbal material which the subject is specifically instructed to ignore. The auditorily presented material has a detrimental effect on the serial recall of visually presented material to the extent that the auditory material changes in physical characteristics in two or more physical dimensions simultaneously. The hypothesis derived from this outcome is that the to-be-remembered material is rehearsed in a restricted-capacity representational space to which the auditory material has obligatory access. Thus the rehearsal space is a general purpose system which can be deployed to store order information about visually presented verbal material and auditorily presented material.

It seems logically plausible that the changing-state effect is a general characteristic of interfering tasks and that the pattern of interference with other agents aside from irrelevant speech might be explicable within the same framework. One such interfering task is articulatory suppression in which subjects articulate some irrelevant material either aloud or silently, rather than it being presented over headphones or loudspeakers. Changing-state effects have been found with articulatory suppression in a range of settings (Jones, Farrand, Stuart, & Morris, 1995; Macken & Jones, 1995). Articulation that changed in state between utterances produced substantial disruption of serial recall, but a smaller disruptive effect was also found when the articulated utterances remained the same (e.g. "the-the-the"). A plausible explanation for this is that irrelevant articulation places a further attentional demand on the subject. Such an explanation might predict that changing-state articulatory suppression would disrupt recall more than changing-state irrelevant speech because there would be an effect of changing state added to the effect caused by attentional load. This does not appear to be the case, and it is notable that the effect of steady-state articulatory suppression does not always reach statistical significance. An alternative explanation is also available, however. It is suggested that the slight disruption to recall evident with steady-state articulatory suppression is caused by voice "drift" or "dither" on these occasions, providing some changing-state information that is absent from recorded synthesised speech. These are relatively minor technical difficulties that should not obscure the important point that changing-state effects are not confined to irrelevant speech and that they may be a general characteristic of interfering tasks, a factor superordinate to the modality of either the memory task or the interfering agent.

More radically, the idea emerged that changing state might be a concept that could be applied to tasks that were non-verbal. Similarity of action to the auditory domain might occur at one or more levels. At the lowest level, one possibility might be that changing-state spatial stimuli are particularly disruptive of spatial short-term memory. A somewhat more revolutionary suggestion is that verbal changing-state stimuli might interfere with a spatial task. A logical sequel to this might be that representation of spatial materials in memory share important characteristics with representations of verbal or auditory materials.

It turns out that the results are encouraging to the most radical position, and that there is essentially no functional distinction between serial spatial and serial verbal memory. The evidence takes two broad forms. Earlier studies suggested that serial position curves for spatial material are characterised by restricted recency; that is, spatial materials do not show the usual improvement in recall for the last one or two items in a list as occurs in memory for auditory, and to a lesser extent, visual verbal lists (Broadbent & Broadbent, 1981; Philips & Christie, 1977). However, a recent series of studies has shown a pattern for spatial materials rather more like that typically found for visually presented verbal material. Jones et al. (1995) employed a method whereby a series of dots were presented one at a time on a screen, and once the last dot had disappeared the screen remained blank throughout a retention interval. Following this, all the stimuli were represented simultaneously on a response screen, the task of the subject being to point and click with a mouse at the dots in the order in which they had been presented. As each dot was chosen, the shading changed from black to grey, to indicate which items had already been chosen. This method has produced serial recall curves for spatial items with relatively good recall for the first items, giving way to poor performance in the middle of the list, with some improvement over the last few items of the list.

That the rehearsal-space is not restricted to verbal material is demonstrated by the logical and empirical considerations given earlier (see also Jones & Morris, 1992b; Jones, 1993), so the important factor appears not to be that the visually presented material is verbal, and could perhaps be recoded into an articulatory-verbal form which might share a common phonological structure with auditorily presented speech sounds. The method used by Jones et al. (1995) was designed specifically to avoid the possibility that the spatial material would be verbally recoded by presenting the dots in random positions within a 350 × 350 matrix on which grid lines were not shown. The changing-state hypothesis, as mentioned earlier, predicts that the effect of irrelevant changing-state material will occur on the serial recall of any material presented transiently and sequentially. This is supported by the discovery of serial recall curves for spatial material which resemble those for verbal material when testing human subjects. If these are also subject to the changing-state effect, this is powerful evidence in favour of an object-oriented, unitary model.

Further experiments of Jones et al. (1995) examined whether the changing-state effect found with irrelevant speech held for the spatial memory task described earlier. This was indeed the case, with steady-state sound producing minimal interference but changing-state auditory materials producing substantial disruption of the spatial task (see Fig. 9.6). Also, the pattern of disruption by articulatory suppression of the spatial task was equivalent to that found with visual verbal material by Macken and Jones (1995), that is, articulatory suppression exhibited a changing-state effect on the serial spatial memory task. These results are further complemented by the finding that memory for visually presented verbal items was disrupted by a changing-state spatio-motor task, but not by a steady-state version of the task (Jones et al., 1995).

The pattern of disruption of serial memory, therefore, appears to be independent of modality but critically dependent on the object-based processes of changing state. Parsimony dictates that a single process, rather than dual equivalent processes manipulating different forms of material in exactly the same manner, should be employed to explain the equivalence of results for these and other behavioural tests. It seems reasonable to conclude that spatial and verbal materials share a common level of representation, contrary to earlier views. Accepting that processes connected with serial order share a common level of representation does not mean that for other types of performance spatial and verbal stimuli cannot be shown to be relatively distinct one from another. Clearly, it is easy to imagine that if we measure how different stimuli are one from another, visuo-spatial stimuli and auditory-verbal stimuli will be very distinct. These differences however do not speak to the issue of commonality of representation, only of distinctiveness; such stimuli are distinct from one another by virtue of having very different attributes.

THEORETICAL ISSUES CONCERNING THE O-OER MODEL

Proceduralism and the O-OER Model

A major trend in current theorising about memory is an attempt to link memory theories and observed data with other biological functions, to relate memory theory more closely to its biological foundations, and distance it from an over-literal reliance on the computer metaphor of distinct memory stores or receptacles, and a central processing unit that operates on these stores. Work on distributed memory models (Humphreys, Bain, & Pike, 1989; Metcalfe Eich, 1982; Murdock, 1983) has suggested alternatives to localising memory items at a discrete address separate from the rest of the

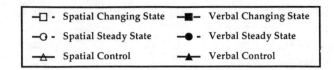

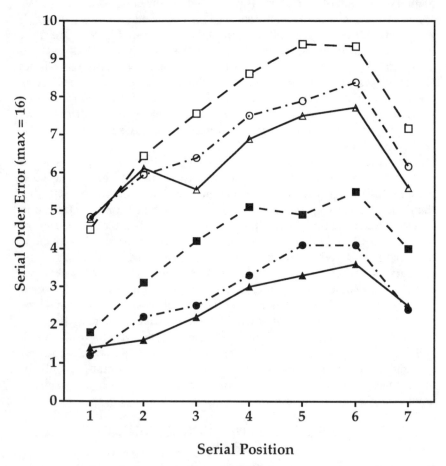

FIG. 9.6.   Effects of changing-state and steady-state irrelevant speech on verbal and spatial serial short-term memory tasks. The upper group of curves are based on performance in a spatial task in which subjects have to recall the order of appearance of a set of dots. For the lower group of curves a verbal task was used in which syllables were recalled. Data from Jones et al. (1995).

processing system, and has, additionally, shown how a single distributed memory model can account for a number of effects previously ascribed to separate memory systems (Anderson, Silverstein, Ritz, & Jones, 1977; Humphreys et al., 1989). Nevertheless many of these models still regard memory as separate from other cognitive functions; short-term memory is still sometimes regarded as simply an interface between perception and cognition rather than an active part of the processing system. This is shown in the way that memory models are often applied only to phenomena derived from memory research paradigms, although attempts are being made to reconcile memory with high-level cognitive function (Weber, Goldstein, & Busemeyer, 1991).

A natural complement to such work, which is based around the concept of a workspace or "working" memory system (Baddeley, 1986, 1992; Newell & Simon, 1972) is to consider the relationship between memory and perceptual processing (see also Cowan, 1988, 1995). Memory is dependent on the results of "peripheral" perceptual processes, and, as demonstrated by the addition of irrelevant speech to the serial recall paradigm, it is not immune to the effects of such processes during a task that supposedly relies solely on memory capacities. Proceduralism within memory theory refers to the idea that memory representations are identical to the representations of perceptual processing. This theoretical stance, which is shared by the O-OER model, has been most clearly articulated by Crowder (1993, p. 139), who has suggested that pure memory is a mythical construct, rather, "... memory storage for an experience resides in the same neural units that processed that experience when it happened in the first place". Thus the model derives much of its explanatory power by suggesting that the interference effects observed are a natural consequence of automatic activation of processing units by changing-state stimuli, which are already in use to form the representations needed to store item and serial order information for immediate or delayed recall. This couples the model firmly to the external environment, providing a bridge between perception and memory (so-called peripheral and central cognitive functions) which has previously been lacking (Baddeley, 1992).

The relationship to perceptual processing via psychoacoustic research on auditory scene analysis (Bregman, 1990) overcomes a logical flaw inherent in many theories of "central" cognitive functioning (Fodor, 1983), that the form of the representations fed to central processors is assumed to reflect the output of peripheral processes, but little attention is paid to the functionality of these processes, which logically should be given a priori consideration. The function of peripheral processes, and the representational formats these processes use, constrain the forms of activity available to memory and rehearsal processes. The proceduralist position avoids this dilemma by identifying the structure of representations within memory via the representations used within perceptual processing.

The perceptual representations within the O-OER model exist at a fairly high "object-centred" level of representation, and consist of propositions about the object derived from various sensory modalities. This is clearly seen in the unitary nature of the model which is much more dependent on the information conveyed than on the source from which it originated. Thus, in proceduralist terms, the model suggests that all stimuli are processed to the degree in which they can be analysed in terms of their physical structure and redescribed propositionally in terms of changing state. These propositional statements concerning serially presented information are structured as chained streams of information that correspond to the products of a high-level analysis of complex auditory stimuli, and obey the same rules, whether they have been visually presented or self-generated (Macken & Jones, 1995). The model is therefore consistent with the principle that serial order performance is a consequence of extended attentional processing. By this account, rehearsal is a form of attending to stimuli no longer present in the external environment by reactivating their internal perceptual representations. Rote rehearsal thus involves the reactivation of the representations of the originally presented items. As such, it is clearly a system that must be concerned with not only what the items presented were (item information), but also when they were presented (order information). It can be thought of as a form of attention that extends over a period of time, by attending to representations of items when the items themselves are no longer present.

The unitary nature of the O-OER model seems, on first consideration, to be at odds with a strict proceduralist position. If memory resides in the processing units, and not in an abstract memory store, it may be supposed that visually presented information should persist along the visual pathways of the brain, and not at some abstract level where it is equipotential with auditory information. This position, however, is dependent on the hidden assumption that the visual information is not analysed to any great degree beyond that necessary for low-level visual scene analysis to occur. This assumption can easily be seen to be false in the basic paradigm in which the visually presented material is verbal. It is clear that the irrelevant auditory information is having an effect on the visually presented to-be-remembered information, but at what level does this effect occur? The O-OER model provides a solution by suggesting that information is processed to an amodal level, to allow conjunctions of auditory and visual features that are concerned with the same "objects" in the external world.

Allowing that there is an abstract level of processing to which verbal material has been subjected, there is no reason to deny (given the experimental results reported here) that this level of processing may also be appropriate for the rehearsal and maintenance of spatial material. It is also noteworthy from a proceduralist point of view that physiological evidence concerning single cell responses in the auditory cortex to species-specific vocalisations shows no evidence for any increase in responsiveness to normal versus reversed vocalisations, suggesting that no special classes of biologically significant responses exist at this level that could form the core of a speech-specific memory system (Glass & Wollberg, 1983).

Modularity and the O-OER Model

This extension of the proceduralist position beyond immediate perceptual processing implies that information must be represented in a universal form to allow as many processes as possible to operate on it, which calls into question the modularity assumption that pervades mainstream cognitive science. Arguments have been put forward to support the modular view of brain function on the basis of evidence from physiology (Marr, 1976), neuropsychology (Shallice, 1988), philosophy (Fodor, 1983) and cognitive science (Simon, 1970). Against this, it has been pointed out that the brain evolved as a whole, rather than being put together from separate parts, and thus a number of essential interdependencies are to be expected. Natural "designs" for organisms are haphazard, consisting of a series of adaptations making use of the available material (referred to in the computer science literature as "kludges"), a biological constraint that is in conflict with the idea of a clean-cut, elegant modular structure. To argue against the modular assumption of brain function entirely would be to go beyond the evidence presented here in favour of the O-OER model, but as the O-OER model is a unitary memory model, it is appropriate to justify this on theoretical as well as the empirical grounds already covered.

An example of the modular assumption of cognitive neuroscience is presented by Ellis and Young (1988) in terms of a modular hi-fi stack. This has advantages over an enclosed unit in terms of ease of addition of new component parts (evolution of new functions), and continued functioning of the system as a whole despite damage to any single component (developmental or acquired brain damage). This is an updated version of Simon's (1970) parable of the watchmakers, but is based on a hidden premise that there is an external designer (albeit either divine or Darwinian) who oversees the system. The analogy also breaks down because it makes the false assumption that the brain, like the machine, has only one type of input at a time, and that these are never correlated (i.e. object-based). Both the watchmaker and the hi-fi stack analogies rely for their force on the idea of an end-goal or finished product, which is a meaningless concept when applied to evolutionary theory. Newly evolved functions, whether physical or mental, must of necessity emerge from existing structures and capabilities. This does not deny the essential principle articulated most clearly by Marr (1976) that the structure of each task should be made as independent as possible, but it neglects the pragmatic difficulty, that attempts to integrate different systems and approaches—vital to a coordinated biological organism acting in an unpredictable but potentially hostile environment—are fraught with difficulty. Components designed independently of each other often do not fit well together, and to stretch the hi-fi analogy, they must be designed with reference to each other, or they will not fit at all[2].

The modular assumption as it is generally conceived in psychology (and explicitly stated by Fodor, 1983, and Shallice, 1988) consists of a sequential "pass-oriented" organisation in which each identifiable processing stage or module is insulated from the influence of parallel or subsequent levels of processing. It is curious, then, that a normally functioning human brain does not allow us to perceive more modular-based dissociations (back to the "binding" problem). Artificial Intelligence techniques (particularly black-board systems and connectionist architectures) in contrast, demonstrate the great increase in computational power that can be bought by allowing rich interactions to occur between locally specialised functions. The possibility that this may also occur in natural intelligence is largely ignored in the psychological formulation of the modularity assumption which typically concerns itself with the internal functioning of individual modules. With regard to natural systems, there is also the problem of identifying which of a seemingly infinite set of possible modular structures actually correspond to the "joints" at which cognition can be carved. Neuropsychological evidence of double dissociations of functions is often appealed to at this point (Shallice, 1988) to identify "natural kinds" of cognitive functions. It is necessary to be wary of the conclusive claims sometimes made for this form of research, however, as the task demand characteristics of tests given to neuropsychological patients need to be analysed as deeply as those of experiments carried out using "normal" subjects, particularly so because the means with which the patients perform these tests are regarded to be in some sense "abnormal", directly reflecting the product of a lesioned functional architecture.

An obvious example to give here is the "fractionation" of short-term memory function (see Vallar & Shallice, 1990, for a review which contrasts several different theoretical interpretations) between auditory and visual modalities which has been frequently observed (Basso, Spinnler, Vallar, & Zanobio, 1982; Shallice & Warrington, 1970, 1974; Vallar & Baddeley, 1984; Warrington & Shallice, 1969, 1972). In contrast, the O-OER model predicts that the important distinctive features are the types of activity in each modality meeting the requirements of serial order and changing state. This has not yet been addressed by any neuropsychological testing procedure within the O-OER framework. There is evidence to suggest from animal

---

[2] Biologically, the example has been given of the evolution of the giraffe; any physical specialisation such as an elongated neck requires an amendment to the cardiovascular system to pump the blood to the brain against the increased gravitational resistance (Marshall, 1984).

testing, however, that the insulo-temporal region of the auditory cortex may act in a supramodal temporal sequencing manner similar to that predicted by the O-OER model. Lesions in the I-T area of the cat have been shown to upset the perception of visual and somatosensory as well as auditory temporal patterns (Colativa, 1972, 1974). Spatial material, similarly, seems to be organised in terms of topographic spatial "maps" which show observable physiological responses in the same area of the brain (the circumstriate visual cortex) dependent on the spatial location of the stimuli, and independent of whether the form of the stimuli is visual or auditory.

The penultimate point to note with regard to modular functioning within short-term memory models relates to the integration of information within such models. There is inherent within this formulation the implication of some form of homunculus explanation. The central system needed to link all the separate stores for different forms of information needs to have properties that may be beyond our capacity to model (Fodor, 1983). It needs to have some form of understanding of the representations stored by the sub-systems in order to solve the binding problem, the question of how to deal with stimuli that qualify for inclusion into more than one store (e.g. speech with lip-movements, Campbell & Dodd, 1980; Jones, 1993). If this problem is not tackled, the models of separate functional components will reflect the modern cognitive science equivalent of the blocks-world paradigm which preoccupied the field of artificial intelligence throughout the 1970s, producing models and programs that ran successfully only in "toy" domains, and did not scale-up to real-world applications. Related to this is the final problem concerned with the extent to which we can claim to be making real theoretical progress simply by assigning functions to one module or another. There seems to be no principled limit that has yet been reached to the number or nature of modules that can be postulated simply for short-term memory to a point where a theory may be unfalsifiable.

Further Work

The O-OER model is primarily a model of serial recall, where the principal means of recall is through a chain of associative cues. The O-OER model also allows access to items through a non-serial recall procedure; the distinction is necessary to account for the differential effects of irrelevant speech on serial recall and tasks with no serial component involved such as the missing item task (Jones & Macken, 1993; Yntema & Trask, 1963). This suggests that a means of accessing the items exists that does not involve tracing the episodic trajectory, and as such is immune to the effects of irrelevant speech. Establishing the mechanisms by which this may take place will require empirical investigation and theoretical elaboration of the model. It seems plausible that an explanation of the missing item task will have to deal with the way in which long-term, semantic levels of representation interact with the episodic level, as in this task the item that is "missing" from a particular episode is only missing with respect to a pre-experimentally familiar set (days of the week, months of the year, etc.). A number of aspects of the model may also require a psychophysical level of investigation, in order, for example, to elaborate the mechanisms whereby multi-modal inputs are combined into object-based representations. Thus, the perceptual processes of segmentation and object formation are an important domain of future work on the model. In general, the model needs to be specified in a more detailed and formal way. For example, the precise mechanism whereby one changing-state stream may interfere with another needs to be established. However, despite the current general descriptive state of the Object-Oriented Episodic Record model, it has nonetheless served as a useful tool in directing investigations of short-term memory.

REFERENCES

Allport, A. (1989). Visual attention. In M.I. Posner (Ed.), *Foundations of cognitive science*. Cambridge, MA: MIT Press.

Anderson, J.A., Silverstein, J.W., Ritz, S.A., & Jones, R.S. (1977). Distinctive features, categorical perception, and probability learning: Some applications of a neural model. *Psychological Review, 84*, 413–451.

Atkinson, R.C., & Shiffrin, R.M. (1968). Human memory: A proposed system and its control processes. In K.W. Spence (Ed.), *The psychology of learning and motivation: Advances in research and theory, Vol. 2*. New York: Academic Press.

Baddeley, A.D. (1986). *Working memory*. Oxford: Oxford University Press.

Baddeley, A.D. (1992). Is Working Memory Working? The fifteenth Bartlett lecture. *Quarterly Journal of Experimental Psychology, 44A*, 1–31.

Baddeley, A.D., & Hitch, G.J. (1974). Working memory. In G. Bower (Ed.), *Recent advances in learning and motivation, Vol. 3*, (pp. 47–90). London: Academic Press.

Basso, A., Spinnler, H., Vallar, G., & Zanobio, M.E. (1982). Left hemisphere damage and selective impairment of auditory verbal short-term memory: A case study. *Neuropsychologia, 20*, 263–274.

Beauvois, M.W., & Meddis, R. (1991). A computer model of auditory stream segregation. In Q. Summerfield (Ed.), *Hearing and speech*, (pp. 517–542). London: Lawrence Erlbaum Associates Ltd.

Bregman, A.S. (1990). *Auditory scene analysis: The perceptual organization of sound*. London: MIT Press.

Bridges, A.M., & Jones, D.M. (in press). Word-dose in the disruption of serial recall by irrelevant speech. *Quarterly Journal of Experimental Psychology*.

Broadbent, D.E. (1984). The Maltese cross: A new simplistic model for memory. *Behavioral and Brain Sciences, 7*, 55–94.

Broadbent, D.E., & Broadbent, M.H.P. (1981). Recency effects in visual memory. *Quarterly Journal of Experimental Psychology, 33A*, 1–15.

Campbell, R., & Dodd, B. (1980). Hearing by eye. *Quarterly Journal of Experimental Psychology, 32*, 85–99.

Colativa, F.B. (1972). Auditory cortical lesions and visual pattern discrimination in cat. *Brain Research, 39*, 437–447.

Colativa, F.B. (1974). Insular-temporal lesions and vibrotactile temporal pattern discrimination in cats. *Psychological Behavior, 12*, 215–218.

Colle, H.A., & Welsh, A. (1976). Acoustic masking in primary memory. *Journal of Verbal Learning and Verbal Behavior, 15*, 17–31.

Colle, H.A. (1980). Auditory encoding in visual short-term recall: Effects of noise intensity and spatial location. *Journal of Verbal Learning and Verbal Behavior, 19*, 722–735.

Cowan, N. (1988). Evolving conceptions of memory storage, selective attention, and mutual constraints within the human information processing system. *Psychological Bulletin, 104*, 163–191.

Cowan, N. (1995). *Attention and memory*. Oxford: Clarendon Press.

Crowder, R.G. (1993). Systems and principles in memory theory: Another critique of pure memory. In A.F. Collins, S.E. Gathercole, M.A. Conway, & P.E. Morris (Eds.), *Theories of memory*, (pp. 139–162). London: Lawrence Erlbaum Associates Ltd.

Ellis, A.W., & Young, A.W. (1988). *Human cognitive neuropsychology*. London: Lawrence Erlbaum Associates Ltd.

Estes, W.K. (1972). An associative basis for coding and organization in memory. In A.W. Melton & E. Martin (Eds.), *Coding processes in human Memory*, (pp. 161–190). New York: Halstead Press.

Fodor, J.A. (1983). *The modularity of mind*. Cambridge MA: MIT Press.

Gathercole, S.E., & Baddeley, A.D. (1990). Phonological memory deficits in language disordered children: Is there a causal connection? *Journal of Memory and Language, 29*, 336–360.

Gathercole, S.E., & Baddeley, A.D. (1993). *Working memory and language*. Hove, UK: Lawrence Erlbaum Associates Ltd.

Glass, I., & Wollberg, Z. (1983). Responses of cells in the auditory cortex of awake squirrel monkeys to normal and reversed species-specific vocalizations. *Hearing Research, 9*, 27–33.

Hall, G. (1980). *Perceptual and associative learning*. Oxford: Oxford University Press.

Hanley, J.R., & Broadbent, C. (1987). The effect of unattended speech on serial recall following auditory presentation. *British Journal of Psychology, 78*, 287–297.

Hellbrück, J., & Kilcher, H. (1993). Effects on mental tasks induced by noise recorded and presented via an artificial head system. In M. Vallet (Ed.), *Noise and man '93*, (pp. 315–322). Arcueil, France: Institut National de Recherche sur les Transports et Leur Sécurité.

Hummel, J.E., & Biederman, I. (1992). Dynamic binding in a neural network for shape recognition. *Psychological Review, 99*(3), 480–517.

Humphreys, M.S., Bain, J.D., & Pike, R. (1989). Different ways to cue a coherent memory system: A theory for episodic, semantic, and procedural tasks. *Psychological Review, 96*(2), 208–233.

Jones, D.M. (1993). Objects, streams and threads of auditory attention. In A.D. Baddeley & L. Weiskrantz (Eds.), *Attention: Selection, awareness and control*, (pp. 87–104). Oxford: Clarendon Press.

Jones, D.M., Farrand, P.A., Stuart, G.P., & Morris, N. (1995). The functional equivalence of verbal and spatial information in short-term memory. *Journal of Experimental Psychology: Learning, Memory and Cognition, 21*, 1008–1018.

Jones, D.M., & Macken, W.J. (1993). Irrelevant tones produce an irrelevant speech effect: Implications for phonological coding in working memory. *Journal of Experimental Psychology: Learning, Memory and Cognition, 19*, 369–381.

Jones, D.M., & Macken, W.J. (1995a). Organizational factors in the irrelevant speech effect: The role of spatial location and timing. *Memory and Cognition, 23*, 192–200.

Jones, D.M., & Macken, W.J. (1995b). Auditory babble and cognitive efficiency: The role of number of voices and their location. *Journal of Experimental Psychology: Applied, 1*, 216–226.

Jones, D.M., & Macken, W.J. (1995c). Phonological similarity in the irrelevant speech effect. Within- or between-stream similarity? *Journal of Experimental Psychology: Learning, Memory and Cognition, 21,* 103–115.

Jones, D.M., Macken, W.J., & Murray, A.C. (1993). Disruption of visual short-term memory by changing state auditory stimuli: The role of segmentation. *Memory and Cognition, 21,* 318–328.

Jones, D.M., Madden, C.A., & Miles, C. (1992). Privileged access by irrelevant speech to short-term memory: The role of changing state. *Quarterly Journal of Experimental Psychology, 44A*(4), 645–669.

Jones, D.M., Miles, C., & Page, J. (1990). Disruption of proof-reading by irrelevant speech: Effects of attention, arousal or memory? *Applied Cognitive Psychology, 4,* 89–108.

Jones, D.M., & Morris, N. (1992a). Irrelevant speech and serial recall: Implications for theories of attention and working memory. *Scandinavian Journal of Psychology, 33,* 212–229.

Jones, D.M., & Morris, N. (1992b). Irrelevant speech and cognition. In D.M. Jones & A.P. Smith (Eds.), *Handbook of human performance,* (pp. 29–53). London: Academic Press.

Knudsen, E.I., duLac, S., & Esterly, S.D. (1987). Computational maps in the brain. *Annual Review of Neuroscience, 10,* 41–66.

LeCompte, D.C. (1994). Extending the irrelevant speech effect beyond serial recall. *Journal of Experimental Psychology: Learning, Memory and Cognition, 20,* 1396–1408.

Lewandowsky, S., & Murdock, B.B. (1989). Memory for serial order. *Psychological Review, 96,* 25–57.

Macken, W.J., & Jones, D.M. (1995). Functional characteristics of the "inner voice" and the "inner ear": Single or double agency? *Journal of Experimental Psychology: Learning, Memory and Cognition, 21,* 436–448.

Marr, D. (1976). Early processing of visual information. *Philosophical Transactions of the Royal Society of London "B", 275,* 483–524.

Marshall, J.C. (1984). Multiple perspectives on modularity. *Cognition, 17,* 209–242.

Metcalfe Eich, J. (1982). A composite holographic associative recall model. *Psychological Review, 89,* 627–661.

Miles, C., Jones, D.M., & Madden, C.A. (1991). Locus of the irrelevant speech effect in short-term memory. *Journal of Experimental Psychology: Learning, Memory and Cognition, 17,* 578–584.

Minsky, M.L. (1968). *Semantic information processing.* Cambridge, MA: MIT Press.

Murdock, B.B. (1983). A distributed memory model for serial order information. *Psychological Review, 90,* 316–338.

Näätänen, R. (1990). The role of attention in auditory information processing as revealed by event-related potentials and other brain measures of cognitive function. *Behavioral and Brain Sciences, 13,* 201–288.

Newell, A., & Simon, H.A. (1972). *Human problem solving.* Englewood Cliffs, NJ: Prentice-Hall.

Öhman, A. (1979). The orienting response, attention, and learning: An information-processing perspective. In H.D. Kimmel, E.H. Van Olst, & J.F. Orlebeke (Eds.), *The orienting reflex in humans* (pp. 443–472). Hillsdale, NJ: Lawrence Erlbaum Associates Inc.

Philips, W.A., & Christie, D.F.M. (1977). Components of visual memory. *Quarterly Journal of Experimental Psychology, 29,* 117–133.

Salamé, P., & Baddeley, A. (1982). Disruption of short-term memory by unattended speech: Implications for the structure of working memory. *Journal of Verbal Learning and Verbal Behavior, 21,* 150–164.

Salamé, P., & Baddeley, A. (1989). Effects of background music on phonological short-term memory. *Quarterly Journal of Experimental Psychology, 22,* 261–273.

Shallice, T. (1988). *From neuropsychology to mental structure.* Cambridge: Cambridge University Press.

Shallice, T., & Warrington, E.K. (1970). Independent functioning of verbal memory stores: A neuropsychological study. *Quarterly Journal of Experimental Psychology, 22,* 261–273.

Shallice, T., & Warrington, E.K. (1974). The dissociation between short term retention of meaningful sounds and verbal material. *Neuropsychologia, 12,* 553–555.

Simon, H.A. (1970). *The sciences of the artificial.* Cambridge, MA: MIT Press.

Smolensky, P. (1986). Information processing in dynamical systems: Foundations of harmony theory. In. D.E. Rumelhart & J.L. McClelland (Eds.), *Parallel distributed processing, Volume 1: Foundations,* (pp. 194–281). Cambridge, MA: MIT Press.

Vallar, G., & Baddeley, A.D. (1984). Fractionation of working memory: Neuropsychological evidence for a phonological short-term store. *Journal of Verbal Learning and Verbal Behavior, 23,* 151–161.

Vallar, G., & Shallice, T. (1990). *Neuropsychological impairments of short-term memory.* Cambridge: Cambridge University Press.

Warrington, E.K., & Shallice, T. (1969). The selective impairment of auditory verbal short-term memory. *Brain, 92,* 885–896.

Warrington, E.K., & Shallice, T. (972). Neuropsychological evidence of visual storage in short-term memory tasks. *Quarterly Journal of Experimental Psychology, 24,* 30–40.

Weber, E.V., Goldstein, W.M., & Busemeyer, J.R. (1991). Beyond strategies: Implications of memory representation and memory processes for models of judgement and decision making. In W.E. Hockley & S. Lewandowsky (Eds.), *Relating theory and data: Essays on human memory in honor of Bennet B. Murdock,* (pp. 75–100). Hillsdale, NJ: Lawrence Erlbaum Associates Inc.

Whitfield, I.C. (1979). The object of the sensory cortex. *Brain, Behavior and Evolution, 16,* 129–154.

Wickelgren, W.A. (1965). Acoustic similarity and intrusion errors in short-term memory. *Journal of Experimental Psychology, 709*(1), 102–108.

Yntema, D.B., & Trask, F.P. (1963). Recall as a search process. *Journal of Verbal Learning and Verbal Behavior, 2,* 65–74.

10 Item, associative, and serial-order information in TODAM

Bennet Murdock
University of Toronto, Canada

TODAM, an acronym for Theory of Distributed Associative Memory, is a general theory of memory that attempts to explain how we store and retrieve item, associative, and serial-order information. Item information allows us to recognise objects and events—names, faces, sounds, the myriad objects and events that make up the world around us. It underlies the feeling of familiarity when we see or hear them. Associative information allows us to remember the relation between two objects or events: lightning and thunder, the taste and smell of a particular food, or the names and faces of our friends. Serial-order information allows us to remember temporal order: the days of the week, the letters of the alphabet, how to spell words, or what our telephone number is.

On a logical basis item, associative, and serial-order information are different. They refer to single objects, pairs of objects, and three or more objects, respectively. There is much experimental evidence supporting these distinctions. The early evidence was reviewed in Murdock (1974), and more will be presented as we go along. No theory of memory can be complete unless it takes these differences into account.

TODAM was an extension of CADAM (Content-Addressable Distributed Associative Memory) developed by Liepa (1977) which in turn borrowed heavily from the distributed-memory models of Anderson (Anderson, 1968, 1970) and Kohonen (1977) and the holographic models of the 1960s and 1970s (e.g. Longuet-Higgins, 1968; Willshaw, 1972). CADAM treated item, associative, and serial-order information separately;

239

TODAM combines them and tries to explicate their interrelationship (see Murdock 1979, 1982, 1983).

The most basic feature of TODAM is that, like the early holographic models, it is a distributed memory model. This means that all information is accumulated in a single memory store. This is in contrast to a localised (or discrete) system where each item or event is stored in a separate location (for an example see Collins & Loftus, 1975).

As a metaphor, imagine we throw a number of objects, one at a time, into a small pond. Each object creates its own distinctive pattern of wave activity, and this wave activity accumulates. At first the pond is smooth. The first object makes its own wave pattern and the second object adds to them. So we have the first and the second, but the first dies down when the second one occurs. Then the third comes along and the first two die down a bit when the third occurs. Suppose α is the attenuation or damping factor (technically, parameter). If O_j is the j-th object and P_j is the wave activity on the pond after the j-th object has been thrown in then

$$P_0 = 0,$$
$$P_1 = O_1,$$
$$P_2 = \alpha\, O_1 + O_2,$$
$$P_3 = \alpha\, P_2 + O_3 = \alpha^2\, O_1 + \alpha\, O_2 + O_3,$$

or in general

$$P_j = \alpha\, P_{j-1} + O_j.$$

This simple scheme captures the essence of the matched-filter model of Anderson (1973) The matched-filter model was incorporated as the basic mechanism for the storage and retrieval of item information in TODAM. The objects correspond to items or events we experience in everyday life (or the list of items we see in a laboratory study of recognition memory) and the pond is our memory, the repository of the events we have experienced. The attenuation factor accounts for forgetting, and it produces pure recency. The most recent events are the sharpest or clearest, and as their age increases the clarity decreases.

How does retrieval occur? We have old objects and new objects; the old objects are in memory (were thrown into the pond), but the new objects are not in memory (were not thrown into the pond). The wave pattern of old objects matches (to a degree) the wave pattern on the surface of the pond at the time of test; the wave pattern of new objects does not. The goodness of match depends on the value of α and the serial position (age) of the item. As a parameter, $0 < \alpha < 1$ so the closer to one the less forgetting in general, and the more recent the item the better the match in particular.

Let me put this more formally. Although TODAM uses vectors to represent items, let me start with scalars (random variables) to introduce the ideas. Suppose the objects are represented by independent random samples all sampled from a common feature distribution which is normally distributed with mean 0 and unit variance (i.e. $\sigma^2 = 1$). Let these samples be $Z_1, Z_2, \ldots Z_L$ (for L items in the list) and

$$M = \sum_{l=1}^{L} \alpha_l Z_l$$

where M is the memory and α_l is a function of α and l (specifically, $\alpha_l = \alpha^{L-l}$). Then for an old item Z_k from Serial Position k the expected value (E) of the product of the probe item with memory is

$$E[Z_k M] = E[Z_k \sum_{l=1}^{L} \alpha_l Z_l]$$

$$= E[Z_k(\alpha_k Z_k + \sum_{l \neq k}^{L} \alpha_l Z_l)] = E[Z_k \alpha_k Z_k + Z_k \sum_{l \neq k}^{L} \alpha_l Z_l]$$

$$= E[Z_k \alpha_k Z_k] + E[Z_k \sum_{l \neq k}^{L} \alpha_l Z_l]$$

and since $E[Z_i Z_j] = 0$, $i \neq j$ (the random samples are independent) the second term is zero and

$$E[Z_k M] = \alpha_k E[Z_k^2] = \alpha_k = \alpha^{L-k} \tag{1}$$

because for random variables with mean zero $E[Z^2] = \sigma^2$ and by definition $\sigma^2 = 1$. For a new item, no items match so $E[Z_{New}M] = 0$.

The point is (and this takes a while to get used to) the items in memory (represented by random variables in the model) are independent, so non-target items have no effect on the result of the comparison process.[i] The age of an item does have an effect but this is a function of α. Thus, TODAM is an interference model not a decay model. We have known since McGeoch (1932), for long-term memory, and Waugh and Norman (1965), for short-term memory, that forgetting is due to interference not decay, and the recency effect of Equation 1 is due to α (i.e. interference not decay).

What evidence is there for recency? One example (Fig. 10.1) is a study of picture memory by Nickerson (1968) with intervals ranging from days up to a year. Another example (Fig. 10.2) is a study of recognition memory

---

[i] We can also determine the effect of non-independence (correlation) or similarity among items, but this is beyond the scope of the present paper.

Long-term Recognition

NICK01.PRE

FIG. 10.1   d′ as a function of retention interval for long-term recognition memory. Data from Nickerson (1968).

for words in a list (Murdock & Anderson, 1975) where the hit rate (percentage of old items recognised) decreases regularly as lag (number of items intervening between study and test) increases. Recognition memory tasks almost always show extensive recency effects, and this is very consistent with the model.

Now the objects in the pond are only a metaphor, and the derivations with random variables were only to get us started, but before we move on let us summarise the argument to date and add a new point. TODAM is a distributed memory model; all items are thrown into the same pond and their waves accumulate. All items are stored in a common memory by superposition (addition). According to the model there is no "grandmother cell"—a cell that is special for her. All cells (at least all cells in the memory system) participate in storing all memories.

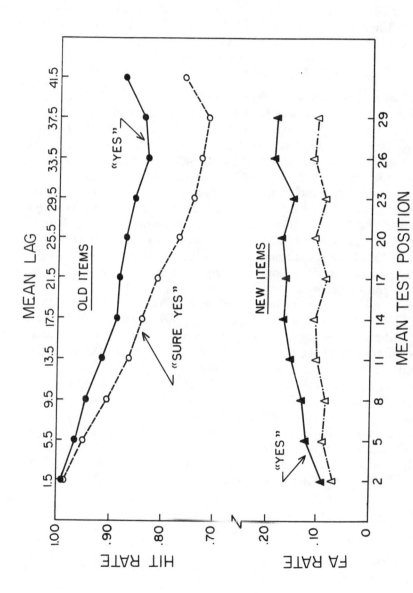

FIG. 10.2 Hit rate and false-alarm rate as a function of lag and test position from a study of short-term recognition memory. Data from Murdock and Anderson (1975).

The new point is retrieval. TODAM is a direct-access model, not a search model. You don't have to search for an item in memory because you know exactly where to look—at the waves on the surface of the pond. Search is a major problem for a localised (or grandmother-cell) type of memory, but not here. There are fuzzy memories and we have to clean them up, but this is a deblurring process not a search process; more on this point later.

THE MATCHED-FILTER MODEL

The matched-filter model (Anderson, 1973) is the original distributed-memory model for recognition. It has four basic assumptions; they deal with representation, storage, retrieval, and decision. The representation assumption says that items can be represented as random vectors; that is, vectors whose elements are normally-distributed, independent random samples from a feature distribution with mean zero and variance $\sigma^2 = 1/N$ where N is the number of elements in the vector. Earlier we talked about random variables; now we have vectors whose elements are random variables (or random samples from some specified feature distribution). You can have N independent vectors in an N-dimensional vector space, so N (the number of elements that is also the dimensionality of the space) must be very large.[ii] But it is estimated that there are 10^{12} neurons and 10^{14} synapses in the brain, so this is not a problem.

These random vectors can be thought of as lists of attributes (e.g. Bower, 1967, Flexser & Tulving 1978, Underwood, 1969, Wickens, 1970) where each attribute is represented by a single random variable. These variables (hence the vector) are the same when an item is repeated, but different (i.e. independent) from item to item. They are random samples from a zero-centred feature distribution so, as noted, $E[Z_i Z_j] = O$, $i \neq j$. The feature distribution has a variance σ^2 of $1/N$ for normalisation. Item vectors are normalised to 1.0 so we are always dealing with unit vectors. The normalisation is approximate (statistical) not exact. The expected value of the dot product of an item with itself is 1.0 but the variance is greater than 0.

If $\mathbf{f}$ is a random vector consisting of N of these random variables, and $\mathbf{f} \bullet \mathbf{f}$ is the dot (or inner) product where $\mathbf{f} \bullet \mathbf{f}$ is

$$\mathbf{f} \bullet \mathbf{f} = \sum_{i=1}^{N} f(i) f(i)$$

then we will always be dealing with unit vectors (vectors of "length" 1) because

---

[ii] Some knowledge of linear algebra is necessary to understand the matched-filter model (and TODAM); for the basic concepts see Jordan (1986).

$$E[\mathbf{f} \bullet \mathbf{f}] = E[\sum_{i=1}^{N} f(i)f(i)] = NE[Z_i Z_i] = NE[Z_i^2] = N\sigma^2 = N(1/N) = 1.$$

The storage assumption (or storage equation) is

$$\mathbf{M}_j = \alpha \mathbf{M}_{j-1} + \mathbf{f}_j \qquad (2)$$

which is exactly what we had before except that we have replaced random variables with random vectors. Thus, if you understood Equation 1 you should have no trouble with Equation 2 if you replace random variables with random vectors.

The retrieval assumption is that the comparison operation (or process) is the dot product. That is, when you compare a probe item with the item information stored in memory then in the model you take the dot product of the probe item with the memory vector. The result of this operation (the output from the memory comparison process) is the input to the decision stage. It is what determines the sense of familiarity when you recognise (or don't recognise) an item or event.

The decision process assumes that there are two matched filters, a positive matched filter for old items and a negative matched filter for new items. The comparison process drives an accumulation of evidence towards an upper criterion or a lower criterion. A response ("yes" or "no") occurs when the accumulation of evidence reaches the upper or lower criterion, respectively. This provides a possible latency mechanism for the model, but as there is not space to deal with latency effects in this paper we won't consider the decision process further.

Evaluation

The matched filter has some strength and weakness, and we will consider these in turn. On the positive side, it is a simple and elegant model for item recognition. Perhaps its most important contribution is to provide a principled account to motivate the application of signal-detection theory to human memory. Egan (1958), Murdock (1965), and Norman and Wickelgren (1965) showed that a signal-detection analysis could be applied to recognition memory, and since then it has become the method of choice for analysing data from recognition-memory experiments. However, the justification was purely empirical—it worked. The matched-filter model provides a possible answer to why it works.

If human memory really worked exactly the way the matched-filter model suggested, then you would get the two strength or familiarity distributions envisioned by signal-detection theory and the 2×2 table of hits, false alarms, misses, and correct rejections would fall out as a result of the location of the criteria (upper and lower boundaries of the accumulation process). In fact, once you know the experimental details (list length and some procedural details) you can easily work out explicit expressions for the means and variances of the strength distributions given the two parameters of the model (N and α).

More generally, the matched-filter model showed in detail that, and how, a distributed-memory model could work. The derivations are all presented in Anderson (1973). You can simulate the model and show that the memory will reject (respond "no" to) new items and accept (respond "yes" to) old items at any accuracy level you specify, even though all the old items have been thrown into the same pond. There is no question that a distributed-memory model works as advertised. The question is whether that is really the way human memory works.

What are the problems? First, it is a specific not a general model of memory. It deals with item information but says nothing about associative or serial-order information. Second, it has no context mechanism and context is crucial in laboratory studies of recognition memory. We do not ask subjects whether they have ever seen or heard the item before; rather, we ask whether they have experienced the item in the experimental context. Thus, you need a context mechanism, and the matched-filter model doesn't have one. Third, it cannot learn. That is, presenting an item will put it in the old item distribution, but repetition increases the mean and variance so as to maintain a constant ratio, so d′ does not increase (Murdock & Lamon, 1988).[iii]

The learning problem is easy to rectify by probabilistic encoding. If you assume that only a random subset of features are encoded on each presentation then the mean increases faster than the standard deviation so d′ increases with repetition the way it should. Specifically, if we revise Equation 2 to be

$$\mathbf{M}_j = \alpha\,\mathbf{M}_{j-1} + p\,\mathbf{f}_j \tag{3}$$

where each feature is encoded with probability p or not encoded with probability 1–p then learning will occur. The other problems however, require more drastic modifications, and that is where TODAM really begins.

ASSOCIATIVE INFORMATION

We represent items as random vectors; how do we represent associations? The traditional way is by connections. In classical conditioning, a conditioned stimulus is associated or connected to the unconditioned

---

[iii] In all fairness it should be pointed out that this result depends on your assumption about how the memory vector is initialised before list presentation; see Murdock and Kahana (1993) for details.

response, and we represent the connection by a line or an arrow. Semantic memory models use a graph-theoretical approach (e.g. Kiss, 1968) where nodes represent the items and links represent the associations or connections between the items.

The Gestaltists (e.g. Asch, 1969; Kohler; 1941, Rock & Ceraso, 1964) thought otherwise. They viewed associations as wholistic entities, but they weren't very clear about just what these wholistic entities were. A possible interpretation was provided by Borsellino and Poggio (1973) who described a mathematical formalism for the storage and retrieval of associative information.

The formalism said that the association between two item vectors could be represented by the mathematical operation of convolution. Convolution (∗) is a particular way of combining or merging two vectors; specifically, cross-multiply all the pairwise elements and sum along the negative diagonals. An example is shown in Fig. 10.3. In terms of components, if there are two vectors $\mathbf{f}$ and $\mathbf{g}$ then the x-th component of $\mathbf{f}{\ast}\mathbf{g}$ is

$$(f * g)(x) = \sum_i f(i)g(x - i). \tag{4}$$

If two vectors are associated by convolution, one can retrieve the other by correlation (#). Correlation can also be carried out by cross-multiplying all pairwise elements but now you sum over the diagonals not the negative diagonals. In terms of components

$$(f\#g)(x) = \sum_i f(i)g(x + i) \tag{5}$$

so the difference between the negative diagonals and the diagonals is reflected in the plus or minus sign in the second subscript on the right-hand side of Equations 4 and 5.

As Borsellino and Poggio (1973) pointed out, convolution and correlation are approximate inverses (like multiplication and division) so retrieval occurs by correlation if the association has been formed by convolution. Specifically, if δ is the delta vector—a particular vector such that $\delta = (\ldots 0,0,0,1,0,0,0, \ldots)$—and if primes (i.e. δ', $\mathbf{g}'$) indicate approximations (i.e. each element of δ' or $\mathbf{g}'$ has approximately the same value as the corresponding element of δ or $\mathbf{g}$ but there is a small plus-or-minus), then

$$\mathbf{f}\#(\mathbf{f} * \mathbf{g}) = (\mathbf{f}\#\mathbf{f}) * \mathbf{g} = \delta' * \mathbf{g} = \mathbf{g}'. \tag{6}$$

Given the representation assumption, for any vector $\mathbf{f}$, $\mathbf{f}\#\mathbf{f} = \delta'$ and δ' (an approximation to δ') convolved with any vector say $\mathbf{g}$ gives $\mathbf{g}'$.

To understand this formalism at a simpler level, think of multiplication and division. If you multiply a by b and then divide the product by a the

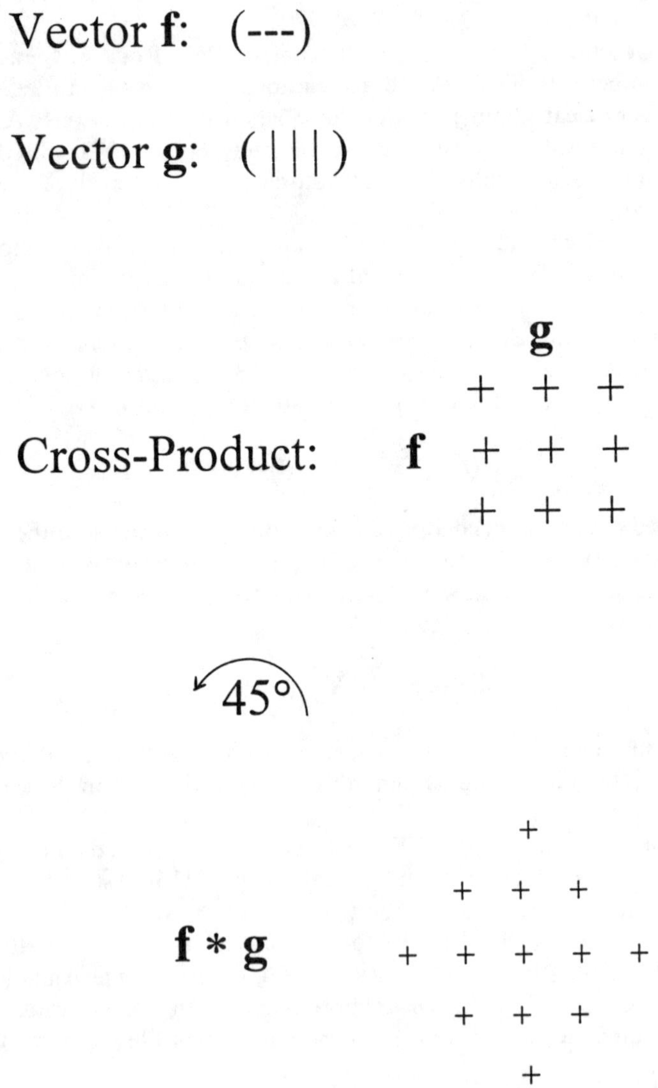

Vector **f**: (---)

Vector **g**: (|||)

$$
\begin{array}{cccc}
 & & \mathbf{g} & \\
 & & + \ + \ + & \\
\text{Cross-Product:} & \mathbf{f} & + \ + \ + & \\
 & & + \ + \ + &
\end{array}
$$

$$
\overset{\nwarrow}{45°}\diagdown
$$

$$
\mathbf{f * g}
\begin{array}{ccccc}
 & & + & & \\
 & + & + & + & \\
+ & + & + & + & + \\
 & + & + & + & \\
 & & + & &
\end{array}
$$

FIG. 10.3 Illustration of convolution (∗). Given two three-element vectors **f** and **g**, form the cross-product matrix (i.e. multiply each row element by each column element), rotate it 45 degrees, and sum the columns to get the convolution **f∗g**.

result is b. The result is exact, not approximate. If you divide the product by b the result is a; because convolution is commutative, the analogous result holds in the Borsellino and Poggio scheme. Thus,

$$\mathbf{g} \# (\mathbf{f} * \mathbf{g}) = \mathbf{g} \# (\mathbf{g} * \mathbf{f}) = (\mathbf{g} \# \mathbf{g}) * \mathbf{f} = \delta' \# \mathbf{f} = \mathbf{f}'. \tag{7}$$

Thus, associative symmetry holds or, in classical terminology, "backward" associations are as strong as "forward" associations. Much supporting evidence has recently been summarised by Kahana (submitted).

The convolution of two item vectors is a "wholistic entity"—it is not **f** or **g** or even like **f** or **g**. Rather it is a new vector of dimension 2N–1 and the items and the associations are independent. That is,

$$E[\mathbf{f} \bullet (\mathbf{f} * \mathbf{g})] = E[\mathbf{g} \bullet (\mathbf{f} * \mathbf{g})] = 0. \tag{8}$$

When a pair of study items is presented, we assume subjects encode both the items and the association. As there must also be some attenuation of the memory vector the simplest storage equation is

$$\mathbf{M}_j = \alpha \mathbf{M}_{j-1} + \mathbf{f}_j + \mathbf{g}_j + \mathbf{f}_j * \mathbf{g}_j. \tag{9a}$$

We need probabilistic encoding in order for learning to occur so

$$\mathbf{M}_j = \alpha \mathbf{M}_{j-1} + p\mathbf{f}_j + p\mathbf{g}_j + p\mathbf{f}_j * p\mathbf{g}_j. \tag{9b}$$

The pf that is associated with pg is the same as the item pf, and likewise for pg.

It is possible for subjects to attend more to the items or more to the associations so let us introduce some attention weights (parameters) γ_1, γ_2, and γ_3 so

$$\mathbf{M}_j = \alpha \mathbf{M}_{j-1} + \gamma_1 (p\mathbf{f}_j) + \gamma_2 (p\mathbf{g}_j) + \gamma_3 (p\mathbf{f}_j * p\mathbf{g}_j). \tag{9c}$$

As attention is limited, presumably the more attention you pay to one the less you pay to the others, so assume a limited-capacity hypothesis, namely

$$\gamma_1 + \gamma_2 + \gamma_3 = 1.0. \tag{10}$$

Equations 9c and 10 are the basic storage equations for item and associative information.

What about retrieval? For item recognition you take the dot product of the probe item with the memory vector and for associative recognition you take the dot product of the convolution of the two probe items with the memory vector. In the latter case, the analysis for intact/rearranged pairs is exactly analogous to the analyses for old/new items in the item-recognition case.[iv] But what about recall?

Recall is a two-stage process. First you correlate the probe item with the memory vector to get an approximation to the target item, but then you must clean up or deblur the approximation in order to generate the item to be recalled. Retroactive-inhibition (RI) studies show important differences between recall and recognition in an A–B, A–C paradigm (Dyne et al., 1990; Postman & Stark, 1969) and recent results by Murdock and Hockley (1989) show no forgetting in associative recognition where cued recall would probably deteriorate, so these effects provide evidence for the dissociation of these two stages (correlation and deblurring).

How does deblurring work? Deblurring is not formally modelled in TODAM because we have been more concerned with memory processes than response processes.[v] Similarly, encoding is part of the perceptual processes and we do not model that either. We simply assume that items can be represented by random vectors, and our knowledge of encoding processes does not yet allow us to construct any 1:1 mapping between real-world stimuli and our idealised representations.

The processes envisaged by TODAM for the storage and retrieval of item and associative information are convolution, correlation, summation, and scalar multiplication (the dot product is a special case of correlation). These are mathematical operations which could readily be implemented in a neural network but we make no attempt to do so. Unlike connectionist models, this is a top-down rather than a bottom-up approach, and I feel the important thing is to get the general principles right before one speculates about the fine-grain details.

Where are these processes carried out? In working memory. Working memory is a "module" in the system architecture which also includes the P-system (perceptual), the Q-system (query), and R-system (response)(Fig. 10.4). The P-system handles encoding, the R-system handles response factors (e.g. deblurring), and M (the memory vector) lives in the Q-system. All communicate with working memory, and that is where these postulated mathematical operations are carried out. As the chapters in this book indicate, there are a variety of views on working memory. A brief account of

---

[iv] For mixed or new pairs (e.g. Dyne, Humphreys, Bain, & Pike, 1990) you must also take the item information into account which leads to the prediction that, as found, the probability of an "old" response will be ordered (most to least) intact, rearranged, mixed (i.e. one old and one new), and new (i.e. two new).

[v] One possibility (Lewandowsky & Li, 1994) is a Hopfield net with anti-learning, but the ramifications of this idea remain to be explored.

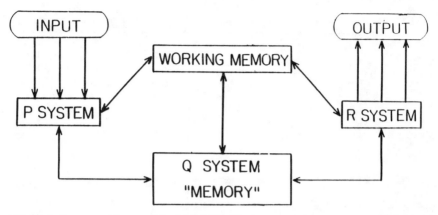

FIG. 10.4   System architecture (Murdock, 1983). The P system is for perception, the Q system is for queries, and the R system is for responses. The memory operations are carried out in working memory.

working memory from a TODAM point of view will be presented in the serial-order section.

Evidence

There is much evidence that is qualitatively consistent with TODAM; that evidence has been summarised elsewhere (Murdock, 1993) and will not be repeated here. Instead, let me focus on three particular effects: the length–difficulty relation, the Tulving-Wiseman function, and the item–associative interaction.

The length–difficulty relation is a classical problem in paired-associate learning. An early analysis by Thurstone showed that the number of trials to learn a list of paired associates should vary as the square root of list length. In an empirical study (Murdock, 1989) two subjects learned lists of 9, 16, 25, 36, 49, 64, 81, and 100 pairs to a criterion of one perfect trial in a study-test procedure with five replications per subject per list length. Data and fits of the model for three of the eight conditions are presented in Fig. 10.5, and the fits are really quite good.

Even though the best-fitting parameters were not identical for the two subjects, none of the parameters varied with list length. Thus, it is the model not the parameters that is doing the work. The values of α were 0.996 and 0.998 for the two subjects, implying that there was almost no forgetting of associations in this task. This seemed very surprising, but was confirmed in some follow-up studies by Murdock and Hockley (1989) and Hockley (1991). Thus, here is a case in which a quantitative fit of the model generated a surprising prediction that was clearly confirmed later.

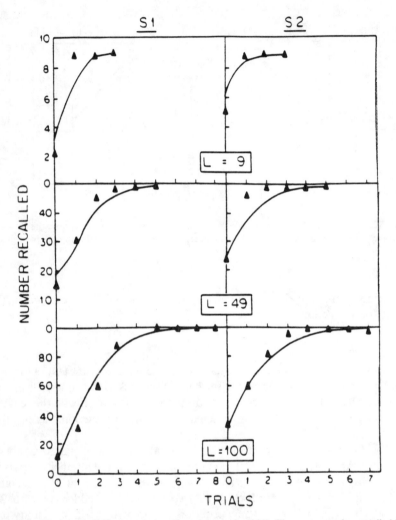

FIG. 10.5   The length–difficulty relation (from Murdock, 1989). The mean number recalled by two subjects (S1 and S2) are shown for lists of 9, 49, and 100 paired associates.

The Tulving-Wiseman function is one way to characterise the relation between item recognition and cued recall. It plots the conditional probability of recognition given recall as a function of the unconditional probability of recognition, and if we call these y and x respectively then

$$y = x + c(1-x) \qquad (11)$$

(Flexser & Tulving, 1978). Loosely speaking, the parameter c indexes the correlation, and plots for three values of c are shown in Fig. 10.6. With a few

Tulving-Wiseman Function

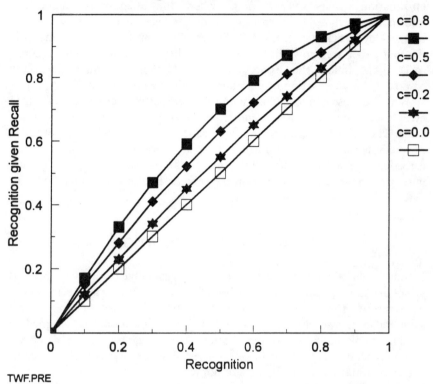

TWF.PRE

FIG. 10.6   The Tulving-Wiseman function for four values of the parameter c. The vertical axis is probability of recognition given recall, the horizontal axis is probability of recognition.

exceptions, the data conform well to the function (Nilsson & Gardiner, 1991) and the best-fitting value of c is about 0.5 (Flexser & Tulving 1978).

However, there are constraints on the function (Hintzman, 1992) and other measures of the correlation may be preferable. Analyses of a large number of studies show that when you make a scatter plot of all the studies with the two variables recall and recognition the correlation is near zero. Thus, cued recall and item recognition are essentially independent, and this is consistent with TODAM (see Equation 8). In principle what little correlation there is could be accounted for by parameter variation across subjects.[vi]

[vi] Metcalfe (1991) reported some simulations that did not show this result, but she may not have picked the right parameters to vary.

The item–associative interaction shows that significant forgetting of item information occurs over a range where the retention of associative information is flat. This surprising result has been reported in two papers by Hockley (Hockley, 1991, 1992). The results from the four experiments in the first paper are shown in Fig. 10.7, and they are distinctly embarrassing to TODAM. In fact, there is no way they could happen if Equation 9c was a complete characterisation of item and associative information.

Why are these results embarrassing? The forgetting parameter acts on **M** every time a new pair is presented, so the forgetting rates should be the same. The problem could be the same as that of the matched-filter model. Presumably both item information and associative information are embedded in some context, and if context changes affected item recognition more than associative information then the desired interaction could occur (Murdock, submitted).

SERIAL-ORDER INFORMATION

It would seem, then, that TODAM can do a reasonable (though not perfect) job of explaining item and associative information. What about serial-order information? There are several possible TODAM approaches, but here I shall focus on the chunking model. The chunking model is designed to explain chunking and serial organisation. Serial organisation is obviously a very important factor in such higher-order cognitive processes as language, concept-formation, thinking, and reasoning.

Miller (1956) in his influential "Magic number 7" paper introduced the term and popularised the notion. As I am using the term, a "chunk" of information is a higher-order unit that can be unpacked into its constituents. A word is a chunk that consists of a sample of letters. We don't think of the letters when we use the word in a sentence, but we could spell the word if we had to. Words go into propositions, propositions go into paragraphs, paragraphs form text, and how this pyramiding occurs is probably the fundamental problem of discourse comprehension.

To extend TODAM to account for chunking in particular and such things as discourse comprehension in general we need three new concepts: multiple convolutions, n-grams, and chunks. If $a*b$ is a two-way convolution, $a*b*c$ is a three-way convolution, $a*b*c*d$ is a four-way convolution, etc. Just as $a*b$ is a vector (although its dimensionality is approximately twice that of its constituents a and b), so $a*b*c$ and $a*b*c*d$ are also vectors, although their dimensionality is approximately three and four times that of their constituents.

We need to have a symbol for multiple convolutions; let us use X (the capital Greek letter chi). It is analogous to Σ for summation; just as

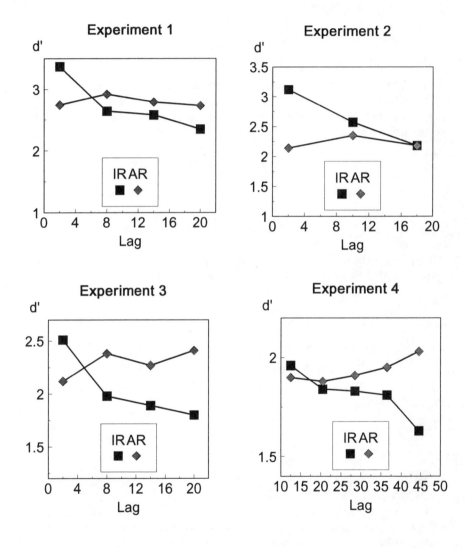

FIG. 10.7 The item–associative interaction (from Hockley, 1991). In each experiment, d' is shown as a function of lag; the squares are for item recognition and the diamonds are for associative recognition.

$$\sum_{i=1}^{n} \mathbf{f}_i = \mathbf{f}_1 + \mathbf{f}_2 + \ldots + \mathbf{f}_n$$

so

$$\mathop{\mathrm{X}}_{i=1}^{n} \mathbf{f}_i = \mathbf{f}_1 * \mathbf{f}_2 * \ldots * \mathbf{f}_n$$

We can also have multiple autoassociations; e.g. $\mathbf{a}*\mathbf{a}$ ($n=2$), $\mathbf{a}*\mathbf{a}*\mathbf{a}$ ($n=3$), etc. This is like squaring or cubing a number or, more generally, raising it to the n-th power. So to symbolise multiple autoassociations let us define any vector $\mathbf{f}$ "star n" as

$$\mathbf{f}*n = \mathbf{f}*\mathbf{f}*\ldots*\mathbf{f} \quad \text{(n times)}$$

or

$$\mathbf{f}*n = \mathbf{f}*\mathbf{f}^{*(n-1)}, \quad \mathbf{f}^{*0} = \delta$$

An n-gram is the n-way autoassociation of the sum of n item vectors. Let us symbolize this by $\mathbf{G}(n)$ where for vectors $\mathbf{a}$, $\mathbf{b}$, and $\mathbf{c}$

$$\mathbf{G}(1) = \mathbf{a}^{*1} = \mathbf{a},$$
$$\mathbf{G}(2) = (\mathbf{a}+\mathbf{b})^{*2} = (\mathbf{a}+\mathbf{b})*(\mathbf{a}+\mathbf{b}) = \mathbf{a}*\mathbf{a} + \mathbf{b}*\mathbf{b} + 2(\mathbf{a}*\mathbf{b}),$$
$$\mathbf{G}(3) = (\mathbf{a}+\mathbf{b}+\mathbf{c})^{*3} = \mathbf{a}*\mathbf{a}*\mathbf{a} + \mathbf{b}*\mathbf{b}*\mathbf{b} + \mathbf{c}*\mathbf{c}*\mathbf{c}$$
$$+ 3(\mathbf{a}*\mathbf{a}*\mathbf{b} + \mathbf{a}*\mathbf{a}*\mathbf{c} + \ldots + \mathbf{b}*\mathbf{c}*\mathbf{c}) + 6(\mathbf{a}*\mathbf{b}*\mathbf{c}),$$

or in general

$$\mathbf{G}(n) = \left(\sum_{i=1}^{n} \mathbf{f}_i\right)^{*n}.$$

Expanding an n-gram is just like raising a series to a power; compare the terms of $\mathbf{G}(2)$ with $(x+y)^2$ or $\mathbf{G}(3)$ with $(x+y+z)^3$.

Just as a multiple convolution or multiple autoconvolution is a vector so an n-gram is a vector even though its kernel consists of the sum of n item vectors. If you expand it you get a number of terms but an n-gram (like a chunk) is a higher-order unit. At encoding it functions as a unit when you are processing a string of items. At retrieval you may have to unpack it but you only use what you need and the rest is noise. This will all be explained shortly in more detail.

A chunk symbolised C(n) is simply the sum of n-grams; thus

$$C(n) = G(1) + G(2) + \ldots + G(n) = \sum_{i=1}^{n} G(i).$$

As n-grams are n-way autoconvolutions of the sum of n item vectors we have

$$C(n) = \sum_{i=1}^{n} G(i) = \sum_{i=1}^{n} \left(\sum_{j=1}^{i} f_j \right)^{*i}.$$

Again a chunk is still a vector because it is a sum of vectors and it serves as the fundamental unit in the chunking model.[vii]

There are three questions: how do we form chunks, how do we unpack chunks, and how do we combine chunks. To my knowledge there is no work on the third question, so all we can consider is the first two. We form chunks and we unpack chunks in working memory.

Assume working memory consists of five storage registers specialised for array processing. It takes three registers for convolution or correlation—one each for a and b, a third for $a*b$ or $a\#b$, a fourth register to accumulate the item information necessary to form n-grams (Σf), and a fifth register to form the chunk (ΣG). Details may be found in Murdock (1993).

The storage equation for forming a single chunk is

$$C_j = \alpha\, C_{j-1} + G_j$$

where G_j is the j-th n-gram. The working memory procedure is very simple: decrement the register containing the item information, add the current item, use the summed item information to form the current n-gram, and add this n-gram to the accumulation of prior n-grams to build the chunk.[viii]

To understand retrieval, item recognition works exactly as before. Take the dot product of the probe item with the register in working memory that contains the item information, and the results are the same as before. Thus, we have the matched-filter model nested in the chunking model, but now it is located in working memory not in the Q-system.[ix] Of course, chunks get stored in the Q-system, but here we are referring to their formation.

[vii] For those who are worried about adding vectors of different dimensionality, the vectors can be thought of as finite-dimensional centre-justified vectors padded with zeros at both ends; see eg. Schonëmann (1987).

[viii] We also have to worry about normalising n-grams and chunks. For details, see Murdock (1995).

[ix] For a delayed test this information is no longer in working memory, but in TODAM2 (Murdock, 1993) we show how it can be retrieved.

Recall is somewhat more complicated. Borrowing an idea from CADAM (Liepa, 1977) we use a multiple convolution of the items retrieved to data as the retrieval cue for the next item. Starting with the delta vector δ and using $\rightarrow$ to indicate deblurring,

$$\delta \# \, C(n) = a' \rightarrow a,$$
$$a \# C(n) = a' + b' \rightarrow b,$$
$$(a*b) \# C(n) = a' + b' + c' \rightarrow c, \quad \text{etc.,}$$

or in general

$$\left(\overset{j-1}{\underset{i=1}{\mathsf{X}}} f_i \right) \# C(n) = f'_j.$$

There are two reasons this works. The first reason is that this is how we built a chunk. We built it one item at a time, so we unpack it one item at a time. The second reason is the filter principle. If we have a multiple convolution of m items, and correlate that with a multiple convolution of a subset of n items, then this subset filters out the remainder. Thus, for $n < m$,

$$\left(\overset{n}{\underset{i=1}{\mathsf{X}}} f_i \right) \# \left(\overset{m}{\underset{j=1}{\mathsf{X}}} f_j \right) = \overset{m}{\underset{k=n+1}{\mathsf{X}}} f_k.$$

This is directly analogous to multiplication and division: $abcde/ade = bc$ or $abc/ab = c$. Thus, Equations 6 and 7 (with $m = 2$) are just a special case of a more general principle. Also, as in multiplication and division, the order of the items does not matter because convolution is commutative. The reason the filter principle works is that

$$\overset{m-1}{\underset{i=1}{\mathsf{X}}} f_i \# C(n) = \overset{m-1}{\underset{i=1}{\mathsf{X}}} f_i \# \left\{ G(m) + \sum_{j=m+1}^{n} G(n) \right\}$$

$$= \overset{m-1}{\underset{i=1}{\mathsf{X}}} f_i \# G(m) + \overset{m-1}{\underset{i=1}{\mathsf{X}}} f_i \# \sum_{j=m+1}^{n} G(n).$$

That is, the probe (a multiple convolution) acts on all higher n-grams but only the next higher n-gram [i.e. $G(m)$] need be considered because the rest is noise.

Suppose we have $(a*b)\# \, M = c'$; how does c' get deblurred to c? Although deblurring is not modelled explicitly in TODAM, it turns out that, due to the construction of n-grams, the target item (i.e. c) will always be twice as strong as its competitors (i.e. **a** and **b**). Any reasonable deblurring scheme should succeed more often than it fails.

Serial recall sometimes goes astray. For instance, you recall the fourth item when you should recall the third item. Mewhort, Popham, and James (1994) and Nairne and Neath (1994) have shown that this is a problem for a chaining model (i.e. it breaks the chain) but it has an interesting implication for the chunking model. Suppose **d** is mistakenly recalled instead of **c**. Then the next retrieval cue is **a∗b∗d** and that should be deblurred to **c**. Thus, a transposition (ABDC) would have occurred. Furthermore, if there were still more items to recall, the retrieval cue **a∗b∗d∗c** is no different from **a∗b∗c∗d** so recall is back on track and the next item recalled should be **e**. Transpositions often occur in middle serial positions (e.g. ABDCE), and this analysis shows how that could happen.

Evidence

Let me briefly describe three applications of the chunking model to serial-order effects. The first application is multiple item probes. In their study list Clark and Shiffrin (1987) presented unrelated word triples which we can represent as ABC, A'B'C', A"B"C", ... (A denotes the first word in the triple, B the second word, and C the third word, but A, A', and A" are three different words). Then they used a variety of test probes. For probe triples the approximate ordering of percent match was ABC > ABC' > BA'C" > ABZ = AB'Z > AYZ > XYZ where X, Y, and Z are new items. This ordering agrees well with the number of matching components in the n-gram (see Table 10.1). The major discrepancy is the AB'C"/ABZ reversal which remains to be explained.

TABLE 10.1
Matches (x) for Each Test Type to Trigram Components (a^3. b^3 ...) and Probability "Yes" for Intact Instruction Condition

Test type	a^3	b^3	c^3	a^2b	a^2c	ab^2	b^2c	ac^2	bc^2	abc	Probability "yes"
				Trigram component							
ABC	x	x	x	x	x	x	x	x	x	x	75
ABC'	x	x	x	x		x					40
AB'C"	x	x	x	x							30
ABZ	x	x	x		x		x				20
AB'Z	x	x									21
AYZ	x										12
XYZ											15

Data are from Clark and Shiffrin (1987).

The second application is to regrouping. If we learn ABC (call it X), DEF (call it Y), GHIJ (call it Z), Johnson (1972) found essentially no positive transfer if we learn ABCD (call it X'), EFG (call it Y'), HIJ (call it Z'). The reason is that the units are different (i.e. $X \neq X'$, $Y \neq Y'$, $Z \neq Z'$). In particular, $E[X \bullet X'] = E[Y \bullet Y'] = E[Z \bullet Z'] = 0$; thus, the fact that some of the components are the same is immaterial.

The third application is the recall–recognition interaction. As detailed in Murdock (1995), tests of item recognition following presentation of a short string of items show mainly recency whereas serial recall shows mainly primacy. Illustrative data are shown in Fig. 10.8 for recognition and in Fig. 10.9 for recall.

To illustrate how the chunking model can mimic these effects, let me present the results of a simulation. Chunks of various sizes (1,2,3, ... ,7) were formed as described earlier. For item recognition, new- and old-item probes were dotted with $C(n)$ ($n = 1$ to 7) and the d' values for each serial position for each set size (n) are shown in Fig. 10.10. All the curves show pure recency and, for each serial position, the set-size differences are quite small.

For recall, we correlated the probe with the chunk and took the best match as the item recalled. If all matches were negative we scored an

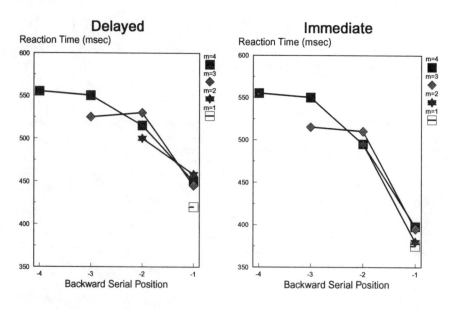

FIG. 10.8 Reaction time as a function of backward serial position for two conditions, a delayed test (D) and an immediate test (I). Data from Monsell.

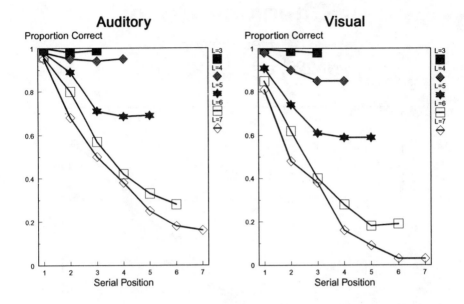

FIG. 10.9   Proportion of correct recalls as a function of serial position for auditory and visual presentation. Data from Drewnowski and Murdock, 1980.

omission. What is retrieved at each step must enter into the retrieval cue for the next step. If the prior recall was successful we used the target item, otherwise we used whatever item had been recalled (i.e. the best match). For further details see Murdock (1995).

The results are shown in Fig. 10.11. The curves essentially show pure primacy (the recency effect is unreliable) and, like the real data, fan out from a common origin so that, at each serial position, the larger the set size the lower the probability of recall. Thus, the chunking model can clearly demonstrate the primacy–recency interaction that is so characteristic of the experimental data.

However, one problem should be acknowledged. The error gradients from this simulation did not show the right pattern. In this and other simulations they either showed primacy or were more-or-less flat across serial positions. Generally error gradients are sharply peaked around the target serial position (Lee & Estes, 1977; Nairne, 1991). Whether this problem can be rectified by some minor modification remains to be seen.

In general, however, the chunking model seems to do a creditable job. There are only three parameters (N, α, and p) and none of these parameters varies with serial position. It is a process model, and it can be fully implemented using a working memory with five registers for array

Chunking Model
Recognition
N=229, al=0.8, p=0.5, rho=0

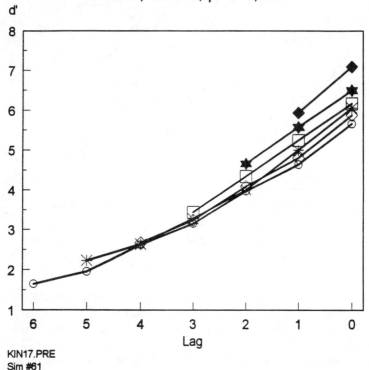

KIN17.PRE
Sim #61

FIG. 10.10   d' as a function of lag from a simulation of the chunking model (Murdock, in press). Data are shown for chunk sizes 2–7.

processing. Most important, it meets the requirement for chunking; it shows how single items can be formed into a higher-order unit and retrieved from this higher-order unit on demand.

A chunk can represent the structure in any ordered set of items whether it be a short list of nonsense syllables or a proposition in a sentence. Of course, propositions have some additional structure because one must distinguish between functions and arguments, but a chunk could be the glue that holds them together. Chunks preserve order information (ABC is not the same as CBA) and different items make different chunks (ABC is not the same as ADC even though there are common items). Finally, chunks can be combined into higher-order metachunks but, as noted, no work on this problem has been done as yet.

Chunking Model
Recall
N=229, al=0.8, p=0.5, rho=0

Recall Probability

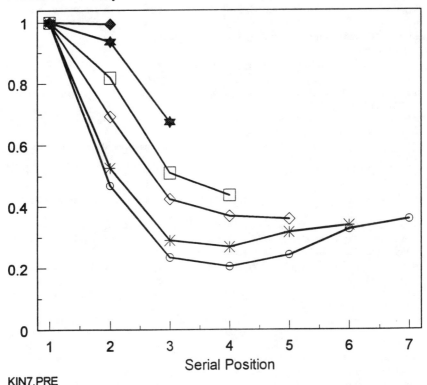

KIN7.PRE
Sim #58

FIG. 10.11   Recall probability as a function of serial position from a simulation of the chunking model (Murdock, 1995). Data are shown for chunk sizes 2–7.

SUMMARY

TODAM is a general model for the storage and retrieval of item, associative, and serial-order information. Based on the convolution/correlation formalism of Borsellino and Poggio (1973), it shows how you can do item recognition and cued recall and also how you can form higher-order chunks. The motivation behind this enterprise is to develop a comprehensive model of human memory. Obviously the fit of the model to the data is not perfect, but as the building and testing of the model continues, we hope that the rough edges will be smoothed off and that TODAM can contribute to our understanding of the detailed workings of human memory.

ACKNOWLEDGEMENTS

Preparation of this paper was supported by Grant APA-146 from the Natural Sciences and Engineering Council of Canada. The author is grateful to Steven Sloman for many helpful comments on the manuscript.

REFERENCES

Anderson, J.A. (1968). A memory storage model utilizing spatial correlation functions. *Kybernetik, 5*, 113–119.

Anderson, J.A. (1970). Two models for memory organization using interacting traces. *Mathematical Biosciences, 8*, 137–160.

Anderson, J.A. (1973). A theory for the recognition of items from short memorized lists. *Psychological Review, 80*, 417–438.

Asch, S.E. (1969). A reformulation of the problem of associations. *American Psychologist, 24*, 92–102.

Borsellino, A., & Poggio, T. (1973). Convolution and correlation algebras. *Kybernetik, 122*, 113–122.

Bower, G.H. (1967). A multicomponent theory of the memory trace. In K.W. Spence & J.T. Spence (Eds.), *The psychology of learning and motivation: Advances in research and theory.* Vol. 1 (pp. 229–325). New York: Academic Press.

Clark, S.E., & Shiffrin, R.M. (1987). Recognition of multiple-item probes. *Memory & Cognition, 15*, 367–378.

Collins, A.M., & Loftus, E.F. (1975). A spreading-activation theory of semantic processing. *Psychological Review, 82*, 407–428.

Drewnowski, A., & Murdock, B.B. (1980). The role of auditory features in memory span for words. *Journal of Experimental Psychology: Human Learning and Memory, 6*, 319–332.

Dyne, A.M., Humphreys, M.S., Bain, J.D., & Pike, R. (1990). Associative interference effects in recognition and recall. *Journal of Experimental Psychology: Learning, Memory, and Cognition, 16*, 813–824.

Egan, J.P. (1958). *Recognition memory and the operating characteristic.* Technical Note AFCRC-TN-58-51, Indiana University, Hearing and Communication Laboratory.

Flexser, A.J., & Tulving, E. (1978). Retrieval independence in recognition and recall. *Psychological Review, 85*, 153–171.

Hintzman, D.L. (1992). Mathematical constraints and the Tulving-Wiseman Law. *Psychological Review, 99*, 536–542.

Hockley, W.E. (1991). Recognition memory for item and associative information: A comparison of forgetting rates. In W.E. Hockley & S. Lewandowsky (Eds.), *Relating theory and data: Essays on human memory in honor of Bennet B. Murdock*, (pp. 227–248). Hillsdale, NJ: Lawrence Erlbaum Associates Inc.

Hockley, W.E. (1992). Item versus associative information: Further comparisons of forgetting rates. *Journal of Experimental Psychology: Learning, Memory, and Cognition, 18*, 1321–1330.

Johnson, N.F. (1972). Organization and the concept of a memory code. In A.W. Melton & E. Martin (Eds.), *Coding processes in human memory*, (pp. 125–159). Washington, DC: Winston.

Jordan, M.I. (1986). An introduction to linear algebra in parallel distributed processing. In D.E. Rumelhart & J.L. McClelland (Eds.), *Parallel distributed processing Vol.1: Foundations*, (pp. 365–422). Cambridge, MA: MIT Press.

Kahana, M.J. (submitted). Associative symmetry for unrelated word triplets: Implications for theories of serial order.

Kiss, G.R. (1968). Words, associations, and networks. *Journal of Verbal Learning and Verbal Behavior, 7*, 707–713.

Kohler, W. (1941). On the nature of association. *Proceedings of the American Philosophical Society, 84*, 489–502.

Kohonen, T. (1977). *Associative memory: A system-theoretical approach*. Berlin: Springer-Verlag.

Lee, C.L., & Estes, W.K. (1977). Order and position in primary memory for letter strings. *Journal of Verbal Learning and Verbal Behavior, 16*, 395–418.

Lewandowsky, S., & Li, S-C. (1994). Memory for serial order revisited. *Psychological Review, 101*, 534–538.

Liepa, P. (1977). *Models of content addressable distributed associative memory (CADAM)*. Unpublished manuscript, University of Toronto.

Longuet-Higgins, H.C. (1968). Holographic model of temporal recall. *Nature, 217*, 104–106.

McGeoch, J.A. (1932). Forgetting and the law of disuse. *Psychological Review, 39*, 352–370.

Metcalfe, J. (1991). Recognition failure and the composite memory trace in CHARM. *Psychological Review, 98*, 529–553.

Mewhort, D.J.K., Popham, D., & James, G. (1994). On serial recall: A critique of chaining in TODAM. *Psychological Review, 101*, 534–538.

Miller, G.A. (1956). The magical number seven, plus or minus two: Some limits on our capacity for processing information. *Psychological Review, 63*, 81–96.

Murdock, B.B. (1965). Signal-detection theory and short-term memory. *Journal of Experimental Psychology, 70*, 443–447.

Murdock, B.B. (1974). *Human memory: Theory and data*. Potomac, MD: Lawrence Erlbaum Associates Inc.

Murdock, B.B. (1979). Convolution and correlation in perception and memory. In L.G. Nilsson (Ed.), *Perspectives in memory research: Essays in honor of Uppsala University's 500th Anniversary*, (pp. 105–119). Hillsdale, NJ: Lawrence Erlbaum Associates.

Murdock, B.B. (1982). A theory for the storage and retrieval of item and associative information. *Psychological Review, 89*, 609–626.

Murdock, B.B. (1983). A distributed memory model for serial-order information. *Psychological Review, 90*, 316–338.

Murdock, B.B. (1989). Learning in a distributed memory model. In C. Izawa (Ed.), *Current issues in cognitive processes: The Tulane Floweree symposium on cognition*, (pp. 69–106). Hillsdale, NJ: Lawrence Erlbaum Associates Inc.

Murdock, B.B. (1992). Serial organization in a distributed memory model. In A.F. Healy, S.M. Kosslyn, & R.M. Shiffrin (Eds.), *From learning theory to connectionist theory: Essays in honour of William K. Estes*, Vol 1, (pp. 201–225). Hillsdale, NJ: Lawrence Erlbaum Associates Inc.

Murdock, B.B. (1993). TODAM2: A model for the storage and retrieval of item, associative, and serial-order information. *Psychological Review, 100*, 183–203.

Murdock, B.B. (1995). Primacy and recency in the chunking model. In C. Weaver, S. Mannes, & R. Fletcher (Eds.), *Discourse comprehension: Models of processing revisited*, (pp. 49–64). Hillsdale, NJ: Lawrence Erlbaum Associates Inc.

Murdock, B.B. (1995). Developing TODAM: Three models for serial-order information. *Memory & Cognition, 23*, 631–645.

Murdock, B.B. (submitted). Item and associative information in TODAM2.

Murdock, B.B., & Anderson, R.E. (1975). Encoding, storage, and retrieval of item information. In R.L. Solso (Ed.), *Information processing and cognition: The Loyola symposium*, (pp. 145–194). Hillsdale, NJ: Lawrence Erlbaum Associates Inc.

Murdock, B.B., & Hockley, W.E. (1989). Short-term memory for associations. In G.H. Bower (Ed.), *The psychology of learning and motivation: Advances in research and theory*, Vol. 24, (pp. 71–108). New York: Academic Press.

Murdock, B.B., & Kahana, M.J. (1993). An analysis of the list-strength effect. *Journal of Experimental Psychology: Learning Memory, and Cognition, 19*, 689–697.

Murdock, B.B., & Lamon, M. (1988). The replacement effect: Repeating some items while replacing others. *Memory & Cognition, 16*, 91–101.

Nairne, J.S. (1991). Positional uncertainty in long-term memory. *Memory & Cognition, 19*, 332–340.

Nairne, J.S., & Neath, I. (1994). A critique of the retrieval/deblurring assumptions of TODAM. *Psychological Review, 101*, 528–533.

Nickerson, R.S. (1968). A note on long-term recognition memory for pictorial material. *Psychonomic Science, 11*, 58.

Nilsson, L-G., & Gardiner, J.M. (1991). Memory theory and the boundary conditions of the Tulving-Wiseman Law. In W.E. Hockley & S. Lewandowsky (Eds.), *Relating theory and data: Essays on human memory in honour of B.B. Murdock*, (pp. 57–74). Hillsdale, NJ: Lawrence Erlbaum Associates Inc.

Norman, D.A., & Wickelgren, W. (1965). Short-term recognition memory for single digits and pairs of digits. *Journal of Experimental Psychology, 70*, 479–489.

Postman, L. Stark, K. (1969). Role of response availability in transfer and interference. *Journal of Experimental Psychology, 79*, 168–77.

Rock, I., & Ceraso, J. (1964). Toward a cognitive theory of associative learning. In C. Scheerer (Ed.), *Cognition: Theory, Research, Promise*, (pp. 110–146). New York: Harper & Row.

Schonëmann, P.H. (1987). Some algebraic relations between involutions, convolutions, and correlations with applications to holographic memories. *Biological Cybernetiks, 56*, 367–374.

Underwood, B.J. (1969). Attributes of memory. *Psychological Review, 76*, 559–573.

Waugh, N.C., & Norman, D.A. (1965). Primary memory. *Psychological Review, 72*, 89–104.

Wickens, D.D. (1970). Encoding categories of words: An empirical approach to meaning. *Psychological Review, 77*, 1–15.

Willshaw, D.J. (1972). A simple network capable of inductive generalization. *Proceedings of the Royal Society, Series B, 182*, 233–247.

11 How many words can working memory hold? A model and a method

Richard Schweickert, Cathrin Hayt, Lora Hersberger, and Lawrence Geuntert
Purdue University, Indiana, USA

Working memory is often described as a system for temporarily storing and manipulating information during cognitive tasks (Baddeley, 1986, p.34). The role of working memory in cognition is analogous to that of the hands in performance. The capacity for holding is important, but what really matters is the ability to transform what is held. Although other memory systems are not static, they tend to be passive. We say, for example, that activation spreads in the semantic memory system. But working memory is an active system, where thoughts are formulated and ideas are grasped.

The storage aspect is easier to investigate with current techniques than the processing aspect, and we begin the chapter by considering storage. The verbal part of working memory holds words; how many words can it hold? We can only go a little way towards answering this question without discussing processing. Storage capacity is best understood in terms of parameters describing processing of speech. From this topic we turn to the role of temporary storage in information processing, using queueing networks to model the system. Items in working memory are either actively being processed or passively being stored. We propose a queueing network model to find estimates of the number of items in each state separately.

This chapter is concerned with a specific question about working memory, namely the number of items that can be held in it at once. Of course, there are many other working memory phenomena to account for. Excellent surveys of the phenomena are given in the two recent books by

267

Baddeley (1986) and Cowan (1995); each author gives a review and a theory. Mathematical models giving good accounts of several phenomena include the feature model of Neath and Nairne (in press), and the neural network model of Burgess and Hitch (1992, this volume). Models with large scope have obvious advantages, with the corresponding disadvantage of needing a considerable number of assumptions and parameters. The models presented here have the disadvantage of being limited in scope, with the compensating advantage of needing few assumptions and parameters.

STORAGE CAPACITY

The memory span for a type of material is the number of items in a list that can be immediately recalled in order, half the time. Although memory span has been studied for over 100 years, and its basis in inner speech has always been obvious, it is only relatively recently that the implications of its intimate association with speech have been appreciated. The two major phenomena related to speech are that memory span is smaller when items are phonologically similar (Conrad, 1964; Hintzman, 1967), and when items take longer to pronounce (Baddeley, Thomson, & Buchanan, 1975; Mackworth, 1963).

Memory span is important as a variable for theoretical reasons, but in practical applications, such as devising phone numbers, one is rarely interested in producing a list of items that can only be recalled half the time. Usually the goal is to find a list that can be recalled a large percentage of the time, and probabilities of recall over a range are of interest. The basic idea used by Broadbent (1958), Baddeley et al. (1975) and Mackworth (1963) to explain memory span was that a list endures in working memory for a limited amount of time. This idea easily explains the word length effect. The idea was extended in a model proposed in Schweickert and Boruff (1986) to predict the probability of correct recall of any list from the time required to say it. According to the model, the probability that a list can be immediately recalled is the probability that recall can be completed before the representation has degraded. If recall is through speech, then

$$\text{Prob[Correct Recall]} = \text{Prob}[U \leqslant T_v],$$

where U is the time the subject requires to utter the list, and T_v is the duration of the verbal memory representation.

It is assumed that as time increases, degradation increases, but no assumption is made about why this would be so. It is convenient to think of decay as the mechanism of degradation, but other mechanisms are possible (see, e.g. Neath & Nairne, in press).

The duration of the verbal representation is assumed to be a random variable, fluctuating from trial to trial. Several kinds of materials were used in the Schweickert and Boruff (1986) study, including, for example, digits and colour names. The same probability distribution for T_v gave good predictions for all materials. This suggests that the distribution of T_v is a characteristic of the working memory system.

Nonetheless, Schweickert and Boruff (1986) noted that the equation given earlier somewhat underestimated the probability of correct recall for digits, the material that subjects had most experience with in daily life, and somewhat overestimated the probability of correct recall for nonsense syllables, the material that subjects had least experience with. This suggests that familiarity with the items may lead to improved performance.

In the following experiment subjects became highly familiar with all of the items in the course of 30 sessions. The result is two opposing tendencies; the usual word length effect together with a reverse word length effect.

Method

Subjects. Two subjects each completed four practice sessions followed by 30 test sessions. Each session lasted about an hour and a half. The subjects were female college students, paid by the hour.

Materials. Five types of material were used: letters, colour names, prepositions, shape names, and words (three-letter concrete nouns). To make the probability of correct guessing by chance low, each material pool contained 20 items. The pools are given in Appendix A.

Design and Procedure. Lists of items of a given material were all presented together in a block. The order of presentation of materials within sessions was governed by six 5 × 5 Latin squares. The lengths of the lists were from three to nine items, inclusive. Each block began with three practice trials, followed by five test trials of each of the seven list lengths. List lengths were randomised within the blocks.

At the beginning of each trial, a list appeared on the computer monitor. On pronunciation trials, subjects read the list aloud with no requirement to remember it. On recall trials, subjects read the list aloud, and then attempted to recall it by speaking aloud. A voice key connected to a computer indicated the onset and offset of speech as the subject read the list aloud. During recall, the experimenter recorded whether the list was correctly recalled or not. The time to read the list on pronunciation trials will be called pronunciation time. On recall trials the time to read the list aloud will be called rehearsal time, because the subject was actually rehearsing the list by reading.

In each session, there were two blocks for each material, one for pronunciation and one for immediate recall. In half the sessions all the pronunciation blocks preceded all the recall blocks, and in the other sessions this order was reversed.

Results

Table 11.1 gives pronunciation time (seconds), rehearsal time, and probability of correct recall for Subject 1, and Table 11.2 gives these data for Subject 2.

Memory. By examining recall for lists of a certain fixed length, say seven items, in Table 11.1 one can clearly see that the longer the pronunciation time or rehearsal time for a material, the worse the probability of correct recall tends to be. This tendency is the word length effect (Baddeley et al., 1975; Mackworth, 1963). However, by looking carefully at the Table, one finds many exceptions to the rule that probability of correct recall decreases with word length.

These results are different from those in Schweickert and Boruff (1986). In that study, a good account of probability of correct recall was produced using the same normally distributed representation duration for each material. For the highly practised subjects in this experiment, however, the duration of the representation in memory was not the same for every material. This is clear from Fig. 11.1, which shows probability of correct recall as a function of rehearsal time for the two subjects. If the duration of the representation were the same for every material, all the curves in the Figure would be superimposed. Instead, the time required to rehearse a list of span length, i.e. a list whose recall probability is 0.5, tends to be *longer* for longer items. Shape names take the longest to say, and the rehearsal time for lists of span length is the longest. This outcome is contrary to the usual word length effect.

Another reverse word length effect, produced in a different way from the reversal reported here, was found by Caplan, Rochon, and Waters (1992). Their finding led them to conclude that the phonological structure of an item, rather than its actual duration, determines probability of recall. But see Baddeley and Andrade (1994) and Caplan and Waters (1994) for further discussion.

Although there is a reversal of the word length effect in our data, this is not an unintuitive outcome for practised subjects. A completely unfamiliar item is a string of phonemes, and virtually every phoneme must be remembered for the item to be recalled. This is one reason why Gathercole and Baddeley (1990) found working memory capacity of children to be correlated with ability to learn new vocabulary. They note that for familiar words, higher-level representations have developed, and can be used to support recall. Familiarity also has a role in the feature model of Nairne

TABLE 11.1
Probability of Correct Recall, Pronunciation Time, and Rehearsal Time; Subject 1

				List Length			
	3	4	5	6	7	8	9
Letters							
Prob. Correct	1.000	1.000	0.971	0.853	0.602	0.235	0.026
Pronunciation							
Mean	0.634	0.950	1.254	1.537	1.938	2.252	2.507
Variance	0.085	0.116	0.122	0.101	0.126	0.200	0.184
Rehearsal							
Mean	0.667	0.951	1.297	1.659	2.072	2.451	2.896
Variance	0.043	0.069	0.084	0.104	0.132	0.180	0.202
Words							
Prob. Correct	0.986	0.979	0.927	0.704	0.319	0.052	0.029
Pronunciation							
Mean	0.778	1.140	1.561	1.886	2.296	2.715	3.126
Variance	0.018	0.044	0.145	0.061	0.081	0.125	0.118
Rehearsal							
Mean	0.827	1.195	1.561	1.967	2.380	3.013	3.254
Variance	0.032	0.071	0.059	0.081	0.194	0.029	0.151
Prepositions							
Prob. Correct	1.000	0.980	0.914	0.818	0.422	0.138	0.036
Pronunciation							
Mean	0.805	1.148	1.494	1.887	2.283	2.649	3.043
Variance	0.025	0.052	0.046	0.078	0.121	0.088	0.110
Rehearsal							
Mean	0.867	1.212	1.617	2.018	2.428	2.840	3.275
Variance	0.029	0.046	0.046	0.083	0.102	0.114	0.112
Colours							
Prob. Correct	1.000	1.000	0.993	0.835	0.497	0.189	0.000
Pronunciation							
Mean	0.871	1.245	1.623	2.070	2.445	2.881	3.293
Variance	0.029	0.042	0.035	0.072	0.081	0.103	0.133
Rehearsal							
Mean	0.889	1.273	1.656	2.099	2.499	2.945	3.430
Variance	0.032	0.038	0.044	0.071	0.070	0.115	0.289
Shapes							
Prob. Correct	1.000	0.987	0.860	0.514	0.135	0.014	0.000
Pronunciation							
Mean	1.232	1.793	2.325	2.853	3.343	3.899	4.444
Variance	0.081	0.119	0.157	0.176	0.158	0.182	0.208
Rehearsal							
Mean	1.254	1.831	2.399	2.972	3.537	4.037	4.637
Variance	0.080	0.128	0.143	0.164	0.216	0.168	0.263

TABLE 11.2
Probability of Correct Recall, Pronunciation Time, and Rehearsal Time; Subject 2

	List Length						
	3	*4*	*5*	*6*	*7*	*8*	*9*
Letters							
Prob. Correct	1.000	0.986	0.979	0.887	0.730	0.346	0.085
Pronunciation							
Mean	0.733	1.121	1.470	1.836	2.191	2.566	2.929
Variance	0.024	0.051	0.063	0.093	0.090	0.109	0.149
Rehearsal							
Mean	0.677	1.104	1.468	1.959	2.293	2.743	3.130
Variance	0.050	0.060	0.072	0.092	0.120	0.115	0.172
Words							
Prob. Correct	0.993	0.993	0.925	0.624	0.359	0.090	0.007
Pronunciation							
Mean	0.919	1.283	1.663	2.051	2.458	2.827	3.196
Variance	0.047	0.041	0.071	0.066	0.098	0.077	0.095
Rehearsal							
Mean	0.873	1.239	1.664	2.145	2.581	3.010	3.433
Variance	0.039	0.027	0.073	0.078	0.102	0.133	0.192
Prepositions							
Prob. Correct	1.000	0.993	0.966	0.878	0.534	0.209	0.047
Pronunciation							
Mean	0.922	1.284	1.638	2.049	2.424	2.777	3.123
Variance	0.027	0.035	0.037	0.060	0.074	0.059	0.074
Rehearsal							
Mean	0.883	1.208	1.647	2.067	2.488	2.897	3.287
Variance	0.034	0.030	0.053	0.068	0.116	0.088	0.115
Colours							
Prob. Correct	1.000	1.000	0.966	0.838	0.479	0.149	0.021
Pronunciation							
Mean	1.000	1.368	1.750	2.160	2.549	2.927	3.357
Variance	0.079	0.064	0.031	0.067	0.055	0.076	0.081
Rehearsal							
Mean	0.920	1.353	1.764	2.234	2.696	3.151	3.635
Variance	0.032	0.102	0.053	0.086	0.130	0.139	0.190
Shapes							
Prob. Correct	0.993	0.959	0.801	0.548	0.158	0.014	0.000
Pronunciation							
Mean	1.336	1.850	2.374	2.868	3.363	3.879	4.357
Variance	0.081	0.090	0.115	0.148	0.143	0.127	0.164
Rehearsal							
Mean	1.621	2.200	2.790	3.356	3.993	4.574	5.039
Variance	0.105	0.090	0.160	0.173	0.261	0.280	0.353

(1990), because degraded traces are compared with undegraded traces in secondary memory to find the best match. Brown and Hulme (1995) and Neath and Nairne (in press) propose that words are made of segments which must be output in the proper order for correct recall; presumably the segments develop with familiarity.

Even more factors come into play with familiarity. For example, content words are better recalled than function words, when word length is equated (Tehan & Humphreys, 1988), and items from the same semantic category are better recalled than items from different categories (Poirier & Saint-Aubin, 1995). An earlier paper proposed that multinomial tree models may account for the way these factors affect the probability of recall of individual items (Schweickert, 1993). In a variety of ways, familiarity leads to a richer representation in secondary memory.

Whatever the representation in secondary memory may be, we propose that it tends to favour long words over short words, for closed word pools. This hypothesis may explain a result of Hulme, Maughan, and Brown (1991). Subjects were given unfamiliar Italian words in an immediate recall experiment. Recall was relatively poor, of course, but improved after subjects studied the words for a few days. The improvement was greater for the longer words.

In our experiment, increasing the length of the items produces two competing tendencies. On the one hand, the longer the items, the greater the time required to output the list, so the greater the chance of degradation. On the other hand, the longer the items, the more distinctive they tend to be, and hence the greater the chances of guessing an item correctly from a partially degraded representation. Highly practised subjects are probably better able to reconstruct the partially degraded representation of an item. The more familiar the items are, the better subjects are able to discriminate among the remnants.

A Model.   If we assume the representation duration is different for each material, the data can be accounted for with the equation in the introduction,

$$\text{Prob[Correct Recall]} = \text{Prob}[U \leqslant T_v].$$

Here U is the time to say a particular list, and T_v is the duration of the representation in memory. We will use a simplification that worked well in Schweickert and Boruff (1986). We simply substitute v, the mean time to say a list of a given length and material, for the random variable U. Then,

$$\text{Prob[Correct Recall]} = \text{Prob}[v < T_v]$$
$$= 1 - \text{Prob}[T_v < v].$$

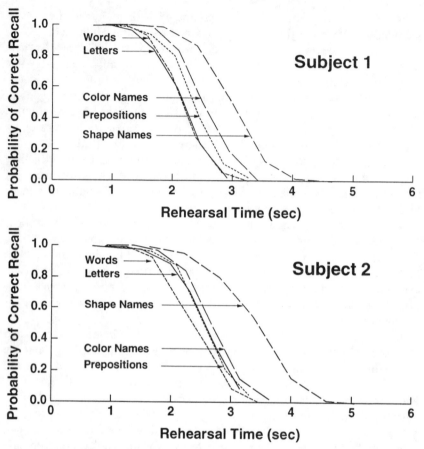

FIG. 11.1.   Probability of correct recall as a function of rehearsal duration, for Subject 1 (top) and Subject 2 (bottom).

If we assume the duration of the representation, T_v, is normally distributed, with mean τ_v and variance σ, then

$$\text{Prob[Correct Recall]} = 1 - \text{Prob}[(T_v - \tau_v)/\sigma \leqslant (v - \tau_v)/\sigma]$$
$$= 1 - \text{NP}[(v - \tau_v)/\sigma],$$

where NP[z] is the normal cumulative distribution function evaluated at the number z.

The parameters can be estimated with standard statistical software. The mean, τ_v, and standard deviation, σ, were estimated for each material with Statistica (StatSoft, 1994), using the logistic distribution as an approximation to the normal. Table 11.3 gives the parameter estimates and goodness

TABLE 11.3
Parameter Estimates (msec) and Goodness of Fit Statistics
For Predicting Probability of Correct Recall

Material	τ_v	σ	R^2	χ^2 (5df)
Subject 1				
Letters	2.16	0.39	0.9958	1.80
Words	2.16	0.38	0.9994	1.32
Prepositions	2.35	0.41	0.9997	0.04
Colour Names	2.53	0.43	0.9972	5.26
Shape Names	2.99	0.46	0.9991	0.98
Subject 2				
Letters	2.55	0.45	0.9990	0.33
Words	2.36	0.52	0.9955	0.73
Prepositions	2.54	0.44	0.9994	0.13
Colour Names	2.68	0.44	0.9998	0.24
Shape Names	3.40	0.55	0.9946	3.23

of fit statistics. More details about the parameter estimation procedure are given in Appendix B.

It is clear from Table 11.3 that the parameter τ_v, the duration of the memory representation, is different for the different materials. The longer the items, the greater the value of τ_v. The relation between the duration of the memory representation and the length of the items is nearly linear. We arbitrarily chose lists of length 7 for reference and conducted a linear regression analysis for predicting τ_v from v (7), the time to rehearse seven items.

For Subject 1,

$$\tau_v \text{ sec } = 0.92 \text{ sec } + 0.59v \text{ (7) sec } \quad (R^2 = 0.90)$$

and for Subject 2,

$$\tau_v \text{ sec } = 1.11 \text{ sec } + 0.57v \text{ (7) sec } \quad (R^2 = 0.90).$$

The large values of R^2 indicate that rehearsal time for seven items is a pretty good predictor of trace duration. Further, there is remarkable agreement between the two subjects for both the slopes and intercepts.

Why does the duration of the representation in memory increase with the time required to say an item? We briefly consider two hypotheses, one based on unique substrings and the other based on recency.

An item can often be distinguished from the other items in its pool if only a small distinctive fragment of the item is intact in working memory. At recall the entire item may be reconstructed from the fragment. Neath and Nairne (in press) call the fragments segments. Although they are not specific about what segments are, they assume the number of them in an item increases linearly with word length.

With the data here, we can evaluate a specific candidate for distinctive fragments; minimal unique substrings. A substring of an item in a pool is unique if the substring is contained in no other item in the pool. A unique substring is minimal if no proper substring of it is unique. Even if an item is long, e.g. *trapezoid*, it can have a short substring uniquely identifying it, e.g. the /z/ in *trapezoid*. A plausible hypothesis is that the number of items recalled is the number of items whose minimal unique substrings have been maintained. If so, one would expect that the span would be greater the smaller the minimal unique substrings.

For each material, the span was estimated by linear interpolation as the length of a list recalled correctly with probability 0.5. The pronunciation of each item was determined (*American Heritage Dictionary*, 1992), and the number of symbols in the smallest minimal unique substring was calculated. The correlation over materials between span and the mean size of the smallest minimal unique substring was –0.82 for Subject 1 and –0.61 for Subject 2. The modest size of these correlations suggests that minimal unique substrings are not the most important variable to pursue.

Another hypothesis, developed in conjunction with Marie Poirier and Jeff Oliver, is that the representation duration τ_v increases with word length because of the contribution due to recency. When the subjects read the items aloud, they are giving themselves an auditory presentation of the list, and hence producing a recency effect for the last items. There is some evidence that the size of the recency effect is not influenced by word length (e.g. Baddeley, Lewis, & Vallar, 1984). Then, the time it takes to say the last items is simply added to the representation duration, and of course this extra time is longer the longer the word length. This hypothesis looks promising, but further data on recency will be needed to evaluate it.

Speaking Times.   According to the model, the time required to utter a list is an important factor in predicting immediate recall, perhaps the most important factor. Therefore, we will analyse the speaking times in some detail. The most striking fact about the speaking times is how linear they appear to be as a function of list length. The linearity is evident in Figs. 11.2 and 11.3; the pronunciation times, although not illustrated, appear linear as well.

Usually, subjects took more time for rehearsal than for mere pronunciation. For Subject 1, pronunciation times are shorter than rehearsal times for every material and every list length. For Subject 2, although pronunciation time and rehearsal time are both linear functions of

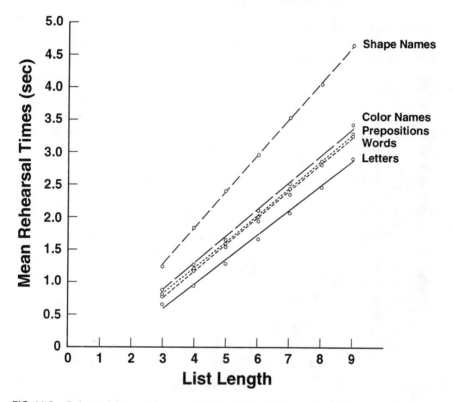

FIG. 11.2.   Rehearsal time as a function of list length for Subject 1. Straight lines were fitted by eye.

list length, the lines cross, having different slopes. With letters, for example, pronunciation times are longer than rehearsal times for short list lengths, but the order is reversed for long list lengths. It is not surprising that more processing is required for rehearsal of the items than for mere pronunciation.

The speaking times are not as simple as they first appear, however. In Figs. 11.2 and 11.3 it is apparent that if the lines relating rehearsal time to list length were extrapolated, the intercept, the time to pronounce a list of length 0, would be negative. This negative value is anomalous, because the time to pronounce a list of length 0 should be 0. One possibility is that the time to rehearse is not exactly a linear function of list length for short list lengths. In fact, pronunciation times collected by Chase (1977) and by Sternberg, Monsell, Knoll, & Wright (1978) display a small, but significant curve, concave up, most evident at small list lengths of 1 and 2. Their data suggest that we might also have a slight curve. This suggestion is supported by a regression analysis.

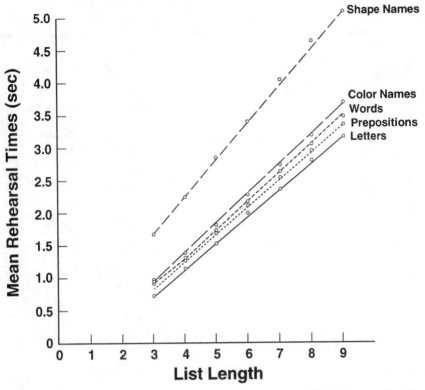

FIG. 11.3.   Rehearsal time as a function of list length for Subject 2. Straight lines were fitted by eye.

A quadratic regression equation was used to predict rehearsal time, v (k), for a list of length k, as

$$v (k) = b_0 + b_1 k + b_2 k^2.$$

The two subjects differ with respect to curvature. For Subject 1, the coefficient of list length squared, b_2, was significantly different from 0, for all materials except shapes. The details are given in Table 11.4. For Subject 2, the quadratic coefficient is not significantly different from 0, except for colours. The results for Subject 1 agree with those of Chase (1977) and Sternberg et al. (1978) who found a slight bow in the curve for speaking time as a function of list length.

Here is our explanation for the nonlinearity. Suppose when the subject says the list aloud, there are two stages in processing each item, including the first is the silent processing of the item, including

TABLE 11.4
Quadratic Regression Coefficients For Predicting Rehearsal Time, v (k),
from List Length, k, as $v(k) = b_0 + b_1 k + b_2 k^2$

Material	b_0	b_1	b_2	R^2
Subject 1				
Letters	−0.120	0.221***	0.013**	0.9997
Words	−0.191*	0.331***	0.006**	0.9999
Prepositions	−0.037	0.266***	0.011**	0.9999
Colour Names	−0.138	0.316***	0.009**	0.9998
Shape Names	−0.503**	0.595***	−0.003	0.9998
Subject 2				
Letters	−0.578**	0.421***	−0.001	0.9990
Words	−0.314*	0.383***	0.002	0.9992
Prepositions	−0.384*	0.403***	0.003	0.9993
Colour Names	−0.290**	0.387***	0.005*	0.9999
Shape Names	−0.285	0.646***	−0.006	0.9993

A coefficient significantly different from 0 is marked with an asterisk; * for
$P < 0.05$, ** for $P < 0.01$, *** for $P < 0.001$.

encoding, identifying, and so on, up to the point of overt speech. The second
stage is the actual speaking. Suppose for item i, the time required by the first
stage is T_{Ai} and the time required by the second stage is T_{Bi}. The voice key
does not come on until the overt speaking of the first item begins, so the
silent processing time T_{A1} is not measured. Then the measured time to say a
list of one item would be $v(1) = T_{B1}$.

For a list of length 2, suppose the silent processing of the second item is
carried out in parallel with speaking the first item aloud. The subject will
start to say item 2 aloud as soon as both T_{A2} and T_{B1} are done. Then the
time to say a list of length 2 would be

$$v(2) = \max\{T_{B1}, T_{A2}\} + T_{B2}.$$

The expression grows more complicated as the list length increases. For
example, the time to pronounce three items is

$$v(3) = \max\{\max\{T_{B1}, T_{A2}\} + T_{B2}, T_{A2} + T_{A3}\} + T_{B3}.$$

In this model, the time to say a list of length k is rather complicated.
However, there are two situations in which it becomes a simple linear
function. The first is when the time to speak an item aloud is always longer
than the silent processing of an item. Then the time to say a list of two items
is simply $T_{B1} + T_{B2}$. With this assumption, the time to pronounce a list of

length k would be $T_{B1} + T_{B2} + \ldots + T_{Bk}$. Then, if the time to say each item is the same (i.e. has the same probability distribution), the time to say a list of k items is simply

$$\upsilon\,(k) = kT_B, \tag{1}$$

where T_B is the time to say an item. This is a linear function of list length k, passing through the origin.

The second condition in which the model predicts that time to say a list is a linear function of list length is when the silent processing of an item is always longer than the time to say an item. Then the time to pronounce a list of length k is $T_{A2} + T_{A3} + \ldots + T_{Ak} + T_{Bk}$. If the silent processing time for each item is the same (i.e. has the same probability distribution), this expression simplifies to

$$\upsilon\,(k) = (k - 1)T_A + T_B, \tag{2}$$

where T_A is the silent processing time for an item, and T_B is the time to say an item. This expression too is a linear function of k, but it does not pass through the origin because the intercept is $T_B - T_A$. The intercept must be negative, because the equation is for the case when the silent processing time T_A is always longer than the speaking time T_B. Note further that the slope, T_A, is predicted to be greater than the absolute value of the intercept, $T_A - T_B$.

From the regression coefficients in Table 11.4, it appears that Equation 2 applies to Subject 2. The intercept, b_0, is negative for each material. With the exception of letters, the linear regression coefficient, b_1, is greater than the absolute value of the intercept. Finally, the quadratic coefficient, b_2, is not significantly different from 0, except for colours.

Subject 1 may fall into this condition for shapes, because the quadratic regression coefficient is not significantly different from 0, and the qualitative predictions for this condition are satisfied.

Although it is encouraging that for the most part these qualitative predictions are satisfied, there is a problem with a quantitative prediction of Equation 2. To be specific, if Equation 2 is true for every trial, the intercept added to the linear regression coefficient is supposed to be an estimate of the time to say an item, T_B. However, these estimates are quite small. For example, for Subject 2, T_B is estimated to be 0.070 seconds for words, but this seems small for the time to say a word aloud.

The following explanation, although untidy, seems likely to be true if the model is true. Equation 2 is linear with a negative intercept. Equation 1 is linear, but with an intercept of 0. The subjects' responses probably do not fall exclusively into the conditions required for one equation or the other.

Instead, the speaking times are a mixture of the various forms taken by the general equation, including Equations 1 and 2 as special cases. Contributions from trials on which Equation 1 holds pull the intercept closer to 0 than it would be if only Equation 2 held.

The function relating list length and the time to say a list is linear only in special circumstances. The nonlinear form occurs when the time to say an item is sometimes longer than the silent processing of an item, and sometimes shorter. The expression in this case is neither simple nor linear, and it turns out that there can be a slight bow in the function, concave up or concave down. A numerical example is worked out in Appendix C. The data of Subject 1 are in the nonlinear form for the materials other than shapes, because the quadratic regression coefficients are significantly greater than 0 (see Table 11.4). It is worth noting that the model does not predict speaking time to depend literally on list length squared. Rather, the quadratic regression coefficient is significant sometimes because it is an index of whether the function is slightly concave up or concave down.

Earlier, we supposed the time for processing an item when a list was uttered was made of two parts, the time for silent processing, T_A, and the time for overt speech, T_B. It is reasonable to ask which of these two component times is the better predictor of the trace duration, τ_v. Unfortunately, these data are not able to resolve the question because separate estimates of T_A and T_B are not available. We can look at the relation between representation duration and rehearsal time in more detail in another way, however.

Representation Duration and Rehearsal Time. In Table 11.4, rehearsal time for Subject 1 is predicted from list length with an intercept, a linear component, and a quadratic component. Which of these three components is most important, that is, which regression coefficient in Table 11.4 is the best predictor of trace duration? The coefficients are approximately linearly related to each other, and each coefficient alone predicts the representation duration pretty well. Nonetheless, it turns out that the linear component is most important.

For Subject 1, the linear regression coefficient, b_1, alone accounts for 92% of the variance. This is greater than the variance accounted for by the intercept, b_0, alone (87%), and by the quadratic coefficient, b_2, alone (88%). Not only does the linear regression coefficient account for more variance than the other two coefficients, but when all three coefficients are used in a multiple regression equation, the variance accounted for is 93%, only a slight increase over the variance accounted for by using b_1 alone.

In other words, the coefficient b_1 is doing almost all the work. This makes sense because the term b_1 is a direct estimate of processing time for an item, but the other two terms are not. The term b_2 is not a direct measure of a relevant quantity, rather it is a measure of the degree to which the two quantities T_A and T_B are close in value. The intercept, b_0, was not significantly different from 0 for some materials.

If the model described here is true, the quadratic regression coefficient is significantly different from 0 in just those situations when the linear coefficient b_1 is not a pure estimate of T_A nor of T_B. Therefore, although we have established that b_1 is the most important regression coefficient, we cannot go further to establish whether T_A or T_B is the most important time parameter.

Our discussion of memory span has become a discussion of the processes involved in speaking. This is not an accident. Working memory is often defined as memory in the service of processing, so the study of working memory and the study of processing are intertwined. In the process model for speaking, we assumed that each item arrived at Processor A and then was sent to Processor B. We implicitly assumed that if an item arrived at Processor B while it was busy, the item would be stored temporarily until Processor B was available. This storage space, by definition, is part of working memory.

There is a fundamental difference in the way an error is made for an item on a processor compared with an item in storage. For an item on a processor, an error might occur from a miscalculation, but the item would not ordinarily be lost. For an item in storage, an error would ordinarily arise from loss, but not from a miscalculation. In a span task, the percentage of errors arising from miscalculations is probably smaller than the percentage arising from loss. For this reason, it would be useful to be able to partition the time an item spends in the system into time spent on processors and time spent in storage. There is no clear way to do this in a typical span task. The problem is that in a span task, the items are presented and recalled in separate phases of the task. At first this may seem ideal if the goal is to separate storage and processing. Unfortunately, analytic leverage is lost because parameters for the two phases are typically different, e.g. presentation rate is different from recall rate.

In the next section we will show that if the subject operates in a continuous rather than a "batch" mode, then time spent in processing can be separated from time spent in storage. The technique we propose for this is based on queueing networks. Queueing networks provide a framework for thinking about processing and memory space in an integrated way. Queueing models for processing have been proposed by Fisher (1982) and by Miller (1993). Queueing models have been proposed for working memory by Bower (1967) and Reitman (1970). They noted that queueing models can account in a natural way for several phenomena, such as serial position curves. These phenomena are beyond the scope of this chapter, and the interested reader is referred to their papers for details.

PROCESSING AND STORAGE IN
QUEUEING NETWORKS

Consider a task such as repeating a message (shadowing), or simultaneous translation, in which stimulus items arrive continually, one by one, and responses are emitted continually, one by one. The items are presented at a rate of λ_{in} items per second and the corresponding responses are made at a rate of λ_{out} items per second.

Although the input rate may be slow enough for the system to keep up with on the average, the processing time varies from item to item, and as a result there will be occasions when a new item arrives at a processor while it is still busy with a previous item. New items arriving at a busy processor would be lost from the system unless there is a temporary store where items can queue until the processor is available. The queues are part of the working memory system.

Figure 11.4 represents the subject's information processing system as a queueing network. Circular nodes represent processors that operate on items, and arrows represent channels for transmission. If a processor is busy, the items (or features of items) ready to use it wait in a queue, represented by a rectangle preceding the node. (It is customary in diagrams to use rectangles containing slots as symbols for queues. This is not intended to be an assumption that the queues are limited to holding a certain specific number of items.)

In Fig. 11.4, stimulus items are produced at the source (represented by a dot), and pass through three processors in sequence. Items are produced as responses at the last processor. The response items are transmitted to the listener. In addition, the responses produce feedback, such as the sound of the subject's voice or the tactile sensations produced by pressing keys. The feedback enters the system again, at the first processor. The feedback pathway is represented in the Figure by the arrow from the last processor back to the first one.

In a typical memory span task, recall begins after all the items have been presented. Feedback from the recalled items enters the perceptual system, where room is available because the items remaining to be

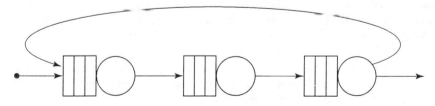

FIG. 11.4. A queueing network with feedback.

recalled have moved on. In a typical memory span task, feedback does not compete for space with items remaining to be recalled. In contrast, when the system is performing a continuous task, after a steady state is reached, feedback from old recalled items is intermixed with new items. As the feedback from an old item is processed, the space it requires is probably about the same as it required when it was new. If the feedback is only discarded near the motor end of the system, about half the system will be occupied with feedback from old items. As a result, the number of new items in the system in a continuous task would be about half the memory span.

Suppose over some interval of time the subject is correctly reciting all the items presented in a continuous task, without guessing, and without omissions or inserts. After an item has been presented, it is in the system for an interval of time, called the *sojourn time*, and then the response for the item is given. When the items first begin to arrive, the number of items in the system increases from 0, to 1, to 2, but eventually this number reaches a steady state, where it fluctuates up and down around some mean number of items.

Two equations for queueing networks may well be equations of human short-term memory. These are the balance equation and Little's Law. We begin with balance.

The Rate-in-equals-rate-out Principle. A balance equation can be written in a very general form (see, e.g. Hillier & Lieberman, 1974, p.393), but for our purposes a specific statement is important: In a steady state, the rate at which new to-be-remembered items enter the system equals the rate at which new to-be-remembered items leave it. This common rate is called the *throughput*. It is clear that if the rate-in-equals-rate-out principle did not hold for the new items at some node, new items would pile up at it, or new items would somehow be leaving faster than they arrive. Balance holds at every node, and also for the system as a whole. At any node, the mean input rate of new items equals the mean output rate of new items, $\lambda_{new,in} = \lambda_{new,out}$, and the same is true for the entire system.

For the old items produced by feedback, balance does not hold at every node, because the old items are not passed through the motor system a second time. Somewhere along the line, almost all the old items produced by feedback are lost. Hence, balance does not hold for the old items, nor for the total number of old and new items.

Little's Law. Little's Law applies to a system in a steady state. Let $N(t)$ be the number of new items in the system at time t, and let $E[N]$ be the mean number of new items in the system, over all times t. Let the throughput rate for new items be λ. Finally, let τ be the mean time for which a new item is in the system, the sojourn time. Then, Little's Law says that under very general conditions,

$$E[N] = \lambda\tau,$$

(Little, 1961). In words, if we consider only the new items, the mean number of items in the system equals the mean throughput × the mean sojourn time.

As with the balance equation, Little's Law need not apply to the feedback from old items, nor to the total of the old and new items. In the remainder of the chapter, when we mention the number of items in the system, the throughput, or the sojourn time we will be referring to new items only.

Little's Law relates three quantities characterising the queueing system. Usually, investigations of working memory have focused on the number of items in the system, N, but Little's Law indicates that equally important roles are played by the throughput λ and the sojourn time, τ.

It is instructive to consider the limitations of working memory in the light of this equation. In her queueing network model of working memory, Reitman (1970) noted that any real system will have an upper limit on the number of items it can contain, and also a limit on the time for which an item can reside. In addition, there will be a limit on the rate at which items can be processed. Each of these limits can be the one that effectively limits performance in a given situation. Decay and interference may both operate, with parameters of the situation determining which is most crucial.

It may seem at first that Little's Law is obvious. But note that the quantities in it are expected values, and ordinarily the expected value of a product of random variables does not equal the product of their expected values. Further, Little's Law is valid for almost any distributions of the random variables involved.

It is also worth noting that Little's Law applies not only to the entire system, but to every subsystem that can be conceived of as a queue (see, e.g. Allen, 1990). It applies, for example, to an individual node together with its queue. If the mean number of new items either waiting in the queue for node i or being processed at node i is $E[N_i]$, the mean throughput rate for new items at node i is λ_i, and the mean time waiting or being processed at node i is τ_i for new items, then Little's Law applied to the subsystem i is

$$E[N_i] = \lambda_i\tau_i.$$

Also, Little's Law applies to the queue alone at a node i. For new items, if $E[N_{iq}]$ is the mean number of items in the queue at node i, τ_{iq} is the mean time spent waiting in this queue, and λ_{iq} is the throughput, then

$$E[N_{iq}] = \lambda_{iq}\tau_{iq}.$$

If we assume no new item uses the same processor or queue more than once, then in these equations, the throughput for each processor and queue is simply λ, the throughput for the system as a whole.

Little's Law helps in understanding the consequences of changes in the capacity of the system. Suppose the mean number of items in the system is restricted somehow, by an experimental manipulation, or by brain damage. It may not be apparent at first, but even if the subject's processing times are unchanged, the rate at which items can be processed, the throughput, will drop. The reason is that by Little's Law, if E[N] is decreased, there must be a decrease in the throughput or the sojourn time, or both. This suggests that subjects with a span lower than average would have slower reading speeds as a consequence.

How Many Processors Are There?

If we assume each processor holds no more than one item at a time, we can obtain a lower bound for the number of processors in the system from Little's Law. The time an item spends in the system can be divided into two mutually exclusive parts; the time on processors and the time waiting in queues. But the time on processors can be determined from an ordinary reaction time experiment with every aspect of the task the same as usual, except that only one item is presented at a time. With only one item in the system, there will be no time spent waiting in queues, so a measure of pure processing time can be obtained. Let this processing time be τ_p and let the time waiting in queues be τ_q. Then the sojourn time is $\tau = \tau_p + \tau_q$.

Suppose when the throughput rate is λ the error rate is negligible. Let E[N_p] be the expected number of items on processors. Then by Little's Law, $E[N_p] = \lambda\tau_p$. Because we have assumed that each processor holds no more than one item, the number of processors m must exceed the number of items on processors, so $m \geqslant E[N_p] = \lambda\tau_p$.

To our knowledge, estimates of λ and reaction time have not been gathered in the same experiment. Until more exact estimates are available, we can obtain a useful approximation by finding estimates of λ and of reaction time from different experiments on the same material. Useful data on letters of the alphabet are available. In our experiment described earlier, the pronunciation rate for letters was 3.6 for Subject 1 and 3.1 for subject 2. These estimates were obtained from Tables 11.1 and 11.2 by dividing 9 by the pronunciation time for nine items. A rough estimate is adequate for our bound, so let us say λ is approximately 3 items/sec.

An estimate of the reaction time to name letters is available in Table 1 of Greenberg (1988, p.33). The experiment was on priming, which is not relevant for our purposes, but the conditions in which the letter to be named was not a constituent of the prime are a reasonable approximation to a pure letter naming task. Averaging the reaction times in these conditions, we obtain an estimate of about 500msec. This leads to the bound of 3 items/sec $\times$ 0.5 sec = 1.5 items. As the number of processors must be an integer, we conclude that the number of processors, m, is greater than or equal to 2.

There must be one more processor, for motor output. One way to see this is to notice that if the output is speech, then the reaction time is measured just as the subject begins output. At that point the item still remains in the system, so the total processing time from when the item enters the system until it has completely left the system is the reaction time, RT, plus the motor time. An estimate of the motor time is the reciprocal of the rate, $1/\lambda$. Then the lower bound for the number of processors is $\lambda(RT + 1/\lambda) = 1.5 + 1$. We conclude that m $\geqslant$ 3. This is obviously only a rough estimate, but as it is plausible we have illustrated three processors in the queueing network in Fig. 11.4.

Our lower bound on the number of sequential processors is in the same neighbourhood as an earlier estimate of the number of parallel processors in a queueing system. In a queueing model for a different task, visual search, and using a different technique, based on Erlang's loss formula, Fisher estimated that there are four processors simultaneously available in the visual system (Fisher, 1982; Fisher, Duffy, Young, & Pollatsek 1988). These processors are all assumed to be available when items are displayed simultaneously on a screen. The underlying assumptions are different from ours; for example, our estimate includes a processor for speech which we assumed to operate on only one item at a time. Nonetheless, the agreement is encouraging.

Estimating the Number of Items in Queue

Suppose the task is typing items as they appear on the screen. The rate at which the items appear on the screen is controlled by the experimenter. If the system is in a steady state, the subject will type the responses at the same rate as the items are presented. By sampling the system periodically during the task, say, every 25msec, the computer can accumulate records from which statistics such as the mean number of items in the system can be calculated.

Suppose the experimenter manipulates a factor that changes the mean processing time for exactly one processor, leaving the other processors unchanged, and leaving the rate of presentation unchanged. Of course, increasing the mean processing time for a processor will increase the mean time that new items spend in the system. By Little's Law, the number of new items in the system will increase.

It might seem at first that the average number of new items waiting in queues would also increase. This intuition is wrong, for the following reason. If the time required per item by a certain processor, say Processor A, is increased, the queue preceding Processor A will tend to be longer. This tends to increase the average number of new items waiting in queues. However, Processor A will be completing fewer items per second, and therefore it will be sending fewer items per second to the queue following it. This tends to decrease the average number of new items waiting in queues. The result of these two competing monotonic tendencies is that the mean number of items waiting in queues will first decrease and then increase as the mean processing time for Processor A is increased.

When the mean processing time for a processor is increased, there are three possible patterns for the mean number of new items waiting in queues, $E[N_q]$. If the entire range of processing times is considered, then $E[N_q]$ will first decrease and then increase as the processing time is increased. If instead only part of the range of processing times is considered, then one might observe only the increasing section of the function relating $E[N_q]$ and processing time, or only the decreasing section.

It may be that not every processor has a queue preceding it and a queue following it. If a processor has no queue preceding it, then increasing its processing time will only decrease the number of items waiting in queues. If a processor has no queue following it, then increasing its processing time will only increase the number of items waiting in queues.

To look for these patterns, we need a way to determine the mean number of new items waiting in queues. Suppose an experimental factor increases the processing time for a single processor. For every level of the factor, the task can be carried out with continual presentation and with single presentation. With continual presentation, new items are presented at a rate λ, and $E[N]$, the mean number of new items in the system, is determined, as described earlier. The mean, $E[N]$, is the sum of two means; the mean number of new items on processors plus the mean number waiting in queues, $E[N] = E[N_p] + E[N_q]$. The value of $E[N_p]$ can be determined from the reaction times in the single presentation mode. In this mode, only one item is presented at a time, so there is no time spent waiting in queue. The mean response time, then, is the mean processing time, τ_p. By Little's Law,

$$E[N_p] = \lambda \tau_p.$$

The value of τ_p can then be determined, and the value of $E[N_q]$ determined by subtraction.

The behaviour of the queues in a queueing network can be quite complicated. When the processing time of a certain processor is changed, the queues preceding and following that processor will change, but queues elsewhere in the system will change as well, until the system achieves a steady state. An experimenter can realistically expect to selectively influence a single processor, but not a single queue.

To investigate the behaviour of a queueing network with feedback, a simulation of the network in Fig. 11.4 was conducted with **MICROSAINT** (Micro Analysis and Design, 1985). The mean durations of the three processes in the Figure were denoted τ_A, τ_B, and τ_C, respectively, going from left to right.

In the simulations, a list of 2000 items was presented at the rate of one item every (simulated) 500msec. Each item arrived, and was processed by A, B, and C in that order. If a processor was busy, the item was placed on the queue preceding the processor. When an item was placed on a processor, the processing time was randomly chosen from a gamma distribution. The means of the distributions used are given in Table 11.5. To simulate the fact that as mean processing time increases, the variance increases as well, for each gamma distribution the standard deviation was equal to one-fourth the mean.

When an item left Processor C, it was returned as feedback to the system, to either Processor A or to the queue for Processor A, depending on whether Processor A was busy or not. We do not know when feedback from old items is discarded in the human memory system. In our simulations, feedback from old items went through Processors A and B, with processing times the same as for new items. Feedback from old items was discarded at Processor C, without taking any time on processor C.

To obtain the simulated data in Table 11.5, three runs were made, with different random number seeds. The data are averages over the three. A trial

TABLE 11.5
Simulations of the Queueing Network in Fig.
11.4 For Various Mean Processing Times
(msec)

τ_A	τ_C		
	200	300	400
Mean Number of New Items in The System			
75	1.082	1.233	1.474
125	1.154	1.310	1.618
225	1.418	1.750	2.065
Mean Number of New Items Waiting in Queue			
75	0.132	0.083	0.124
125	0.104	0.060	0.168
225	0.168	0.300	0.415

For each cell, the value of τ_B was 200. The throughput λ was 2 items/1000msec.

with 2000 items may not seem feasible for an experiment on humans at first. But because the items arrive at the rate of two per second, the time required for 2000 items would be 1000 seconds, or about 17 minutes.

The results of the simulations are in Table 11.5. The top panel of the table gives the mean number of new items in the system, i.e. the number of new items in working memory. The mean number of new items increases monotonically with the mean processing time for Processor A, and also for Processor C. However, the second panel of the Table shows that the mean number of new items waiting in queues first decreases with increasing processing time, and then increases. In the last row and in the last column, the means increase monotonically, one of the three predicted patterns.

For applications, it is important to note that these results were obtained in simulations in which the mean number of new items in the system was relatively constant over time. When the system is operating near its limits, even if the throughput is low enough for the system to handle on the average, a queue can become temporarily congested. These congestions may lead to violations of the three predicted patterns. In an experiment on humans, temporary congestion of a queue would immediately be detected because it would lead to a large number of errors.

SUMMARY

We began with a model for the probability that a subject can correctly recall a list in order. The usual effect of increasing word length is to decrease the memory span, while the time required to pronounce a list of span length remains invariant. With highly practised subjects, we found a reverse effect of word length; the longer the items, the longer the time required to pronounce a list of span length. A tentative explanation was offered in terms of the recency effect. With auditory presentation, the probability of recall of the last few items can be independent of word length. Then, the time spent recalling those last few items will increase with word length, leading to an increase in the time to pronounce a list of span length.

Although the time to pronounce a list increases approximately linearly with the number of items in the list, there is a slight bow concave up in the curve. We explain the bowing with a model in which the overt pronunciation of one item goes on concurrently with the covert processing of the next item.

Although the need to recall a list in order occurs from time to time in daily life, the memory part of working memory has a more ubiquitous role as a buffer for mental processes. We described these buffers in terms of queueing theory. We estimated that there are at least three processors in the sequence of events from presentation of an item to the pronunciation of the item. The number of items in queues can be estimated by comparing the reaction times when items are presented alone with the sojourn times when the items are presented continually. The number of words that can be held in working memory is the number on processors plus the number in queues. If an experimenter can selectively influence the rate at which a certain processor works, then the experimenter can determine whether the processor has a queue preceding it, or following it, or both. The capacity of working memory is most often stated in terms of the number of items it holds, but a queueing model emphasises two equally important quantities, the rate at which the items are processed, and the time they sojourn in the system.

ACKNOWLEDGEMENTS

I thank Donald L. Fisher, Jeff Oliver, and Marie Poirier for helpful discussions. Kim Nowicki carried out the simulations. A program for calculating unique substrings was written by Xiaojian Li. Portions of this work were supported by grant MH38675 from the National Institute for Mental Health and by grant 9123865-DBS from the National Science Foundation.

REFERENCES

Allen, A.O. (1990). *Probability, statistics, and queueing theory with computer science applications* (2nd edn.). Boston: Academic Press.

American Heritage Dictionary of the English Language. (1992). Boston: Houghton Mifflin.

Baddeley, A. (1986). *Working memory.* Oxford: Clarendon Press.

Baddeley, A., & Andrade, J. (1994). Reversing the word-length effect: A comment on Caplan, Rochon, and Waters. *Quarterly Journal of Experimental Psychology, 47A,* 1047–1054.

Baddeley, A.D., Lewis, V.J., & Vallar, G. (1984). Exploring the articulatory loop. *Quarterly Journal of Experimental Psychology, 36,* 233–252.

Baddeley, A.D., Thomson, N., & Buchanan, M. (1975). Word length and the structure of short-term memory. *Journal of Verbal Learning and Verbal Behavior, 14,* 575–589.

Bower, G.H. (1967). A descriptive theory of memory. In D.P. Kimple (Ed.), *Proceedings of the second conference on learning, remembering, and forgetting,* (pp. 112–185). New York: New York Academy of Sciences.

Broadbent, D.E. (1958). *Perception and communication.* London: Pergamon Press.

Brown, G.D.A., & Hulme, C. (1995). Modeling item length effects in memory span: No rehearsal needed? *Journal of Memory and Language, 34,* 594–621.

Burgess, N., & Hitch, G.J. (1992). Towards a neural network model of the articulatory loop. *Journal of Memory and Language, 31,* 429–460.

Caplan, D., Rochon, E., & Waters, G.S. (1992). Articulatory and phonological determinants of word length effects in span tasks. *Quarterly Journal of Experimental Psychology, 45A,* 177–192.

Caplan, D., & Waters, G.S. (1994). Articulatory length and phonological similarity in span tasks: A reply to Baddeley and Andrade. *Quarterly Journal of Experimental Psychology, 47A,* 1055–1062.

Chase, W.G. (1977). Does memory scanning involve implicit speech? In S. Dornic (Ed.), *Attention and performance VI.* Hillsdale, NJ: Lawrence Erlbaum Associates Inc.

Conrad, R. (1964). Acoustic confusion in immediate memory. *British Journal of Psychology, 55,* 75–84.

Cowan, N. (1992). Verbal memory span and the timing of spoken recall. *Journal of Memory and Language, 31,* 668–684.

Cowan, N. (1995). *Attention and memory: An integrated framework.* Oxford: Oxford University Press.

Fisher, D.L. (1982). Limited channel models of automatic detection: Capacity and scanning in visual search. *Psychological Review, 89,* 662–692.

Fisher, D.L., Duffy, S.A., Young, C., & Pollatsek, A. (1988). Understanding the central processing limit in consistent-mapping visual search tasks. *Journal of Experimental Psychology: Human Perception and Performance, 14,* 253–266.

Gathercole, S.E., & Baddeley, A.D. (1990). The role of phonological memory in vocabulary acquisition: A study of young children learning new names. *British Journal of Psychology, 81,* 439–454.

Greenberg, S.N. (1988). Are letter codes always activated? *Perception & Psychophysics, 44,* 331–338.

Hillier, F.S., & Lieberman, G.J. (1974). *Operations research* (2nd edn.). San Francisco: Holden-Day.

Hintzman, D.L. (1967). Articulate coding in short-term memory. *Journal of Verbal Learning and Verbal Behavior, 6,* 312–316.

Hulme, C., Maughan, S., & Brown, G.D.A. (1991). Memory for familiar and unfamiliar words: Evidence for a long-term memory contribution to short-term memory span. *Journal of Memory & Language, 30,* 685–701.

Johnson, N.I., & Kotz, S. (1970). *Distributions in statistics: Continuous univariate distributions 2.* Boston: Houghton Mifflin.

Little, J.D.C. (1961). A proof of the queueing formula: $L = \lambda W$. *Operations Research, 9,* 383–387.

Mackworth, J.F. (1963). The duration of the visual image. *Canadian Journal of Psychology, 17,* 62–81.

Micro Analysis and Design. (1985). *MICROSAINT* [Computer program]. Concord, MA: MGA Inc.

Miller, J.O. (1993). A queue-series model for reaction time, with discrete stage and continuous-flow models as special cases. *Psychological Review, 100,* 702–715.

Nairne, J.S. (1990). A feature model of immediate memory. *Memory & Cognition, 18,* 251–269.

Neath, I., & Nairne, J.S. (in press). Word-length effects in immediate memory: Overwriting trace decay theory. *Psychonomic Bulletin & Review.*

Poirier, M., & Saint-Aubin, J. (1995). Memory for related and unrelated words: Further evidence concerning the influence of semantic factors on immediate serial recall. *Quarterly Journal of Experimental Psychology, 48A,* 384–404.

Reitman, J.S. (1970). Computer simulation of an information-processing model of short term memory. In D.A. Norman (Ed.), *Models of memory,* (pp. 117–151). New York: Academic Press.

Schweickert, R. (1993). A multinomial processing tree model for degradation and redintegration in immediate recall. *Memory & Cognition, 21,* 168–175.

Schweickert, R., & Boruff, B. (1986). Short-term memory capacity: Magic number or magic spell? *Journal of Experimental Psychology: Learning, Memory, and Cognition, 12,* 419–425.

StatSoft. (1994). *Statistica* [Computer program]. StatSoft, Inc., 2325 East 13th St., Tulsa, OK 74104, USA.

Sternberg, S., Monsell, S., Knoll, R.L., & Wright, C.E. (1978). The latency and duration of rapid movement sequences: Comparisons of speech and typewriting. In G.E. Stelmach (Ed.), *Information processing in motor control and learning,* (pp. 117–152). New York: Academic Press.

Tehan, G. & Humphreys, M.S. (1988). Articulatory loop explanations of memory span and pronunciation rate correspondence: A cautionary note. *Bulletin of the Psychonomic Society, 26,* 293–296.

APPENDIX A

Stimulus Materials

Letters: b c d f g h j k l m n p q r s t v w x z
Prepositions: through towards since until down from near over with for like into at up in of as on to by
Words: boy bed arm key dog fig box fly hat net van cow pin jar rug fox hub bud inn ant
Colours: red orange yellow green blue purple black white brown gray silver pink rust beige maroon aqua gold tan turquoise scarlet
Shapes: quadrilateral parallelogram semicircle trapezoid rectangle pentagon triangle oval circle hexagon heart diamond square club rhombus cross star ring spiral spade

APPENDIX B

Parameter Estimation Procedure

An excellent approximation to the normal cumulative distribution can be obtained from that of the logistic distribution, by using the formula $NP(x/c) = 1/(1 + \exp x)$, where $c = 15\pi/16\sqrt{3}$ (Johnson & Kotz, 1970). $NP(x/c)$ is the cumulative normal probability at x/c, and the expression on the right-hand side is the cumulative logistic probability at x. Parameters for the logistic distribution were found with the User Defined Nonlinear Regression routine in Statistica, with the loss function to be minimised specified as the chi-square, that is, the sum of [(PRED − OBS) **2]/PRED, where OBS is the observed value and PRED is the corresponding predicted value. The parameters of the best-fitting logistic distribution were then converted to the parameters of a normal distribution approximating it via the formula just quoted.

APPENDIX C

Speaking Time as a Function of List Length

The general expression v (k) for the time to say a list of length k can be concave up or concave down. Consider list lengths 1, 2, and 3. The function v (k) is linear if v (3) − 2v (2) + v (1) is 0, concave up if this expression is positive, and concave down if it is negative.

In the text, equations for v (1), v (2), and v (3) are given. By substituting the values TA2 = TB2 = 2, TA3 = TB1 = 1, it will be found that T(1) = 1, T(2) = 4, and T (3) = 4 + TB3. Then

$$v\ (3) - 2v\ (2) + v\ (1) = TB3 - 3.$$

Depending on whether TB3 is greater than 3 or less than 3, the function v (k) is concave up or concave down.

Author Index

Subject Index